PERCEPTIONS OF A RENEGADE MIND

ickonic
publishing

First published in July 2021.

ickonic
publishing

New Enterprise House
St Helens Street
Derby
DE1 3GY
UK

email: gareth.icke@davidicke.com

Copyright © 2021 David Icke

No part of this book may be reproduced
in any form without permission from
the Publisher, except for the quotation
of brief passages in criticism

Cover Design: Gareth Icke
Book Design: Neil Hague

British Library Cataloguing-in
Publication Data
A catalogue record for this book is
available from the British Library

ISBN 978-18384153-1-0

Printed and bound by
CPI Group (UK) Ltd, Croydon, CR0 4YY

PERCEPTIONS OF A RENEGADE MIND

DAVID ICKE

Dedication:

To *Freeeeeedom!*

ICK◉NIC
THE ALTERNATIVE

NEW. DIFFERENT. REVOLUTIONARY

HUNDREDS OF CUTTING EDGE DOCUMENTARIES, FEATURE FILMS, SERIES & PODCASTS.

SIGN UP NOW AT ICKONIC.COM

THE LIFE STORY OF DAVID ICKE

RENEGADE

THE FEATURE LENGTH FILM

AVAILABLE NOW AT DAVIDICKE.COM

Renegade:

Adjective

'Having rejected tradition: Unconventional.'

Merriam-Webster Dictionary

Acquiescence to tyranny is the death of the spirit

You may be 38 years old, as I happen to be. And one day, some great opportunity stands before you and calls you to stand up for some great principle, some great issue, some great cause. And you refuse to do it because you are afraid … You refuse to do it because you want to live longer … You're afraid that you will lose your job, or you are afraid that you will be criticised or that you will lose your popularity, or you're afraid that somebody will stab you, or shoot at you or bomb your house; so you refuse to take the stand.

Well, you may go on and live until you are 90, but you're just as dead at 38 as you would be at 90. And the cessation of breathing in your life is but the belated announcement of an earlier death of the spirit.

Martin Luther King

How the few control the many and always have – the many do whatever they're told

'Forward, the Light Brigade!'
Was there a man dismayed?
Not though the soldier knew
Someone had blundered.
Theirs not to make reply,
Theirs not to reason why,
Theirs but to do and die.
Into the valley of Death
Rode the six hundred.

Cannon to right of them,
Cannon to left of them,
Cannon in front of them
Volleyed and thundered;
Stormed at with shot and shell,
Boldly they rode and well,
Into the jaws of Death,
Into the mouth of hell
Rode the six hundred

Alfred Lord Tennyson (1809-1892)

The mist is lifting slowly
I can see the way ahead
And I've left behind the empty streets
That once inspired my life
And the strength of the emotion
Is like thunder in the air
'Cos the promise that we made each other
Haunts me to the end

The secret of your beauty
And the mystery of your soul
I've been searching for in everyone I meet
And the times I've been mistaken
It's impossible to say
And the grass is growing
Underneath our feet

The words that I remember
From my childhood still are true
That there's none so blind
As those who will not see
And to those who lack the courage
And say it's dangerous to try
Well they just don't know
That love eternal will not be denied

I know you're out there somewhere
Somewhere, somewhere
I know you're out there somewhere
Somewhere you can hear my voice
I know I'll find you somehow
Somehow, somehow
I know I'll find you somehow
And somehow I'll return again to you

The Moody Blues

Are you a gutless wonder - or a Renegade Mind?

Monuments put from pen to paper,
Turns me into a gutless wonder,
And if you tolerate this,
Then your children will be next.
Gravity keeps my head down,
Or is it maybe shame ...

Manic Street Preachers

Rise like lions after slumber
In unvanquishable number.
Shake your chains to earth like dew
Which in sleep have fallen on you.
Ye are many – they are few.

Percy Shelley

Contents

CHAPTER ONE

I'm thinking' –
Oh, but *are* you?

Think for yourself and let others enjoy the privilege of doing so too
Voltaire

French-born philosopher, mathematician and scientist René Descartes became famous for his statement in Latin in the 17th century which translates into English as: 'I think, therefore I am.'

On the face of it that is true. Thought reflects perception and perception leads to both behaviour and self-identity. In that sense 'we' are what we think. But who or what is doing the thinking and is thinking the only route to perception? Clearly, as we shall see, 'we' are not always the source of 'our' perception, indeed with regard to humanity as a whole this is rarely the case; and thinking is far from the only means of perception. Thought is the village idiot compared with other expressions of consciousness that we all have the potential to access and tap into. This has to be true when we *are* those other expressions of consciousness which are infinite in nature. We have forgotten this, or, more to the point, been manipulated to forget.

These are not just the esoteric musings of the navel. The whole foundation of human control and oppression is control of perception. Once perception is hijacked then so is behaviour which is dictated by perception. Collective perception becomes collective behaviour and collective behaviour is what we call human society. Perception is all and those behind human control know that which is why perception is the target 24/7 of the psychopathic manipulators that I call the Global Cult. They know that if they dictate perception they will dictate behaviour and collectively dictate the nature of human society. They are further aware that perception is formed from information received and if they control the circulation of information they will to a vast extent direct human behaviour. Censorship of information and opinion has become globally Nazi-like in recent years and never more blatantly than since the illusory 'virus pandemic' was triggered out of China in 2019 and across the world in 2020. Why have billions submitted to house arrest and accepted fascistic societies in a way they would have never believed possible? Those controlling the information spewing from government, mainstream media and Silicon Valley (all controlled by the same Global Cult networks) told them they were in danger from a 'deadly virus' and only by submitting to house arrest and conceding their most basic of freedoms could they and their families be protected. This monumental and provable lie became the *perception* of the billions and therefore the *behaviour* of the billions. In those few words you have the whole structure and modus operandi of human control. Fear is a perception – **F**alse **E**motion **A**ppearing **R**eal – and fear is the currency of control. In short … get them by the balls (or give them the impression that you have) and their hearts and minds will follow. Nothing grips the dangly bits and freezes the rear-end more comprehensively than fear.

World number 1

There are two 'worlds' in what appears to be one 'world' and the prime difference between them is knowledge. First we have the mass of human society in which the population is maintained in coldly-calculated ignorance through control of information and the 'education' (indoctrination) system. That's all you really need to control to enslave billions in a perceptual delusion in which what are perceived to be *their* thoughts and opinions are ever-repeated mantras that the system has been downloading all their lives through 'education', media, science, medicine, politics and academia in which the personnel and advocates are themselves overwhelmingly the perceptual products of the same repetition. Teachers and academics in general are processed by the same programming machine as everyone else, but unlike the great majority they never leave the 'education' program. It gripped them as students and continues to grip them as programmers of subsequent generations of students. The programmed become the programmers – the programmed programmers. The same can largely be said for scientists, doctors and politicians and not least because as the American writer Upton Sinclair said: 'It is difficult to get a man to understand something when his salary depends upon his not understanding it.' If your career and income depend on thinking the way the system demands then you will – bar a few free-minded exceptions – concede your mind to the Perceptual Mainframe that I call the Postage Stamp Consensus. This is a tiny band of perceived knowledge and possibility 'taught' (downloaded) in the schools and universities, pounded out by the mainstream media and on which all government policy is founded. Try thinking, and especially speaking and acting, outside of the 'box' of consensus and see what that does for your career in the Mainstream Everything which bullies, harasses, intimidates and ridicules the population into compliance. Here we have the simple structure which enslaves most of humanity in a perceptual prison cell for an entire lifetime and I'll go deeper into this process shortly. Most of what humanity is taught as fact is nothing more than programmed belief. American science fiction author Frank Herbert was right when he said: 'Belief can be manipulated. Only knowledge is dangerous.' In the 'Covid' age belief is promoted and knowledge is censored. It was always so, but never to the extreme of today.

World number 2

A 'number 2' is slang for 'doing a poo' and how appropriate that is when this other 'world' is doing just that on humanity every minute of every day. World number 2 is a global network of secret societies and semi-secret groups dictating the direction of society via governments, corporations and authorities of every kind. I have spent more than 30 years uncovering and exposing this network that I call the Global Cult and knowing its agenda is what has made my books so accurate in predicting current and past events. Secret societies are secret for a reason. They want to keep their hoarded knowledge to themselves and their chosen initiates and to hide it from the population which they seek through ignorance to control and subdue. The whole foundation of the division between World 1 and World 2 is *knowledge*. What number 1 knows number 2 must not. Knowledge they have worked so hard to keep secret includes (a) the agenda to enslave humanity in a centrally-controlled global dictatorship, and (b) the nature of reality and life itself. The latter (b) must be suppressed to allow the former (a) to prevail as I shall be explaining. The way the Cult manipulates and interacts with the population can be likened to a spider's web. The 'spider' sits at the centre in the shadows and imposes its will through the web with each strand represented in World number 2 by a secret society, satanic or semi-secret group, and in World number 1 – the world of the seen – by governments, agencies of government, law enforcement, corporations, the banking system, media conglomerates and Silicon Valley (Fig 1 overleaf). The spider and the web connect and coordinate all these organisations to pursue the same global outcome while the population sees them as individual entities working randomly and independently. At the level of the web governments *are* the banking system *are* the corporations *are* the media *are* Silicon Valley *are* the World Health Organization working from their inner cores as one unit. Apparently unconnected countries, corporations, institutions, organisations and people are on the *same team* pursuing the same global outcome. Strands in the web immediately around the spider are the most secretive and exclusive secret societies and their membership is emphatically restricted to the Cult inner-circle emerging through the generations from

Figure 1: The global web through which the few control the many. (Image Neil Hague.)

particular bloodlines for reasons I will come to. At the core of the core you would get them in a single room. That's how many people are dictating the direction of human society and its transformation through the 'Covid' hoax and other means. As the web expands out from the spider we meet the secret societies that many people will be aware of – the Freemasons, Knights Templar, Knights of Malta, Opus Dei, the inner sanctum of the Jesuit Order, and such like. Note how many are connected to the Church of Rome and there is a reason for that. The Roman Church was established as a revamp, a rebranding, of the relocated 'Church' of Babylon and the Cult imposing global tyranny today can be tracked back to Babylon and Sumer in what is now Iraq.

Inner levels of the web operate in the unseen away from the public eye and then we have what I call the cusp organisations located at the point where the hidden meets the seen. They include a series of satellite organisations answering to a secret society founded in London in the late 19th century called the Round Table and among them are the Royal Institute of International Affairs (UK, founded in 1920); Council on Foreign Relations (US, 1921); Bilderberg Group (worldwide, 1954); Trilateral Commission (US/worldwide, 1972); and the Club of Rome (worldwide, 1968) which was created to exploit environmental concerns to justify the centralisation of global power to 'save the planet'. The Club of Rome instigated with others the human-caused climate change hoax which has led to all the 'green new deals' demanding that very centralisation of control. Cusp organisations, which include endless 'think tanks' all over the world, are designed to coordinate a single global policy between political and business leaders, intelligence personnel, media organisations and anyone who can influence the direction of policy in their own sphere of operation. Major players and regular attenders will know what is happening – or some of it – while others come and go and are kept overwhelmingly in the dark about the big picture. I refer to these cusp groupings as semi-secret in that they can be publicly identified, but what goes on at the inner-core is kept very much 'in house' even from most of their members and participants through a fiercely-imposed system of compartmentalisation. Only let them know what they need to know to serve your interests and no more. The structure of secret societies serves as a perfect example of this principle. Most Freemasons never get higher than the bottom three levels of 'degree' (degree of knowledge) when there are 33 official degrees of the Scottish Rite. Initiates only qualify for the next higher 'compartment' or degree if those at that level choose to allow them. Knowledge can be carefully assigned only to those considered 'safe'. I went to my local Freemason's lodge a few years ago when they were having an 'open day' to show how cuddly they were and when I chatted to some of them I was astonished at how little the rank and file knew even about the most ubiquitous symbols they use. The mushroom technique – keep them in the dark and feed them bullshit – applies to most people in the web as well as the population as a whole. Sub-divisions of the web mirror in theme and structure transnational corporations which have a headquarters somewhere in the world dictating to all their subsidiaries in different countries. Subsidiaries operate in their methodology and branding to the same centrally-dictated plan and policy in pursuit of particular ends. The Cult web functions in the same way. Each country has its own web as a subsidiary of the global one. They consist of networks of secret societies, semi-secret groups and bloodline families and their job is to impose the will of the spider and the global web in their particular country. Subsidiary networks control and manipulate the national political system, finance, corporations, media, medicine, etc. to ensure that they follow the globally-dictated Cult agenda. These networks were the means through which the 'Covid' hoax could be played out with almost every country responding in the same way.

The 'Yessir' pyramid

Compartmentalisation is the key to understanding how a tiny few can dictate the lives of billions when combined with a top-down sequence of imposition and acquiescence. The inner core of the Cult sits at the peak of the pyramidal hierarchy of human society (Fig 2 overleaf). It imposes its will – its agenda for the world – on the level immediately below which acquiesces to that imposition. This level then imposes the Cult will on the level below them which acquiesces and imposes on the next level. Very quickly we meet levels in the hierarchy that have no idea there even is a Cult, but the sequence of imposition and acquiescence

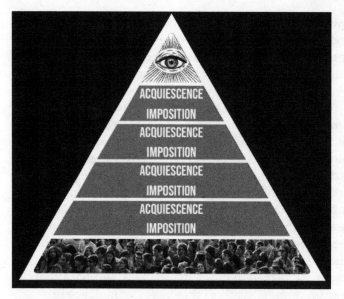

Figure 2: The simple sequence of imposition and compliance that allows a handful of people at the peak of the pyramid to dictate the lives of billions.

continues down the pyramid in just the same way. 'I don't know why we are doing this but the order came from "on-high" and so we better just do it.' Alfred Lord Tennyson said of the cannon fodder levels in his poem *The Charge of the Light Brigade*: 'Theirs not to reason why; theirs but to do and die.' The next line says that 'into the valley of death rode the six hundred' and they died because they obeyed without question what their perceived 'superiors' told them to do. In the same way the population capitulated to 'Covid'. The whole hierarchical pyramid functions like this to allow the very few to direct the enormous many. Eventually imposition-acquiescence-imposition-acquiescence comes down to the mass of the population at the foot of the pyramid. If they acquiesce to those levels of the hierarchy imposing on them (governments/law enforcement/doctors/media) a circuit is completed between the population and the handful of super-psychopaths in the Cult inner core at the top of the pyramid. Without a circuit-breaking refusal to obey, the sequence of imposition and acquiescence allows a staggeringly few people to impose their will upon the entirety of humankind. We are looking at the very sequence that has subjugated billions since the start of 2020. Our freedom has not been taken from us. Humanity has given it away. Fascists do not impose fascism because there are not enough of them. Fascism is imposed by the population acquiescing to fascism. Put another way allowing their perceptions to be programmed to the extent that leads to the population giving their freedom away by giving their perceptions – their mind – away. If this circuit is not broken by humanity ceasing to cooperate with their own enslavement then nothing can change. For that to happen people have to critically think and see through the lies and window dressing and then summon the backbone to act upon what they see. The Cult spends its days working to stop either happening and its methodology is systematic and highly detailed, but it can be overcome and that is what this book is all about.

The Life Program

Okay, back to world number 1 or the world of the 'masses'. Observe the process of what we call 'life' and it is a perceptual download from cradle to grave. The Cult has created a global structure in which perception can be programmed and the program continually topped-up with what appears to be constant confirmation that the program is indeed true reality. The important word here is 'appears'. This is the structure, the fly-trap, the Postage Stamp Consensus or Perceptual Mainframe, which represents that incredibly narrow band of perceived possibility delivered by the 'education' system, mainstream media, science and medicine. From the earliest age the download begins with parents who have themselves succumbed to the very programming their children are about to go through. Most parents don't do this out of malevolence and mostly it is quite the opposite. They do what they believe is best for their children and that is what the program has told them is best. Within three or four years comes the major transition from parental programming to full-blown state (Cult) programming in school, college and university where perceptually-programmed teachers and academics pass on their programming to the next generations. Teachers who resist are soon marginalised and their careers ended while children who resist are called a problem child for whom Ritalin may need to be prescribed. A few years after entering the 'world' children are under the control of authority figures representing the state telling them when they have to be there, when they can leave and when they can speak, eat, even go to the toilet. This is calculated preparation for a lifetime of obeying authority in all its forms. Reflex-action fear of authority is instilled by authority from the start. Children soon learn the carrot and stick consequences of obeying or defying authority which is underpinned daily for the rest of their life. Fortunately I daydreamed through this crap and never obeyed authority simply because it told me to. This approach to my alleged 'betters' continues to this day. There can be consequences of pursuing open-minded freedom in a world of closed-minded conformity. I spent a lot of time in school corridors after being ejected from the classroom for not taking some of it seriously and now I spend a lot of time being ejected from Facebook, YouTube and Twitter. But I can tell you that being true to yourself and not compromising your self-respect is far more exhilarating than bowing to authority for authority's sake. You don't have to be a sheep to the shepherd (authority) and the sheep dog (fear of not obeying authority).

The perceptual download continues throughout the formative years

8   **Perceptions of a Renegade Mind**

in school, college and university while script-reading 'teachers', 'academics' 'scientists', 'doctors' and 'journalists' insist that ongoing generations must be as programmed as they are. Accept the program or you will not pass your 'exams' which confirm your 'degree' of programming. It is tragic to think that many parents pressure their offspring to work hard at school to download the program and qualify for the next stage at college and university. The late, great, American comedian George Carlin said: 'Here's a bumper sticker I'd like to see: We are proud parents of a child who has resisted his teachers' attempts to break his spirit and bend him to the will of his corporate masters.' Well, the best of luck finding many of those, George. Then comes the moment to leave the formal programming years in academia and enter the 'adult' world of work. There you meet others in your chosen or prescribed arena who went through the same Postage Stamp Consensus program before you did. There is therefore overwhelming agreement between almost everyone on the basic foundations of Postage Stamp reality and the rejection, even contempt, of the few who have a mind of their own and are prepared to use it. This has two major effects. Firstly, the consensus confirms to the programmed that their download is really how things are. I mean, everyone knows that, right? Secondly, the arrogance and ignorance of Postage Stamp adherents ensure that anyone questioning the program will have unpleasant consequences for seeking their own truth and not picking their perceptions from the shelf marked: 'Things you must believe without question and if you don't you're a dangerous lunatic conspiracy theorist and a harebrained nutter'.

Every government, agency and corporation is founded on the same Postage Stamp prison cell and you can see why so many people believe the same thing while calling it their own 'opinion'. Fusion of governments and corporations in pursuit of the same agenda was the definition of fascism described by Italian dictator Benito Mussolini. The pressure to conform to perceptual norms downloaded for a lifetime is incessant and infiltrates society right down to family groups that become censors and condemners of their own 'black sheep' for not, ironically, being sheep. We have seen an explosion of that in the 'Covid' era. Cult-owned global media unleashes its propaganda all day every day in support of the Postage Stamp and targets with abuse and ridicule anyone in the public eye who won't bend their mind to the will of the tyranny. Any response to this is denied (certainly in my case). They don't want to give a platform to expose official lies. Cult-owned-and-created Internet giants like Facebook, Google, YouTube and Twitter delete you for having an unapproved opinion. Facebook boasts that its AI censors delete 97-percent of 'hate speech' before anyone even reports it. Much of that 'hate speech' will simply be an opinion that Facebook and its masters don't want people to see. Such perceptual oppression is widely known as fascism. Even Facebook executive Benny Thomas, a 'CEO Global Planning Lead', said in comments secretly recorded by investigative journalism operation Project Veritas that Facebook is 'too powerful' and should be broken up:

> I mean, no king in history has been the ruler of two billion people, but Mark Zuckerberg is … And he's 36. That's too much for a 36-year-old … You should not have power over two billion people. I just think that's wrong.

Thomas said Facebook-owned platforms like Instagram, Oculus, and WhatsApp needed to be separate companies. 'It's too much power when they're all one together'. That's the way the Cult likes it, however. We have an executive of a Cult organisation in Benny Thomas that doesn't know there is a Cult such is the compartmentalisation. Thomas said that Facebook and Google 'are no longer companies, they're countries'. Actually they are more powerful than countries on the basis that if you control information you control perception and control human society.

I love my oppressor

Another expression of this psychological trickery is for those who realise they are being pressured into compliance to eventually convince themselves to believe the official narratives to protect their self-respect from accepting the truth that they have succumbed to meek and subservient compliance. Such people become some of the most vehement defenders of the system. You can see them everywhere screaming abuse at those who prefer to think for themselves and by doing so reminding the compliers of their own capitulation to conformity. 'You are talking dangerous nonsense you Covidiot!!' Are you trying to convince me or yourself? It is a potent form of Stockholm syndrome which is defined as: 'A psychological condition that occurs when a victim of abuse identifies and attaches, or bonds, positively with their abuser.' An example is hostages bonding and even 'falling in love' with their kidnappers. The syndrome has been observed in domestic violence, abused children, concentration camp inmates, prisoners of war and many and various Satanic cults. These are some traits of Stockholm syndrome listed at goodtherapy.org:

- Positive regard towards perpetrators of abuse or captor [see 'Covid'].
- Failure to cooperate with police and other government authorities when it comes to holding perpetrators of abuse or kidnapping accountable [or in the case of 'Covid' cooperating with the police to enforce and defend their captors' demands].
- Little or no effort to escape [see 'Covid'].
- Belief in the goodness of the perpetrators or kidnappers [see 'Covid'].

- Appeasement of captors. This is a manipulative strategy for maintaining one's safety. As victims get rewarded – perhaps with less abuse or even with life itself – their appeasing behaviours are reinforced [see 'Covid'].
- Learned helplessness. This can be akin to 'if you can't beat 'em, join 'em'. As the victims fail to escape the abuse or captivity, they may start giving up and soon realize it's just easier for everyone if they acquiesce all their power to their captors [see 'Covid'].
- Feelings of pity toward the abusers, believing they are actually victims themselves. Because of this, victims may go on a crusade or mission to 'save' [protect] their abuser [see the venom unleashed on those challenging the official 'Covid' narrative].
- Unwillingness to learn to detach from their perpetrators and heal. In essence, victims may tend to be less loyal to themselves than to their abuser [*definitely* see 'Covid'].

Ponder on those traits and compare them with the behaviour of great swathes of the global population who have defended governments and authorities which have spent every minute destroying their lives and livelihoods and those of their children and grandchildren since early 2020 with fascistic lockdowns, house arrest and employment deletion to 'protect' them from a 'deadly virus' that their abusers' perceptually created to bring about this very outcome. We are looking at mass Stockholm syndrome. All those that agree to concede their freedom will believe those perceptions are originating in their own independent 'mind' when in fact by conceding their reality to Stockholm syndrome they have by definition conceded any independence of mind. Listen to the 'opinions' of the acquiescing masses in this 'Covid' era and what gushes forth is the repetition of the official version of everything delivered unprocessed, unfiltered and unquestioned. The whole programming dynamic works this way. I must be free because I'm told that I am and so I think that I am.

You can see what I mean with the chapter theme of 'I'm thinking – Oh, but *are* you?' The great majority are not thinking, let alone for themselves. They are repeating what authority has told them to believe which allows them to be controlled. Weaving through this mentality is the fear that the 'conspiracy theorists' are right and this again explains the often hysterical abuse that ensues when you dare to contest the official narrative of anything. Denial is the mechanism of hiding from yourself what you don't want to be true. Telling people what they want to hear is easy, but it's an infinitely greater challenge to tell them what they would rather not be happening. One is akin to pushing against an open door while the other is met with vehement resistance no matter what the scale of evidence. I don't want it to be true so I'll convince myself that it's not. Examples are everywhere from the denial that a partner is cheating despite all the signs to the reflex-action rejection of any idea that world events in which country after country act in exactly the same way are centrally coordinated. To accept the latter is to accept that a force of unspeakable evil is working to destroy your life and the lives of your children with nothing too horrific to achieve that end. Who the heck wants that to be true? But if we don't face reality the end is duly achieved and the consequences are far worse and ongoing than breaking through the walls of denial today with the courage to make a stand against tyranny.

Connect the dots – but how?

A crucial aspect of perceptual programming is to portray a world in which everything is random and almost nothing is connected to anything else. Randomness cannot be coordinated by its very nature and once you perceive events as random the idea they could be connected is waved away as the rantings of the tinfoil-hat brigade. You can't plan and coordinate random you idiot! No, you can't, but you can hide the coldly-calculated and long-planned behind the *illusion* of randomness. A foundation manifestation of the Renegade Mind is to scan reality for patterns that connect the apparently random and turn pixels and dots into pictures. This is the way I work and have done so for more than 30 years. You look for similarities in people, modus operandi and desired outcomes and slowly, then ever quicker, the picture forms. For instance: There would seem to be no connection between the 'Covid pandemic' hoax and the human-caused global-warming hoax and yet they are masks (appropriately) on the same face seeking the same outcome. Those pushing the global warming myth through the Club of Rome and other Cult agencies are driving the lies about 'Covid' – Bill Gates is an obvious one, but they are endless. Why would the same people be involved in both when they are clearly not connected? Oh, but they *are*. Common themes with personnel are matched by common goals. The 'solutions' to both 'problems' are centralisation of global power to impose the will of the few on the many to 'save' humanity from 'Covid' and save the planet from an 'existential threat' (we need 'zero Covid' and 'zero carbon emissions'). These, in turn, connect with the 'dot' of globalisation which was coined to describe the centralisation of global power in every area of life through incessant political and corporate expansion, trading blocks and superstates like the European Union. If you are the few and you want to control the many you have to centralise power and decision-making. The more you centralise power the more power the few at the centre will have over the many; and the more that power is centralised the more power those at the centre have to centralise even quicker. The momentum of centralisation gets faster and faster which is exactly the process we have witnessed. In this way the hoaxed 'pandemic' and the fakery of human-caused global warming serve the interests of globalisation and the seizure of global power in the hands of the Cult inner-circle which is behind 'Covid', 'climate change' *and* globalisation. At this point random 'dots' become a clear and obvious picture or pattern.

Klaus Schwab, the classic Bond villain who founded the Cult's Gates-funded World Economic Forum, published a book in 2020, *The Great Reset*, in which he used the 'problem' of 'Covid' to justify a total transformation of human society to 'save' humanity from 'climate change'. Schwab said: 'The pandemic represents a rare but narrow window of opportunity to reflect, reimagine, and reset our world.' What he didn't mention is that the Cult he serves is behind both hoaxes as I show in my book *The Answer*. He and the Cult don't have to reimagine the world. They know precisely what they want and that's why they destroyed human society with 'Covid' to 'build back better' in their grand design. Their job is not to imagine, but to get humanity to imagine and agree with their plans while believing it's all random. It must be pure coincidence that 'The Great Reset' has long been the Cult's code name for the global imposition of fascism and replaced previous code-names of the 'New World Order' used by Cult frontmen like Father George Bush and the 'New Order of the Ages' which emerged from Freemasonry and much older secret societies. New Order of the Ages appears on the reverse of the Great Seal of the United States as 'Novus ordo seclorum' underneath the Cult symbol used since way back of the pyramid and all seeing-eye (Fig 3). The pyramid is the hierarchy of human control headed by the illuminated eye that symbolises the force behind the Cult which I will expose in later chapters. The term 'Annuit Coeptis' translates as 'He favours our undertaking'. We are told the 'He' is the Christian god, but 'He' is not as I will be explaining.

Figure 3: The all-seeing eye of the Cult 'god' on the Freemason-designed Great Seal of the United States and also on the dollar bill.

Having you on

Two major Cult techniques of perceptual manipulation that relate to all this are what I have called since the 1990s Problem-Reaction-Solution (PRS) and the Totalitarian Tiptoe (TT). They can be uncovered by the inquiring mind with a simple question: Who benefits? The answer usually identifies the perpetrators of a given action or happening through the concept of 'he who most benefits from a crime is the one most likely to have committed it'. The Latin 'Cue bono?' – Who benefits? – is widely attributed to the Roman orator and statesman Marcus Tullius Cicero. No wonder it goes back so far when the concept has been relevant to human behaviour since history was recorded. Problem-Reaction-Solution is the technique used to manipulate us every day by covertly creating a problem (or the illusion of one) and offering the solution to the problem (or the illusion of one). In the first phase you create the problem and blame someone or something else for why it has happened. This may relate to a financial collapse, terrorist attack, war, global warming or pandemic, anything in fact that will allow you to impose the 'solution' to change society in the way you desire at that time. The 'problem' doesn't have to be real. PRS is manipulation of perception and all you need is the population to believe the problem is real. Human-caused global warming and the 'Covid pandemic' only have to be *perceived* to be real for the population to accept the 'solutions' of authority. I refer to this technique as NO-Problem-Reaction-Solution. Billions did not meekly accept house arrest from early 2020 because there was a real deadly 'Covid pandemic' but because they perceived – believed – that to be the case. The antidote to Problem-Reaction-Solution is to ask who benefits from the proposed solution. Invariably it will be anyone who wants to justify more control through deletion of freedom and centralisation of power and decision-making.

The two world wars were Problem-Reaction-Solutions that transformed and realigned global society. Both were manipulated into being by the Cult as I have detailed in books since the mid-1990s. They dramatically centralised global power, especially World War Two, which led to the United Nations and other global bodies thanks to the overt and covert manipulations of the Rockefeller family and other Cult bloodlines like the Rothschilds. The UN is a stalking horse for full-blown world government that I will come to shortly. The land on which the UN building stands in New York was donated by the Rockefellers and the same Cult family was behind Big Pharma scalpel and drug 'medicine' and the creation of the World Health Organization as part of the UN. They have been stalwarts of the eugenics movement and funded Hitler's race-purity expert' Ernst Rudin. The human-caused global warming hoax has been orchestrated by the Club of Rome through the UN which is manufacturing both the 'problem' through its Intergovernmental Panel on Climate Change and imposing the 'solution' through its Agenda 21 and Agenda 2030 which demand the total centralisation of global power to 'save the world' from a climate hoax the United Nations is itself perpetrating. What a small world the Cult can be seen to be particularly among the inner circles. The bedfellow of Problem-Reaction-Solution is the Totalitarian Tiptoe which became the Totalitarian Sprint in 2020. The technique is fashioned to hide the carefully-coordinated behind the cover of apparently random events. You start the sequence at 'A' and you know you are heading for 'Z'. You don't want people to know that and each step on the journey is presented as a random happening while all the steps strung together lead in the same direction. The speed may have quickened dramatically in recent times, but you can still see the incremental approach of the Tiptoe in the case of 'Covid' as each new imposition takes us deeper into fascism. Tell people they have to do this or that to get back to 'normal', then this and this and this. With each new demand adding to the ones that went before the population's freedom is deleted until it disappears. The spider wraps its web around the flies more comprehensively with each new diktat. I'll highlight this in more detail when I get to the 'Covid' hoax and how it has been pulled off. Another prime example of the Totalitarian Tiptoe is how the Cult-created European Union went from a 'free-trade zone' to a centralised bureaucratic dictatorship through the Tiptoe of incremental centralisation of power until nations became mere administrative units for Cult-owned dark suits in Brussels.

The antidote to ignorance is knowledge which the Cult seeks vehemently to deny us, but despite the systematic censorship to that end the Renegade Mind can overcome this by vociferously seeking out the facts no matter the impediments put in the way. There is also a method of thinking and perceiving – *knowing* – that doesn't even need names, dates, place-type facts to identify the patterns that reveal the story. I'll get to that in the final chapter. All you need to know about the manipulation of human society and to what end is still out there – *at the time of writing* – in the form of books, videos and websites for those that really want to breach the walls of programmed perception. To access this knowledge requires the abandonment of the mainstream media as a source of information in the awareness that this is owned and controlled by the Cult and therefore promotes mass perceptions that suit the Cult. Mainstream media lies all day, every day. That is its function and very reason for being. Where it does tell the truth, here and there, is only because the truth and the Cult agenda very occasionally coincide. If you look for fact and insight to the BBC, CNN and virtually all the rest of them you are asking to be conned and perceptually programmed.

Know the outcome and you'll see the journey

Events seem random when you have no idea where the world is being taken. Once you do the random becomes the carefully planned. Know the outcome and you'll see the journey is a phrase I have been using for a long time to give context to daily happenings that appear unconnected. Does a problem, or illusion of a problem, trigger a proposed 'solution' that further drives society in the direction of the outcome? Invariably the answer will be yes and the random – *abracadabra* – becomes the clearly coordinated. So what is this outcome that unlocks the door to a massively expanded understanding of daily events? I will summarise its major aspects – the fine detail is in my other books – and those new to this information will see that the world they thought they were living in is a very different place. The foundation of the Cult agenda is the incessant centralisation of power and all such centralisation is ultimately in pursuit of Cult control on a global level. I have described for a long time the planned world structure of top-down dictatorship as the Hunger Games Society. The term obviously comes from the movie series which portrayed a world in which a few living in military-protected hi-tech luxury were the overlords of a population condemned to abject poverty in isolated 'sectors' that were not allowed to interact. 'Covid' lockdowns and travel bans anyone? The 'Hunger Games' pyramid of structural control has the inner circle of the Cult at the top with pretty much the entire population at the bottom under their control through dependency for survival on the Cult. The whole structure is planned to be protected and enforced by a military-police state (Fig 4).

Here you have the reason for the global lockdowns of the fake

Figure 4: The Hunger Games Society structure I have long warned was planned and now the 'Covid' hoax has made it possible. This is the real reason for lockdowns.

pandemic to coldly destroy independent incomes and livelihoods and make everyone dependent on the 'state' (the Cult that controls the 'states'). I have warned in my books for many years about the plan to introduce a 'guaranteed income' – a barely survivable pittance – designed to impose dependency when employment was destroyed by AI technology and now even more comprehensively at great speed by the 'Covid' scam. Once the pandemic was played and lockdown consequences began to delete independent income the authorities began to talk right on cue about the need for a guaranteed income and a 'Great Reset'. Guaranteed income will be presented as benevolent governments seeking to help a desperate people – desperate as a direct result of actions of the same governments. The truth is that such payments are a trap. You will only get them if you do exactly what the authorities demand including mass vaccination (genetic manipulation). We have seen this theme already in Australia where those dependent on government benefits have them reduced if parents don't agree to have their children vaccinated according to an insane health-destroying government-dictated schedule. Calculated economic collapse applies to governments as well as people. The Cult wants rid of countries through the creation of a world state with countries broken up into regions ruled by a world government and super states like the European Union. Countries must be bankrupted, too, to this end and it's being achieved by the trillions in 'rescue packages' and furlough payments, trillions in lost taxation, and money-no-object spending on 'Covid' including constant all-medium advertising (programming) which has made the media dependent on government for much of its income. The day of reckoning is coming – as planned – for government spending and given that it has been made possible by printing money and not by production/taxation there is inflation on the way that has the potential to wipe out monetary value. In that case there will be no need for the Cult to steal your money. It just won't be worth anything (see the German Weimar Republic before the Nazis took over). Many have been okay with lockdowns while getting a percentage of their income from so-called furlough payments without having to work. Those payments are dependent, however, on people having at least a theoretical job with a business considered non-essential and ordered to close. As these business go under because they are closed by lockdown after lockdown the furlough stops and it will for everyone eventually. Then what? The 'then what?' is precisely the idea.

Hired hands

Between the Hunger Games Cult elite and the dependent population is planned to be a vicious military-police state (a fusion of the two into one force). This has been in the making for a long time with police looking ever more like the military and carrying weapons to match. The pandemic scam has seen this process accelerate so fast as lockdown house arrest is brutally enforced by carefully recruited fascist minds and gormless system-servers. The police and military are planned to merge into a centrally-directed world army in a global structure headed by a world government which wouldn't be elected even by the election fixes now in place. The world army is not planned even to be human and instead wars would be fought, primarily against the population, using robot technology controlled by artificial intelligence. I have been warning about this for decades and now militaries around the world are being transformed by this very AI technology. The global regime that I describe is a particular form of fascism known as a technocracy in which decisions are not made by clueless and co-opted politicians but by unelected technocrats – scientists, engineers, technologists and bureaucrats. Cult-owned-and-controlled Silicon Valley giants are examples of technocracy and they already have far more power to direct world events than governments. They are with their censorship *selecting* governments. I know that some are calling the 'Great Reset' a Marxist communist takeover, but fascism and Marxism are different labels for the same tyranny. Tell those who lived in fascist Germany and Stalinist Russia that there was a difference in the way their freedom was deleted and their lives controlled. I could call it a fascist technocracy or a Marxist technocracy and they would be equally accurate. The Hunger Games society with its world government structure would oversee a world army, world central bank and single world cashless currency imposing its will on a microchipped population (Fig 5). Scan its different elements and see how the illusory pandemic is forcing society in this very

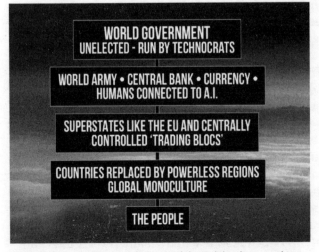

direction at great speed. Leaders of 23 countries and the World Health Organization (WHO) backed the idea in March, 2021, of a global treaty for 'international cooperation' in 'health emergencies' and nations should 'come together as a global community for peaceful cooperation that extends beyond this

Figure 5: The structure of global control the Cult has been working towards for so long and this has been enormously advanced by the 'Covid' illusion.

crisis'. Cut the Orwellian bullshit and this means another step towards global government. The plan includes a cashless digital money system that I first warned about in 1993. Right at the start of 'Covid' the deeply corrupt Tedros Adhanom Ghebreyesus, the crooked and merely gofer 'head' of the World Health Organization, said it was possible to catch the 'virus' by touching cash and it was better to use cashless means. The claim was ridiculous nonsense and like the whole 'Covid' mind-trick it was nothing to do with 'health' and everything to do with pushing every aspect of the Cult agenda. As a result of the Tedros lie the use of cash has plummeted. The Cult script involves a single world digital currency that would eventually be technologically embedded in the body. China is a massive global centre for the Cult and if you watch what is happening there you will know what is planned for everywhere. The Chinese government is developing a digital currency which would allow fines to be deducted immediately via AI for anyone caught on camera breaking its fantastic list of laws and the money is going to be programmable with an expiry date to ensure that no one can accrue wealth except the Cult and its operatives.

Serfdom is so smart

The Cult plan is far wider, extreme, and more comprehensive than even most conspiracy researchers appreciate and I will come to the true depths of deceit and control in the chapters 'Who controls the Cult?' and 'Escaping Wetiko'. Even the world that we know is crazy enough. We are being deluged with ever more sophisticated and controlling technology under the heading of 'smart'. We have smart televisions, smart meters, smart cards, smart cars, smart driving, smart roads, smart pills, smart patches, smart watches, smart skin, smart borders, smart pavements, smart streets, smart cities, smart communities, smart environments, smart growth, smart planet ... smart *everything* around us. Smart technologies and methods of operation are designed to interlock to create a global Smart Grid connecting the entirety of human society including human minds to create a centrally-dictated 'hive' mind. 'Smart cities' is code for densely-occupied megacities of total surveillance and control through AI. Ever more destructive frequency communication systems like 5G have been rolled out without any official testing for health and psychological effects (colossal). 5G/6G/7G systems are needed to run the Smart Grid and each one becomes more destructive of body and mind. Deleting independent income is crucial to forcing people into these AI-policed prisons by ending private property ownership (except for the Cult elite). The Cult's Great Reset now openly foresees a global society in which no one will own any possessions and everything will be rented while the Cult would own literally everything under the guise of government and corporations. The aim has been to use the lockdowns to destroy sources of income on a mass scale and when the people are destitute and in unrepayable amounts of debt (problem) Cult assets come forward with the pledge to write-off debt in return for handing over all property and possessions (solution). Everything – literally everything including people – would be connected to the Internet via AI. I was warning years ago about the coming Internet of Things (IoT) in which all devices and technology from your car to your fridge would be plugged into the Internet and controlled by AI. Now we are already there with much more to come. The next stage is the Internet of Everything (IoE) which is planned to include the connection of AI to the human brain and body to replace the human mind with a centrally-controlled AI mind. Instead of perceptions being manipulated through control of information and censorship those perceptions would come direct from the Cult through AI. What do you think? You think whatever AI decides that you think. In human terms there would be no individual 'think' any longer. Too incredible? The ravings of a lunatic? Not at all. Cult-owned crazies in Silicon Valley have been telling us the plan for years without explaining the real motivation and calculated implications. These include Google executive and 'futurist' Ray Kurzweil who highlights the year 2030 for when this would be underway. He said:

> Our thinking ... will be a hybrid of biological and non-biological thinking ... humans will be able to extend their limitations and 'think in the cloud' ... We're going to put gateways to the cloud in our brains ... We're going to gradually merge and enhance ourselves ... In my view, that's the nature of being human – we transcend our limitations.

> As the technology becomes vastly superior to what we are then the small proportion that is still human gets smaller and smaller and smaller until it's just utterly negligible.

The sales-pitch of Kurzweil and Cult-owned Silicon Valley is that this would make us 'super-human' when the real aim is to make us post-human and no longer 'human' in the sense that we have come to know. The entire global population would be connected to AI and become the centrally-controlled 'hive-mind' of externally-delivered perceptions. The Smart Grid being installed to impose the Cult's will on the world is being constructed to allow particular locations – even one location – to control the whole global system. From these prime control centres, which absolutely include China and Israel, anything connected to the Internet would be switched on or off and manipulated at will. Energy systems could be cut, communication via the Internet taken down, computer-controlled driverless autonomous vehicles driven off the road, medical devices switched off, the potential is limitless given how much AI and Internet connections now run human society. We have seen nothing yet if we allow this to continue. Autonomous vehicle makers are working with law enforcement to produce cars designed to automatically pull over if they detect a police or emergency vehicle flashing from up to 100 feet away. At a police stop the car would be unlocked and the window rolled down automatically. Vehicles would only take you where the computer (the state) allowed. The end of petrol vehicles and speed limiters on all new cars in the UK and EU from 2022 are steps leading to electric computerised transport over which ultimately you have no control. The picture is far bigger even than the Cult global network or web and that will become clear when I get to the nature of the 'spider'. There is a connection between all these happenings and the instigation of DNA-manipulating 'vaccines' (which aren't 'vaccines') justified by the 'Covid' hoax. That connection is the unfolding plan to transform the human body from a biological to a synthetic biological state and this is why synthetic biology is such a fast-emerging discipline of mainstream science. 'Covid vaccines' are infusing self-replicating synthetic genetic material into the cells to cumulatively take us on the Totalitarian Tiptoe from Human 1.0 to the synthetic biological Human 2.0 which will be physically and perceptually attached to the Smart Grid to one hundred percent control every thought, perception and deed. Humanity needs to wake up and *fast*.

This is the barest explanation of where the 'outcome' is planned to go but it's enough to see the journey happening all around us. Those new to this information will already see 'Covid' in a whole new context. I will add much more detail as we go along, but for the minutiae evidence see my mega-works, *The Answer*, *The Trigger* and *Everything You Need to Know But Have Never Been Told*.

Now – how does a Renegade Mind see the 'world'?

CHAPTER TWO

Renegade Perception

It is one thing to be clever and another to be wise
George R.R. Martin

A simple definition of the difference between a programmed mind and a Renegade Mind would be that one sees only dots while the other connects them to see the picture. Reading reality with accuracy requires the observer to (a) know the planned outcome and (b) realise that everything, but *everything*, is connected.

The entirety of infinite reality is connected – that's its very nature – and with human society an expression of infinite reality the same must apply. Simple cause and effect is a connection. The effect is triggered by the cause and the effect then becomes the cause of another effect. Nothing happens in isolation because it *can't*. Life in whatever reality is simple choice and consequence. We make choices and these lead to consequences. If we don't like the consequences we can make different choices and get different consequences which lead to other choices and consequences. The choice and the consequence are not only connected they are indivisible. You can't have one without the other as an old song goes. A few cannot control the world unless those being controlled allow that to happen – cause and effect, choice and consequence. Control – who has it and who doesn't – is a two-way process, a symbiotic relationship, involving the controller and controlled. 'They took my freedom away!!' Well, yes, but you also gave it to them. Humanity is subjected to mass control because humanity has acquiesced to that control. This is all cause and effect and literally a case of give and take. In the same way world events of every kind are connected and the Cult works incessantly to sell the illusion of the random and coincidental to maintain the essential (to them) perception of dots that hide the picture. Renegade Minds know this and constantly scan the world for patterns of connection. This is absolutely pivotal in understanding the happenings in the world and without that perspective clarity is impossible. First you know the planned outcome and then you identify the steps on the journey – the day-by-day apparently random which, when connected in relation to the outcome, no longer appear as individual events, but as the proverbial *chain* of events leading in the same direction. I'll give you some examples:

Political puppet show

We are told to believe that politics is 'adversarial' in that different parties with different beliefs engage in an endless tussle for power. There may have been some truth in that up to a point – and only a point – but today divisions between 'different' parties are rhetorical not ideological. Even the rhetorical is fusing into one-speak as the parties eject any remaining free thinkers while others succumb to the ever-gathering intimidation of anyone with the 'wrong' opinion. The Cult is not a new phenomenon and can be traced back thousands of years as my books have documented. Its intergenerational initiates have been manipulating events with increasing effect the more that global power has been centralised. In ancient times the Cult secured control through the system of monarchy in which 'special' bloodlines (of which more later) demanded the right to rule as kings and queens simply by birthright and by vanquishing others who claimed the same birthright. There came a time, however, when people had matured enough to see the unfairness of such tyranny and demanded a say in who governed them. Note the word – *governed* them. Not served them – *governed* them, hence government defined as 'the political direction and control exercised over the actions of the members, citizens, or inhabitants of communities, societies, and states; direction of the affairs of a state, community, etc.' Governments exercise control over rather than serve just like the monarchies before them. Bizarrely there are still countries like the United Kingdom which are ruled by a monarch *and* a government that officially answers to the monarch. The UK head of state and that of Commonwealth countries such as Canada, Australia and New Zealand is 'selected' by who in a *single family* had unprotected sex with whom and in what order. Pinch me it can't be true. Ouch! Shit, it is. The demise of monarchies in most countries offered a potential vacuum in which some form of free and fair society could arise and the Cult had that base covered. Monarchies had served its interests but they couldn't continue in the face of such widespread opposition and, anyway, replacing a 'royal' dictatorship that people could see with a dictatorship 'of the people' hiding behind the concept of 'democracy' presented far greater manipulative possibilities and ways of hiding coordinated tyranny behind the illusion of 'freedom'.

Democracy is quite wrongly defined as government selected by the population. This is not the case at all. It is government selected by *some* of the population (and then only in theory). This 'some' doesn't even have to be the majority as we have seen so often in first-past-the-post elections in which the so-called majority party wins fewer votes than the 'losing' parties combined. Democracy can give total power to a party in government from a minority of the votes cast. It's a sleight of hand to sell tyranny as freedom. Seventy-four million Trump-supporting Americans didn't vote for the 'Democratic' Party of Joe Biden in the distinctly dodgy election in 2020 and yet far from acknowledging the wishes and feelings of that great percentage of American society the Cult-owned Biden government set out from day one to destroy them and their right to a voice and opinion. Empty shell Biden and his Cult handlers said they were doing this to 'protect democracy'. Such is the level of lunacy and sickness to which politics has descended. Connect the dots and relate them to the desired outcome – a world government run by self-appointed technocrats and no longer even elected politicians. While operating through its political agents in government the Cult is at the same time encouraging public distain for politicians by putting idiots and incompetents in theoretical power on the road to deleting them. The idea is to instil a public reaction that says of the technocrats: 'Well, they couldn't do any worse than the pathetic politicians.' It's all about controlling perception and Renegade Minds can see through that while programmed minds cannot when they are ignorant of both the planned outcome and the manipulation techniques employed to secure that end. This knowledge can be learned, however, and fast if people choose to get informed.

Politics may at first sight appear very difficult to control from a central point. I mean look at the 'different' parties and how would you be able to oversee them all and their constituent parts? In truth, it's very straightforward because of their structure. We are back to the pyramid of imposition and acquiescence. Organisations are structured in the same way as the system as a whole. Political parties are not open forums of free expression. They are hierarchies. I was a national spokesman for the British Green Party which claimed to be a different kind of politics in which influence and power was devolved; but I can tell you from direct experience – and it's far worse now – that Green parties are run as hierarchies like all the others however much they may try to hide that fact or kid themselves that it's not true. A very few at the top of all political parties are directing policy and personnel. They decide if you are elevated in the party or serve as a government minister and to do that you have to be a yes man or woman. Look at all the maverick political thinkers who never ascended the greasy pole. If you want to progress within the party or reach 'high-office' you need to fall into line and conform. Exceptions to this are rare indeed. Should you want to run for parliament or Congress you have to persuade the local or state level of the party to select you and for that you need to play the game as dictated by the hierarchy. If you secure election and wish to progress within the greater structure you need to go on conforming to what is acceptable to those running the hierarchy from the peak of the pyramid. Political parties are perceptual gulags and the very fact that there are party 'Whips' appointed to 'whip' politicians into voting the way the hierarchy demands exposes the ridiculous idea that politicians are elected to serve the people they are supposed to represent. Cult operatives and manipulation has long seized control of major parties that have any chance of forming a government and at least most of those that haven't. A new party forms and the Cult goes to work to infiltrate and direct. This has reached such a level today that you see video compilations of 'leaders' of all parties whether Democrats, Republicans, Conservative, Labour and Green parroting the same Cult mantra of 'Build Back Better' and the 'Great Reset' which are straight off the Cult song-sheet to describe the transformation of global society in response to the Cult-instigated hoaxes of the 'Covid pandemic' and human-caused 'climate change'. To see Caroline Lucas, the Green Party MP that I knew when I was in the party in the 1980s, speaking in support of plans proposed by Cult operative Klaus Schwab representing the billionaire global elite is a real head-shaker.

Many parties – one master

The party system is another mind-trick and was instigated to change the nature of the dictatorship by swapping 'royalty' for dark suits that people believed – though now ever less so – represented their interests. Understanding this trick is to realise that a single force (the Cult) controls all parties either directly in terms of the major ones or through manipulation of perception and ideology with others. You don't need to manipulate Green parties to demand your transformation of society in the name of 'climate change' when they are obsessed with the lie that this is essential to 'save the planet'. You just give them a platform and away they go serving your interests while believing they are being environmentally virtuous. America's political structure is a perfect blueprint for how the two or multi-party system is really a one-party state. The Republican Party is controlled from one step back in the shadows by a group made up of billionaires and their gofers known as neoconservatives or Neocons. I have exposed them in fine detail in my books and they were the driving force behind the policies of the imbecilic presidency of Boy George Bush which included 9/11 (see *The Trigger* for a comprehensive demolition of the official story), the subsequent 'war on terror' (war *of* terror) and the invasions of Afghanistan and Iraq. The latter was a No-Problem-Reaction-Solution based on claims by Cult operatives, including Bush and British Prime Minister Tony Blair, about Saddam Hussein's 'weapons of mass destruction' which did not exist as war criminals Bush and Blair well knew.

The Democratic Party has its own 'Neocon' group controlling from the background which I call the 'Democons' and here's the penny-drop – the Neocons and Democons answer to the same masters one step further back into the shadows (Fig 6). At that level of the Cult the Republican and Democrat parties are controlled by the same people and no matter which is in power the Cult is in power. This is how it works in almost every country and certainly in Britain with Conservative, Labour, Liberal Democrat and Green parties now all on the same page whatever the rhetoric may be in their feeble attempts to appear different. Neocons operated at the time of Bush through a think tank called The Project for the New American Century which in September, 2000, published a document entitled *Rebuilding America's Defenses: Strategies, Forces, and Resources For a New Century* demanding that America fight 'multiple, simultaneous major theatre wars' as a 'core mission' to force regime-

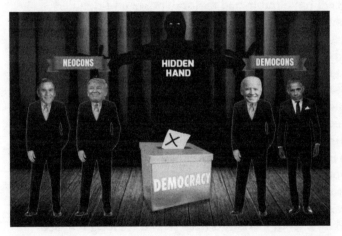

Figure 6: Different front people, different parties – same control system.

change in countries including Iraq, Libya and Syria. Neocons arranged for Bush ('Republican') and Blair ('Labour Party') to front-up the invasion of Iraq and when they departed the Democons orchestrated the targeting of Libya and Syria through Barack Obama ('Democrat') and British Prime Minister David Cameron ('Conservative Party'). We have 'different' parties and 'different' people, but the same unfolding script. The more the Cult has seized the reigns of parties and personnel the more their policies have transparently pursued the same agenda to the point where the fascist 'Covid' impositions of the Conservative junta of Jackboot Johnson in Britain were opposed by the Labour Party because they were not fascist enough. The Labour Party is likened to the US Democrats while the Conservative Party is akin to a British version of the Republicans and on both sides of the Atlantic they all speak the same language and support the direction demanded by the Cult although some more enthusiastically than others. It's a similar story in country after country because it's all centrally controlled. Oh, but what about

Trump? I'll come to him shortly. Political 'choice' in the 'party' system goes like this: You vote for Party A and they get into government. You don't like what they do so next time you vote for Party B and they get into government. You don't like what they do when it's pretty much the same as Party A and why wouldn't that be with both controlled by the same force? Given that only two, sometimes three, parties have any chance of forming a government to get rid of Party B that you don't like you have to vote again for Party A which … you don't like. This, ladies and gentlemen, is what they call 'democracy' which we are told – wrongly – is a term interchangeable with 'freedom'.

The cult of cults

At this point I need to introduce a major expression of the Global Cult known as Sabbatian-Frankism. Sabbatian is also spelt as Sabbatean. I will summarise here. I have published major exposés and detailed background in other works. Sabbatian-Frankism combines the names of two frauds posing as 'Jewish' men, Sabbatai Zevi (1626-1676), a rabbi, black magician and occultist who proclaimed he was the Jewish messiah; and Jacob Frank (1726-1791), the Polish 'Jew', black magician and occultist who said he was the reincarnation of 'messiah' Zevi and biblical patriarch Jacob. They worked across two centuries to establish the Sabbatian-Frankist cult that plays a major, indeed central, role in the manipulation of human society by the Global Cult which has its origins much further back in history than Sabbatai Zevi. I should emphasise two points here in response to the shrill voices that will scream 'anti-Semitism': (1) Sabbatian-Frankists are NOT Jewish and only pose as such to hide their cult behind a Jewish façade; and (2) my information about this cult has come from Jewish sources who have long realised that their society and community has been infiltrated and taken over by interloper Sabbatian-Frankists. Infiltration has been the foundation technique of Sabbatian-Frankism from its official origin in the 17th century. Zevi's Sabbatian sect attracted a massive following described as the biggest messianic movement in Jewish history, spreading as far as Africa and Asia, and he promised a return for the Jews to the 'Promised Land' of Israel. Sabbatianism was not Judaism but an inversion of everything that mainstream Judaism stood for. So much so that this sinister cult would have a feast day when Judaism had a fast day and whatever was forbidden in Judaism the Sabbatians were encouraged and even commanded to do. This included incest and what would be today called Satanism. Members were forbidden to marry outside the sect and there was a system of keeping their children ignorant of what they were part of until they were old enough to be trusted not to unknowingly reveal anything to outsiders. The same system is employed to this day by the Global Cult in general which Sabbatian-

Frankism has enormously influenced and now largely controls.

Zevi and his Sabbatians suffered a setback with the intervention by the Sultan of the Islamic Ottoman Empire in the Middle East and what is now the Republic of Turkey where Zevi was located. The Sultan gave him the choice of proving his 'divinity', converting to Islam or facing torture and death. Funnily enough Zevi chose to convert or at least appear to. Some of his supporters were disillusioned and drifted away, but many did not with 300 families also converting – only in theory – to Islam. They continued behind this Islamic smokescreen to follow the goals, rules and rituals of Sabbatianism and became known as 'crypto-Jews' or the 'Dönmeh' which means 'to turn'. This is rather ironic because they didn't 'turn' and instead hid behind a fake Islamic persona. The process of appearing to be one thing while being very much another would become the calling card of Sabbatianism especially after Zevi's death and the arrival of the Satanist Jacob Frank in the 18th century when the cult became Sabbatian-Frankism and plumbed still new depths of depravity and infiltration which included – still includes – human sacrifice and sex with children. Wherever Sabbatians go paedophilia and Satanism follow and is it really a surprise that Hollywood is so infested with child abuse and Satanism when it was established by Sabbatian-Frankists and is still controlled by them? Hollywood has been one of the prime vehicles for global perceptual programming and manipulation. How many believe the version of 'history' portrayed in movies when it is a travesty and inversion (again) of the truth? Rabbi Marvin Antelman describes Frankism in his book, *To Eliminate the Opiate*, as 'a movement of complete evil' while Jewish professor Gershom Scholem said of Frank in *The Messianic Idea in Judaism*: 'In all his actions [he was] a truly corrupt and degenerate individual ... one of the most frightening phenomena in the whole of Jewish history.' Frank was excommunicated by traditional rabbis, as was Zevi, but Frank was undeterred and enjoyed vital support from the House of Rothschild, the infamous banking dynasty whose inner-core are Sabbatian-Frankists and not Jews. Infiltration of the Roman Church and Vatican was instigated by Frank with many Dönmeh 'turning' again to convert to Roman Catholicism with a view to hijacking the reins of power. This was the ever-repeating modus operandi and continues to be so. Pose as an advocate of the religion, culture or country that you want to control and then manipulate your people into the positions of authority and influence largely as advisers, administrators and Svengalis for those that appear to be in power. They did this with Judaism, Christianity (Christian Zionism is part of this), Islam and other religions and nations until Sabbatian-Frankism spanned the world as it does today.

Sabbatian Saudis and the terror network

One expression of the Sabbatian-Frankist Dönmeh within Islam is the
ruling family of Saudi Arabia, the House of Saud, through which came
the vile distortion of Islam known as Wahhabism. This is the violent
creed followed by terrorist groups like Al-Qaeda and ISIS or Islamic
State. Wahhabism is the hand-chopping, head-chopping 'religion' of
Saudi Arabia which is used to keep the people in a constant state of fear
so the interloper House of Saud can continue to rule. Al-Qaeda and
Islamic State were lavishly funded by the House of Saud while being
created and directed by the Sabbatian-Frankist network in the United
States that operates through the Pentagon, CIA and the government in
general of whichever 'party'. The front man for the establishment of
Wahhabism in the middle of the 18th century was a Sabbatian-Frankist
'crypto-Jew' posing as Islamic called Muhammad ibn Abd al-Wahhab.
His daughter would marry the son of Muhammad bin Saud who
established the first Saudi state before his death in 1765 with support
from the British Empire. Bin Saud's successors would establish modern
Saudi Arabia in league with the British and Americans in 1932 which
allowed them to seize control of Islam's major shrines in Mecca and
Medina. They have dictated the direction of Sunni Islam ever since while
Iran is the major centre of the Shiite version and here we have the source
of at least the public conflict between them. The Sabbatian network has
used its Wahhabi extremists to carry out Problem-Reaction-Solution
terrorist attacks in the name of 'Al-Qaeda' and 'Islamic State' to justify a
devastating 'war on terror', ever-increasing surveillance of the
population and to terrify people into compliance. Another insight of the
Renegade Mind is the streetwise understanding that just because a
country, location or people are attacked doesn't mean that those
apparently representing that country, location or people are not behind
the attackers. Often they are *orchestrating* the attacks because of the
societal changes that can be then justified in the name of 'saving the
population from terrorists'.

I show in great detail in *The Trigger* how Sabbatian-Frankists were the
real perpetrators of 9/11 and not '19 Arab hijackers' who were blamed
for what happened. Observe what was justified in the name of 9/11
alone in terms of Middle East invasions, mass surveillance and control
that fulfilled the demands of the Project for the New American Century
document published by the Sabbatian Neocons. What appear to be
enemies are on the deep inside players on the same Sabbatian team.
Israel and Arab 'royal' dictatorships are all ruled by Sabbatians and the
recent peace agreements between Israel and Saudi Arabia, the United
Arab Emirates (UAE) and others are only making formal what has
always been the case behind the scenes. Palestinians who have been
subjected to grotesque tyranny since Israel was bombed and terrorised

into existence in 1948 have never stood a chance. Sabbatian-Frankists have controlled Israel (so the constant theme of violence and war which Sabbatians love) and they have controlled the Arab countries that Palestinians have looked to for real support that never comes. 'Royal families' of the Arab world in Saudi Arabia, Bahrain, UAE, etc., are all Sabbatians with allegiance to the aims of the cult and not what is best for their Arabic populations. They have stolen the oil and financial resources from their people by false claims to be 'royal dynasties' with a genetic right to rule and by employing vicious militaries to impose their will.

Satanic 'illumination'

The Satanist Jacob Frank formed an alliance in 1773 with two other Sabbatians, Mayer Amschel Rothschild (1744-1812), founder of the Rothschild banking dynasty, and Jesuit-educated fraudulent Jew, Adam Weishaupt, and this led to the formation of the Bavarian Illuminati, firstly under another name, in 1776. The Illuminati would be the manipulating force behind the French Revolution (1789-1799) and was also involved in the American Revolution (1775-1783) before and after the Illuminati's official creation. Weishaupt would later become (in public) a Protestant Christian in archetypal Sabbatian style. I read that his name can be decoded as Adam-Weis-haupt or 'the first man to lead those who know'. He wasn't a leader in the sense that he was a subordinate, but he did lead those below him in a crusade of transforming human society that still continues today. The theme was confirmed as early as 1785 when a horseman courier called Lanz was reported to be struck by lighting and extensive Illuminati documents were found in his saddlebags. They made the link to Weishaupt and detailed the plan for world takeover. Current events with 'Covid' fascism have been in the making for a very long time. Jacob Frank was jailed for 13 years by the Catholic Inquisition after his arrest in 1760 and on his release he headed for Frankfurt, Germany, home city and headquarters of the House of Rothschild where the alliance was struck with Mayer Amschel Rothschild and Weishaupt. Rothschild arranged for Frank to be given the title of Baron and he became a wealthy nobleman with a big following of Jews in Germany, the Austro-Hungarian Empire and other European countries. Most of them would have believed he was on their side.

The name 'Illuminati' came from the Zohar which is a body of works in the Jewish mystical 'bible' called the Kabbalah. 'Zohar' is the foundation of Sabbatian-Frankist belief and in Hebrew 'Zohar' means 'splendour', 'radiance', 'illuminated', and so we have 'Illuminati'. They claim to be the 'Illuminated Ones' from their knowledge systematically hidden from the human population and passed on through generations of carefully-chosen initiates in the global secret society network or Cult. Hidden knowledge includes an awareness of the Cult agenda for the world and the nature of our collective reality that I will explore later. Cult 'illumination' is symbolised by the torch held by the Statue of Liberty which was gifted to New York by French Freemasons in Paris who knew exactly what it represents. 'Liberty' symbolises the goddess worshipped in Babylon as Queen Semiramis or Ishtar. The significance of this will become clear. Notice again the ubiquitous theme of inversion with the Statue of 'Liberty' really symbolising mass control (Fig 7). A mirror-image statute stands on an island in the River Seine in Paris from where New York Liberty originated (Fig 8). A large replica of the Liberty flame stands on top of the Pont de l'Alma tunnel in Paris where Princess Diana died in a Cult ritual described in *The Biggest Secret*. Lucifer 'the

Figure 7: The Cult goddess of Babylon disguised as the Statue of Liberty holding the flame of Lucifer the 'light bringer'.

Figure 8: Liberty's mirror image in Paris where the New York version originated.

light bringer' is related to all this (and much more as we'll see) and 'Lucifer' is a central figure in Sabbatian-Frankism and its associated Satanism. Sabbatians reject the Jewish Torah, or Pentateuch, the 'five books of Moses' in the Old Testament known as Genesis, Exodus, Leviticus, Numbers, and Deuteronomy which are claimed by Judaism and Christianity to have been dictated by 'God' to Moses on Mount Sinai. Sabbatians say these do not apply to them and they seek to replace them with the Zohar to absorb Judaism and its followers into their inversion which is an expression of a much greater global inversion. They want to

delete all religions and force humanity to worship a one-world religion –
Sabbatian Satanism that also includes worship of the Earth goddess.
Satanic themes are being more and more introduced into mainstream
society and while Christianity is currently the foremost target for
destruction the others are planned to follow.

Marx brothers

Rabbi Marvin Antelman connects the Illuminati to the Jacobins in *To
Eliminate the Opiate* and Jacobins were the force behind the French
Revolution. He links both to the Bund der Gerechten, or League of the
Just, which was the network that inflicted communism/Marxism on the
world. Antelman wrote:

> The original inner circle of the Bund der Gerechten consisted of born
> Catholics, Protestants and Jews [Sabbatian-Frankist infiltrators], and those
> representatives of respective subdivisions formulated schemes for the ultimate
> destruction of their faiths. The heretical Catholics laid plans which they felt
> would take a century or more for the ultimate destruction of the church; the
> apostate Jews for the ultimate destruction of the Jewish religion.

Sabbatian-created communism connects into this anti-religion agenda
in that communism does not allow for the free practice of religion. The
Sabbatian 'Bund' became the International Communist Party and
Communist League and in 1848 'Marxism' was born with the
Communist Manifesto of Sabbatian assets Karl Marx and Friedrich
Engels. It is absolutely no coincidence that Marxism, just a different
name for fascist and other centrally-controlled tyrannies, is being
imposed worldwide as a result of the 'Covid' hoax and nor that
Marxist/fascist China was the place where the hoax originated. The
reason for this will become very clear in the chapter 'Covid: The
calculated catastrophe'. The so-called 'Woke' mentality has hijacked
traditional beliefs of the political left and replaced them with far-right
make-believe 'social justice' better known as Marxism. Woke will,
however, be swallowed by its own perceived 'revolution' which is really
the work of billionaires and billionaire corporations feigning being
'Woke'. Marxism is being touted by Wokers as a replacement for
'capitalism' when we don't have 'capitalism'. We have cartelism in
which the market is stitched up by the very Cult billionaires and
corporations bankrolling Woke. Billionaires love Marxism which keeps
the people in servitude while they control from the top. Terminally naïve
Wokers think they are 'changing the world' when it's the Cult that is
doing the changing and when they have played their vital part and
become surplus to requirements they, too, will be targeted. The
Illuminati-Jacobins were behind the period known as 'The Terror' in the

French Revolution in 1793 and 1794 when Jacobin Maximillian de Robespierre and his Orwellian 'Committee of Public Safety' killed 17,000 'enemies of the Revolution' who had once been 'friends of the Revolution'. Karl Marx (1818-1883), whose Sabbatian creed of Marxism has cost the lives of at least 100 million people, is a hero once again to Wokers who have been systematically kept ignorant of real history by their 'education' programming. As a result they now promote a Sabbatian 'Marxist' abomination destined at some point to consume them. Rabbi Antelman, who spent decades researching the Sabbatian plot, said of the League of the Just and Karl Marx:

> Contrary to popular opinion Karl Marx did not originate the Communist Manifesto. He was paid for his services by the League of the Just, which was known in its country of origin, Germany, as the Bund der Geaechteten.

Antelman said the text attributed to Marx was the work of other people and Marx 'was only repeating what others already said'. Marx was 'a hired hack – lackey of the wealthy Illuminists'. Marx famously said that religion was the 'opium of the people' (part of the Sabbatian plan to demonise religion) and Antelman called his books, *To Eliminate the Opiate*. Marx was born Jewish, but his family converted to Christianity (Sabbatian modus operandi) and he attacked Jews, not least in his book, *A World Without Jews*. In doing so he supported the Sabbatian plan to destroy traditional Jewishness and Judaism which we are clearly seeing today with the vindictive targeting of orthodox Jews by the Sabbatian government of Israel over 'Covid' laws. I don't follow any religion and it has done much damage to the world over centuries and acted as a perceptual straightjacket. Renegade Minds, however, are always asking *why* something is being done. It doesn't matter if they agree or disagree with what is happening – *why* is it happening is the question. The 'why?' can be answered with regard to religion in that religions create interacting communities of believers when the Cult wants to dismantle all discourse, unity and interaction (see 'Covid' lockdowns) and the ultimate goal is to delete all religions for a one-world religion of Cult Satanism worshipping their 'god' of which more later. We see the same 'why?' with gun control in America. I don't have guns and don't want them, but why is the Cult seeking to disarm the population at the same time that law enforcement agencies are armed to their molars and why has every tyrant in history sought to disarm people before launching the final takeover? They include Hitler, Stalin, Pol Pot and Mao who followed confiscation with violent seizing of power. You know it's a Cult agenda by the people who immediately race to the microphones to exploit dead people in multiple shootings. Ultra-Zionist Cult lackey Senator Chuck Schumer was straight on the case after ten people were killed in Boulder, Colorado in March, 2121. Simple rule ... if Schumer wants it the Cult wants it and the same with his ultra-Zionist mate the wild-eyed Senator Adam Schiff. At the same time they were calling for the disarmament of Americans, many of whom live a long way from a police response, Schumer, Schiff and the rest of these pampered clowns were sitting on Capitol Hill behind a razor-wired security fence protected by thousands of armed troops in addition to their own armed bodyguards. Mom and pop in an isolated home? They're just potential mass shooters.

Zion Mainframe

Sabbatian-Frankists and most importantly the Rothschilds were behind the creation of 'Zionism', a political movement that demanded a Jewish homeland in Israel as promised by Sabbatai Zevi. The very symbol of Israel comes from the German meaning of the name Rothschild. Dynasty founder Mayer Amschel Rothschild changed the family name from Bauer to Rothschild, or 'Red-Shield' in German, in deference to the six-pointed 'Star of David' hexagram displayed on the family's home in Frankfurt. The symbol later appeared on the flag of Israel after the Rothschilds were centrally involved in its creation. Hexagrams are not a uniquely Jewish symbol and are widely used in occult ('hidden') networks often as a symbol for Saturn (see my other books for why). Neither are Zionism and Jewishness interchangeable. Zionism is a political movement and philosophy and not a 'race' or a people. Many Jews oppose Zionism and many non-Jews, including US President Joe Biden, call themselves Zionists as does Israel-centric Donald Trump. America's support for the Israel government is pretty much a gimme with ultra-Zionist billionaires and corporations providing fantastic and dominant funding for both political parties. Former Congresswoman Cynthia McKinney has told how she was approached immediately she ran for office to 'sign the pledge' to Israel and confirm that she would always vote in that country's best interests. All American politicians are approached in this way. Anyone who refuses will get no support or funding from the enormous and all-powerful Zionist lobby that includes organisations like mega-lobby group AIPAC, the American Israel Public Affairs Committee. Trump's biggest funder was ultra-Zionist casino and media billionaire Sheldon Adelson while major funders of the Democratic Party include ultra-Zionist George Soros and ultra-Zionist financial and media mogul, Haim Saban. Some may reel back at the suggestion that Soros is an Israel-firster (Sabbatian-controlled Israel-firster), but Renegade Minds watch the actions not the words and everywhere Soros donates his billions the Sabbatian agenda benefits. In the spirit of Sabbatian inversion Soros pledged $1 billion for a new university network to promote 'liberal values and tackle intolerance'. He made the announcement during his annual speech at the Cult-owned World Economic Forum in Davos, Switzerland, in January, 2020, after his 'harsh criticism' of 'authoritarian rulers' around the world. You can only laugh at such brazen mendacity. How *he* doesn't laugh is the mystery. Translated from the Orwellian 'liberal values and tackle intolerance' means teaching non-white people to hate white people and for white people to loathe themselves for being born white. The reason for that will become clear.

The 'Anti-Semitism' fraud

Zionists support the Jewish homeland in the land of Palestine which has been the Sabbatian-Rothschild goal for so long, but not for the benefit of Jews. Sabbatians and their global Anti-Semitism Industry have skewed public and political opinion to equate opposing the violent extremes of Zionism to be a blanket attack and condemnation of all Jewish people. Sabbatians and their global Anti-Semitism Industry have skewed public and political opinion to equate opposing the violent extremes of Zionism to be a blanket attack and condemnation of all Jewish people. This is nothing more than a Sabbatian protection racket to stop legitimate investigation and exposure of their agendas and activities. The official definition of 'anti-Semitism' has more recently been expanded to include criticism of Zionism – a *political movement* – and this was done to further stop exposure of Sabbatian infiltrators who created Zionism as we know it today in the 19th century. Renegade Minds will talk about these subjects when they know the shit that will come their way. People must decide if they want to know the truth or just cower in the corner in fear of what others will say. Sabbatians have been trying to label me as 'anti-Semitic' since the 1990s as I have uncovered more and more about their background and agendas. Useless, gutless, fraudulent 'journalists' then just repeat the smears without question and on the day I was writing this section a pair of unquestioning repeaters called Ben Quinn and Archie Bland (how appropriate) outright called me an 'anti-Semite' in the establishment propaganda sheet, the London *Guardian*, with no supporting evidence. The Sabbatian Anti-Semitism Industry said so and who are they to question that? They wouldn't dare. Ironically 'Semitic' refers to a group of languages in the Middle East that are almost entirely Arabic. 'Anti-Semitism' becomes 'anti-Arab' which if the consequences of this misunderstanding were not so grave would be hilarious. Don't bother telling Quinn and Bland. I don't want to confuse them, bless 'em. One reason I am dubbed 'anti-Semitic' is that I wrote in the 1990s that Jewish operatives (Sabbatians) were heavily involved in the Russian Revolution when Sabbatians overthrew the Romanov dynasty. This apparently made me 'anti-Semitic'. Oh, really? Here is a section from *The Trigger*:

British journalist Robert Wilton confirmed these themes in his 1920 book *The Last Days of the Romanovs* when he studied official documents from the Russian government to identify the members of the Bolshevik ruling elite between 1917 and 1919. The Central Committee included 41 Jews among 62 members; the Council of the People's Commissars had 17 Jews out of 22 members; and 458 of the 556 most important Bolshevik positions between 1918 and 1919 were occupied by Jewish people. Only 17 were Russian. Then there were the 23 Jews among the 36 members of the vicious Cheka Soviet secret police established in 1917 who would soon appear all across the country.

Professor Robert Service of Oxford University, an expert on 20th century Russian history, found evidence that ['Jewish'] Leon Trotsky had sought to make sure that Jews were enrolled in the Red Army and were disproportionately represented in the Soviet civil bureaucracy that included the Cheka which performed mass arrests, imprisonment and executions of 'enemies of the people'. A US State Department Decimal File (861.00/5339) dated November 13th, 1918, names [Rothschild banking agent in America] Jacob Schiff and a list of ultra-Zionists as funders of the Russian Revolution leading to claims of a 'Jewish plot', but the key point missed by all is they were not 'Jews' – they were Sabbatian-Frankists.

Britain's Winston Churchill made the same error by mistake or otherwise. He wrote in a 1920 edition of the *Illustrated Sunday Herald* that those behind the Russian revolution were part of a 'worldwide conspiracy for the overthrow of civilisation and for the reconstitution of society on the basis of arrested development, of envious malevolence, and impossible equality' (see 'Woke' today because that has been created by the same network). Churchill said there was no need to exaggerate the part played in the creation of Bolshevism and in the actual bringing about of the Russian Revolution 'by these international and for the most part atheistical Jews' ['atheistical Jews' = Sabbatians]. Churchill said it is certainly a very great one and probably outweighs all others: 'With the notable exception of Lenin, the majority of the leading figures are Jews.' He went on to describe, knowingly or not, the Sabbatian modus operandi of placing puppet leaders nominally in power while they control from the background:

Moreover, the principal inspiration and driving power comes from the Jewish leaders. Thus Tchitcherin, a pure Russian, is eclipsed by his nominal subordinate, Litvinoff, and the influence of Russians like Bukharin or Lunacharski cannot be compared with the power of Trotsky, or of Zinovieff, the Dictator of the Red Citadel (Petrograd), or of Krassin or Radek – all Jews. In the Soviet institutions the predominance of Jews is even more astonishing. And the prominent, if not indeed the principal, part in the system of terrorism applied by the Extraordinary Commissions for Combatting Counter-Revolution has been taken by Jews, and in some notable cases by Jewesses.

What I said about seriously disproportionate involvement in the Russian Revolution by Jewish 'revolutionaries' (Sabbatians) is provable fact, but truth is no defence against the Sabbatian Anti-Semitism Industry, its repeater parrots like Quinn and Bland, and the now breathtaking network of so-called 'Woke' 'anti-hate' groups with interlocking leaderships and funding which have the role of discrediting and silencing anyone who gets too close to exposing the Sabbatians. We have seen 'truth is no defence' confirmed in legal judgements with the Saskatchewan Human Rights Commission in Canada decreeing this: 'Truthful statements can be presented in a manner that would meet the definition of hate speech, and not all truthful statements must be free from restriction.' Most 'anti-hate' activists, who are themselves consumed by hatred, are too stupid and ignorant of the world to know how they are being used. They are far too far up their own virtue-signalling arses and it's far too dark for them to see anything.

The 'revolution' game

The background and methods of the 'Russian' Revolution are straight from the Sabbatian playbook seen in the French Revolution and endless others around the world that appear to start as a revolution of the people against tyrannical rule and end up with a regime change to more tyrannical rule overtly or covertly. Wars, terror attacks and regime overthrows follow the Sabbatian cult through history with its agents creating them as Problem-Reaction-Solutions to remove opposition on the road to world domination. Sabbatian dots connect the Rothschilds with the Illuminati, Jacobins of the French Revolution, the 'Bund' or League of the Just, the International Communist Party, Communist League and the Communist Manifesto of Karl Marx and Friedrich Engels that would lead to the Rothschild-funded Russian Revolution. The sequence comes under the heading of 'creative destruction' when you advance to your global goal by continually destroying the status quo to install a new status quo which you then also destroy. The two world wars come to mind. With each new status quo you move closer to your planned outcome. Wars and mass murder are to Sabbatians a collective blood sacrifice ritual. They are obsessed with death for many reasons and one is that death is an inversion of life. Satanists and Sabbatians are obsessed with death and often target churches and churchyards for their rituals. Inversion-obsessed Sabbatians explain the use of inverted symbolism including the *inverted* pentagram and *inverted* cross. The inversion of the cross has been related to targeting Christianity, but the cross was a religious symbol long before Christianity and its inversion is a statement about the Sabbatian mentality and goals more than any single religion.

Sabbatians operating in Germany were behind the rise of the occult-obsessed Nazis and the subsequent Jewish exodus from Germany and Europe to Palestine and the United States after World War Two. The Rothschild dynasty was at the forefront of this both as political manipulators and by funding the operation. Why would Sabbatians help to orchestrate the horrors inflicted on Jews by the Nazis and by Stalin after they organised the Russian Revolution? Sabbatians hate Jews and their religion, that's why. They pose as Jews and secure positions of control within Jewish society and play the 'anti-Semitism' card to protect themselves from exposure through a global network of organisations answering to the Sabbatian-created-and-controlled globe-spanning intelligence network that involves a stunning web of military-intelligence operatives and operations for a tiny country of just nine million. Among them are Jewish assets who are not Sabbatians but have been convinced by them that what they are doing is for the good of Israel and the Jewish community to protect them from what they have been programmed since childhood to believe is a Jew-hating hostile world. The Jewish community is just a highly convenient cover to hide the true nature of Sabbatians. Anyone getting close to exposing their game is accused by Sabbatian place-people and gofers of 'anti-Semitism' and claiming that all Jews are part of a plot to take over the world. I am not saying that. I am saying that Sabbatians – the *real* Jew-haters – have infiltrated the Jewish community to use them both as a cover and an 'anti-Semitic' defence against exposure. Thus we have the Anti-Semitism Industry targeted researchers in this way and most Jewish people think this is justified and genuine. They don't know that their 'Jewish' leaders and institutions of state, intelligence and military are not controlled by Jews at all, but cultists and stooges of Sabbatian-Frankism. I once added my name to a pro-Jewish freedom petition online and the next time I looked my name was gone and text had been added to the petition blurb to attack me as an 'anti-Semite' such is the scale of perceptual programming.

Moving on America

I tell the story in *The Trigger* and a chapter called 'Atlantic Crossing' how particularly after Israel was established the Sabbatians moved in on the United States and eventually grasped control of government administration, the political system via both Democrats and Republicans, the intelligence community like the CIA and National Security Agency (NSA), the Pentagon and mass media. Through this

seriously compartmentalised network Sabbatians and their operatives in
Mossad, Israeli Defense Forces (IDF) and US agencies pulled off 9/11
and blamed it on 19 'Al-Qaeda hijackers' dominated by men from, or
connected to, Sabbatian-ruled Saudi Arabia. The '19' were not even on
the planes let alone flew those big passenger jets into buildings while
being largely incompetent at piloting one-engine light aircraft. 'Hijacker'
Hani Hanjour who is said to have flown American Airlines Flight 77
into the Pentagon with a turn and manoeuvre most professional pilots
said they would have struggled to do was banned from renting a small
plane by instructors at the Freeway Airport in Bowie, Maryland, just *six
weeks* earlier on the grounds that he was an incompetent pilot. The
Jewish population of the world is just 0.2 percent with even that almost
entirely concentrated in Israel (75 percent Jewish) and the United States
(around two percent). This two percent and globally 0.2 percent refers to
Jewish people and not Sabbatian interlopers who are a fraction of that
fraction. What a sobering thought when you think of the fantastic
influence on world affairs of tiny Israel and that the Project for the New
America Century (PNAC) which laid out the blueprint in September,
2000, for America's war on terror and regime change wars in Iraq, Libya
and Syria was founded and dominated by Sabbatians known as
'Neocons'. The document conceded that this plan would not be
supported politically or publicly without a major attack on American
soil and a Problem-Reaction-Solution excuse to send troops to war
across the Middle East. Sabbatian Neocons said:

> ... [The] process of transformation ... [war and regime change] ... is likely to
> be a long one, absent some catastrophic and catalysing event – like a new
> Pearl Harbor.

Four months later many of those who produced that document came
to power with their inane puppet George Bush from the long-time
Sabbatian Bush family. They included Sabbatian Dick Cheney who was
officially vice-president, but really de-facto president for the entirety of
the 'Bush' government. Nine months after the 'Bush' inauguration came
what Bush called at the time 'the Pearl Harbor of the 21st century' and
with typical Sabbatian timing and symbolism 2001 was the 60th
anniversary of the attack in 1941 by the Japanese Air Force on Pearl
Harbor, Hawaii, which allowed President Franklin Delano Roosevelt to
take the United States into a Sabbatian-instigated Second World War that
he said in his election campaign that he never would. The evidence is
overwhelming that Roosevelt and his military and intelligence networks
knew the attack was coming and did nothing to stop it, but they did
make sure that America's most essential naval ships were not in Hawaii
at the time. Three thousand Americans died in the Pearl Harbor attacks

as they did on September 11th. By the 9/11 year of 2001 Sabbatians had widely infiltrated the US government, military and intelligence operations and used their compartmentalised assets to pull off the 'Al-Qaeda' attacks. If you read *The Trigger* it will blow your mind to see the utterly staggering concentration of 'Jewish' operatives (Sabbatian infiltrators) in essential positions of political, security, legal, law enforcement, financial and business power before, during, and after the attacks to make them happen, carry them out, and then cover their tracks – and I do mean *staggering* when you think of that 0.2 percent of the world population and two percent of Americans which are Jewish while Sabbatian infiltrators are a fraction of that. A central foundation of the 9/11 conspiracy was the hijacking of government, military, Air Force and intelligence computer systems in real time through 'back-door' access made possible by Israeli (Sabbatian) 'cyber security' software. Sabbatian-controlled Israel is on the way to rivalling Silicon Valley for domination of cyberspace and is becoming the dominant force in cyber-security which gives them access to entire computer systems and their passcodes across the world. Then add to this that Zionists head (officially) Silicon Valley giants like Google (Larry Page and Sergey Brin), Google-owned YouTube (Susan Wojcicki), Facebook (Mark Zuckerberg and Sheryl Sandberg), and Apple (Chairman Arthur D. Levinson), and that ultra-Zionist hedge fund billionaire Paul Singer has a $1 billion stake in Twitter which is only nominally headed by 'CEO' pothead Jack Dorsey. As cable news host Tucker Carlson said of Dorsey: 'There used to be debate in the medical community whether dropping a ton of acid had permanent effects and I think that debate has now ended.' Carlson made the comment after Dorsey told a hearing on Capitol Hill (if you cut through his bullshit) that he believed in free speech so long as he got to decide what you can hear and see. These 'big names' of Silicon Valley are only front men and women for the Global Cult, not least the Sabbatians, who are the true controllers of these corporations. Does anyone still wonder why these same people and companies have been ferociously censoring and banning people (like me) for exposing any aspect of the Cult agenda and especially the truth about the 'Covid' hoax which Sabbatians have orchestrated?

The Jeffrey Epstein paedophile ring was a Sabbatian operation. He was officially 'Jewish' but he was a Sabbatian and women abused by the ring have told me about the high number of 'Jewish' people involved. The Epstein horror has Sabbatian written all over it and matches perfectly their modus operandi and obsession with sex and ritual. Epstein was running a Sabbatian blackmail ring in which famous people with political and other influence were provided with young girls for sex while everything was being filmed and recorded on hidden cameras and microphones at his New York house, Caribbean island and other properties. Epstein survivors have described this surveillance system to me and some have gone public. Once the famous politician or other figure knew he or she was on video they tended to do whatever they were told. Here we go again …when you've got them by the balls their hearts and minds will follow. Sabbatians use this blackmail technique on a wide scale across the world to entrap politicians and others they need to act as demanded. Epstein's private plane, the infamous 'Lolita Express', had many well-known passengers including Bill Clinton while Bill Gates has flown on an Epstein plane and met with him four years after Epstein had been jailed for paedophilia. They subsequently met many times at Epstein's home in New York according to a witness who was there. Epstein's infamous side-kick was Ghislaine Maxwell, daughter of Mossad agent and ultra-Zionist mega-crooked British businessman, Bob Maxwell, who at one time owned the *Daily Mirror* newspaper. Maxwell was murdered at sea on his boat in 1991 by Sabbatian-controlled Mossad when he became a liability with his business empire collapsing as a former Mossad operative has confirmed (see *The Trigger*).

Money, money, money, funny money ...

Before I come to the Sabbatian connection with the last three US presidents I will lay out the crucial importance to Sabbatians of controlling banking and finance. Sabbatian Mayer Amschel Rothschild set out to dominate this arena in his family's quest for total global control. What is freedom? It is, in effect, choice. The more choices you have the freer you are and the fewer your choices the more you are enslaved. In the global structure created over centuries by Sabbatians the biggest decider and restrictor of choice is … money. Across the world if you ask people what they would like to do with their lives and why they are not doing that they will reply 'I don't have the money'. This is the idea. A global elite of multi-billionaires are described as 'greedy' and that is true on one level; but control of money – who has it and who doesn't – is not primarily about greed. It's about control. Sabbatians have seized ever more control of finance and sucked the wealth of the world out of the hands of the population. We talk now, after all, about the 'One-percent' and even then the wealthiest are a lot fewer even than that. This has been made possible by a money scam so outrageous and so vast it could rightly be called the scam of scams founded on creating 'money' out of nothing and 'loaning' that with interest to the population. Money out of nothing is called 'credit'. Sabbatians have asserted control over governments and banking ever more completely through the centuries and secured financial laws that allow banks to lend hugely more than they have on deposit in a confidence trick known as fractional reserve lending. Imagine if you could lend money that doesn't exist and charge the recipient interest for doing so. You would end up in jail. Bankers by contrast end up in mansions, private jets, Malibu and Monaco.

Banks are only required to keep a fraction of their deposits and wealth in their vaults and they are allowed to lend 'money' they don't have called 'credit. Go into a bank for a loan and if you succeed the banker will not move any real wealth into your account. They will type into your account the amount of the agreed 'loan' – say £100,000. This is not wealth that really exists; it is non-existent, fresh-air, created-out-of-nothing 'credit' which has never, does not, and will never exist except in theory. Credit is backed by nothing except wind and only has buying power because people think that it has buying power and accept it in return for property, goods and services. I have described this situation as like those cartoon characters you see chasing each other and when they run over the edge of a cliff they keep running forward on fresh air until one of them looks down, realises what's happened, and they all crash into the ravine. The whole foundation of the Sabbatian financial system is to stop people looking down except for periodic moments when they want to crash the system (as in 2008 and 2020 ongoing) and reap the rewards from all the property, businesses and wealth their borrowers had signed over as 'collateral' in return for a 'loan' of fresh air. Most people think that money is somehow created by governments when it comes into existence from the start as a debt through banks 'lending' illusory money called credit. Yes, the very currency of exchange is a *debt* from day one issued as an interest-bearing loan. Why don't governments create money interest-free and lend it to their people interest-free? Governments are controlled by Sabbatians and the financial system is controlled by Sabbatians for whom interest-free money would be a nightmare come true. Sabbatians underpin their financial domination through their global network of central banks, including the privately-owned US Federal Reserve and Britain's Bank of England, and this is orchestrated by a privately-owned central bank coordination body called the Bank for International Settlements in Basle, Switzerland, created by the usual suspects including the Rockefellers and Rothschilds. Central bank chiefs don't answer to governments or the people. They answer to the Bank for International Settlements or, in other words, the Global Cult which is dominated today by Sabbatians.

Built-in disaster

There are so many constituent scams within the overall banking scam. When you take out a loan of thin-air credit only the amount of that loan is theoretically brought into circulation to add to the amount in circulation; but you are paying back the principle plus interest. The additional interest is not created and this means that with every 'loan' there is a shortfall in the money in circulation between what is borrowed and what has to be paid back. There is never even close to enough money in circulation to repay all outstanding public and private debt including interest. Coldly weaved in the very fabric of the system is the certainty that some will lose their homes, businesses and possessions to the banking 'lender'. This is less obvious in times of 'boom' when the amount of money in circulation (and the debt) is expanding through more people wanting and getting loans. When a downturn comes and the money supply contracts it becomes painfully obvious that there is not enough money to service all debt and interest. This is less obvious in times of 'boom' when the amount of money in circulation (and the debt) is expanding through more people wanting and getting loans. When a downturn comes and the money supply contracts and it becomes painfully obvious – as in 2008 and currently – that there is not enough money to service all debt and interest. Sabbatian banksters have been leading the human population through a calculated series of booms (more debt incurred) and busts (when the debt can't be repaid and the banks get the debtor's tangible wealth in exchange for non-existent 'credit'). With each 'bust' Sabbatian bankers have absorbed more of the world's tangible wealth and we end up with the One-percent. Governments are in bankruptcy levels of debt to the same system and are therefore owned by a system they do not control. The Federal Reserve, 'America's central bank', is privately-owned and American presidents only nominally appoint its chairman or woman to maintain the illusion that it's an arm of government. It's not. The 'Fed' is a cartel of private banks which handed billions to its associates and friends after the crash of 2008 and has been Sabbatian-controlled since it was manipulated into being in 1913 through the covert trickery of Rothschild banking agents Jacob Schiff and Paul Warburg, and the Sabbatian Rockefeller family. Somehow from a Jewish population of two-percent and globally 0.2 percent (Sabbatian interlopers remember are far smaller) ultra-Zionists headed the Federal Reserve for 31 years between 1987 and 2018 in the form of Alan Greenspan, Bernard Bernanke and Janet Yellen (now Biden's Treasury Secretary) with Yellen's deputy chairman a Israeli-American duel citizen and ultra-Zionist Stanley Fischer, a former governor of the Bank of Israel. Ultra-Zionist Fed chiefs spanned the presidencies of Ronald Reagan ('Republican'), Father George Bush ('Republican'), Bill Clinton ('Democrat'), Boy George Bush ('Republican') and Barack Obama ('Democrat'). We should really add the pre-Greenspan chairman, Paul Adolph Volcker, 'appointed' by Jimmy Carter ('Democrat') who ran the Fed between 1979 and 1987 during the Carter and Reagan administrations before Greenspan took over. Volcker was a long-time associate and business partner of the Rothschilds. No matter what the 'party' officially in power the United

States economy was directed by the same force. Here are members of the Obama, Trump and Biden administrations and see if you can make out a common theme.

Barack Obama ('Democrat')

Ultra-Zionists Robert Rubin, Larry Summers, and Timothy Geithner ran the US Treasury in the Clinton administration and two of them reappeared with Obama. Ultra-Zionist Fed chairman Alan Greenspan had manipulated the crash of 2008 through deregulation and jumped ship just before the disaster to make way for ultra-Zionist Bernard Bernanke to hand out trillions to Sabbatian 'too big to fail' banks and businesses, including the ubiquitous ultra-Zionist Goldman Sachs which has an ongoing staff revolving door operation between itself and major financial positions in government worldwide. Obama inherited the fallout of the crash when he took office in January, 2009, and fortunately he had the support of his ultra-Zionist White House Chief of Staff Rahm Emmanuel, son of a terrorist who helped to bomb Israel into being in 1948, and his ultra-Zionist senior adviser David Axelrod, chief strategist in Obama's two successful presidential campaigns. Emmanuel, later mayor of Chicago and former senior fundraiser and strategist for Bill Clinton, is an example of the Sabbatian policy after Israel was established of migrating insider families to America so their children would be born American citizens. 'Obama' chose this financial team throughout his administration to respond to the Sabbatian-instigated crisis:

Timothy Geithner (ultra-Zionist) Treasury Secretary; Jacob J. Lew, Treasury Secretary; Larry Summers (ultra-Zionist), director of the White House National Economic Council; Paul Adolph Volcker (Rothschild business partner), chairman of the Economic Recovery Advisory Board; Peter Orszag (ultra-Zionist), director of the Office of Management and Budget overseeing all government spending; Penny Pritzker (ultra-Zionist), Commerce Secretary; Jared Bernstein (ultra-Zionist), chief economist and economic policy adviser to Vice President Joe Biden; Mary Schapiro (ultra-Zionist), chair of the Securities and Exchange Commission (SEC); Gary Gensler (ultra-Zionist), chairman of the Commodity Futures Trading Commission (CFTC); Sheila Bair (ultra-Zionist), chair of the Federal Deposit Insurance Corporation (FDIC); Karen Mills (ultra-Zionist), head of the Small Business Administration (SBA); Kenneth Feinberg (ultra-Zionist), Special Master for Executive [bail-out] Compensation. Feinberg would be appointed to oversee compensation (with strings) to 9/11 victims and families in a campaign to stop them having their day in court to question the official story. At the same time ultra-Zionist Bernard Bernanke was chairman of the Federal Reserve and these are only some of the ultra-Zionists with allegiance to Sabbatian-controlled Israel in the Obama government. Obama's biggest corporate donor was ultra-Zionist Goldman Sachs which had employed many in his administration.

Donald Trump ('Republican')

Trump claimed to be an outsider (he wasn't) who had come to 'drain the swamp'. He embarked on this goal by immediately appointing ultra-Zionist Steve Mnuchin, a Goldman Sachs employee for 17 years, as his Treasury Secretary. Others included Gary Cohn (ultra-Zionist), chief operating officer of Goldman Sachs, his first Director of the National Economic Council and chief economic adviser, who was later replaced by Larry Kudlow (ultra-Zionist). Trump's senior adviser throughout his four years in the White House was his sinister son-in-law Jared Kushner, a life-long friend of Israel Prime Minister Benjamin Netanyahu. Kushner is the son of a convicted crook who was pardoned by Trump in his last days in office. Other ultra-Zionists in the Trump administration included: Stephen Miller, Senior Policy Adviser; Avrahm Berkowitz, Deputy Adviser to Trump and his Senior Adviser Jared Kushner; Ivanka Trump, Adviser to the President, who converted to Judaism when she married Jared Kushner; David Friedman, Trump lawyer and Ambassador to Israel; Jason Greenblatt, Trump Organization executive vice president and chief legal officer, who was made Special Representative for International Negotiations and the Israeli-Palestinian Conflict; Rod Rosenstein, Deputy Attorney General; Elliot Abrams, Special Representative for Venezuela, then Iran; John Eisenberg, National Security Council Legal Adviser and Deputy Council to the President for National Security Affairs; Anne Neuberger, Deputy National Manager, National Security Agency; Ezra Cohen-Watnick, Acting Under Secretary of Defense for Intelligence; Elan Carr, Special Envoy to monitor and combat anti-Semitism; Len Khodorkovsky, Deputy Special Envoy to monitor and combat anti-Semitism; Reed Cordish, Assistant to the President, Intragovernmental and Technology Initiatives. Trump Vice President Mike Pence and Secretary of State Mike Pompeo, both Christian Zionists, were also vehement supporters of Israel and its goals and ambitions.

Donald 'free-speech believer' Trump pardoned a number of financial and violent criminals while ignoring calls to pardon Julian Assange and Edward Snowden whose crimes are revealing highly relevant information about government manipulation and corruption and the widespread illegal surveillance of the American people by US 'security' agencies. It's so good to know that Trump is on the side of freedom and justice and not mega-criminals with allegiance to Sabbatian-controlled Israel. These included a pardon for Israeli spy Jonathan Pollard who was jailed for life in 1987 under the Espionage Act. Aviem Sella, the Mossad agent who recruited Pollard, was also pardoned by Trump while Assange sat in jail and Snowden remained in exile in Russia. Sella had 'fled' (was helped to escape) to Israel in 1987 and was never extradited despite being charged under the Espionage Act. A Trump White House statement said that Sella's clemency had been 'supported by Benjamin Netanyahu, Ron Dermer, Israel's US Ambassador, David Friedman, US Ambassador to Israel and Miriam Adelson, wife of leading Trump donor Sheldon Adelson who died shortly before. Other friends of Jared Kushner were pardoned along with Sholom Weiss who was believed to be serving the longest-ever white-collar prison sentence of more than 800 years in 2000. The sentence was commuted of Ponzi-schemer Eliyahu Weinstein who defrauded Jews and others out of $200 million. I did mention that Assange and Snowden were ignored, right? Trump gave Sabbatians almost everything they asked for in military and political support, moving the US Embassy from Tel Aviv to Jerusalem with its critical symbolic and literal implications for Palestinian statehood, and the 'deal of the Century' designed by Jared Kushner and David Friedman which gave the Sabbatian Israeli government the green light to substantially expand its already widespread program of building illegal Jewish-only settlements in the occupied land of the West Bank. This made a two-state 'solution' impossible by seizing all the land of a potential Palestinian homeland and that had been the plan since 1948 and then 1967 when the Arab-controlled Gaza Strip, West Bank, Sinai Peninsula and Syrian Golan Heights were occupied by Israel. All the talks about talks and road maps and delays have been buying time until the West Bank was physically occupied by Israeli real estate. Trump would have to be a monumentally ill-informed idiot not to see that this was the plan he was helping to complete. The Trump administration was in so many ways the Kushner administration which means the Netanyahu administration which means the Sabbatian administration. I understand why many opposing Cult fascism in all its forms gravitated to Trump, but he was a crucial part of the Sabbatian plan and I will deal with this in the next chapter.

Joe Biden ('Democrat')

A barely cognitive Joe Biden took over the presidency in January, 2021, along with his fellow empty shell, Vice-President Kamala Harris, as the latest Sabbatian gofers to enter the White House. Names on the door may have changed and the 'party' – the force behind them remained the same as Zionists were appointed to a stream of pivotal areas relating to Sabbatian plans and policy. They included: Janet Yellen, Treasury Secretary, former head of the Federal Reserve, and still another ultra-Zionist running the US Treasury after Mnuchin (Trump), Lew and Geithner (Obama), and Summers and Rubin (Clinton); Anthony Blinken,

Secretary of State; Wendy Sherman, Deputy Secretary of State (so that's 'Biden's' Sabbatian foreign policy sorted); Jeff Zients, White House coronavirus coordinator; Rochelle Walensky, head of the Centers for Disease Control; Rachel Levine, transgender deputy health secretary (that's 'Covid' hoax policy under control); Merrick Garland, Attorney General; Alejandro Mayorkas, Secretary of Homeland Security; Cass Sunstein, Homeland Security with responsibility for new immigration laws; Avril Haines, Director of National Intelligence; Anne Neuberger, National Security Agency cybersecurity director (note, cybersecurity); David Cohen, CIA Deputy Director; Ronald Klain, Biden's Chief of Staff (see Rahm Emanuel); Eric Lander, a 'leading geneticist', Office of Science and Technology Policy director (see Smart Grid, synthetic biology agenda); Jessica Rosenworcel, acting head of the Federal Communications Commission (FCC) which controls Smart Grid technology policy and electromagnetic communication systems including 5G. How can it be that so many pivotal positions are held by two-percent of the American population and 0.2 percent of the world population administration after administration no matter who is the president and what is the party? It's a coincidence? Of course it's not and this is why Sabbatians have built their colossal global web of interlocking 'anti-hate' hate groups to condemn anyone who asks these glaring questions as an 'anti-Semite'. The way that Jewish people horrifically abused in Sabbatian-backed Nazi Germany are exploited to this end is stomach-turning and disgusting beyond words.

Political fusion

Sabbatian manipulation has reversed the roles of Republicans and Democrats and the same has happened in Britain with the Conservative and Labour Parties. Republicans and Conservatives were always labelled the 'right' and Democrats and Labour the 'left', but look at the policy positions now and the Democrat-Labour 'left' has moved further to the 'right' than Republicans and Conservatives under the banner of 'Woke', the Cult-created far-right tyranny. Where once the Democrat-Labour 'left' defended free speech and human rights they now seek to delete them and as I said earlier despite the 'Covid' fascism of the Jackboot Johnson Conservative government in the UK the Labour Party of leader Keir Starmer demanded even more extreme measures. The Labour Party has been very publicly absorbed by Sabbatians after a political and media onslaught against the previous leader, the weak and inept Jeremy Corbyn, over made-up allegations of 'anti-Semitism' both by him and his party. The plan was clear with this 'anti-Semite' propaganda and what was required in response was a swift and decisive 'fuck off' from Corbyn and a statement to expose the Anti-Semitism Industry (Sabbatian) attempt to silence Labour criticism of the Israeli government (Sabbatians) and purge the party of all dissent against the extremes of ultra-Zionism (Sabbatians). Instead Corbyn and his party fell to their knees and appeased the abusers which, by definition, is impossible. Appeasing one demand leads only to a new demand to be appeased until takeover is complete. Like I say – 'fuck off' would have been a much more effective policy and I have used it myself with great effect over the years when Sabbatians are on my case which is most of the time. I consider that fact a great compliment, by the way. The outcome of the Labour Party capitulation is that we now have a Sabbatian-controlled Conservative Party 'opposed' by a Sabbatian-controlled Labour Party in a one-party Sabbatian state that hurtles towards the extremes of tyranny (the Sabbatian cult agenda). In America the situation is the same. Labour's Keir Starmer spends his days on his knees with his tongue out pointing to Tel Aviv, or I guess now Jerusalem, while Boris Johnson has an 'anti-Semitism czar' in the form of former Labour MP John Mann who keeps Starmer company on his prayer mat.

Sabbatian influence can be seen in Jewish members of the Labour Party who have been ejected for criticism of Israel including those from families that suffered in Nazi Germany. Sabbatians despise real Jewish people and target them even more harshly because it is so much more difficult to dub them 'anti-Semitic' although in their desperation they do try.

CHAPTER THREE

The Pushbacker sting

Until you realize how easy it is for your mind to be manipulated, you remain the puppet of someone else's game
Evita Ochel

I will use the presidencies of Trump and Biden to show how the manipulation of the one-party state plays out behind the illusion of political choice across the world. No two presidencies could – on the face of it – be more different and apparently at odds in terms of direction and policy.

A Renegade Mind sees beyond the obvious and focuses on outcomes and consequences and not image, words and waffle. The Cult embarked on a campaign to divide America between those who blindly support its agenda (the mentality known as 'Woke') and those who are pushing back on where the Cult and its Sabbatians want to go. This presents infinite possibilities for dividing and ruling the population by setting them at war with each other and allows a perceptual ring fence of demonisation to encircle the Pushbackers in a modern version of the Little Big Horn in 1876 when American cavalry led by Lieutenant Colonel George Custer were drawn into a trap, surrounded and killed by Native American tribes defending their land of thousands of years from being seized by the government. In this modern version the roles are reversed and it's those defending themselves from the Sabbatian government who are surrounded and the government that's seeking to destroy them. This trap was set years ago and to explain how we must return to 2016 and the emergence of Donald Trump as a candidate to be President of the United States. He set out to overcome the best part of 20 other candidates in the Republican Party before and during the primaries and was not considered by many in those early stages to have a prayer of living in the White House. The Republican Party was said to have great reservations about Trump and yet somehow he won the nomination. When you know how American politics works – politics in general – there is no way that Trump could have become the party's candidate unless the Sabbatian-controlled 'Neocons' that run the Republican Party wanted that to happen. We saw the proof in emails and documents made public by WikiLeaks that the Democratic Party hierarchy, or Democons, systematically undermined the campaign of Bernie Sanders to make sure that Sabbatian gofer Hillary Clinton won the nomination to be their presidential candidate. If the Democons could do that then the Neocons in the Republican Party could have derailed Trump in the same way. But they didn't and at that stage I began to conclude that Trump could well be the one chosen to be president. If that was the case the 'why' was pretty clear to see – the goal of dividing America between Cult agenda-supporting Wokers and Pushbackers who gravitated to Trump because he was telling them what they wanted to hear. His constituency of support had been increasingly ignored and voiceless for decades and profoundly through the eight years of Sabbatian puppet Barack Obama. Now here was someone speaking their language of pulling back from the incessant globalisation of political and economic power, the exporting of American jobs to China and elsewhere by 'American' (Sabbatian) corporations, the deletion of free speech, and the mass immigration policies that had further devastated job opportunities for the urban working class of all races and the once American heartlands of the Midwest.

Beware the forked tongue

Those people collectively sighed with relief that at last a political leader was apparently on their side, but another trait of the Renegade Mind is that you look even harder at people telling you what you want to hear than those who are telling you otherwise. Obviously as I said earlier people wish what they want to hear to be true and genuine and they are much more likely to believe that than someone saying what they don't want to here and don't want to be true. Sales people are taught to be skilled in eliciting by calculated questioning what their customers want to hear and repeating that back to them as their own opinion to get their targets to like and trust them. Assets of the Cult are also sales people in the sense of selling perception. To read Cult manipulation you have to play the long and expanded game and not fall for the Vaudeville show of party politics. Both American parties are vehicles for the Cult and they exploit them in different ways depending on what the agenda requires at that moment. Trump and the Republicans were used to be the focus of dividing America and isolating Pushbackers to open the way for a Biden presidency to become the most extreme in American history by advancing the full-blown Woke (Cult) agenda with the aim of destroying and silencing Pushbackers now labelled Nazi Trump supporters and white supremacists.

Sabbatians wanted Trump in office for the reasons described by ultra-Zionist Saul Alinsky (1909-1972) who was promoting the Woke philosophy through 'community organising' long before anyone had heard of it. In those days it still went by its traditional name of Marxism. The reason for the manipulated Trump phenomenon was laid out in Alinsky's 1971 book, *Rules for Radicals,* which was his blueprint for overthrowing democratic and other regimes and replacing them with Sabbatian Marxism. Not surprisingly his to-do list was evident in the Sabbatian French and Russian 'Revolutions' and that in China which will become very relevant in the next chapter about the 'Covid' hoax. Among Alinsky's followers have been the deeply corrupt Barack Obama, House Speaker Nancy Pelosi and Hillary Clinton who described him as a 'hero'. All three are Sabbatian stooges with Pelosi personifying the arrogant corrupt idiocy that so widely fronts up for the Cult inner core. Predictably as a Sabbatian advocate of the 'light-bringer' Alinsky features Lucifer on the dedication page of his book as the original radical who gained his own kingdom ('Earth' as we shall see). One of Alinsky's golden radical rules was to pick an individual and focus all attention, hatred and blame on them and not to target faceless bureaucracies and corporations. *Rules for Radicals* is really a Sabbatian handbook with its contents repeatedly employed all over the world for centuries and why wouldn't Sabbatians bring to power their designer-villain to be used as the individual on which all attention, hatred and blame was bestowed? This is what they did and the only question for me is how much Trump knew that and how much he was manipulated. A bit of both, I suspect. This was Alinsky's Trump technique from a man who died in 1972. The technique has spanned history:

> Pick the target, freeze it, personalize it, polarize it. Don't try to attack abstract corporations or bureaucracies. Identify a responsible individual. Ignore attempts to shift or spread the blame.

From the moment Trump came to illusory power everything was about him. It wasn't about Republican policy or opinion, but all about Trump. Everything he did was presented in negative, derogatory and abusive terms by the Sabbatian-dominated media led by Cult operations such as CNN, MSNBC, *The New York Times* and the Jeff Bezos-owned *Washington Post* – 'Pick the target, freeze it, personalize it, polarize it.' Trump was turned into a demon to be vilified by those who hated him and a demi-god loved by those who worshipped him. This, in turn, had his supporters, too, presented as equally demonic in preparation for the punchline later down the line when Biden was about to take office. It was here's a Trump, there's a Trump, everywhere a Trump, Trump. Virtually every news story or happening was filtered through the lens of 'The Donald'. You loved him or hated him and which one you chose was said to define you as Satan's spawn or a paragon of virtue. Even supporting some Trump policies or statements and not others was enough for an assault on your character. No shades of grey were or are allowed. Everything is black and white (literally and figuratively). A Californian I knew had her head utterly scrambled by her hatred for Trump while telling people they should love each other. She was so totally consumed by Trump Derangement Syndrome as it became to be known that this glaring contradiction would never have occurred to her. By definition anyone who criticised Trump or praised his opponents was a hero and this lady described Joe Biden as 'a kind, honest gentleman' when he's a provable liar, mega-crook and vicious piece of work to boot. Sabbatians had indeed divided America using Trump as the fall-guy and all along the clock was ticking on the consequences for his supporters.

In hock to his masters

Trump gave Sabbatians via Israel almost everything they wanted in his four years. Ask and you shall receive was the dynamic between himself and Benjamin Netanyahu orchestrated by Trump's ultra-Zionist son-in-law Jared Kushner, his ultra-Zionist Ambassador to Israel, David Friedman, and ultra-Zionist 'Israel adviser', Jason Greenblatt. The last two were central to the running and protecting from collapse of his business empire, the Trump Organisation, and colossal business failures made him forever beholding to Sabbatian networks that bailed him out. By the start of the 1990s Trump owed $4 billion to banks that he couldn't pay and almost $1billion of that was down to him personally and not his companies. This mega-disaster was the result of building two new casinos in Atlantic City and buying the enormous Taj Mahal operation which led to crippling debt payments. He had borrowed fantastic sums from 72 banks with major Sabbatian connections and although the scale of debt should have had him living in a tent alongside the highway they never foreclosed. A plan was devised to lift Trump from the mire by BT Securities Corporation and Rothschild Inc. and the case was handled by Wilber Ross who had worked for the Rothschilds for 27 years. Ross would be named US Commerce Secretary after Trump's election. Another crucial figure in saving Trump was ultra-Zionist 'investor' Carl Icahn who bought the Taj Mahal casino. Icahn was made special economic adviser on financial regulation in the Trump administration. He didn't stay long but still managed to find time to make a tidy sum of a reported $31.3 million when he sold his holdings affected by the price of steel three days before Trump imposed a 235 percent tariff on steel imports. What amazing bits of luck these people have. Trump and Sabbatian operatives have long had a close association and his mentor and legal adviser from the early 1970s until 1986 was the dark and genetically corrupt ultra-Zionist Roy Cohn who was chief counsel to Senator Joseph McCarthy's 'communist' witch-hunt in the 1950s. *Esquire* magazine published an article about Cohn with the headline 'Don't

mess with Roy Cohn'. He was described as the most feared lawyer in
New York and 'a ruthless master of dirty tricks ... [with] ... more than
one Mafia Don on speed dial'. Cohn's influence, contacts, support and
protection made Trump a front man for Sabbatians in New York with
their connections to one of Cohn's many criminal employers, the
'Russian' Sabbatian Mafia. Israel-centric media mogul Rupert Murdoch
was introduced to Trump by Cohn and they started a long friendship.
Cohn died in 1986 weeks after being disbarred for unethical conduct by
the Appellate Division of the New York State Supreme Court. The
wheels of justice do indeed run slow given the length of Cohn's crooked
career.

QAnon-sense

We are asked to believe that Donald Trump with his fundamental
connections to Sabbatian networks and operatives has been leading the
fight to stop the Sabbatian agenda for the fascistic control of America
and the world. Sure he has. A man entrapped during his years in the
White House by Sabbatian operatives and whose biggest financial donor
was casino billionaire Sheldon Adelson who was Sabbatian to his
DNA?? Oh, do come on. Trump has been used to divide America and
isolate Pushbackers on the Cult agenda under the heading of 'Trump
supporters', 'insurrectionists' and 'white supremacists'. The US
Intelligence/Mossad Psyop or psychological operation known as
QAnon emerged during the Trump years as a central pillar in the
Sabbatian campaign to lead Pushbackers into the trap set by those that
wished to destroy them. I knew from the start that QAnon was a scam
because I had seen the same scenario many times before over 30 years
under different names and I had written about one in particular in the
books. 'Not again' was my reaction when QAnon came to the fore. The
same script is pulled out every few years and a new name added to the
letterhead. The story always takes the same form: 'Insiders' or 'the good
guys' in the government-intelligence-military 'Deep State' apparatus
were going to instigate mass arrests of the 'bad guys' which would
include the Rockefellers, Rothschilds, Barack Obama, Hillary Clinton,
George Soros, etc., etc. Dates are given for when the 'good guys' are
going to move in, but the dates pass without incident and new dates are
given which pass without incident. The central message to Pushbackers
in each case is that they don't have to do anything because there is 'a
plan' and it is all going to be sorted by the 'good guys' on the inside.
'Trust the plan' was a QAnon mantra when the only plan was to
misdirect Pushbackers into putting their trust in a Psyop they believed
to be real. Beware, beware, those who tell you what you want to hear
and always check it out. Right up to Biden's inauguration QAnon was
still claiming that 'the Storm' was coming and Trump would stay on as

president when Biden and his cronies were arrested and jailed. It was never going to happen and of course it didn't, but what did happen as a result provided that punchline to the Sabbatian Trump/QAnon Psyop.

On January 6th, 2021, a very big crowd of Trump supporters gathered in the National Mall in Washington DC down from the Capitol Building to protest at what they believed to be widespread corruption and vote fraud that stopped Trump being re-elected for a second term as president in November, 2020. I say as someone that does not support Trump or Biden that the evidence is clear that major vote-fixing went on to favour Biden, a man with cognitive problems so advanced he can often hardly string a sentence together without reading the words written for him on the Teleprompter. Glaring ballot discrepancies included serious questions about electronic voting machines that make vote rigging a comparative cinch and hundreds of thousands of paper votes that suddenly appeared during already advanced vote counts and virtually all of them for Biden. Early Trump leads in crucial swing states suddenly began to close and disappear. The pandemic hoax was used as the excuse to issue almost limitless numbers of mail-in ballots with no checks to establish that the recipients were still alive or lived at that address. They were sent to streams of people who had not even asked for them. Private organisations were employed to gather these ballots and who knows what they did with them before they turned up at the counts. The American election system has been manipulated over decades to become a sick joke with more holes than a Swiss cheese for the express purpose of dictating the results. Then there was the criminal manipulation of information by Sabbatian tech giants like Facebook, Twitter and Google-owned YouTube which deleted pro-Trump, anti-Biden accounts and posts while everything in support of Biden was left alone. Sabbatians wanted Biden to win because after the dividing of America it was time for full-on Woke and every aspect of the Cult agenda to be unleashed.

Hunter gatherer

Extreme Silicon Valley bias included blocking information by the *New York Post* exposing a Biden scandal that should have ended his bid for president in the final weeks of the campaign. Hunter Biden, his monumentally corrupt son, is reported to have sent a laptop to be repaired at a local store and failed to return for it. Time passed until the laptop became the property of the store for non-payment of the bill. When the owner saw what was on the hard drive he gave a copy to the FBI who did nothing even though it confirmed widespread corruption in which the Joe Biden family were using his political position, especially when he was vice president to Obama, to make multiple millions in countries around the world and most notably Ukraine and

China. Hunter Biden's one-time business partner Tony Bobulinski went public when the story broke in the *New York Post* to confirm the corruption he saw and that Joe Biden not only knew what was going on he also profited from the spoils. Millions were handed over by a Chinese company with close connections – like all major businesses in China – to the Chinese communist party of President Xi Jinping. Joe Biden even boasted at a meeting of the Cult's World Economic Forum that as vice president he had ordered the government of Ukraine to fire a prosecutor. What he didn't mention was that the same man just happened to be investigating an energy company which was part of Hunter Biden's corrupt portfolio. The company was paying him big bucks for no other reason than the influence his father had. Overnight Biden's presidential campaign should have been over given that he had lied publicly about not knowing what his son was doing. Instead almost the entire Sabbatian-owned mainstream media and Sabbatian-owned Silicon Valley suppressed circulation of the story. This alone went a mighty way to rigging the election of 2020. Cult assets like Mark Zuckerberg at Facebook also spent hundreds of millions to be used in support of Biden and vote 'administration'.

The Cult had used Trump as the focus to divide America and was now desperate to bring in moronic, pliable, corrupt Biden to complete the double-whammy. No way were they going to let little things like the will of the people thwart their plan. Silicon Valley widely censored claims that the election was rigged because it *was* rigged. For the same reason anyone claiming it was rigged was denounced as a 'white supremacist' including the pathetically few Republican politicians willing to say so. Right across the media where the claim was mentioned it was described as a 'false claim' even though these excuses for 'journalists' would have done no research into the subject whatsoever. Trump won seven million more votes than any sitting president had ever achieved while somehow a cognitively-challenged soon to be 78-year-old who was hidden away from the public for most of the campaign managed to win more votes than any presidential candidate in history. It makes no sense. You only had to see election rallies for both candidates to witness the enthusiasm for Trump and the apathy for Biden. Tens of thousands would attend Trump events while Biden was speaking in empty car parks with often only television crews attending and framing their shots to hide the fact that no one was there. It was pathetic to see footage come to light of Biden standing at a podium making speeches only to TV crews and party fixers while reading the words written for him on massive Teleprompter screens. So, yes, those protestors on January 6th had a point about election rigging, but some were about to walk into a trap laid for them in Washington by the Cult Deep State and its QAnon Psyop. This was the Capitol Hill riot ludicrously dubbed an 'insurrection'.

The spider and the fly

Renegade Minds know there are not two 'sides' in politics, only one side, the Cult, working through all 'sides'. It's a stage show, a puppet show, to direct the perceptions of the population into focusing on diversions like parties and candidates while missing the puppeteers with their hands holding all the strings. The Capitol Hill 'insurrection' brings us back to the Little Big Horn. Having created two distinct opposing groupings – Woke and Pushbackers – the trap was about to be sprung. Pushbackers were to be encircled and isolated by associating them all in the public mind with Trump and then labelling Trump as some sort of Confederate leader. I knew immediately that the Capitol riot was a set-up because of two things. One was how easy the rioters got into the building with virtually no credible resistance and secondly I could see – as with the 'Covid' hoax in the West at the start of 2020 – how the Cult could exploit the situation to move its agenda forward with great speed. My experience of Cult techniques and activities over more than 30 years has showed me that while they do exploit situations they haven't themselves created this never happens with events of fundamental agenda significance. Every time major events giving cultists the excuse to rapidly advance their plan you find they are manipulated into being for the specific reason of providing that excuse – Problem-Reaction-Solution. Only a tiny minority of the huge crowd of Washington protestors sought to gain entry to the Capitol by smashing windows and breaching doors. That didn't matter. The whole crowd and all Pushbackers, even if they did not support Trump, were going to be lumped together as dangerous insurrectionists and conspiracy theorists. The latter term came into widespread use through a CIA memo in the 1960s aimed at discrediting those questioning the nonsensical official story of the Kennedy assassination and it subsequently became widely employed by the media. It's still being used by inept 'journalists' with no idea of its origin to discredit anyone questioning anything that authority claims to be true. When you are perpetrating a conspiracy you need to discredit the very word itself even though the dictionary definition of conspiracy is merely 'the activity of secretly planning with other people to do something bad or illegal' and 'a general agreement to keep silent about a subject for the purpose of keeping it secret'. On that basis there are conspiracies almost wherever you look. For obvious reasons the Cult and its lapdog media have to claim there are no conspiracies even though the word appears in state laws as with conspiracy to defraud, to murder, and to corrupt public morals.

Agent provocateurs are widely used by the Cult Deep State to manipulate genuine people into acting in ways that suit the desired outcome. By genuine in this case I mean protestors genuinely supporting Trump and claims that the election was stolen. In among them, however, were agents of the state wearing the garb of Trump supporters and QAnon to pump-prime the Capital riot which some genuine Trump supporters naively fell for. I described the situation as 'Come into my parlour said the spider to the fly'. Leaflets appeared through the Woke paramilitary arm Antifa, the anti-fascist fascists, calling on supporters to turn up in Washington looking like Trump supporters even though they hated him. Some of those arrested for breaching the Capitol Building were sourced to Antifa and its stable mate Black Lives Matter. Both organisations are funded by Cult billionaires and corporations. One man charged for the riot was according to his lawyer a former FBI agent who had held top secret security clearance for 40 years. Attorney Thomas Plofchan said of his client, 66-year-old Thomas Edward Caldwell:

> He has held a Top Secret Security Clearance since 1979 and has undergone multiple Special Background Investigations in support of his clearances. After retiring from the Navy, he worked as a section chief for the Federal Bureau of Investigation from 2009-2010 as a GS-12 [mid-level employee].

> He also formed and operated a consulting firm performing work, often classified, for U.S government customers including the US. Drug Enforcement Agency, Department of Housing and Urban Development, the US Coast Guard, and the US Army Personnel Command.

A judge later released Caldwell pending trial in the absence of evidence about a conspiracy or that he tried to force his way into the building. *The New York Post* reported a 'law enforcement source' as saying that 'at least two known Antifa members were spotted' on camera among Trump supporters during the riot while one of the rioters arrested was John Earle Sullivan, a seriously extreme Black Lives Matter Trump-hater from Utah who was previously arrested and charged in July, 2020, over a BLM-Antifa riot in which drivers were threatened and one was shot. Sullivan is the founder of Utah-based Insurgence USA which is an affiliate of the Cult-created-and-funded Black Lives Matter movement. Footage appeared and was then deleted by Twitter of Trump supporters calling out Antifa infiltrators and a group was filmed changing into pro-Trump clothing before the riot. Security at the building was *pathetic* – as planned. Colonel Leroy Fletcher Prouty, a man with long experience in covert operations working with the US security apparatus, once described the tell-tale sign to identify who is involved in an assassination. He said:

No one has to direct an assassination – it happens. The active role is played secretly by permitting it to happen. This is the greatest single clue. Who has the power to call off or reduce the usual security precautions?

This principle applies to many other situations and certainly to the Capitol riot of January 6th, 2021.

The sting

With such a big and potentially angry crowd known to be gathering near the Capitol the security apparatus would have had a major police detail to defend the building with National Guard troops on standby given the strength of feeling among people arriving from all over America encouraged by the QAnon Psyop and statements by Donald Trump. Instead Capitol Police 'security' was flimsy, weak, and easily breached. The same number of officers was deployed as on a regular day and that is a blatant red flag. They were not staffed or equipped for a possible riot that had been an obvious possibility in the circumstances. No protective and effective fencing worth the name was put in place and there were no contingency plans. The whole thing was basically a case of standing aside and waving people in. Once inside police mostly backed off apart from one Capitol police officer who ridiculously shot dead unarmed Air Force veteran protestor Ashli Babbitt without a warning as she climbed through a broken window. The 'investigation' refused to name or charge the officer after what must surely be considered a murder in the circumstances. They just lifted a carpet and swept. The story was endlessly repeated about five people dying in the 'armed insurrection' when there was no report of rioters using weapons. Apart from Babbitt the other four died from a heart attack, strokes and apparently a drug overdose. Capitol police officer Brian Sicknick was reported to have died after being bludgeoned with a fire extinguisher when he was alive after the riot was over and died later of what the Washington Medical Examiner's Office said was a stroke. Sicknick had no external injuries. The lies were delivered like rapid fire. There was a narrative to build with incessant repetition of the lie until the lie became the accepted 'everybody knows that' truth. The 'Big Lie' technique of Nazi Propaganda Minister Joseph Goebbels is constantly used by the Cult which was behind the Nazis and is today behind the 'Covid' and 'climate change' hoaxes. Goebbels said:

> If you tell a lie big enough and keep repeating it, people will eventually come to believe it. The lie can be maintained only for such time as the State can shield the people from the political, economic and/or military consequences of the lie. It thus becomes vitally important for the State to use all of its powers to repress dissent, for the truth is the mortal enemy of the lie, and thus by

extension, the truth is the greatest enemy of the State.

Most protestors had a free run of the Capitol Building. This allowed pictures to be taken of rioters in iconic parts of the building including the Senate chamber which could be used as propaganda images against all Pushbackers. One Congresswoman described the scene as 'the worst kind of non-security anybody could ever imagine'. Well, the first part was true, but someone obviously did imagine it and made sure it happened. Some photographs most widely circulated featured people wearing QAnon symbols and now the Psyop would be used to dub all QAnon followers with the ubiquitous fit-all label of 'white supremacist' and 'insurrectionists'. When a Muslim extremist called Noah Green drove his car at two police officers at the Capitol Building killing one in April, 2021, there was no such political and media hysteria. They were just disappointed he wasn't white.

The witch-hunt

Government prosecutor Michael Sherwin, an aggressive, dark-eyed, professional Rottweiler led the 'investigation' and to call it over the top would be to understate reality a thousand fold. Hundreds were tracked down and arrested for the crime of having the wrong political views and people were jailed who had done nothing more than walk in the building, committed no violence or damage to property, took a few pictures and left. They were labelled a 'threat to the Republic' while Biden sat in the White House signing executive orders written for him that were dismantling 'the Republic'. Even when judges ruled that a mother and son should not be in jail the government kept them there. Some of those arrested have been badly beaten by prison guards in Washington and lawyers for one man said he suffered a fractured skull and was made blind in one eye. Meanwhile a woman is shot dead for no reason by a Capitol Police officer and we are not allowed to know who he is never mind what has happened to him although that will be *nothing*. The Cult's QAnon/Trump sting to identify and isolate Pushbackers and then target them on the road to crushing and deleting them was a resounding success. You would have thought the Russians had invaded the building at gunpoint and lined up senators for a firing squad to see the political and media reaction. Congresswoman Alexandria Ocasio-Cortez is a child in a woman's body, a terrible-twos, me, me, me, Woker narcissist of such proportions that words have no meaning. She said she thought she was going to die when 'insurrectionists' banged on her office door. It turned out she wasn't even in the Capitol Building when the riot was happening and the 'banging' was a Capitol Police officer. She referred to herself as a 'survivor' which is an insult to all those true survivors of violent and sexual abuse while she lives her pampered and privileged life talking drivel for a living. Her Woke colleague and fellow mega-narcissist Rashida Tlaib broke down describing the devastating effect on her, too, of *not being* in the building when the rioters were there. Ocasio-Cortez and Tlaib are members of a fully-Woke group of Congresswomen known as 'The Squad' along with Ilhan Omar and Ayanna Pressley. The Squad from what I can see can be identified by its vehement anti-white racism, anti-white men agenda, and, as always in these cases, the absence of brain cells on active duty.

The usual suspects were on the riot case immediately in the form of Democrat ultra-Zionist senators and operatives Chuck Schumer and Adam Schiff demanding that Trump be impeached for 'his part in the insurrection'. The same pair of prats had led the failed impeachment of Trump over the invented 'Russia collusion' nonsense which claimed Russia had helped Trump win the 2016 election. I didn't realise that Tel Aviv had been relocated just outside Moscow. I must find an up-to-date map. The Russia hoax was a Sabbatian operation to keep Trump occupied and impotent and to stop any rapport with Russia which the Cult wants to retain as a perceptual enemy to be pulled out at will. Puppet Biden began attacking Russia when he came to office as the Cult seeks more upheaval, division and war across the world. A two-year stage show 'Russia collusion inquiry' headed by the not-very-bright former 9/11 FBI chief Robert Mueller, with support from 19 lawyers, 40 FBI agents plus intelligence analysts, forensic accountants and other staff, devoured tens of millions of dollars and found no evidence of Russia collusion which a ten-year-old could have told them on day one. Now the same moronic Schumer and Schiff wanted a second impeachment of Trump over the Capitol 'insurrection' (riot) which the arrested development of Schumer called another 'Pearl Harbor' while others compared it with 9/11 in which 3,000 died and, in the case of CNN, with the Rwandan genocide in the 1990s in which an estimated 500,000 to 600,000 were murdered, between 250, 000 and 500,000 women were raped, and populations of whole towns were hacked to death with machetes. To make those comparisons purely for Cult political reasons is beyond insulting to those that suffered and lost their lives and confirms yet again the callous inhumanity that we are dealing with. Schumer is a monumental idiot and so is Schiff, but they serve the Cult agenda and do whatever they're told so they get looked after. Talking of idiots – another inane man who spanned the Russia and Capitol impeachment attempts was Senator Eric Swalwell who had the nerve to accuse Trump of collusion with the Russians while sleeping with a Chinese spy called Christine Fang or 'Fang Fang' which is straight out of a Bond film no doubt starring Klaus Schwab as the bloke living on a secret island and controlling laser weapons positioned in space and pointing at world capitals. Fang Fang plays the part of Bond's infiltrator girlfriend which I'm sure she would enjoy rather more than sharing a bed with the brainless Swalwell, lying back and thinking of China. The FBI eventually warned Swalwell about Fang Fang which gave her time to escape back to the Chinese dictatorship. How very thoughtful of them. The second Trump impeachment also failed and hardly surprising when an impeachment is supposed to remove a sitting president and by the time it happened Trump was no longer president. These people are running your country America, well, officially anyway. Terrifying isn't it?

Outcomes tell the story - always

The outcome of all this – and it's the *outcome* on which Renegade Minds focus, not the words – was that a vicious, hysterical and obviously pre-planned assault was launched on Pushbackers to censor, silence and discredit them and even targeted their right to earn a living. They have since been condemned as 'domestic terrorists' that need to be treated like Al-Qaeda and Islamic State. 'Domestic terrorists' is a label the Cult has been trying to make stick since the period of the Oklahoma bombing in 1995 which was blamed on 'far-right domestic terrorists'. If you read *The Trigger* you will see that the bombing was clearly a Problem-Reaction-Solution carried out by the Deep State during a Bill Clinton administration so corrupt that no dictionary definition of the term would even nearly suffice. Nearly 30, 000 troops were deployed from all over America to the empty streets of Washington for Biden's inauguration. Ten thousand of them stayed on with the pretext of protecting the capital from insurrectionists when it was more psychological programming to normalise the use of the military in domestic law enforcement in support of the Cult plan for a police-military state. Biden's fascist administration began a purge of 'wrong-thinkers' in the military which means anyone that is not on board with Woke. The Capitol Building was surrounded by a fence with razor wire and the Land of the Free was further symbolically and literally dismantled. The circle was completed with the installation of Biden and the exploitation of the QAnon Psyop.

America had never been so divided since the civil war of the 19th century, Pushbackers were isolated and dubbed terrorists and now, as was always going to happen, the Cult immediately set about deleting what little was left of freedom and transforming American society through a swish of the hand of the most controlled 'president' in American history leading (officially at least) the most extreme regime since the country was declared an independent state on July 4th, 1776. Biden issued undebated, dictatorial executive orders almost by the hour in his opening days in office across the whole spectrum of the Cult wish-list including diluting controls on the border with Mexico allowing thousands of migrants to illegally enter the United States to transform the demographics of America and import an election-changing number of perceived Democrat voters. Then there were Biden deportation amnesties for the already illegally resident (estimated to be as high as 20 or even 30 million). A bill before Congress awarded American citizenship to anyone who could prove they had worked in agriculture for just 180 days in the previous two years as 'Big Ag' secured its slave labour long-term. There were the plans to add new states to the union such as Puerto Rico and making Washington DC a state. They are all parts of a plan to ensure that the Cult-owned Woke Democrats would be permanently in power.

Border – what border?

I have exposed in detail in other books how mass immigration into the United States and Europe is the work of Cult networks fuelled by the tens of billions spent to this and other ends by George Soros and his global Open Society (open borders) Foundations. The impact can be seen in America alone where the population has increased by *100 million* in little more than 30 years mostly through immigration. I wrote in *The Answer* that the plan was to have so many people crossing the southern border that the numbers become unstoppable and we are now there under Cult-owned Biden. El Salvador in Central America puts the scale of what is happening into context. A third of the population now lives in the United States, much of it illegally, and many more are on the way. The methodology is to crush Central and South American countries economically and spread violence through machete-wielding psychopathic gangs like MS-13 based in El Salvador and now operating in many American cities. Biden-imposed lax security at the southern border means that it is all but open. He said before his 'election' that he wanted to see a surge towards the border if he became president and that was the green light for people to do just that after election day to create the human disaster that followed for both America and the migrants. When that surge came the imbecilic Alexandria Ocasio-Cortez said it wasn't a 'surge' because they are 'children, not insurgents' and the term 'surge' (used by Biden) was a claim of 'white supremacists'. This disingenuous lady may one day enter the realm of the most basic intelligence, but it won't be any time soon.

Sabbatians and the Cult are in the process of destroying America by importing violent people and gangs in among the genuine to terrorise American cities and by overwhelming services that cannot cope with the sheer volume of new arrivals. Something similar is happening in Europe as Western society in general is targeted for demographic and cultural transformation and upheaval. The plan demands violence and crime to create an environment of intimidation, fear and division and Soros has been funding the election of district attorneys across America who then stop prosecuting many crimes, reduce sentences for violent crimes and free as many violent criminals as they can. Sabbatians are creating the chaos from which order – their order – can respond in a classic Problem-Reaction-Solution. A Freemasonic moto says 'Ordo Ab Chao' (Order out of Chaos) and this is why the Cult is constantly creating chaos to impose a new 'order'. Here you have the reason the Cult is constantly creating chaos. The 'Covid' hoax can be seen with those entering the United States by plane being forced to take a 'Covid' test while migrants flooding through southern border processing facilities do not. Nothing is put in the way of mass migration and if that means ignoring the government's own 'Covid' rules then so be it. They know it's all bullshit anyway. Any pushback on this is denounced as 'racist' by Wokers and Sabbatian fronts like the ultra-Zionist Anti-Defamation League headed by the appalling Jonathan Greenblatt which at the same time argues that Israel should not give citizenship and voting rights to more Palestinian Arabs or the 'Jewish population' (in truth the Sabbatian network) will lose control of the country.

Society-changing numbers

Biden's masters have declared that countries like El Salvador are so dangerous that their people must be allowed into the United States for humanitarian reasons when there are fewer murders in large parts of many Central American countries than in US cities like Baltimore. That is not to say Central America cannot be a dangerous place and Cult-controlled American governments have been making it so since way back, along with the dismantling of economies, in a long-term plan to drive people north into the United States. Parts of Central America are very dangerous, but in other areas the story is being greatly exaggerated to justify relaxing immigration criteria. Migrants are being offered free healthcare and education in the United States as another incentive to head for the border and there is no requirement to be financially independent before you can enter to prevent the resources of America being drained. You can't blame migrants for seeking what they believe will be a better life, but they are being played by the Cult for dark and nefarious ends. The numbers since Biden took office are huge. In February, 2021, more than 100,000 people were known to have tried to enter the US illegally through the southern border (it was 34,000 in the same month in 2020) and in March it was 170,000 – a 418 percent increase on March, 2020. These numbers are only known people, not the ones who get in unseen. The true figure for migrants illegally crossing the border in a single month was estimated by one congressman at 250,000 and that number will only rise under Biden's current policy. Gangs of murdering drug-running thugs that control the Mexican side of the border demand money – thousands of dollars – to let migrants cross the Rio Grande into America. At the same time gun battles are breaking out on the border several times a week between rival Mexican drug gangs (which now operate globally) who are equipped with sophisticated military-grade weapons, grenades and armoured vehicles. While the Capitol Building was being 'protected' from a non-existent 'threat' by thousands of troops, and others were still deployed at the time in the Cult Neocon war in Afghanistan, the southern border of America was left to its fate. This is not incompetence, it is cold calculation.

By March, 2021, there were 17,000 unaccompanied children held at border facilities and many of them are ensnared by people traffickers for paedophile rings and raped on their journey north to America. This is not conjecture – this is fact. Many of those designated children are in reality teenage boys or older. Meanwhile Wokers posture their self-purity for encouraging poor and tragic people to come to America and face this nightmare both on the journey and at the border with the disgusting figure of House Speaker Nancy Pelosi giving disingenuous speeches about caring for migrants. The woman's evil. Wokers condemned Trump for having children in cages at the border (so did Obama, *Shhhh*), but now they are sleeping on the floor without access to a shower with one border facility 729 percent over capacity. The Biden insanity even proposed flying migrants from the southern border to the northern border with Canada for 'processing'. The whole shambles is being overseen by ultra-Zionist Secretary of Homeland Security, the moronic liar Alejandro Mayorkas, who banned news cameras at border facilities to stop Americans seeing what was happening. Mayorkas said there was not a ban on news crews; it was just that they were not allowed to film. Alongside him at Homeland Security is another ultra-Zionist Cass Sunstein appointed by Biden to oversee new immigration laws. Sunstein despises conspiracy researchers to the point where he suggests they should be banned or *taxed* for having such views. The man is not bonkers or anything. He's perfectly well-adjusted, but adjusted to what is the question. Criticise what is happening and you are a 'white supremacist' when earlier non-white immigrants also oppose the numbers which effect their lives and opportunities. Black people in poor areas are particularly damaged by uncontrolled immigration and the increased competition for work opportunities with those who will work for less. They are also losing voting power as Hispanics become more dominant in former black areas. It's a downward spiral for them while the billionaires behind the policy drone on about how much they care about black people and 'racism'. None of this is about compassion for migrants or black people – that's just wind and air. Migrants are instead being mercilessly exploited to transform America while the countries they leave are losing their future and the same is true in Europe. Mass immigration may now be the work of Woke Democrats, but it can be traced back to the 1986 Immigration Reform and Control Act (it wasn't) signed into law by Republican hero President Ronald Reagan which gave amnesty to millions living in the United States illegally and other incentives for people to head for the southern border. Here we have the one-party state at work again.

Save me syndrome

Almost every aspect of what I have been exposing as the Cult agenda was on display in even the first days of 'Biden' with silencing of Pushbackers at the forefront of everything. A Renegade Mind will view the Trump years and QAnon in a very different light to their supporters and advocates as the dots are connected. The QAnon/Trump Psyop has given the Cult all it was looking for. We may not know how much, or little, that Trump realised he was being used, but that's a side issue. This pincer movement produced the desired outcome of dividing America and having Pushbackers isolated. To turn this around we have to look at new routes to empowerment which do not include handing our power to other people and groups through what I will call the 'Save Me Syndrome' – 'I want someone else to do it so that I don't have to'. We have seen this at work throughout human history and the QAnon/Trump Psyop is only the latest incarnation alongside all the others. Religion is an obvious expression of this when people look to a 'god' or priest to save them or tell them how to be saved and then there are 'save me' politicians like Trump. Politics is a diversion and not a 'saviour'. It is a means to block positive change, not make it possible.

Save Me Syndrome always comes with the same repeating theme of handing your power to whom or what you believe will save you while your real 'saviour' stares back from the mirror every morning. Renegade Minds are constantly vigilant in this regard and always asking the question 'What can I do?' rather than 'What can someone else do for me?' Gandhi was right when he said: 'You must be the change you want to see in the world.' We are indeed the people we have been waiting for. We are presented with a constant raft of reasons to concede that power to others and forget where the real power is. Humanity has the numbers and the Cult does not. It has to use diversion and division to target the unstoppable power that comes from unity. Religions, governments, politicians, corporations, media, QAnon, are all different manifestations of this power-diversion and dilution. Refusing to give your power to governments and instead handing it to Trump and QAnon is not to take a new direction, but merely to recycle the old one with new names on the posters. I will explore this phenomenon as we proceed and how to break the cycles and recycles that got us here through the mists of repeating perception and so repeating history.

For now we shall turn to the most potent example in the entire human story of the consequences that follow when you give your power away. I am talking, of course, of the 'Covid' hoax.

CHAPTER FOUR

'Covid': Calculated catastrophe

Facts are threatening to those invested in fraud
DaShanne Stokes

We can easily unravel the real reason for the 'Covid pandemic' hoax by employing the Renegade Mind methodology that I have outlined this far. We'll start by comparing the long-planned Cult outcome with the 'Covid pandemic' outcome. Know the outcome and you'll see the journey.

I have highlighted the plan for the Hunger Games Society which has been in my books for so many years with the very few controlling the very many through ongoing dependency. To create this dependency it is essential to destroy independent livelihoods, businesses and employment to make the population reliant on the state (the Cult) for even the basics of life through a guaranteed pittance income. While independence of income remained these Cult ambitions would be thwarted. With this knowledge it was easy to see where the 'pandemic' hoax was going once talk of 'lockdowns' began and the closing of all but perceived 'essential' businesses to 'save' us from an alleged 'deadly virus'. Cult corporations like Amazon and Walmart were naturally considered 'essential' while mom and pop shops and stores had their doors closed by fascist decree. As a result with every new lockdown and new regulation more small and medium, even large businesses not owned by the Cult, went to the wall while Cult giants and their frontmen and women grew financially fatter by the second. Mom and pop were denied an income and the right to earn a living and the wealth of people like Jeff Bezos (Amazon), Mark Zuckerberg (Facebook) and Sergei Brin and Larry Page (Google/Alphabet) have reached record levels. The Cult was increasing its own power through further dramatic concentrations of wealth while the competition was being destroyed and brought into a state of dependency. Lockdowns have been instigated to secure that very end and were never anything to do with health. My brother Paul spent 45 years building up a bus repair business, but lockdowns meant buses were running at a fraction of normal levels for months on end. Similar stories can told in their hundreds of millions worldwide. Efforts of a lifetime coldly destroyed by Cult multi-billionaires and their lackeys in government and law enforcement who continued to earn their living from the taxation of the people while denying the right of the same people to earn theirs. How different it would have been if those making and enforcing these decisions had to face the same financial hardships of those they affected, but they never do.

Gates of Hell

Behind it all in the full knowledge of what he is doing and why is the psychopathic figure of Cult operative Bill Gates. His puppet Tedros at the World Health Organization declared 'Covid' a pandemic in March, 2020. The WHO had changed the definition of a 'pandemic' in 2009 just a month before declaring the 'swine flu pandemic' which would not have been so under the previous definition. The same applies to 'Covid'. The definition had included… 'an infection by an infectious agent, occurring simultaneously in different countries, with a significant mortality rate relative to the proportion of the population infected'. The new definition removed the need for 'significant mortality'. The 'pandemic' has been fraudulent even down to the definition, but Gates demanded economy-destroying lockdowns, school closures, social distancing, mandatory masks, a 'vaccination' for every man, woman and child on the planet and severe consequences and restrictions for those that refused. Who gave him this power? The Cult did which he serves like a little boy in short trousers doing what his daddy tells him. He and his psychopathic missus even smiled when they said that much worse was to come (what they knew was planned to come). Gates responded in the matter-of-fact way of all psychopaths to a question about the effect on the world economy of what he was doing:

Well, it won't go to zero but it will shrink. Global GDP is probably going to take the biggest hit ever [Gates was smiling as he said this] … in my lifetime this will be the greatest economic hit. But you don't have a choice. People act as if you have a choice. People don't feel like going to the stadium when they might get infected … People are deeply affected by seeing these stats, by knowing they could be part of the transmission chain, old people, their parents and grandparents, could be affected by this, and so you don't get to say ignore what is going on here.

There will be the ability to open up, particularly in rich countries, if things are done well over the next few months, but for the world at large normalcy only returns when we have largely vaccinated the entire population.

The man has no compassion or empathy. How could he when he's a psychopath like all Cult players? My own view is that even beyond that he is very seriously mentally ill. Look in his eyes and you can see this along with his crazy flailing arms. You don't do what he has done to the world population since the start of 2020 unless you are mentally ill and at the most extreme end of psychopathic. You especially don't do it when to you know, as we shall see, that cases and deaths from 'Covid' are fakery and a product of monumental figure massaging. 'These stats' that Gates referred to are based on a 'test' that's not testing for the 'virus' as he has known all along. He made his fortune with big Cult support as an infamously ruthless software salesman and now buys global control of 'health' (death) policy without the population he affects having any say. It's a breathtaking outrage. Gates talked about people being deeply affected by fear of 'Covid' when that was because of *him* and his global network lying to them minute-by-minute supported by a lying media that he seriously influences and funds to the tune of hundreds of millions. He's handed big sums to media operations including the BBC, NBC, Al Jazeera, Univision, *PBS NewsHour, ProPublica, National Journal, The Guardian, The Financial Times, The Atlantic, Texas Tribune, USA Today* publisher Gannett, *Washington Monthly, Le Monde,* Center for Investigative Reporting, Pulitzer Center on Crisis Reporting, National Press Foundation, International Center for Journalists, Solutions Journalism Network, the Poynter Institute for Media Studies, and many more. Gates is everywhere in the 'Covid' hoax and the man must go to prison – or a mental facility – for the rest of his life and his money distributed to those he has taken such enormous psychopathic pleasure in crushing.

The Muscle

The Hunger Games global structure demands a police-military state – a fusion of the two into one force – which viciously imposes the will of the Cult on the population and protects the Cult from public rebellion. In that regard, too, the 'Covid' hoax just keeps on giving. Often unlawful, ridiculous and contradictory 'Covid' rules and regulations have been policed across the world by moronic automatons and psychopaths made faceless by face-nappy masks and acting like the Nazi SS and fascist blackshirts and brownshirts of Hitler and Mussolini. The smallest departure from the rules decreed by the psychos in government and their clueless gofers were jumped upon by the face-nappy fascists. Brutality against public protestors soon became commonplace even on girls, women and old people as the brave men with the batons – the Face-Nappies as I call them – broke up peaceful protests and handed out fines like confetti to people who couldn't earn a living let alone pay hundreds of pounds for what was once an accepted human right. Robot Face-Nappies of Nottingham police in the English East Midlands fined one group £11,000 for attending a child's birthday party. For decades I charted the transformation of law enforcement as genuine, decent officers were replaced with psychopaths and the brain dead who would happily and brutally do whatever their masters told them. Now they were let loose on the public and I would emphasise the point that none of this just happened. The step-by-step change in the dynamic between police and public was orchestrated from the shadows by those who knew where this was all going and the same with the perceptual reframing of those in all levels of authority and official administration through 'training courses' by organisations such as Common Purpose which was created in the late 1980s and given a massive boost in Blair era Britain until it became a global phenomenon. Supposed public 'servants' began to view the population as the enemy and the same was true of the police. This was the start of the explosion of behaviour manipulation organisations and networks preparing for the all-war on the human psyche unleashed with the dawn of 2020. I will go into more detail about this later in the book because it is a core part of what is happening.

Police desecrated beauty spots to deter people gathering and arrested women for walking in the countryside alone 'too far' from their homes. We had arrogant, clueless sergeants in the Isle of Wight police where I live posting on Facebook what they insisted the population must do or else. A schoolmaster sergeant called Radford looked young enough for me to ask if his mother knew he was out, but he was posting what he *expected* people to do while a Sergeant Wilkinson boasted about fining lads for meeting in a McDonald's car park where they went to get a lockdown takeaway. Wilkinson added that he had even cancelled their order. What a pair of prats these people are and yet they have increasingly become the norm among Jackboot Johnson's Yellowshirts once known as the British police. This was the theme all over the world with police savagery common during lockdown protests in the United States, the Netherlands, and the fascist state of Victoria in Australia under its tyrannical and again moronic premier Daniel Andrews. Amazing how tyrannical and moronic tend to work as a team and the same combination could be seen across America as arrogant, narcissistic Woke governors and mayors such as Gavin Newsom (California), Andrew Cuomo (New York), Gretchen Whitmer (Michigan), Lori Lightfoot (Chicago) and Eric Garcetti (Los Angeles) did their Nazi and Stalin impressions with the full support of the compliant brutality of their enforcers in uniform as they arrested small business owners defying fascist shutdown orders and took them to jail in ankle shackles and handcuffs. This happened to bistro owner Marlena Pavlos-Hackney in Gretchen Whitmer's fascist state of Michigan when police arrived to enforce an order by a state-owned judge for 'putting the community at risk' at a time when other states like Texas were dropping restrictions and migrants were pouring across the southern border without any 'Covid' questions at all. I'm sure there are many officers appalled by what they are ordered to do, but not nearly enough of them. If they were truly appalled they would not do it. As the months passed every opportunity was taken to have the military involved to make their presence on the streets ever more familiar and 'normal' for the longer-term goal of police-military fusion.

Another crucial element to the Hunger Games enforcement network has been encouraging the public to report neighbours and others for 'breaking the lockdown rules'. The group faced with £11,000 in fines at the child's birthday party would have been dobbed-in by a neighbour with a brain the size of a pea. The technique was most famously employed by the Stasi secret police in communist East Germany who had public informants placed throughout the population. A police chief in the UK says his force doesn't need to carry out 'Covid' patrols when they are flooded with so many calls from the public reporting other people for visiting the beach. Dorset police chief James Vaughan said people were so enthusiastic about snitching on their fellow humans they were now operating as an auxiliary arm of the police: 'We are still getting around 400 reports a week from the public, so we will respond to reports …We won't need to be doing hotspot patrols because people are very quick to pick the phone up and tell us.' Vaughan didn't say that this is a pillar of all tyrannies of whatever complexion and the means to hugely extend the reach of enforcement while spreading distrust among the people and making them wary of doing anything that might get them reported. Those narcissistic Isle of Wight sergeants Radford and Wilkinson never fail to add a link to their Facebook posts where the public can inform on their fellow slaves. Neither would be self-aware enough to realise they were imitating the Stasi which they might well never have heard of. Government psychologists that I will expose later laid out a policy to turn communities against each other in the same way.

A coincidence? Yep, and I can knit fog

I knew from the start of the alleged pandemic that this was a Cult operation. It presented limitless potential to rapidly advance the Cult agenda and exploit manipulated fear to demand that every man, woman and child on the planet was 'vaccinated' in a process never used on humans before which infuses self-replicating *synthetic* material into human cells. Remember the plan to transform the human body from a biological to a synthetic biological state. I'll deal with the 'vaccine' (that's not actually a vaccine) when I focus on the genetic agenda. Enough to say here that mass global 'vaccination' justified by this 'new virus' set alarms ringing after 30 years of tracking these people and their methods. The 'Covid' hoax officially beginning in China was also a big red flag for reasons I will be explaining. The agenda potential was so enormous that I could dismiss any idea that the 'virus' appeared naturally. Major happenings with major agenda implications never occur without Cult involvement in making them happen. My questions were twofold in early 2020 as the media began its campaign to induce global fear and hysteria: Was this alleged infectious agent released on purpose by the Cult or did it even exist at all? I then did what I always do in these situations. I sat, observed and waited to see where the evidence and information would take me. By March and early April synchronicity was strongly – and ever more so since then – pointing me in the direction of *there is no 'virus'*. I went public on that with derision even from swathes of the alternative media that voiced a scenario that the Chinese government released the 'virus' in league with Deep State elements in the United States from a top-level bio-lab in Wuhan where the 'virus' is said to have first appeared. I looked at that possibility, but I didn't buy it for several reasons. Deaths from the 'virus' did not in any way match what they would have been with a 'deadly bioweapon' and it is much more effective if you sell the *illusion* of an infectious agent rather than having a real one unless you can control through injection who has it and who doesn't. Otherwise you lose control of events. A made-up 'virus' gives you a blank sheet of paper on which you can make it do whatever you like and have any symptoms or mutant 'variants' you choose to add while a real infectious agent would limit you to what it actually does. A phantom disease allows you to have endless ludicrous 'studies' on the 'Covid' dollar to widen the perceived impact by inventing ever more 'at risk' groups including one study which said those who walk slowly may be almost four times more likely to die from the 'virus'. People are in psychiatric wards for less.

A real 'deadly bioweapon' can take out people in the hierarchy that are not part of the Cult, but essential to its operation. Obviously they don't want that. Releasing a real disease means you immediately lose control of it. Releasing an illusory one means you don't. Again it's vital that people are extra careful when dealing with what they want to hear. A bioweapon unleashed from a Chinese laboratory in collusion with the American Deep State may fit a conspiracy narrative, but is it true? Would it not be far more effective to use the excuse of a 'virus' to justify the real bioweapon – the 'vaccine'? That way your disease agent does not have to be transmitted and arrives directly through a syringe. I saw a French virologist Luc Montagnier quoted in the alternative media as saying he had discovered that the alleged 'new' severe acute respiratory syndrome coronavirus , or SARS-CoV-2, was made artificially and included elements of the human immunodeficiency 'virus' (HIV) and a parasite that causes malaria. SARS-CoV-2 is alleged to trigger an alleged illness called Covid-19. I remembered Montagnier's name from my research years before into claims that an HIV 'retrovirus' causes AIDs – claims that were demolished by Berkeley virologist Peter Duesberg who showed that no one had ever proved that HIV causes acquired immunodeficiency syndrome or AIDS. Claims that become accepted as fact, publicly and medically, with no proof whatsoever are an ever-recurring story that profoundly applies to 'Covid'. Nevertheless, despite the lack of proof, Montagnier's team at the Pasteur Institute in Paris had a long dispute with American researcher Robert Gallo over which of them discovered and isolated the HIV 'virus' and with *no evidence* found it to cause AIDS. You will see later that there is also no evidence that any 'virus' causes any disease or that there is even such a thing as a 'virus' in the way it is said to exist. The claim to have 'isolated' the HIV 'virus' will be presented in its real context as we come to the shocking story – and it is a story – of SARS-CoV-2 and so will Montagnier's assertion that he identified the full SARS-CoV-2 genome.

Hoax in the making

We can pick up the 'Covid' story in 2010 and the publication by the Rockefeller Foundation of a document called 'Scenarios for the Future of Technology and International Development'. The inner circle of the Rockefeller family has been serving the Cult since John D. Rockefeller (1839-1937) made his fortune with Standard Oil. It is less well known that the same Rockefeller – the Bill Gates of his day – was responsible for establishing what is now referred to as 'Big Pharma', the global network of pharmaceutical companies that make outrageous profits dispensing scalpel and drug 'medicine' and are obsessed with pumping vaccines in ever-increasing number into as many human arms and backsides as possible. John D. Rockefeller was the driving force behind the creation of the 'education' system in the United States and elsewhere specifically designed to program the perceptions of generations thereafter. The Rockefeller family donated exceptionally valuable land in New York for the United Nations building and were central in establishing the World Health Organization in 1948 as an agency of the UN which was created from the start as a Trojan horse and stalking horse for world government. Now enter Bill Gates. His family and the Rockefellers have long been extremely close and I have seen genealogy which claims that if you go back far enough the two families fuse into the same bloodline. Gates has said that the Bill and Melinda Gates Foundation was inspired by the Rockefeller Foundation and why not when both are serving the same Cult? Major tax-exempt foundations are overwhelmingly criminal enterprises in which Cult assets fund the Cult agenda in the guise of 'philanthropy' while avoiding tax in the process. Cult operatives can become mega-rich in their role of front men and women for the psychopaths at the inner core and they, too, have to be psychopaths to knowingly serve such evil. Part of the deal is that a big percentage of the wealth gleaned from representing the Cult has to be spent advancing the ambitions of the Cult and hence you have the Rockefeller Foundation, Bill and Melinda Gates Foundation (and *so* many more) and people like George Soros with his global Open Society Foundations spending their billions in pursuit of global Cult control. Gates is a global public face of the Cult with his interventions in world affairs including Big Tech influence; a central role in the 'Covid' and 'vaccine' scam; promotion of the climate change shakedown; manipulation of education; geoengineering of the skies; and his food-control agenda as the biggest owner of farmland in America, his GMO promotion and through other means. As one writer said: 'Gates monopolizes or wields disproportionate influence over the tech industry, global health and vaccines, agriculture and food policy (including biopiracy and fake food), weather modification and other climate technologies, surveillance, education and media.' The almost limitless wealth secured through Microsoft and other not-allowed-to-fail ventures (including vaccines) has been ploughed into a long, long list of Cult projects designed to enslave the entire human race. Gates and the Rockefellers have been working as one unit with the Rockefeller-established World Health Organization leading global 'Covid' policy controlled by Gates through his mouth-piece Tedros. Gates became the WHO's biggest funder when Trump announced that the American government would cease its donations, but Biden immediately said he would restore the money when he took office in January, 2021. The Gates Foundation (the Cult) owns through limitless funding the world health system and the major players across the globe in the 'Covid' hoax.

Okay, with that background we return to that Rockefeller Foundation document of 2010 headed 'Scenarios for the Future of Technology and International Development' and its 'imaginary' epidemic of a virulent and deadly influenza strain which infected 20 percent of the global population and killed eight million in seven months. The Rockefeller scenario was that the epidemic destroyed economies, closed shops, offices and other businesses and led to governments imposing fierce rules and restrictions that included mandatory wearing of face masks and body-temperature checks to enter communal spaces like railway stations and supermarkets. The document predicted that even after the height of the Rockefeller-envisaged epidemic the authoritarian rule would continue to deal with further pandemics, transnational terrorism,

environmental crises and rising poverty. Now you may think that the
Rockefellers are our modern-day seers or alternatively, and rather more
likely, that they well knew what was planned a few years further on.
Fascism had to be imposed, you see, to 'protect citizens from risk and
exposure'. The Rockefeller scenario document said:

> During the pandemic, national leaders around the world flexed their authority
> and imposed airtight rules and restrictions, from the mandatory wearing of
> face masks to body-temperature checks at the entries to communal spaces like
> train stations and supermarkets. Even after the pandemic faded, this more
> authoritarian control and oversight of citizens and their activities stuck and
> even intensified. In order to protect themselves from the spread of increasingly
> global problems – from pandemics and transnational terrorism to
> environmental crises and rising poverty – leaders around the world took a
> firmer grip on power.
>
> At first, the notion of a more controlled world gained wide acceptance and
> approval. Citizens willingly gave up some of their sovereignty – and their
> privacy – to more paternalistic states in exchange for greater safety and
> stability. Citizens were more tolerant, and even eager, for top-down direction
> and oversight, and national leaders had more latitude to impose order in the
> ways they saw fit.
>
> In developed countries, this heightened oversight took many forms: biometric
> IDs for all citizens, for example, and tighter regulation of key industries whose
> stability was deemed vital to national interests. In many developed countries,
> enforced cooperation with a suite of new regulations and agreements slowly
> but steadily restored both order and, importantly, economic growth.

There we have the prophetic Rockefellers in 2010 and three years
later came their paper for the Global Health Summit in Beijing, China,
when government representatives, the private sector, international
organisations and groups met to discuss the next 100 years of 'global
health'. The Rockefeller Foundation-funded paper was called 'Dreaming
the Future of Health for the Next 100 Years and more prophecy ensued
as it described a dystopian future: 'The abundance of data, digitally
tracking and linking people may mean the 'death of privacy' and may
replace physical interaction with transient, virtual connection,
generating isolation and raising questions of how values are shaped in
virtual networks.' Next in the 'Covid' hoax preparation sequence came a
'table top' simulation in 2018 for another 'imaginary' pandemic of a
disease called Clade X which was said to kill 900 million people. The
exercise was organised by the Gates-funded Johns Hopkins University's
Center for Health Security in the United States and this is the very same

university that has been compiling the disgustingly and systematically erroneous global figures for 'Covid' cases and deaths. Similar Johns Hopkins health crisis scenarios have included the Dark Winter exercise in 2001 and Atlantic Storm in 2005.

Nostradamus 201

For sheer predictive genius look no further prophecy-watchers than the Bill Gates-funded Event 201 held only six weeks before the 'coronavirus pandemic' is supposed to have broken out in China and Event 201 was based on a scenario of a global 'coronavirus pandemic'. Melinda Gates, the great man's missus, told the BBC that he had 'prepared for years' for a coronavirus pandemic which told us what we already knew. Nostradamugates had predicted in a TED talk in 2015 that a pandemic was coming that would kill a lot of people and demolish the world economy. My god, the man is a machine – possibly even literally. Now here he was only weeks before the real thing funding just such a simulated scenario and involving his friends and associates at Johns Hopkins, the World Economic Forum Cult-front of Klaus Schwab, the United Nations, Johnson & Johnson, major banks, and officials from China and the Centers for Disease Control in the United States. What synchronicity – Johns Hopkins would go on to compile the fraudulent 'Covid' figures, the World Economic Forum and Schwab would push the 'Great Reset' in response to 'Covid', the Centers for Disease Control would be at the forefront of 'Covid' policy in the United States, Johnson & Johnson would produce a 'Covid vaccine', and everything would officially start just weeks later in China. Spooky, eh? They were even accurate in creating a simulation of a 'virus' pandemic because the 'real thing' would also be a simulation. Event 201 was not an exercise preparing for something that might happen; it was a rehearsal for what those in control knew was *going* to happen and very shortly. Hours of this simulation were posted on the Internet and the various themes and responses mirrored what would soon be imposed to transform human society. News stories were inserted and what they said would be commonplace a few weeks later with still more prophecy perfection. Much discussion focused on the need to deal with misinformation and the 'anti-vax movement' which is exactly what happened when the 'virus' arrived – was said to have arrived – in the West.

Cult-owned social media banned criticism and exposure of the official 'virus' narrative and when I said there *was* no 'virus' in early April, 2020, I was banned by one platform after another including YouTube, Facebook and later Twitter. The mainstream broadcast media in Britain was in effect banned from interviewing me by the Tony-Blair-created government broadcasting censor Ofcom headed by career government bureaucrat Melanie Dawes who was appointed just as the 'virus' hoax was about to play out in January, 2020. At the same time the Ickonic media platform was using Vimeo, another ultra-Zionist-owned operation, while our own player was being created and they deleted in an instant hundreds of videos, documentaries, series and shows to confirm their unbelievable vindictiveness. We had copies, of course, and they had to be restored one by one when our player was ready. These people have no class. Sabbatian Facebook promised free advertisements for the Gates-controlled World Health Organization narrative while deleting 'false claims and conspiracy theories' to stop 'misinformation' about the alleged coronavirus. All these responses could be seen just a short while earlier in the scenarios of Event 201. Extreme censorship was absolutely crucial for the Cult because the official story was so ridiculous and unsupportable by the evidence that it could never survive open debate and the free-flow of information and opinion. If you can't win a debate then don't have one is the Cult's approach throughout history. Facebook's little boy front man – front boy – Mark Zuckerberg equated 'credible and accurate information' with official sources and exposing their lies with 'misinformation'.

Silencing those that can see

The censorship dynamic of Event 201 is now the norm with an army of narrative-supporting 'fact-checker' organisations whose entire reason for being is to tell the public that official narratives are true and those exposing them are lying. One of the most appalling of these 'fact-checkers' is called NewsGuard founded by ultra-Zionist Americans Gordon Crovitz and Steven Brill. Crovitz is a former publisher of *The Wall Street Journal*, former Executive Vice President of Dow Jones, a member of the Council on Foreign Relations (CFR), and on the board of the American Association of Rhodes Scholars. The CFR and Rhodes Scholarships, named after Rothschild agent Cecil Rhodes who plundered the gold and diamonds of South Africa for his masters and the Cult, have featured widely in my books. NewsGuard don't seem to like me for some reason – I really can't think why – and they have done all they can to have me censored and discredited which is, to quote an old British politician, like being savaged by a dead sheep. They are, however, like all in the censorship network, very well connected and funded by organisations themselves funded by, or connected to, Bill Gates. As you would expect with anything associated with Gates NewsGuard has an offshoot called HealthGuard which 'fights online health care hoaxes'. How very kind. Somehow the NewsGuard European Managing Director Anna-Sophie Harling, a remarkably young-looking woman with no broadcasting experience and little hands-on work in journalism, has somehow secured a position on the 'Content Board' of UK government broadcast censor Ofcom. An executive of an organisation seeking to discredit dissidents of the official narratives is making decisions for the government broadcast 'regulator' about content?? Another appalling 'fact-checker' is Full Fact funded by George Soros and global censors Google and Facebook.

It's amazing how many activists in the 'fact-checking', 'anti-hate', arena turn up in government-related positions – people like UK Labour Party activist Imran Ahmed who heads the Center for Countering Digital Hate founded by people like Morgan McSweeney, now chief of staff to the Labour Party's hapless and useless 'leader' Keir Starmer. Digital Hate – which is what it really is – uses the American spelling of Center to betray its connection to a transatlantic network of similar organisations which in 2020 shapeshifted from attacking people for 'hate' to attacking them for questioning the 'Covid' hoax and the dangers of the 'Covid vaccine'. It's just a coincidence, you understand. This is one of Imran Ahmed's hysterical statements: 'I would go beyond calling anti-vaxxers conspiracy theorists to say they are an extremist group that pose a national security risk.' No one could ever accuse this prat of understatement and he's including in that those parents who are now against vaccines after their children were damaged for life or killed by them. He's such a nice man. Ahmed does the rounds of the Woke media getting soft-ball questions from spineless 'journalists' who never ask what right he has to campaign to destroy the freedom of speech of others while he demands it for himself. There also seems to be an overrepresentation in Ofcom of people connected to the narrative-worshipping BBC. This incredible global network of narrative-support was super-vital when the 'Covid' hoax was played in the light of the mega-whopper lies that have to be defended from the spotlight cast by the most basic intelligence.

Setting the scene

The Cult plays the long game and proceeds step-by-step ensuring that everything is in place before major cards are played and they don't come any bigger than the 'Covid' hoax. The psychopaths can't handle events where the outcome isn't certain and as little as possible – preferably nothing – is left to chance. Politicians, government and medical officials who would follow direction were brought to illusory power in advance by the Cult web whether on the national stage or others like state governors and mayors of America. For decades the dynamic between officialdom, law enforcement and the public was changed from one of service to one of control and dictatorship. Behaviour manipulation networks established within government were waiting to impose the coming 'Covid' rules and regulations specifically designed to subdue and rewire the psyche of the people in the guise of protecting health. These included in the UK the Behavioural Insights Team part-owned by the British government Cabinet Office; the Scientific Pandemic Insights Group on Behaviours (SPI-B); and a whole web of intelligence and military groups seeking to direct the conversation on social media and control the narrative. Among them are the cyberwarfare (on the people) 77th Brigade of the British military which is also coordinated through the Cabinet Office as civilian and military leadership continues to combine in what they call the Fusion Doctrine. The 77th Brigade is a British equivalent of the infamous Israeli (Sabbatian) military cyberwarfare and Internet manipulation operation Unit 8200 which I expose at length in *The Trigger*. Also carefully in place were the medical and science advisers to government – many on the payroll past or present of Bill Gates – and a whole alternative structure of unelected government stood by to take control when elected parliaments were effectively closed down once the 'Covid' card was slammed on the table. The structure I have described here and so much more was installed in every major country through the Cult networks. The top-down control hierarchy looks like this: The Cult – Cult-owned Gates – the World Health Organization and Tedros – Gates-funded or controlled chief medical officers and science 'advisers' (dictators) in each country – political 'leaders'– law enforcement – The People. Through this simple global communication and enforcement structure the policy of the Cult could be imposed on virtually the entire human population so long as they acquiesced to the fascism. With everything in place it was time for the button to be pressed in late 2019/early 2020.

These were the prime goals the Cult had to secure for its will to prevail:

1) Locking down economies, closing all but designated 'essential' businesses (Cult-owned corporations were 'essential'), and putting the population under house arrest was an imperative to destroy independent income and employment and ensure dependency on the Cult-controlled state in the Hunger Games Society. Lockdowns had to be established as the global blueprint from the start to respond to the 'virus' and followed by pretty much the entire world.

2) The global population had to be terrified into believing in a deadly 'virus' that didn't actually exist so they would unquestioningly obey authority in the belief that authority must know how best to protect them and their families. Software salesman Gates would suddenly morph into the world's health expert and be promoted as such by the Cult-owned media.

3) A method of testing that wasn't testing for the 'virus', but was only claimed to be, had to be in place to provide the illusion of 'cases' and

subsequent 'deaths' that had a very different cause to the 'Covid-19' that would be scribbled on the death certificate.

4) Because there was no 'virus' and the great majority testing positive with a test not testing for the 'virus' would have no symptoms of anything the lie had to be sold that people without symptoms (without the 'virus') could still pass it on to others. This was crucial to justify for the first time quarantining – house arresting – healthy people. Without this the economy-destroying lockdown of *everybody* could not have been credibly sold.

5) The 'saviour' had to be seen as a vaccine which beyond evil drug companies were working like angels of mercy to develop as quickly as possible, with all corners cut, to save the day. The public must absolutely not know that the 'vaccine' had nothing to do with a 'virus' or that the contents were ready and waiting with a very different motive long before the 'Covid' card was even lifted from the pack.

I said in March, 2020, that the 'vaccine' would have been created way ahead of the 'Covid' hoax which justified its use and the following December an article in the New York *Intelligencer* magazine said the Moderna 'vaccine' had been 'designed' by January, 2020. This was 'before China had even acknowledged that the disease could be transmitted from human to human, more than a week before the first confirmed coronavirus case in the United States'. The article said that by the time the first American death was announced a month later 'the vaccine had already been manufactured and shipped to the National Institutes of Health for the beginning of its Phase I clinical trial'. The 'vaccine' was actually 'designed' long before that although even with this timescale you would expect the article to ask how on earth it could have been done that quickly. Instead it asked why the 'vaccine' had not been rolled out then and not months later. Journalism in the mainstream is truly dead. I am going to detail in the next chapter why the 'virus' has never existed and how a hoax on that scale was possible, but first the foundation on which the Big Lie of 'Covid' was built.

The test that doesn't test

Fraudulent 'testing' is the bottom line of the whole 'Covid' hoax and was the means by which a 'virus' that did not exist *appeared* to exist. They could only achieve this magic trick by using a test not testing for the 'virus'. To use a test that *was* testing for the 'virus' would mean that every test would come back negative given there was no 'virus'. They chose to exploit something called the RT-PCR test invented by American

biochemist Kary Mullis in the 1980s who said publicly that his PCR test
… *cannot detect infectious disease*. Yes, the 'test' used worldwide to detect
infectious 'Covid' to produce all the illusory 'cases' and 'deaths'
compiled by Johns Hopkins and others *cannot detect infectious disease*.
This fact came from the mouth of the man who invented PCR and was
awarded the Nobel Prize in Chemistry in 1993 for doing so. Sadly, and
incredibly conveniently for the Cult, Mullis died in August, 2019, at the
age of 74 just before his test would be fraudulently used to unleash
fascism on the world. He was said to have died from pneumonia which
was an irony in itself. A few months later he would have had 'Covid-19'
on his death certificate. I say the timing of his death was convenient
because had he lived Mullis, a brilliant, honest and decent man, would
have been vociferously speaking out against the use of his test to detect
'Covid' when it was never designed, or able, to do that. I know that to be
true given that Mullis made the same point when his test was used to
'detect' – not detect – HIV. He had been seriously critical of the
Gallo/Montagnier claim to have isolated the HIV 'virus' and shown it to
cause AIDS for which Mullis said there was no evidence. AIDS is
actually not a disease but a series of diseases from which people die all
the time. When they die from those *same diseases* after a positive 'test' for
HIV then AIDS goes on their death certificate. I think I've heard that
before somewhere. Countries instigated a policy with 'Covid' that
anyone who tested positive with a test not testing for the 'virus' and
died of any other cause within 28 days and even longer 'Covid-19' had
to go on the death certificate. Cases have come from the test that can't
test for infectious disease and the deaths are those who have died of
anything after testing positive with a test not testing for the 'virus'. I'll
have much more later about the death certificate scandal.

   Mullis was deeply dismissive of the now US 'Covid' star Anthony
Fauci who he said was a liar who didn't know anything about anything
– 'and I would say that to his face – nothing.' He said of Fauci: 'The man
thinks he can take a blood sample, put it in an electron microscope and if
it's got a virus in there you'll know it – he doesn't understand electron
microscopy and he doesn't understand medicine and shouldn't be in a
position like he's in.' That position, terrifyingly, has made him the
decider of 'Covid' fascism policy on behalf of the Cult in his role as
director since 1984 of the National Institute of Allergy and Infectious
Diseases (NIAID) while his record of being wrong is laughable; but
being wrong, so long as it's the *right kind* of wrong, is why the Cult loves
him. He'll say anything the Cult tells him to say. Fauci was made Chief
Medical Adviser to the President immediately Biden took office. Biden
was installed in the White House by Cult manipulation and one of his
first decisions was to elevate Fauci to a position of even more control.
This is a coincidence? Yes, and I identify as a flamenco dancer called

Lola. How does such an incompetent criminal like Fauci remain in that pivotal position in American health since *the 1980s*? When you serve the Cult it looks after you until you are surplus to requirements. Kary Mullis said prophetically of Fauci and his like: 'Those guys have an agenda and it's not an agenda we would like them to have ... they make their own rules, they change them when they want to, and Tony Fauci does not mind going on television in front of the people who pay his salary and lie directly into the camera.' Fauci has done that almost daily since the 'Covid' hoax began. Lying is in Fauci's DNA. To make the situation crystal clear about the PCR test this is a direct quote from its inventor Kary Mullis:

> It [the PCR test] doesn't tell you that you're sick and doesn't tell you that the thing you ended up with was really going to hurt you ...'

Ask yourself why governments and medical systems the world over have been using this very test to decide who is 'infected' with the SARS-CoV-2 'virus' and the alleged disease it allegedly causes, 'Covid-19'. The answer to that question will tell you what has been going on. By the way, here's a little show-stopper – the 'new' SARS-CoV-2 'virus' was 'identified' as such right from the start using ... *the PCR test not testing for the 'virus'*. If you are new to this and find that shocking then stick around. I have hardly started yet. Even worse, other 'tests', like the 'Lateral Flow Device' (LFD), are considered so useless that they have to be *confirmed* by the PCR test! Leaked emails written by Ben Dyson, adviser to UK 'Health' Secretary Matt Hancock, said they were 'dangerously unreliable'. Dyson, executive director of strategy at the Department of Health, wrote: 'As of today, someone who gets a positive LFD result in (say) London has at best a 25 per cent chance of it being a true positive, but if it is a self-reported test potentially as low as 10 per cent (on an optimistic assumption about specificity) or as low as 2 per cent (on a more pessimistic assumption).' These are the 'tests' that schoolchildren and the public are being urged to have twice a week or more and have to isolate if they get a positive. Each fake positive goes in the statistics as a 'case' no matter how ludicrously inaccurate and the 'cases' drive lockdown, masks and the pressure to 'vaccinate'. The government said in response to the email leak that the 'tests' were accurate which confirmed yet again what shocking bloody liars they are. The real false positive rate is *100 percent* as we'll see. In another 'you couldn't make it up' the UK government agreed to pay £2.8 billion to California's Innova Medical Group to supply the irrelevant lateral flow tests. The company's primary test-making centre is in China. Innova Medical Group, established in March, 2020, is owned by Pasaca Capital Inc, chaired by Chinese-American millionaire Charles Huang who was born in Wuhan.

How it works – and how it doesn't

The RT-PCR test, known by its full title of Polymerase chain reaction, is used across the world to make millions, even billions, of copies of a DNA/RNA genetic information sample. The process is called 'amplification' and means that a tiny sample of genetic material is amplified to bring out the detailed content. I stress that it is not testing for an infectious disease. It is simply amplifying a sample of genetic material. In the words of Kary Mullis: 'PCR is … just a process that's used to make a whole lot of something out of something.' To emphasise the point companies that make the PCR tests circulated around the world to 'test' for 'Covid' warn on the box that it can't be used to detect 'Covid' or infectious disease and is for research purposes only. It's okay, rest for a minute and you'll be fine. This is the test that produces the 'cases' and 'deaths' that have been used to destroy human society. All those global and national medical and scientific 'experts' demanding this destruction to 'save us' *KNOW* that the test is not testing for the 'virus' and the cases and deaths they claim to be real are an almost unimaginable fraud. Every one of them and so many others including politicians and psychopaths like Gates and Tedros must be brought before Nuremburg-type trials and jailed for the rest of their lives. The more the genetic sample is amplified by PCR the more elements of that material become sensitive to the test and by that I don't mean sensitive for a 'virus' but for elements of the genetic material which is *naturally* in the body or relates to remnants of old conditions of various kinds lying dormant and causing no disease. Once the amplification of the PCR reaches a certain level *everyone* will test positive. So much of the material has been made sensitive to the test that everyone will have some part of it in their body. Even lying criminals like Fauci have said that once PCR amplifications pass 35 cycles everything will be a false positive that cannot be trusted for the reasons I have described. I say, like many proper doctors and scientists, that 100 percent of the 'positives' are false, but let's just go with Fauci for a moment.

He says that any amplification over 35 cycles will produce false positives and yet the US Centers for Disease Control (CDC) and Food and Drug Administration (FDA) have recommended up to 40 *cycles* and the National Health Service (NHS) in Britain admitted in an internal document for staff that it was using 45 *cycles* of amplification. A long list of other countries has been doing the same and at least one 'testing' laboratory has been using 50 *cycles*. Have you ever heard a doctor, medical 'expert' or the media ask what level of amplification has been used to claim a 'positive'. The 'test' comes back 'positive' and so you have the 'virus', end of story. Now we can see how the government in

Tanzania could send off samples from a goat and a pawpaw fruit under human names and both came back positive for 'Covid-19'. Tanzania president John Magufuli mocked the 'Covid' hysteria, the PCR test and masks and refused to import the DNA-manipulating 'vaccine'. The Cult hated him and an article sponsored by the Bill Gates Foundation appeared in the London *Guardian* in February, 2021, headed 'It's time for Africa to rein in Tanzania's anti-vaxxer president'. Well, 'reined in' he shortly was. Magufuli appeared in good health, but then, in March, 2021, he was dead at 61 from 'heart failure'. He was replaced by Samia Hassan Suhulu who is connected to Klaus Schwab's World Economic Forum and she immediately reversed Magufuli's 'Covid' policy. A sample of cola tested positive for 'Covid' with the PCR test in Germany while American actress and singer-songwriter Erykah Badu tested positive in one nostril and negative in the other. Footballer Ronaldo called the PCR test 'bullshit' after testing positive three times and being forced to quarantine and miss matches when there was nothing wrong with him. The mantra from Tedros at the World Health Organization and national governments (same thing) has been test, test, test. They know that the more tests they can generate the more fake 'cases' they have which go on to become 'deaths' in ways I am coming to. The UK government has its Operation Moonshot planned to test multiple millions every day in workplaces and schools with free tests for everyone to use twice a week at home in line with the Cult plan from the start to make testing part of life. A government advertisement for an 'Interim Head of Asymptomatic Testing Communication' said the job included responsibility for delivering a 'communications strategy' (propaganda) 'to support the expansion of asymptomatic testing that *normalises testing as part of everyday life*'. More tests means more fake 'cases', 'deaths' and fascism. I have heard of, and from, many people who booked a test, couldn't turn up, and yet got a positive result through the post for a test they'd never even had. The whole thing is crazy, but for the Cult there's method in the madness. Controlling and manipulating the level of amplification of the test means the authorities can control whenever they want the number of apparent 'cases' and 'deaths'. If they want to justify more fascist lockdown and destruction of livelihoods they keep the amplification high. If they want to give the illusion that lockdowns and the 'vaccine' are working then they lower the amplification and 'cases' and 'deaths' will appear to fall. In January, 2021, the Cult-owned World Health Organization suddenly warned laboratories about over-amplification of the test and to lower the threshold. Suddenly headlines began appearing such as: 'Why ARE "Covid" cases plummeting?' This was just when the vaccine rollout was underway and I had predicted months before they would make cases appear to fall through amplification tampering when the 'vaccine' came.

These people are so predictable.

Cow vaccines?

The question must be asked of what is on the test swabs being poked far up the nose of the population to the base of the brain? A nasal swab punctured one woman's brain and caused it to leak fluid. Most of these procedures are being done by people with little training or medical knowledge. Dr Lorraine Day, former orthopaedic trauma surgeon and Chief of Orthopaedic Surgery at San Francisco General Hospital, says the tests are really a *'vaccine'*. Cows have long been vaccinated this way. She points out that masks have to cover the nose and the mouth where it is claimed the 'virus' exists in saliva. Why then don't they take saliva from the mouth as they do with a DNA test instead of pushing a long swab up the nose towards the brain? The ethmoid bone separates the nasal cavity from the brain and within that bone is the cribriform plate. Dr Day says that when the swab is pushed up against this plate and twisted the procedure is 'depositing things back there'. She claims that among these 'things' are nanoparticles that can enter the brain. Researchers have noted that a team at the Gates-funded Johns Hopkins have designed tiny, star-shaped micro-devices that can latch onto intestinal mucosa and release drugs into the body. Mucosa is the thin skin that covers the inside surface of parts of the body such as *the nose* and mouth and produces mucus to protect them. The Johns Hopkins micro-devices are called 'theragrippers' and were 'inspired' by a parasitic worm that digs its sharp teeth into a host's intestines. Nasal swabs are also coated in the sterilisation agent ethylene oxide. The US National Cancer Institute posts this explanation on its website:

> At room temperature, ethylene oxide is a flammable colorless gas with a sweet odor. It is used primarily to produce other chemicals, including antifreeze. In smaller amounts, ethylene oxide is used as a pesticide and a sterilizing agent. The ability of ethylene oxide to damage DNA makes it an effective sterilizing agent but also accounts for its cancer-causing activity.

The Institute mentions lymphoma and leukaemia as cancers most frequently reported to be associated with occupational exposure to ethylene oxide along with stomach and breast cancers. How does anyone think this is going to work out with the constant testing regime being inflicted on adults and children at home and at school that will accumulate in the body anything that's on the swab?

Doctors know best

It is vital for people to realise that 'hero' doctors 'know' only what the Big Pharma-dominated medical authorities tell them to 'know' and if they refuse to 'know' what they are told to 'know' they are out the door. They are mostly not physicians or healers, but repeaters of the official narrative – or else. I have seen alleged professional doctors on British television make shocking statements that we are supposed to take seriously. One called 'Dr' Amir Khan, who is actually telling patients how to respond to illness, said that men could take the birth pill to 'help slow down the effects of Covid-19'. In March, 2021, another ridiculous 'Covid study' by an American doctor proposed injecting men with the female sex hormone progesterone as a 'Covid' treatment. British doctor Nighat Arif told the BBC that face coverings were now going to be part of ongoing normal. Yes, the vaccine protects you, she said (evidence?) … but the way to deal with viruses in the community was always going to come down to hand washing, face covering and keeping a physical distance. That's not what we were told before the 'vaccine' was circulating. Arif said she couldn't imagine ever again going on the underground or in a lift without a mask. I was just thanking my good luck that she was not my doctor when she said – in March, 2021 – that if 'we are *behaving* and we are doing all the right things' she thought we could 'have our nearest and dearest around us at home … around *Christmas* and *New Year!* Her patronising delivery was the usual school teacher talking to six-year-olds as she repeated every government talking point and probably believed them all. If we have learned anything from the 'Covid' experience surely it must be that humanity's perception of doctors needs a fundamental rethink. NHS 'doctor' Sara Kayat told her television audience that the 'Covid vaccine' would '100 percent prevent hospitalisation and death'. Not even Big Pharma claimed that. We have to stop taking 'experts' at their word without question when so many of them are clueless and only repeating the party line on which their careers depend. That is not to say there are not brilliants doctors – there are and I have spoken to many of them since all this began – but you won't see them in the mainstream media or quoted by the psychopaths and yes-people in government.

Remember the name – Christian Drosten

German virologist Christian Drosten, Director of Charité Institute of Virology in Berlin, became a national star after the pandemic hoax began. He was feted on television and advised the German government on 'Covid' policy. Most importantly to the wider world Drosten led a group that produced the 'Covid' testing protocol for the PCR test. What a remarkable feat given the PCR cannot test for infectious disease and even more so when you think that Drosten said that his method of testing for SARS-CoV-2 was developed 'without having virus material available'. *He developed a test for a 'virus' that he didn't have and had never seen.* Let that sink in as you survey the global devastation that came from what he did. The whole catastrophe of Drosten's 'test' was based on the alleged genetic sequence published by Chinese scientists on the Internet. We will see in the next chapter that this alleged 'genetic sequence' has never been produced by China or anyone and cannot be when there *is no* SARS-CoV-2. Drosten, however, doesn't seem to let little details like that get in the way. He was the lead author with Victor Corman from the same Charité Hospital of the paper 'Detection of 2019 novel coronavirus (2019-nCoV) by real-time PCR' published in a magazine called *Eurosurveillance*. This became known as the Corman-Drosten paper. In November, 2020, with human society devastated by the effects of the Corman-Drosten test baloney, the protocol was publicly challenged by 22 international scientists and independent researchers from Europe, the United States, and Japan. Among them were senior molecular geneticists, biochemists, immunologists, and microbiologists. They produced a document headed 'External peer review of the RTPCR test to detect SARS-Cov-2 Reveals 10 Major Flaws At The Molecular and Methodological Level: Consequences For False-Positive Results'. The flaws in the Corman-Drosten test included the following:

- The test is non-specific because of erroneous design
- Results are enormously variable
- The test is unable to discriminate between the whole 'virus' and viral fragments
- It doesn't have positive or negative controls
- The test lacks a standard operating procedure
- It is unsupported by proper peer view

The scientists said the PCR 'Covid' testing protocol was not founded on science and they demanded the Corman-Drosten paper be retracted by *Eurosurveillance*. They said all present and previous Covid deaths, cases, and 'infection rates' should be subject to a massive retroactive inquiry. Lockdowns and travel restrictions should be reviewed and relaxed and those diagnosed through PCR to have 'Covid-19' should not be forced to isolate. Dr Kevin Corbett, a health researcher and nurse educator with a long academic career producing a stream of peer-reviewed publications at many UK universities, made the same point about the PCR test debacle. He said of the scientists' conclusions: 'Every scientific rationale for the development of that test has been totally destroyed by this paper. It's like Hiroshima/Nagasaki to the Covid test.' He said that China hadn't given them an isolated 'virus' when Drosten developed the test. Instead they had developed the test from *a sequence in a gene bank.*' Put another way … *they made it up!* The scientists were supported in this contention by a Portuguese appeals court which ruled in November, 2020, that PCR tests are unreliable and it is unlawful to quarantine people based solely on a PCR test. The point about China not providing an isolated virus must be true when the 'virus' has never been isolated to this day and the consequences of that will become clear. Drosten and company produced this useless 'protocol' right on cue in January, 2020, just as the 'virus' was said to be moving westward and it somehow managed to successfully pass a peer-review in 24 hours. In other words there was no peer-review for a test that would be used to decide who had 'Covid' and who didn't across the world. The Cult-created, Gates-controlled World Health Organization immediately recommended all its nearly 200 member countries to use the Drosten PCR protocol to detect 'cases' and 'deaths'. The sting was underway and it continues to this day.

So who is this Christian Drosten that produced the means through which death, destruction and economic catastrophe would be justified? His education background, including his doctoral thesis, would appear to be somewhat shrouded in mystery and his track record is dire as with another essential player in the 'Covid' hoax, the Gates-funded Professor Neil Ferguson at the Gates-funded Imperial College in London of whom more shortly. Drosten predicted in 2003 that the alleged original SARS 'virus' (SARS-1') was an epidemic that could have serious effects on economies and an effective vaccine would take at least two years to produce. Drosten's answer to every alleged 'outbreak' is a vaccine which you won't be shocked to know. What followed were just 774 official deaths worldwide and none in Germany where there were only nine cases. That is even if you believe there ever was a SARS 'virus' when the evidence is zilch and I will expand on this in the next chapter. Drosten claims to be co-discoverer of 'SARS-1' and developed a test for it in 2003. He was screaming warnings about 'swine flu' in 2009 and how it was a widespread infection far more severe than any dangers from a vaccine could be and people should get vaccinated. It would be helpful for Drosten's vocal chords if he simply recorded the words 'the virus is deadly and you need to get vaccinated' and copies could be handed out whenever the latest made-up threat comes along. Drosten's swine flu epidemic never happened, but Big Pharma didn't mind with governments spending hundreds of millions on vaccines that hardly anyone bothered to use and many who did wished they hadn't. A study in 2010 revealed that the risk of dying from swine flu, or H1N1, was no higher than that of the annual seasonal flu which is what at least most of 'it' really was as in the case of 'Covid-19'. A media investigation into Drosten asked how with such a record of inaccuracy he could be *the* government adviser on these issues. The answer to that question is the same with Drosten, Ferguson and Fauci – they keep on giving the authorities the 'conclusions' and 'advice' they want to hear. Drosten certainly produced the goods for them in January, 2020, with his PCR protocol garbage and provided the foundation of what German internal medicine specialist Dr Claus Köhnlein, co-author of *Virus Mania*, called the 'test pandemic'. The 22 scientists in the *Eurosurveillance* challenge called out conflicts of interest within the Drosten 'protocol' group and with good reason. Olfert Landt, a regular co-author of Drosten 'studies', owns the biotech company TIB Molbiol Syntheselabor GmbH in Berlin which manufactures and sells the tests that Drosten and his mates come up with. They have done this with SARS, Enterotoxigenic E. coli (ETEC), MERS, Zika 'virus', yellow fever, and now 'Covid'. Landt told the *Berliner Zeitung* newspaper:

> The testing, design and development came from the Charité [Drosten and Corman]. We simply implemented it immediately in the form of a kit. And if we don't have the virus, which originally only existed in Wuhan, we can make a synthetic gene to simulate the genome of the virus. That's what we did very quickly.

This is more confirmation that the Drosten test was designed without access to the 'virus' and only a synthetic simulation which is what SARS-CoV-2 really is – a computer-generated synthetic fiction. It's quite an enterprise they have going here. A Drosten team decides what the test for something should be and Landt's biotech company flogs it to governments and medical systems across the world. His company must have made an absolute fortune since the 'Covid' hoax began. Dr Reiner Fuellmich, a prominent German consumer protection trial lawyer in Germany and California, is on Drosten's case and that of Tedros at the World Health Organization for crimes against humanity with a class-action lawsuit being prepared in the United States and other legal action in Germany.

Why China?

Scamming the world with a 'virus' that doesn't exist would seem impossible on the face of it, but not if you have control of the relatively few people that make policy decisions and the great majority of the global media. Remember it's not about changing 'real' reality it's about controlling *perception* of reality. You don't have to make something happen you only have make people *believe* that it's happening. Renegade Minds understand this and are therefore much harder to swindle. 'Covid-19' is not a 'real' 'virus'. It's a mind virus, like a computer virus, which has infected the minds, not the bodies, of billions. It all started, publically at least, in China and that alone is of central significance. The Cult was behind the revolution led by its asset Mao Zedong, or Chairman Mao, which established the People's Republic of China on October 1st, 1949. It should have been called The Cult's Republic of

China, but the name had to reflect the recurring illusion that vicious dictatorships are run by and for the people (see all the 'Democratic Republics' controlled by tyrants). In the same way we have the 'Biden' Democratic Republic of America officially ruled by a puppet tyrant (at least temporarily) on behalf of Cult tyrants. The creation of Mao's merciless communist/fascist dictatorship was part of a frenzy of activity by the Cult at the conclusion of World War Two which, like the First World War, it had instigated through its assets in Germany, Britain, France, the United States and elsewhere. Israel was formed in 1948; the Soviet Union expanded its 'Iron Curtain' control, influence and military power with the Warsaw Pact communist alliance in 1955; the United Nations was formed in 1945 as a Cult precursor to world government; and a long list of world bodies would be established including the World Health Organization (1948), World Trade Organization (1948 under another name until 1995), International Monetary Fund (1945) and World Bank (1944). Human society was redrawn and hugely centralised in the global Problem-Reaction-Solution that was World War Two. All these changes were significant. Israel would become the headquarters of the Sabbatians and the revolution in China would prepare the ground and control system for the events of 2019/2020.

Renegade Minds know there are no borders except for public consumption. The Cult is a seamless, borderless global entity and to understand the game we need to put aside labels like borders, nations, countries, communism, fascism and democracy. These delude the population into believing that countries are ruled within their borders by a government of whatever shade when these are mere agencies of a global power. America's illusion of democracy and China's communism/fascism are subsidiaries – vehicles – for the same agenda. We may hear about conflict and competition between America and China and on the lower levels that will be true; but at the Cult level they are branches of the same company in the way of the McDonald's example I gave earlier. I have tracked in the books over the years support by US governments of both parties for Chinese Communist Party infiltration of American society through allowing the sale of land, even military facilities, and the acquisition of American business and university influence. All this is underpinned by the infamous stealing of intellectual property and technological know-how. Cult-owned Silicon Valley corporations waive their fraudulent 'morality' to do business with human-rights-free China; Cult-controlled Disney has become China's PR department; and China in effect owns 'American' sports such as basketball which depends for much of its income on Chinese audiences. As a result any sports player, coach or official speaking out against China's horrific human rights record is immediately condemned or fired by the China-worshipping National Basketball Association. One of the first acts of China-controlled Biden was to issue an executive order telling federal agencies to stop making references to the 'virus' by the 'geographic location of its origin'. Long-time Congressman Jerry Nadler warned that criticising China, America's biggest rival, leads to hate crimes against Asian people in the United States. So shut up you bigot. China is fast closing in on Israel as a country that must not be criticised which is apt, really, given that Sabbatians control them both. The two countries have developed close economic, military, technological and strategic ties which include involvement in China's 'Silk Road' transport and economic initiative to connect China with Europe. Israel was the first country in the Middle East to recognise the establishment of Mao's tyranny in 1950 months after it was established.

Project Wuhan – the 'Covid' Psyop

I emphasise again that the Cult plays the long game and what is happening to the world today is the result of centuries of calculated manipulation following a script to take control step-by-step of every aspect of human society. I will discuss later the common force behind all this that has spanned those centuries and thousands of years if the truth be told. Instigating the Mao revolution in China in 1949 with a 2020 'pandemic' in mind is not only how they work – the 71 years between them is really quite short by the Cult's standards of manipulation preparation. The reason for the Cult's Chinese revolution was to create a fiercely-controlled environment within which an extreme structure for human control could be incubated to eventually be unleashed across the world. We have seen this happen since the 'pandemic' emerged from China with the Chinese control-structure founded on AI technology and tyrannical enforcement sweep across the West. Until the moment when the Cult went for broke in the West and put its fascism on public display Western governments had to pay some lip-service to freedom and democracy to not alert too many people to the tyranny-in-the-making. Freedoms were more subtly eroded and power centralised with covert government structures put in place waiting for the arrival of 2020 when that smokescreen of 'freedom' could be dispensed with. The West was not able to move towards tyranny before 2020 anything like as fast as China which was created as a tyranny and had no limits on how fast it could construct the Cult's blueprint for global control. When the time came to impose that structure on the world it was the same Cult-owned Chinese communist/fascist government that provided the excuse – the 'Covid pandemic'. It was absolutely crucial to the Cult plan for the Chinese response to the 'pandemic' – draconian lockdowns of the entire population – to become the blueprint that Western countries would follow to destroy the livelihoods and freedom of their people. This is why the Cult-owned, Gates-owned, WHO Director-General Tedros said early on:

> The Chinese government is to be congratulated for the extraordinary measures
> it has taken to contain the outbreak. China is actually setting a new standard
> for outbreak response and it is not an exaggeration.

Forbes magazine said of China: '... those measures protected untold
millions from getting the disease'. The Rockefeller Foundation 'epidemic
scenario' document in 2010 said 'prophetically':

> However, a few countries did fare better – China in particular. The Chinese
> government's quick imposition and enforcement of mandatory quarantine for
> all citizens, as well as its instant and near-hermetic sealing off of all borders,
> saved millions of lives, stopping the spread of the virus far earlier than in other
> countries and enabling a swifter post-pandemic recovery.

Once again – *spooky.*

The first official story was the 'bat theory' or rather the bat diversion.
The source of the 'virus outbreak' we were told was a "wet market' in
Wuhan where bats and other animals are bought and eaten in
horrifically unhygienic conditions. Then another story emerged through
the alternative media that the 'virus' had been released on purpose or by
accident from a BSL-4 (biosafety level 4) laboratory in Wuhan not far
from the wet market. The lab was reported to create and work with
lethal concoctions and bioweapons. Biosafety level 4 is the highest in the
World Health Organization system of safety and containment. Renegade
Minds are aware of what I call designer manipulation. The ideal for the
Cult is for people to buy its prime narrative which in the opening
salvoes of the 'pandemic' was the wet market story. It knows, however,
that there is now a considerable worldwide alternative media of
researchers sceptical of anything governments say and they are often
given a version of events in a form they can perceive as credible while
misdirecting them from the real truth. In this case let them think that the
conspiracy involved is a 'bioweapon virus' released from the Wuhan lab
to keep them from the real conspiracy – *there is no 'virus'.* The WHO's
current position on the source of the outbreak at the time of writing
appears to be: 'We haven't got a clue, mate.' This is a good position to
maintain mystery and bewilderment. The inner circle will know where
the 'virus' came from – *nowhere.* The bottom line was to ensure the
public believed there *was* a 'virus' and it didn't much matter if they
thought it was natural or had been released from a lab. The belief that
there was a 'deadly virus' was all that was needed to trigger global
panic and fear. The population was terrified into handing their power to
authority and doing what they were told. They had to or they were 'all

gonna die'.

In March, 2020, information began to come my way from real doctors and scientists and my own additional research which had my intuition screaming: 'Yes, that's it! *There is no virus.*' The 'bioweapon' was not the 'virus'; it was the *'vaccine'* already being talked about that would be the bioweapon. My conclusion was further enhanced by happenings in Wuhan. The 'virus' was said to be sweeping the city and news footage circulated of people collapsing in the street (which they've never done in the West with the same 'virus'). The Chinese government was building 'new hospitals' in a matter of ten days to 'cope with demand' such was the virulent nature of the 'virus'. Yet in what seemed like no time the 'new hospitals' closed – even if they even opened – and China declared itself 'virus-free'. It was back to business as usual. This was more propaganda to promote the Chinese draconian lockdowns in the West as the way to 'beat the virus'. Trouble was that we subsequently had lockdown after lockdown, but never business as usual. As the people of the West and most of the rest of the world were caught in an ever-worsening spiral of lockdown, social distancing, masks, isolated old people, families forced apart, and livelihood destruction, it was party-time in Wuhan. Pictures emerged of thousands of people enjoying pool parties and concerts. It made no sense until you realised there never was a 'virus' and the whole thing was a Cult set-up to transform human society out of one its major global strongholds – China.

How is it possible to deceive virtually the entire world population into believing there is a deadly virus when there is not even a 'virus' let alone a deadly one? It's nothing like as difficult as you would think and that's clearly true because it happened.

Postscript: See end of book Postscript for more on the 'Wuhan lab virus release' story which the authorities and media were pushing heavily in the summer of 2021 to divert attention from the truth that the 'Covid virus' is pure invention.

CHAPTER FIVE

There *is no 'virus'*

You can fool some of the people all of the time, and all of the people some of the time, but you cannot fool all of the people all of the time
Abraham Lincoln

The greatest form of mind control is repetition. The more you repeat the same mantra of alleged 'facts' the more will accept them to be true. It becomes an 'everyone knows that, mate'. If you can also censor any other version or alternative to your alleged 'facts' you are pretty much home and cooking.

By the start of 2020 the Cult owned the global mainstream media almost in its entirety to spew out its 'Covid' propaganda and ignore or discredit any other information and view. Cult-owned social media platforms in Cult-owned Silicon Valley were poised and ready to unleash a campaign of ferocious censorship to obliterate all but the official narrative. To complete the circle many demands for censorship by Silicon Valley were led by the mainstream media as 'journalists' became full-out enforcers for the Cult both as propagandists and censors. Part of this has been the influx of young people straight out of university who have become 'journalists' in significant positions. They have no experience and a headful of programmed perceptions from their years at school and university at a time when today's young are the most perceptually-targeted generations in known human history given the insidious impact of technology. They enter the media perceptually prepared and ready to repeat the narratives of the system that programmed them to repeat its narratives. The BBC has a truly pathetic 'specialist disinformation reporter' called Marianna Spring who fits this bill perfectly. She is clueless about the world, how it works and what is really going on. Her role is to discredit anyone doing the job that a proper journalist would do and system-serving hacks like Spring wouldn't dare to do or even see the need to do. They are too busy licking the arse of authority which can never be wrong and, in the case of the BBC propaganda programme, *Panorama*, contacting payments systems such as PayPal to have a donations page taken down for a film company making documentaries questioning vaccines. Even the BBC soap opera *EastEnders* included a disgracefully biased scene in which an inarticulate white working class woman was made to look foolish for questioning the 'vaccine' while a well-spoken black man and Asian woman promoted the government narrative. It ticked every BBC box and the fact that the black and minority community was resisting the 'vaccine' had nothing to do with the way the scene was written. The BBC has become a disgusting tyrannical propaganda and censorship operation that should be defunded and disbanded and a free media take its place with a brief to stop censorship instead of demanding it. A BBC 'interview' with Gates goes something like: 'Mr Gates, sir, if I can call you sir, would you like to tell our audience why you are such a great man, a wonderful humanitarian philanthropist, and why you should absolutely be allowed as a software salesman to decide health policy for approaching eight billion people? Thank you, sir, please sir.' Propaganda programming has been incessant and merciless and when all you hear is the same story from the media, repeated by those around you who have only heard the same story, is it any wonder that people on a grand scale believe absolute mendacious garbage to be true? You are about to see, too, why this level of information control is necessary when the official 'Covid' narrative is so nonsensical and unsupportable by the evidence.

Structure of Deceit

The pyramid structure through which the 'Covid' hoax has been manifested is very simple and has to be to work. As few people as possible have to be involved with full knowledge of what they are doing – and why – or the real story would get out. At the top of the pyramid are the inner core of the Cult which controls Bill Gates who, in turn, controls the World Health Organization through his pivotal funding and his puppet Director-General mouthpiece, Tedros. Before he was appointed Tedros was chair of the Gates-founded Global Fund to 'fight against AIDS, tuberculosis and malaria', a board member of the Gates-funded 'vaccine alliance' GAVI, and on the board of another Gates-funded organisation. Gates owns him and picked him for a specific reason – Tedros is a crook and worse. 'Dr' Tedros (he's not a medical doctor, the first WHO chief not to be) was a member of the tyrannical Marxist government of Ethiopia for decades with all its human rights abuses. He has faced allegations of corruption and misappropriation of funds and was exposed three times for covering up cholera epidemics while Ethiopia's health minister. Tedros appointed the mass-murdering genocidal Zimbabwe dictator Robert Mugabe as a WHO goodwill ambassador for public health which, as with Tedros, is like appointing a psychopath to run a peace and love campaign. The move was so ridiculous that he had to drop Mugabe in the face of widespread condemnation. American economist David Steinman, a Nobel peace prize nominee, lodged a complaint with the International Criminal Court in The Hague over alleged genocide by Tedros when he was Ethiopia's foreign minister. Steinman says Tedros was a 'crucial decision maker' who directed the actions of Ethiopia's security forces from 2013 to 2015 and one of three officials in charge when those security services embarked on the 'killing' and 'torturing' of Ethiopians. You can see where Tedros is coming from and it's sobering to think that he has been the vehicle for Gates and the Cult to direct the global response to 'Covid'. Think about that. A psychopathic Cult dictates to psychopath Gates who dictates to psychopath Tedros who dictates how countries of the world must respond to a 'Covid virus' never scientifically shown to exist. At the same time psychopathic Cult-owned Silicon Valley information giants like Google, YouTube, Facebook and Twitter announced very early on that they would give the Cult/Gates/Tedros/WHO version of the narrative free advertising and censor those who challenged their intelligence-insulting, mendacious story.

The next layer in the global 'medical' structure below the Cult, Gates and Tedros are the chief medical officers and science 'advisers' in each of the WHO member countries which means virtually all of them. Medical officers and arbiters of science (they're not) then take the WHO policy and recommended responses and impose them on their country's population while the political 'leaders' say they are deciding policy (they're clearly not) by 'following the science' on the advice of the 'experts' – the same medical officers and science 'advisers' (dictators). In this way with the rarest of exceptions the entire world followed the same policy of lockdown, people distancing, masks and 'vaccines' dictated by the psychopathic Cult, psychopathic Gates and psychopathic Tedros who we are supposed to believe give a damn about the health of the world population they are seeking to enslave. That, amazingly, is all there is to it in terms of crucial decision-making. Medical staff in each country then follow like sheep the dictates of the shepherds at the top of the national medical hierarchies – chief medical officers and science 'advisers' who themselves follow like sheep the shepherds of the World Health Organization and the Cult. Shepherds at the national level often have major funding and other connections to Gates and his Bill and Melinda Gates Foundation which carefully hands out money like confetti at a wedding to control the entire global medical system from the WHO down.

Follow the money

Christopher Whitty, Chief Medical Adviser to the UK Government at the centre of 'virus' policy, a senior adviser to the government's Scientific Advisory Group for Emergencies (SAGE), and Executive Board member

of the World Health Organization, was gifted a grant of $40 million by
the Bill and Melinda Gates Foundation for malaria research in Africa.
The BBC described the unelected Whitty as 'the official who will
probably have the greatest impact on our everyday lives of any
individual policymaker in modern times' and so it turned out. What
Gates and Tedros have said Whitty has done like his equivalents around
the world. Patrick Vallance, co-chair of SAGE and the government's
Chief Scientific Adviser, is a former executive of Big Pharma giant
GlaxoSmithKline with its fundamental financial and business
connections to Bill Gates. In September, 2020, it was revealed that
Vallance owned a deferred bonus of shares in GlaxoSmithKline worth
£600,000 while the company was 'developing' a 'Covid vaccine'. Move
along now – nothing to see here – what could possibly be wrong with
that? Imperial College in London, a major player in 'Covid' policy in
Britain and elsewhere with its 'Covid-19' Response Team, is funded by
Gates and has big connections to China while the now infamous
Professor Neil Ferguson, the useless 'computer modeller' at Imperial
College is also funded by Gates. Ferguson delivered the dramatically
inaccurate excuse for the first lockdowns (much more in the next
chapter). The Institute for Health Metrics and Evaluation (IHME) in the
United States, another source of outrageously false 'Covid' computer
models to justify lockdowns, is bankrolled by Gates who is a vehement
promotor of lockdowns. America's version of Whitty and Vallance, the
again now infamous Anthony Fauci, has connections to 'Covid vaccine'
maker Moderna as does Bill Gates through funding from the Bill and
Melinda Gates Foundation. Fauci is director of the National Institute of
Allergy and Infectious Diseases (NIAID), a major recipient of Gates
money, and they are very close. Deborah Birx who was appointed White
House Coronavirus Response Coordinator in February, 2020, is yet
another with ties to Gates. Everywhere you look at the different
elements around the world behind the coordination and decision
making of the 'Covid' hoax there is Bill Gates and his money. They
include the World Health Organization; Centers for Disease Control
(CDC) in the United States; National Institutes of Health (NIH) of
Anthony Fauci; Imperial College and Neil Ferguson; the London School
of Hygiene where Chris Whitty worked; Regulatory agencies like the
UK Medicines & Healthcare products Regulatory Agency (MHRA)
which gave emergency approval for 'Covid vaccines'; Wellcome Trust;
GAVI, the Vaccine Alliance; the Coalition for Epidemic Preparedness
Innovations (CEPI); Johns Hopkins University which has compiled the
false 'Covid' figures; and the World Economic Forum. A
Nationalfile.com article said:

Gates has a lot of pull in the medical world, he has a multi-million dollar relationship with Dr. Fauci, and Fauci originally took the Gates line supporting vaccines and casting doubt on [the drug hydroxychloroquine]. Coronavirus response team member Dr. Deborah Birx, appointed by former president Obama to serve as United States Global AIDS Coordinator, also sits on the board of a group that has received billions from Gates' foundation, and Birx reportedly used a disputed Bill Gates-funded model for the White House's Coronavirus effort. Gates is a big proponent for a population lockdown scenario for the Coronavirus outbreak.

Another funder of Moderna is the Defense Advanced Research Projects Agency (DARPA), the technology-development arm of the Pentagon and one of the most sinister organisations on earth. DARPA had a major role with the CIA covert technology-funding operation In-Q-Tel in the development of Google and social media which is now at the centre of global censorship. Fauci and Gates are extremely close and openly admit to talking regularly about 'Covid' policy, but then why wouldn't Gates have a seat at every national 'Covid' table after his Foundation committed $1.75 billion to the 'fight against Covid-19'. When passed through our Orwellian Translation Unit this means that he has bought and paid for the Cult-driven 'Covid' response worldwide. Research the major 'Covid' response personnel in your own country and you will find the same Gates funding and other connections again and again. Medical and science chiefs following World Health Organization 'policy' sit atop a medical hierarchy in their country of administrators, doctors and nursing staff. These 'subordinates' are told they must work and behave in accordance with the policy delivered from the 'top' of the national 'health' pyramid which is largely the policy delivered by the WHO which is the policy delivered by Gates and the Cult. The whole 'Covid' narrative has been imposed on medical staff by a climate of fear although great numbers don't even need that to comply. They do so through breathtaking levels of ignorance and include doctors who go through life simply repeating what Big Pharma and their hierarchical masters tell them to say and believe. No wonder Big Pharma 'medicine' is one of the biggest killers on Planet Earth.

The same top-down system of intimidation operates with regard to the Cult Big Pharma cartel which also dictates policy through national and global medical systems in this way. The Cult and Big Pharma agendas are the same because the former controls and owns the latter. 'Health' administrators, doctors, and nursing staff are told to support and parrot the dictated policy or they will face consequences which can include being fired. How sad it's been to see medical staff meekly repeating and imposing Cult policy without question and most of those who can see through the deceit are only willing to speak anonymously off the record. They know what will happen if their identity is known.

This has left the courageous few to expose the lies about the 'virus', face masks, overwhelmed hospitals that aren't, and the dangers of the 'vaccine' that isn't a vaccine. When these medical professionals and scientists, some renowned in their field, have taken to the Internet to expose the truth their articles, comments and videos have been deleted by Cult-owned Facebook, Twitter and YouTube. What a real head-shaker to see YouTube videos with leading world scientists and highly qualified medical specialists with an added link underneath to the notorious Cult propaganda website *Wikipedia* to find the 'facts' about the same subject.

HIV – the 'Covid' trial-run

I'll give you an example of the consequences for health and truth that come from censorship and unquestioning belief in official narratives. The story was told by PCR inventor Kary Mullis in his book *Dancing Naked in the Mind Field*. He said that in 1984 he accepted as just another scientific fact that Luc Montagnier of France's Pasteur Institute and Robert Gallo of America's National Institutes of Health had independently discovered that a 'retrovirus' dubbed HIV (human immunodeficiency virus) caused AIDS. They were, after all, Mullis writes, specialists in retroviruses. This is how the medical and science pyramids work. Something is announced or *assumed* and then becomes an everybody-knows-that purely through repetition of the assumption as if it is fact. Complete crap becomes accepted truth with no supporting evidence and only repetition of the crap. This is how a 'virus' that doesn't exist became the 'virus' that changed the world. The HIV-AIDS fairy story became a multi-billion pound industry and the media poured out propaganda terrifying the world about the deadly HIV 'virus' that caused the lethal AIDS. By then Mullis was working at a lab in Santa Monica, California, to detect retroviruses with his PCR test in blood donations received by the Red Cross. In doing so he asked a virologist where he could find a reference for HIV being the cause of AIDS. 'You don't need a reference,' the virologist said … *'Everybody knows it.'* Mullis said he wanted to quote a reference in the report he was doing and he said he felt a little funny about not knowing the source of such an important discovery when everyone else seemed to. The virologist suggested he cite a report by the Centers for Disease Control and Prevention (CDC) on morbidity and mortality. Mullis read the report, but it only said that an organism had been identified and did not say how. The report did not identify the original scientific work. Physicians, however, *assumed* (key recurring theme) that if the CDC was convinced that HIV caused AIDS then proof must exist. Mullis continues:

I did computer searches. Neither Montagnier, Gallo, nor anyone else had published papers describing experiments which led to the conclusion that HIV probably caused AIDS. I read the papers in Science for which they had become well known as AIDS doctors, but all they had said there was that they had found evidence of a past infection by something which was probably HIV in some AIDS patients.

They found antibodies. Antibodies to viruses had always been considered evidence of past disease, not present disease. Antibodies signaled that the virus had been defeated. The patient had saved himself. There was no indication in these papers that this virus caused a disease. They didn't show that everybody with the antibodies had the disease. In fact they found some healthy people with antibodies.

Mullis asked why their work had been published if Montagnier and Gallo hadn't really found this evidence, and why had they been fighting so hard to get credit for the discovery? He says he was hesitant to write 'HIV is the probable cause of AIDS' until he found published evidence to support that. 'Tens of thousands of scientists and researchers were spending billions of dollars a year doing research based on this idea,' Mullis writes. 'The reason had to be there somewhere; otherwise these people would not have allowed their research to settle into one narrow channel of investigation.' He said he lectured about PCR at numerous meetings where people were always talking about HIV and he asked them how they knew that HIV was the cause of AIDS:

Everyone said something. Everyone had the answer at home, in the office, in some drawer. They all knew, and they would send me the papers as soon as they got back. But I never got any papers. Nobody ever sent me the news about how AIDS was caused by HIV.

Eventually Mullis was able to ask Montagnier himself about the reference proof when he lectured in San Diego at the grand opening of the University of California AIDS Research Center. Mullis says this was the last time he would ask his question without showing anger. Montagnier said he should reference the CDC report. 'I read it', Mullis said, and it didn't answer the question. 'If Montagnier didn't know the answer who the hell did?' Then one night Mullis was driving when an interview came on National Public Radio with Peter Duesberg, a prominent virologist at Berkeley and a California Scientist of the Year. Mullis says he finally understood why he could not find references that connected HIV to AIDS – *there weren't any!* No one had ever proved that HIV causes AIDS even though it had spawned a multi-billion pound global industry and the media was repeating this as fact every day in their articles and broadcasts terrifying the shit out of people about AIDS and giving the impression that a positive test for HIV (see 'Covid') was a death sentence. Duesberg was a threat to the AIDS gravy train and the agenda that underpinned it. He was therefore abused and castigated after he told the Proceedings of the National Academy of Sciences there was no good evidence implicating the new 'virus'. Editors rejected his manuscripts and his research funds were deleted. Mullis points out that the CDC has defined AIDS as one of more than 30 diseases *if accompanied* by a positive result on a test that detects antibodies to HIV; but those same diseases are not defined as AIDS cases when antibodies are not detected:

> If an HIV-positive woman develops uterine cancer, for example, she is considered to have AIDS. If she is not HIV positive, she simply has uterine cancer. An HIV-positive man with tuberculosis has AIDS; if he tests negative he simply has tuberculosis. If he lives in Kenya or Colombia, where the test for HIV antibodies is too expensive, he is simply presumed to have the antibodies and therefore AIDS, and therefore he can be treated in the World Health Organization's clinic. It's the only medical help available in some places. And it's free, because the countries that support WHO are worried about AIDS.

Mullis accuses the CDC of continually adding new diseases (see ever more 'Covid symptoms') to the grand AIDS definition and of virtually doctoring the books to make it appear as if the disease continued to spread. He cites how in 1993 the CDC enormously broadened its AIDS definition and county health authorities were delighted because they received $2,500 per year from the Federal government for every reported AIDS case. Ladies and gentlemen, I have just described, via Kary Mullis, the 'Covid pandemic' of 2020 and beyond. Every element is the same and it's been pulled off in the same way by the same networks.

The 'Covid virus' exists? Okay – prove it. Er ... still waiting

What Kary Mullis described with regard to 'HIV' has been repeated with 'Covid'. A claim is made that a new, or 'novel', infection has been found and the entire medical system of the world repeats that as fact exactly as they did with HIV and AIDS. No one in the mainstream asks rather relevant questions such as 'How do you know?' and 'Where is your proof?' The SARS-Cov-2 'virus' and the 'Covid-19 disease' became an overnight 'everybody-knows-that'. The origin could be debated and mulled over, but what you could not suggest was that 'SARS-Cov-2' didn't exist. That would be ridiculous. 'Everybody knows' the 'virus' exists. Well, I didn't for one along with American proper doctors like Andrew Kaufman and Tom Cowan and long-time American proper journalist Jon Rappaport. We dared to pursue the obvious and simple question: 'Where's the evidence?' The overwhelming majority in medicine, journalism and the general public did not think to ask that. After all, *everyone knew* there was a new 'virus'. Everyone was saying so and I heard it on the BBC. Some would eventually argue that the 'deadly virus' was nothing like as deadly as claimed, but few would venture into the realms of its very existence. Had they done so they would have found that the evidence for that claim had gone AWOL as with HIV causes AIDS. In fact, not even that. For something to go AWOL it has to exist in the first place and scientific proof for a 'SARS-Cov-2' can be filed under nothing, nowhere and zilch.

Dr Andrew Kaufman is a board-certified forensic psychiatrist in New York State, a Doctor of Medicine and former Assistant Professor and Medical Director of Psychiatry at SUNY Upstate Medical University, and Medical Instructor of Hematology and Oncology at the Medical School of South Carolina. He also studied biology at the Massachusetts Institute of Technology (MIT) and trained in Psychiatry at Duke University. Kaufman is retired from allopathic medicine, but remains a consultant and educator on natural healing, I saw a video of his very early on in the 'Covid' hoax in which he questioned claims about the 'virus' in the absence of any supporting evidence and with plenty pointing the other way. I did everything I could to circulate his work which I felt was asking the pivotal questions that needed an answer. I can recommend an excellent pull-together interview he did with the website The Last Vagabond entitled *Dr Andrew Kaufman: Virus Isolation, Terrain Theory and Covid-19* and his website is andrewkaufmanmd.com. Kaufman is not only a forensic psychiatrist; he is forensic in all that he does. He always reads original scientific papers, experiments and studies instead of second-third-fourth-hand reports about the 'virus' in the media which are repeating the repeated repetition of the narrative. When he did so with the original Chinese 'virus' papers Kaufman realised that there was no evidence of a 'SARS-Cov-2'. They had never – from the start – shown it to exist and every repeat of this claim worldwide was based on the accepted existence of proof that was nowhere to be found – see Kary Mullis and HIV. Here we go again.

Let's postulate

Kaufman discovered that the Chinese authorities immediately concluded that the cause of an illness that broke out among about 200 initial patients in Wuhan was a 'new virus' when there were no grounds to make that conclusion. The alleged 'virus' was not isolated from other genetic material in their samples and then shown through a system known as Koch's postulates to be the causative agent of the illness. The world was told that the SARS-Cov-2 'virus' caused a disease they called 'Covid-19' which had 'flu-like' symptoms and could lead to respiratory problems and pneumonia. If it wasn't so tragic it would almost be funny. *'Flu-like' symptoms'? Pneumonia? Respiratory disease?* What in *CHINA* and particularly in *Wuhan*, one of the most polluted cities in the world with a resulting epidemic of respiratory disease?? Three hundred thousand people get pneumonia in China every year and there are nearly a billion cases worldwide of 'flu-like symptoms'. These have a whole range of causes – including pollution in Wuhan – but no other possibility was credibly considered in late 2019 when the world was told there was a new and deadly 'virus'. The global prevalence of pneumonia and 'flu-like systems' gave the Cult networks unlimited potential to re-diagnose these other causes as the mythical 'Covid-19' and that is what they did from the very start. Kaufman revealed how Chinese medical and science authorities (all subordinates to the Cult-owned communist government) took genetic material from the lungs of only a few of the first patients. The material contained their own cells, bacteria, fungi and other microorganisms living in their bodies. The only way you could prove the existence of the 'virus' and its responsibility for the alleged 'Covid-19' was to isolate the virus from all the other material – a process also known as 'purification' – and then follow the postulates sequence developed in the late 19th century by German physician and bacteriologist Robert Koch which became the 'gold standard' for connecting an alleged causation agent to a disease:

1. The microorganism (bacteria, fungus, virus, etc.) must be present in every case of the disease and all patients must have the same symptoms. It must also *not be present in healthy individuals*.

2. The microorganism must be isolated from the host with the disease. If the microorganism is a bacteria or fungus it must be grown in a pure culture. If it is a virus, it must be purified (i.e. containing no other material except the virus particles) from a clinical sample.

3. The specific disease, with all of its characteristics, must be reproduced when the infectious agent (the purified virus or a pure culture of bacteria or fungi) is inoculated into a healthy, susceptible host.

4. The microorganism must be recoverable from the experimentally infected host as in step 2.

Not one of these criteria has been met in the case of 'SARS-Cov-2' and 'Covid-19'. Not ONE. *EVER.* Robert Koch refers to bacteria and not viruses. What are called 'viral particles' are so minute (hence masks are useless by any definition) that they could only be seen after the invention of the electron microscope in the 1930s and can still only be observed through that means. American bacteriologist and virologist Thomas Milton Rivers, the so-called 'Father of Modern Virology' who was very significantly director of the Rockefeller Institute for Medical Research in the 1930s, developed a less stringent version of Koch's postulates to identify 'virus' causation known as 'Rivers criteria'. 'Covid' did not pass that process either. Some even doubt whether any 'virus' can be isolated from other particles containing genetic material in the Koch method. Freedom of Information requests in many countries asking for scientific proof that the 'Covid virus' has been purified and isolated and shown to exist have all come back with a 'we don't have that' and when this happened with a request to the UK Department of Health they added this comment:

> However, outside of the scope of the [Freedom of Information Act] and on a discretionary basis, the following information has been advised to us, which may be of interest. Most infectious diseases are caused by viruses, bacteria or fungi. Some bacteria or fungi have the capacity to grow on their own in isolation, for example in colonies on a petri dish. Viruses are different in that they are what we call 'obligate pathogens' – that is, they cannot survive or reproduce without infecting a host ...

> … For some diseases, it is possible to establish causation between a microorganism and a disease by isolating the pathogen from a patient, growing it in pure culture and reintroducing it to a healthy organism. These are known as 'Koch's postulates' and were developed in 1882. However, as our understanding of disease and different disease-causing agents has advanced, these are no longer the method for determining causation [Andrew Kaufman asks why in that case are there two published articles falsely claiming to satisfy Koch's postulates].

> It has long been known that viral diseases cannot be identified in this way as viruses cannot be grown in 'pure culture'. When a patient is tested for a viral illness, this is normally done by looking for the presence of antigens, or viral genetic code in a host with molecular biology techniques [Kaufman asks how you could know the origin of these chemicals without having a pure culture for comparison].

For the record 'antigens' are defined so:

> Invading microorganisms have antigens on their surface that the human body can recognise as being foreign – meaning not belonging to it. When the body recognises a foreign antigen, lymphocytes (white blood cells) produce antibodies, which are complementary in shape to the antigen.

Notwithstanding that this is open to question in relation to 'SARS-Cov-2' the presence of 'antibodies' can have many causes and they are found in people that are perfectly well. Kary Mullis said: 'Antibodies ... had always been considered evidence of past disease, not present disease.'

'Covid' really is a *computer* 'virus'

Where the UK Department of Health statement says 'viruses' are now 'diagnosed' through a 'viral genetic code in a host with molecular biology techniques', they mean ... *the PCR test* which its inventor said cannot test for infectious disease. They have no credible method of connecting a 'virus' to a disease and we will see that there is no scientific proof that any 'virus' causes any disease or there is any such thing as a 'virus' in the way that it is described. Tenacious Canadian researcher Christine Massey and her team made some 40 Freedom of Information requests to national public health agencies in different countries asking for proof that SARS-CoV-2 has been isolated and not one of them could supply that information. Massey said of her request in Canada: 'Freedom of Information reveals Public Health Agency of Canada has no record of 'SARS-COV-2' isolation performed by anyone, anywhere, ever.' If you accept the comment from the UK Department of Health it's because they can't isolate a 'virus'. Even so many 'science' papers claimed to have isolated the 'Covid virus' until they were questioned and had to admit they hadn't. A reply from the Robert Koch Institute in Germany was typical: 'I am not aware of a paper which purified isolated SARS-CoV-2.' So what the hell was Christian Drosten and his gang using to design the 'Covid' testing protocol that has produced all the illusory Covid' cases and 'Covid' deaths when the head of the Chinese version of the CDC admitted there was a problem right from the start in that the 'virus' had never been isolated/purified? Breathe deeply: What they are calling 'Covid' is actually created by a *computer program* i.e. *they made it up* – er, that's it. They took lung fluid, with many sources of genetic material, from one single person alleged to be infected with Covid-19 by a PCR test which they *claimed*, without clear evidence, contained a 'virus'. They used several computer programs to create a model of a theoretical virus genome sequence from more than fifty-six million small sequences of RNA, each of an unknown source, assembling them like a puzzle with no known solution. The computer filled in the gaps with sequences from bits in the gene bank to make it look like a bat SARS-like coronavirus! A wave of the magic wand and poof, an in silico (computer-generated) genome, a scientific fantasy, was created. UK health researcher Dr Kevin Corbett made the same point with this analogy:

    ... It's like giving you a few bones and saying that's your fish. It could be any

fish. Not even a skeleton. Here's a few fragments of bones. That's your fish …
It's all from gene bank and the bits of the virus sequence that weren't there
they made up.

They synthetically created them to fill in the blanks. That's what genetics is; it's
a code. So it's ABBBCCDDD and you're missing some what you think is EEE
so you put it in. It's all synthetic. You just manufacture the bits that are
missing. This is the end result of the geneticization of virology. This is basically
a computer virus.

Further confirmation came in an email exchange between British
citizen journalist Frances Leader and the government's Medicines &
Healthcare Products Regulatory Agency (the Gates-funded MHRA)
which gave emergency permission for untested 'Covid vaccines' to be
used. The agency admitted that the 'vaccine' is not based on an isolated
'virus', but comes from a *computer-generated model*. Frances Leader was
naturally banned from Cult-owned fascist Twitter for making this
exchange public. The process of creating computer-generated alleged
'viruses' is called 'in silico' or 'in silicon' – computer chips – and the
term 'in silico' is believed to originate with biological experiments using
only a computer in 1989. 'Vaccines' involved with 'Covid' are also
produced 'in silico' or by computer not a natural process. If the original
'virus' is nothing more than a made-up computer model how can there
be 'new variants' of something that never existed in the first place? They
are not new 'variants'; they are new *computer models* only minutely
different to the original program and designed to further terrify the
population into having the 'vaccine' and submitting to fascism. You
want a 'new variant'? Click, click, enter – there you go. Tell the medical
profession that you have discovered a 'South African variant', 'UK
variants' or a 'Brazilian variant' and in the usual HIV-causes-AIDS
manner they will unquestioningly repeat it with no evidence whatsoever
to support these claims. They will go on television and warn about the
dangers of 'new variants' while doing nothing more than repeating what
they have been told to be true and knowing that any deviation from that
would be career suicide. Big-time insiders will know it's a hoax, but
much of the medical community is clueless about the way they are being
played and themselves play the public without even being aware they
are doing so. What an interesting 'coincidence' that AstraZeneca and
Oxford University were conducting 'Covid vaccine trials' in the three
countries – the UK, South Africa and Brazil – where the first three
'variants' were claimed to have 'broken out'.

Here's your 'virus' – it's a unicorn
Dr Andrew Kaufman presented a brilliant analysis describing how the

'virus' was imagined into fake existence when he dissected an article published by *Nature* and written by 19 authors detailing *alleged* 'sequencing of a complete viral genome' of the 'new SARS-CoV-2 virus'. This computer-modelled *in silico* genome was used as a template for all subsequent genome sequencing experiments that resulted in the so-called variants which he said now number more than 6,000. The fake genome was constructed from more than 56 million individual short strands of RNA. Those little pieces were assembled into longer pieces by finding areas of overlapping sequences. The computer programs created over two million possible combinations from which the authors simply chose the longest one. They then compared this to a 'bat virus' and the computer 'alignment' rearranged the sequence and filled in the gaps! They called this computer-generated abomination the 'complete genome'. Dr Tom Cowan, a fellow medical author and collaborator with Kaufman, said such computer-generation constitutes scientific fraud and he makes this superb analogy:

> Here is an equivalency: A group of researchers claim to have found a unicorn because they found a piece of a hoof, a hair from a tail, and a snippet of a horn. They then add that information into a computer and program it to re-create the unicorn, and they then claim this computer re-creation is the real unicorn. Of course, they had never actually seen a unicorn so could not possibly have examined its genetic makeup to compare their samples with the actual unicorn's hair, hooves and horn.
>
> The researchers claim they decided which is the real genome of SARS-CoV-2 by 'consensus', sort of like a vote. Again, different computer programs will come up with different versions of the imaginary 'unicorn', so they come together as a group and decide which is the real imaginary unicorn.

This is how the 'virus' that has transformed the world was brought into fraudulent 'existence'. Extraordinary, yes, but as the Nazis said the bigger the lie the more will believe it. Cowan, however, wasn't finished and he went on to identify what he called the real blockbuster in the paper. He quotes this section from a paper written by virologists and published by the CDC and then explains what it means:

> Therefore, we examined the capacity of SARS-CoV-2 to infect and replicate in several common primate and human cell lines, including human adenocarcinoma cells (A549), human liver cells (HUH 7.0), and human embryonic kidney cells (HEK-293T). In addition to Vero E6 and Vero CCL81 cells. ... Each cell line was inoculated at high multiplicity of infection and examined 24h post-infection.

No CPE was observed in any of the cell lines except in Vero cells, which grew to greater than 10 to the 7th power at 24 h post-infection. In contrast, HUH 7.0 and 293T showed only modest viral replication, and A549 cells were incompatible with SARS CoV-2 infection.

Cowan explains that when virologists attempt to prove infection they have three possible 'hosts' or models on which they can test. The first was humans. Exposure to humans was generally not done for ethical reasons and has never been done with SARS-CoV-2 or any coronavirus. The second possible host was animals. Cowan said that forgetting for a moment that they never actually use purified virus when exposing animals they do use solutions that they *claim* contain the virus. Exposure to animals has been done with SARS-CoV-2 in an experiment involving mice and this is what they found: *None of the wild (normal) mice got sick.* In a group of genetically-modified mice, a statistically insignificant number lost weight and had slightly bristled fur, but they experienced nothing like the illness called 'Covid-19'. Cowan said the third method – the one they mostly rely on – is to inoculate solutions they *say* contain the virus onto a variety of tissue cultures. This process had never been shown to kill tissue *unless* the sample material was starved of nutrients and poisoned as *part of the process.* Yes, incredibly, in tissue experiments designed to show the 'virus' is responsible for killing the tissue they starve the tissue of nutrients and add toxic drugs including antibiotics and they do not have control studies to see if it's the starvation and poisoning that is degrading the tissue rather than the 'virus' they allege to be in there somewhere. You want me to pinch you? Yep, I understand. Tom Cowan said this about the whole nonsensical farce as he explains what that quote from the CDC paper really means:

> The shocking thing about the above quote is that using their own methods, the virologists found that solutions containing SARS-CoV-2 – even in high amounts – were NOT, I repeat NOT, infective to any of the three human tissue cultures they tested. In plain English, this means they proved, on their terms, that this 'new coronavirus' is not infectious to human beings. It is ONLY infective to monkey kidney cells, and only then when you add two potent drugs (gentamicin and amphotericin), known to be toxic to kidneys, to the mix.

> My friends, read this again and again. These virologists, published by the CDC, performed a clear proof, on their terms, showing that the SARS-CoV- 2 virus is harmless to human beings. That is the only possible conclusion, but, unfortunately, this result is not even mentioned in their conclusion. They simply say they can provide virus stocks cultured only on monkey Vero cells, thanks for coming.

Cowan concluded: 'If people really understood how this "science" was done, I would hope they would storm the gates and demand honesty, transparency and truth.' Dr Michael Yeadon, former Vice President and Chief Scientific Adviser at drug giant Pfizer has been a vocal critic of the 'Covid vaccine' and its potential for multiple harm. He said in an interview in April, 2021, that 'not one [vaccine] has the virus. He was asked why vaccines normally using a 'dead' version of a disease to activate the immune system were not used for 'Covid' and instead we had the synthetic methods of the 'mRNA Covid vaccine'. Yeadon said that to do the former 'you'd have to have some of [the virus] wouldn't you?' He added: 'No-one's got any – seriously.' Yeadon said that surely they couldn't have fooled the whole world for a year without having a virus, 'but oddly enough ask around – no one's got it'. He didn't know why with all the 'great labs' around the world that the virus had not been isolated – 'Maybe they've been too busy running bad PCR tests and vaccines that people don't need.' What is today called 'science' is not 'science' at all. Science is no longer what is, but whatever people can be manipulated to *believe* that it is. Real science has been hijacked by the Cult to dispense and produce the 'expert scientists' and contentions that suit the agenda of the Cult. How big-time this has happened with the 'Covid' hoax which is entirely based on fake science delivered by fake 'scientists' and fake 'doctors'. The human-caused climate change hoax is also entirely based on fake science delivered by fake 'scientists' and fake 'climate experts'. In both cases real scientists, climate experts and doctors have their views suppressed and deleted by the Cult-owned science establishment, media and Silicon Valley. This is the 'science' that politicians claim to be 'following' and a common denominator of 'Covid' and climate are Cult psychopaths Bill Gates and his mate Klaus Schwab at the Gates-funded World Economic Forum. But, don't worry, it's all just a coincidence and absolutely nothing to worry about. Zzzzzzzz.

What is a 'virus' REALLY?

Dr Tom Cowan is one of many contesting the very existence of viruses let alone that they cause disease. This is understandable when there is no scientific evidence for a disease-causing 'virus'. German virologist Dr Stefan Lanka won a landmark case in 2017 in the German Supreme Court over his contention that there is no such thing as a measles virus. He had offered a big prize for anyone who could prove there is and Lanka won his case when someone sought to claim the money. There is currently a prize of more than 225,000 euros on offer from an Isolate Truth Fund for anyone who can prove the isolation of SARS-CoV-2 and its genetic substance. Lanka wrote in an article headed 'The Misconception Called Virus' that scientists think a 'virus' is causing tissue to become diseased and degraded when in fact it is the *processes they are using* which do that – not a 'virus'. Lanka has done an important job in making this point clear as Cowan did in his analysis of the CDC paper. Lanka says that all claims about viruses as disease-causing pathogens are wrong and based on 'easily recognisable, understandable and verifiable misinterpretations.' Scientists believed they were working with 'viruses' in their laboratories when they were really working with 'typical particles of specific dying tissues or cells ...' Lanka said that the tissue decaying process claimed to be caused by a 'virus' still happens when no alleged 'virus' is involved. It's the *process* that does the damage and not a 'virus'. The genetic sample is deprived of nutrients, removed from its energy supply through removal from the body and then doused in toxic antibiotics to remove any bacteria. He confirms again that establishment scientists do not (pinch me) conduct control experiments to see if this is the case and if they did they would see the claims that 'viruses' are doing the damage is nonsense. He adds that during the measles 'virus' court case he commissioned an independent laboratory to perform just such a control experiment and the result was that the tissues and cells died in the exact same way as with alleged 'infected' material. This is supported by a gathering number of scientists, doctors and researchers who reject what is called 'germ theory' or the belief in the body being infected by contagious sources emitted by other people. Researchers Dawn Lester and David Parker take the same stance in their highly-detailed and sourced book *What Really Makes You Ill – Why everything you thought you knew about disease is wrong* which was recommended to me by a number of medical professionals genuinely seeking the truth. Lester and Parker say there is no provable scientific evidence to show that a 'virus' can be transmitted between people or people and animals or animals and people:

> The definition also claims that viruses are the cause of many diseases, as if this has been definitively proven. But this is not the case; there is no original scientific evidence that definitively demonstrates that any virus is the cause of any disease. The burden of proof for any theory lies with those who proposed it; but none of the existing documents provides 'proof' that supports the claim that 'viruses' are pathogens.

Dr Tom Cowan employs one of his clever analogies to describe the process by which a 'virus' is named as the culprit for a disease when what is called a 'virus' is only material released by cells detoxing themselves from infiltration by chemical or radiation poisoning. The tidal wave of technologically-generated radiation in the 'smart' modern world plus all the toxic food and drink are causing this to happen more than ever. Deluded 'scientists' misread this as a gathering impact of what they wrongly label 'viruses'.

Paper can infect houses

Cowan said in an article for davidicke.com – with his tongue only
mildly in his cheek – that he believed he had made a tremendous
discovery that may revolutionise science. He had discovered that small
bits of paper are alive, 'well alive-ish', can 'infect' houses, and then
reproduce themselves inside the house. The result was that this
explosion of growth in the paper inside the house causes the house to
explode, blowing it to smithereens. His evidence for this new theory is
that in the past months he had carefully examined many of the houses in
his neighbourhood and found almost no scraps of paper on the lawns
and surrounds of the house. There was an occasional stray label, but
nothing more. Then he would return to these same houses a week or so
later and with a few, not all of them, particularly the old and decrepit
ones, he found to his shock and surprise they were littered with stray
bits of paper. He knew then that the paper had infected these houses,
made copies of itself, and blew up the house. A young boy on a bicycle
at one of the sites told him he had seen a demolition crew using
dynamite to explode the house the previous week, but Cowan dismissed
this as the idle thoughts of silly boys because 'I was on to something
big'. He was on to how 'scientists' mistake genetic material in the
detoxifying process for something they call a 'virus'. Cowan said of his
house and paper story:

> If this sounds crazy to you, it's because it should. This scenario is obviously
> nuts. But consider this admittedly embellished, for effect, current viral theory
> that all scientists, medical doctors and virologists currently believe.

He takes the example of the 'novel SARS-Cov2' virus to prove the point.
First they take someone with an undefined illness called 'Covid-19' and
don't even attempt to find any virus in their sputum. Never mind the
scientists still describe how this 'virus', which they have not located
attaches to a cell receptor, injects its genetic material, in 'Covid's' case,
RNA, into the cell. The RNA once inserted exploits the cell to reproduce
itself and makes 'thousands, nay millions, of copies of itself ... Then it
emerges victorious to claim its next victim':

> If you were to look in the scientific literature for proof, actual scientific proof,
> that uniform SARS-CoV2 viruses have been properly isolated from the sputum
> of a sick person, that actual spike proteins could be seen protruding from the
> virus (which has not been found), you would find that such evidence doesn't
> exist.

If you go looking in the published scientific literature for actual pictures, proof, that these spike proteins or any viral proteins are ever attached to any receptor embedded in any cell membrane, you would also find that no such evidence exists. If you were to look for a video or documented evidence of the intact virus injecting its genetic material into the body of the cell, reproducing itself and then emerging victorious by budding off the cell membrane, you would find that no such evidence exists.

The closest thing you would find is electron micrograph pictures of cellular particles, possibly attached to cell debris, both of which to be seen were stained by heavy metals, a process that completely distorts their architecture within the living organism. This is like finding bits of paper stuck to the blown-up bricks, thereby proving the paper emerged by taking pieces of the bricks on its way out.

The Enders baloney

Cowan describes the 'Covid' story as being just as make-believe as his paper story and he charts back this fantasy to a Nobel Prize winner called John Enders (1897-1985), an American biomedical scientist who has been dubbed 'The Father of Modern Vaccines'. Enders is claimed to have 'discovered' the process of the viral culture which 'proved' that a 'virus' caused measles. Cowan explains how Enders did this 'by using the EXACT same procedure that has been followed by every virologist to find and characterize every new virus since 1954'. Enders took throat swabs from children with measles and immersed them in 2ml of milk. Penicillin (100u/ml) and the antibiotic streptomycin (50,g/ml) were added and the whole mix was centrifuged – rotated at high speed to separate large cellular debris from small particles and molecules as with milk and cream, for example. Cowan says that if the aim is to find little particles of genetic material ('viruses') in the snot from children with measles it would seem that the last thing you would do is mix the snot with other material – milk –that also has genetic material. 'How are you ever going to know whether whatever you found came from the snot or the milk?' He points out that streptomycin is a 'nephrotoxic' or poisonous-to-the-kidney drug. You will see the relevance of that shortly. Cowan says that it gets worse, much worse, when Enders describes the culture medium upon which the virus 'grows': 'The culture medium consisted of bovine amniotic fluid (90%), beef embryo extract (5%), horse serum (5%), antibiotics and phenol red as an indicator of cell metabolism.' Cowan asks incredulously: 'Did he just say that the culture medium also contained fluids and tissues that are themselves rich sources of genetic material?' The genetic cocktail, or 'medium', is inoculated onto tissue and cells from rhesus monkey *kidney* tissue. This is where the importance of streptomycin comes in and currently-used antimicrobials and other drugs that are *poisonous to kidneys* and used in ALL modern viral cultures (e.g. gentamicin, streptomycin, and amphotericin). Cowan asks: 'How are you ever going to know from this witch's brew where any genetic material comes from as we now have five different sources of rich genetic material in our mix?' Remember, he says, that all genetic material, whether from monkey kidney tissues, bovine serum, milk, etc., is made from the exact same components. The same central question returns: 'How are you possibly going to know that it was the virus that killed the kidney tissue and not the toxic antibiotic and starvation rations on which you are growing the tissue?' John Enders answered the question himself – *you can't*:

> A second agent was obtained from an uninoculated culture of monkey kidney cells. The cytopathic changes [death of the cells] it induced in the unstained preparations could not be distinguished with confidence from the viruses isolated from measles.

The death of the cells ('cytopathic changes') happened in exactly the same manner, whether they inoculated the kidney tissue with the measles snot or not, Cowan says. 'This is evidence that the destruction of the tissue, the very proof of viral causation of illness, was not caused by anything in the snot because they saw the same destructive effect when the snot was not even used ... the cytopathic, i.e., cell-killing, changes come from the process of the culture itself, not from any virus in any snot, period.' Enders quotes in his 1957 paper a virologist called Ruckle as reporting similar findings 'and in addition has isolated an agent from monkey kidney tissue that is so far indistinguishable from human measles virus'. In other words, Cowan says, these particles called 'measles viruses' are simply and clearly breakdown products of the starved and poisoned tissue. For measles 'virus' see all 'viruses' including the so-called 'Covid virus'. Enders, the 'Father of Modern Vaccines', also said:

> There is a potential risk in employing cultures of primate cells for the production of vaccines composed of attenuated virus, since the presence of other agents possibly latent in primate tissues cannot be definitely excluded by any known method.

Cowan further quotes from a paper published in the journal *Viruses* in May, 2020, while the 'Covid pandemic' was well underway in the media if not in reality. 'EVs' here refers to particles of genetic debris from our own tissues, such as exosomes of which more in a moment: 'The remarkable resemblance between EVs and viruses has caused quite a few problems in the studies focused on the analysis of EVs released during viral infections.' Later the paper adds that to date a reliable method that can actually guarantee a complete separation (of EVs from viruses) DOES NOT EXIST. This was published at a time when a fairy tale 'virus' was claimed in total certainty to be causing a fairy tale 'viral disease' called 'Covid-19' – a fairy tale that was already well on the way to transforming human society in the image that the Cult has worked to achieve for so long. Cowan concludes his article:

> To summarize, there is no scientific evidence that pathogenic viruses exist. What we think of as 'viruses' are simply the normal breakdown products of dead and dying tissues and cells. When we are well, we make fewer of these particles; when we are starved, poisoned, suffocated by wearing masks, or afraid, we make more.

> There is no engineered virus circulating and making people sick. People in laboratories all over the world are making genetically modified products to make people sick. These are called vaccines. There is no virome, no 'ecosystem' of viruses, viruses are not 8%, 50% or 100 % of our genetic material. These are all simply erroneous ideas based on the misconception called a virus.

What is 'Covid'? Load of bollocks

The background described here by Cowan and Lanka was emphasised in the first video presentation that I saw by Dr Andrew Kaufman when he asked whether the 'Covid virus' was in truth a natural defence mechanism of the body called 'exosomes'. These are released by cells when in states of toxicity – see the same themes returning over and over. They are released ever more profusely as chemical and radiation toxicity increases and think of the potential effect therefore of 5G alone as its destructive frequencies infest the human energetic information field with a gathering pace (5G went online in Wuhan in 2019 as the 'virus' emerged). I'll have more about this later. Exosomes transmit a warning to the rest of the body that 'Houston, we have a problem'. Kaufman presented images of exosomes and compared them with 'Covid' under an electron microscope and the similarity was remarkable. They both attach to the same cell receptors (*claimed* in the case of 'Covid'), contain the same genetic material in the form of RNA or ribonucleic acid, and both are found in 'viral cell cultures' with damaged or dying cells. James Hildreth MD, President and Chief Executive Officer of the Meharry Medical College at Johns Hopkins, said: 'The virus is fully an exosome in every sense of the word.' Kaufman's conclusion was that there is no 'virus': 'This entire pandemic is a completely manufactured crisis … there is no evidence of anyone dying from [this] illness.' Dr Tom Cowan and Sally Fallon Morell, authors of *The Contagion Myth*, published a statement with Dr Kaufman in February, 2021, explaining why the 'virus' does not exist and you can read it that in full in the Appendix.

'Virus' theory can be traced to the 'cell theory' in 1858 of German physician Rudolf Virchow (1821-1920) who contended that disease originates from a single cell infiltrated by a 'virus'. Dr Stefan Lanka said that findings and insights with respect to the structure, function and central importance of tissues in the creation of life, which were already known in 1858, comprehensively refute the cell theory. Virchow ignored them. We have seen the part later played by John Enders in the 1950s and Lanka notes that infection theories were only established as a global dogma through the policies and eugenics of the Third Reich in Nazi Germany (creation of the same Sabbatian cult behind the 'Covid' hoax). Lanka said: 'Before 1933, scientists dared to contradict this theory; after 1933, these critical scientists were silenced'. Dr Tom Cowan's view is that ill-heath is caused by too much of something, too little of something, or toxification from chemicals and radiation – not contagion. We must also highlight as a major source of the 'virus' theology a man still called the 'Father of Modern Virology' – Thomas Milton Rivers (1888-1962). There is no way given the Cult's long game policy that it was a coincidence for the 'Father of Modern Virology' to be director of the Rockefeller Institute for Medical Research from 1937 to 1956 when he is credited with making the Rockefeller Institute a leader in 'viral research'. Cult Rockefellers were the force behind the creation of Big Pharma 'medicine', established the World Health Organisation in 1948, and have long and close associations with the Gates family that now runs the WHO during the pandemic hoax through mega-rich Cult gofer and psychopath Bill Gates.

Only a Renegade Mind can see through all this bullshit by asking the questions that need to be answered, not taking 'no' or prevarication for an answer, and certainly not hiding from the truth in fear of speaking it. Renegade Minds have always changed the world for the better and they will change this one no matter how bleak it may currently appear to be.

CHAPTER SIX

Sequence of deceit

If you tell the truth, you don't have to remember anything
Mark Twain

Against the background that I have laid out this far the sequence that took us from an invented 'virus' in Cult-owned China in late 2019 to the fascist transformation of human society can be seen and understood in a whole new context.

We were told that a deadly disease had broken out in Wuhan and the world media began its campaign (coordinated by behavioural psychologists as we shall see) to terrify the population into unquestioning compliance. We were shown images of Chinese people collapsing in the street which never happened in the West with what was supposed to be the same condition. In the earliest days when alleged cases and deaths were few the fear register was hysterical in many areas of the media and this would expand into the common media narrative across the world. The real story was rather different, but we were never told that. The Chinese government, one of the Cult's biggest centres of global operation, said they had discovered a new illness with flu-like and pneumonia-type symptoms in a city with such toxic air that it is overwhelmed with flu-like symptoms, pneumonia and respiratory disease. Chinese scientists said it was a new – 'novel' – coronavirus which they called Sars-Cov-2 and that it caused a disease they labelled 'Covid-19'. There was no evidence for this and the 'virus' has never to this day been isolated, purified and its genetic code established from that. It was from the beginning a computer-generated fiction. Stories of Chinese whistleblowers saying the number of deaths was being supressed or that the 'new disease' was related to the Wuhan bio-lab misdirected mainstream and alternative media into cul-de-sacs to obscure the real truth – there was no 'virus'.

Chinese scientists took genetic material from the lung fluid of just a few people and said they had found a 'new' disease when this material had a wide range of content. There was no evidence for a 'virus' for the very reasons explained in the last two chapters. The 'virus' has never been shown to (a) exist and (b) cause any disease. People were diagnosed on symptoms that are so widespread in Wuhan and polluted

China and with a PCR test that can't detect infectious disease. On this farce the whole global scam was sold to the rest of the world which would also diagnose respiratory disease as 'Covid-19' from symptoms alone or with a PCR test not testing for a 'virus'. Flu miraculously disappeared *worldwide* in 2020 and into 2021 as it was redesignated 'Covid-19'. It was really the same old flu with its 'flu-like' symptoms attributed to 'flu-like' 'Covid-19'. At the same time with very few exceptions the Chinese response of draconian lockdown and fascism was the chosen weapon to respond across the West as recommended by the Cult-owned Tedros at the Cult-owned World Health Organization run by the Cult-owned Gates. All was going according to plan. Chinese scientists – everything in China is controlled by the Cult-owned government – compared their contaminated RNA lung-fluid material with other RNA sequences and said it appeared to be just under 80 percent identical to the SARS-CoV-1 'virus' claimed to be the cause of the SARS (severe acute respiratory syndrome) 'outbreak' in 2003. They decreed that because of this the 'new virus' had to be related and they called it SARS-CoV-2. There are some serious problems with this assumption and *assumption* was all it was. Most 'factual' science turns out to be assumptions repeated into everyone-knows-that. A match of under 80-percent is meaningless. Dr Kaufman makes the point that there's a *96 percent* genetic correlation between humans and chimpanzees, but 'no one would say our genetic material is part of the chimpanzee family'. Yet the Chinese authorities were claiming that a much lower percentage, less than 80 percent, proved the existence of a new 'coronavirus'. For goodness sake human DNA is 60 percent similar to a *banana*.

You are feeling sleepy

The entire 'Covid' hoax is a global Psyop, a psychological operation to program the human mind into believing and fearing a complete fantasy. A crucial aspect of this was what *appeared* to happen in Italy. It was all very well streaming out daily images of an alleged catastrophe in Wuhan, but to the Western mind it was still on the other side of the world in a very different culture and setting. A reaction of 'this could happen to me and my family' was still nothing like as intense enough for the mind-doctors. The Cult needed a Western example to push people over that edge and it chose Italy, one of its major global locations going back to the Roman Empire. An Italian 'Covid' crisis was manufactured in a particular area called Lombardy which just happens to be notorious for its toxic air and therefore respiratory disease. Wuhan, China, déjà vu. An hysterical media told horror stories of Italians dying from 'Covid' in their droves and how Lombardy hospitals were being overrun by a tidal wave of desperately ill people needing treatment after being struck down by the 'deadly virus'. Here was the psychological turning point the Cult had planned. Wow, if this is happening in Italy, the Western mind concluded, this indeed could happen to me and my family. Another point is that Italian authorities responded by following the Chinese blueprint so vehemently recommended by the Cult-owned World Health Organization. They imposed fascistic lockdowns on the whole country viciously policed with the help of surveillance drones sweeping through the streets seeking out anyone who escaped from mass house arrest. Livelihoods were destroyed and psychology unravelled in the way we have witnessed since in all lockdown countries. Crucial to the plan was that Italy responded in this way to set the precedent of suspending freedom and imposing fascism in a 'Western liberal democracy'. I emphasised in an animated video explanation on davidicke.com posted in the summer of 2020 how important it was to the Cult to expand the Chinese lockdown model across the West. Without this, and the bare-faced lie that non-symptomatic people could still transmit a 'disease' they didn't have, there was no way locking down the whole population, sick and not sick, could be pulled off. At just the right time and with no evidence Cult operatives and gofers claimed that people without symptoms could pass on the 'disease'. In the name of protecting the 'vulnerable' like elderly people, who lockdowns would kill by the tens of thousands, we had for the first time healthy people told to isolate as well as the sick. The great majority of people who tested positive had no symptoms because there was nothing wrong with them. It was just a trick made possible by a test not testing for the 'virus'.

Months after my animated video the Gates-funded Professor Neil Ferguson at the Gates-funded Imperial College confirmed that I was right. He didn't say it in those terms, naturally, but he did say it. Ferguson will enter the story shortly for his outrageously crazy 'computer models' that led to Britain, the United States and many other countries following the Chinese and now Italian methods of response. Put another way, following the Cult script. Ferguson said that SAGE, the UK government's scientific advisory group which has controlled 'Covid' policy from the start, wanted to follow the Chinese lockdown model (while they all continued to work and be paid), but they wondered if they could possibly, in Ferguson's words, 'get away with it in Europe'. 'Get away with it'? Who the hell do these moronic, arrogant people think they are? This appalling man Ferguson said that once Italy went into national lockdown they realised they, too, could mimic China:

It's a communist one-party state, we said. We couldn't get away with it in Europe, we thought ... and then Italy did it. And we realised we could.
Behind this garbage from Ferguson is a simple fact: Doing the same

as China in every country was the plan from the start and Ferguson's 'models' would play a central role in achieving that. It's just a coincidence, of course, and absolutely nothing to worry your little head about.

Oops, sorry, our mistake

Once the Italian segment of the Psyop had done the job it was designed to do a very different story emerged. Italian authorities revealed that 99 percent of those who had 'died from Covid-19' in Italy had one, two, three, or more 'co-morbidities' or illnesses and health problems that could have ended their life. The US Centers for Disease Control and Prevention (CDC) published a figure of 94 percent for Americans dying of 'Covid' while having other serious medical conditions – on average two to three (some five or six) other potential causes of death. In terms of death from an unproven 'virus' I say it is 100 percent. The other one percent in Italy and six percent in the US would presumably have died from 'Covid's' flu-like symptoms with a range of other possible causes in conjunction with a test not testing for the 'virus'. Fox News reported that even more startling figures had emerged in one US county in which 410 of 422 deaths attributed to 'Covid-19' had other potentially deadly health conditions. The Italian National Health Institute said later that the average age of people dying with a 'Covid-19' diagnosis in Italy was about 81. Ninety percent were over 70 with ten percent over 90. In terms of other reasons to die some 80 percent had two or more chronic diseases with half having three or more including cardiovascular problems, diabetes, respiratory problems and cancer. Why is the phantom 'Covid-19' said to kill overwhelmingly old people and hardly affect the young? Old people continually die of many causes and especially respiratory disease which you can re-diagnose 'Covid-19' while young people die in tiny numbers by comparison and rarely of respiratory disease. Old people 'die of Covid' because they die of other things that can be redesignated 'Covid' and it really is that simple.

Flu has flown

The blueprint was in place. Get your illusory 'cases' from a test not testing for the 'virus' and redesignate other causes of death as 'Covid-19'. You have an instant 'pandemic' from something that is nothing more than a computer-generated fiction. With near-on a billion people having 'flu-like' symptoms every year the potential was limitless and we can see why flu quickly and apparently miraculously disappeared *worldwide* by being diagnosed 'Covid-19'. The painfully bloody obvious was explained away by the childlike media in headlines like this in the UK *'Independent'*: 'Not a single case of flu detected by Public Health England this year as Covid restrictions suppress virus'. I kid you not. The masking, social distancing and house arrest that did not make the 'Covid virus' disappear somehow did so with the 'flu virus'. Even worse the article, by a bloke called Samuel Lovett, suggested that maybe the masking, sanitising and other 'Covid' measures should continue to keep the flu away. With a ridiculousness that disturbs your breathing (it's 'Covid-19') the said Lovett wrote: 'With widespread social distancing and mask-wearing measures in place throughout the UK, the usual routes of transmission for influenza have been blocked.' He had absolutely no evidence to support that statement, but look at the consequences of him acknowledging the obvious. With flu not disappearing at all and only being relabelled 'Covid-19' he would have to contemplate that 'Covid' was a hoax on a scale that is hard to imagine. You need guts and commitment to truth to even go there and that's clearly something Samuel Lovett does not have in abundance. He would never have got it through the editors anyway.

Tens of thousands die in the United States alone every winter from flu including many with pneumonia complications. CDC figures record *45 million* Americans diagnosed with flu in 2017-2018 of which 61,000 died and some reports claim 80,000. Where was the same hysteria then that we have seen with 'Covid-19'? Some 250,000 Americans are admitted to hospital with pneumonia every year with about 50,000 cases proving fatal. About 65 million suffer respiratory disease every year and three million deaths makes this the third biggest cause of death worldwide. You only have to redesignate a portion of all these people 'Covid-19' and you have an instant global pandemic or the *appearance* of one. Why would doctors do this? They are told to do this and all but a few dare not refuse those who must be obeyed. Doctors in general are not researching their own knowledge and instead take it direct and unquestioned from the authorities that own them and their careers. The authorities say they must now diagnose these symptoms 'Covid-19' and not flu, or whatever, and they do it. Dark suits say put 'Covid-19' on death certificates no matter what the cause of death and the doctors do it. Renegade Minds don't fall for the illusion that doctors and medical staff are all highly-intelligent, highly-principled, seekers of medical truth. *Some are*, but not the majority. They are repeaters, gofers, and yes sir, no sir, purveyors of what the system demands they purvey. The 'Covid' con is not merely confined to diseases of the lungs. Instructions to doctors to put 'Covid-19' on death certificates for anyone dying of *anything* within 28 days (or much more) of a positive test not testing for the 'virus' opened the floodgates. The term dying *with* 'Covid' and not *of* 'Covid' was coined to cover the truth. Whether it was a *with* or an *of* they were all added to the death numbers attributed to the 'deadly virus' compiled by national governments and globally by the Gates-funded Johns Hopkins operation in the United States that was so involved in those 'pandemic' simulations. Fraudulent deaths were added to the ever-growing list of fraudulent 'cases' from false positives from a false test. No wonder Professor Walter Ricciardi, scientific advisor to the Italian minister of health, said after the Lombardy hysteria had done its job that 'Covid' death rates were due to Italy having the second oldest population in the world and to *how hospitals record deaths*:

> The way in which we code deaths in our country is very generous in the sense that all the people who die in hospitals with the coronavirus are deemed to be dying of the coronavirus. On re-evaluation by the National Institute of Health, only 12 per cent of death certificates have shown a direct causality from coronavirus, while 88 per cent of patients who have died have at least one pre-morbidity – many had two or three.

This is extraordinary enough when you consider the propaganda campaign to use Italy to terrify the world, but how can they even say twelve percent were genuine when the 'virus' has not been shown to exist, its 'code' is a computer program, and diagnosis comes from a test not testing for it? As in China, and soon the world, 'Covid-19' in Italy was a redesignation of diagnosis. Lies and corruption were to become the real 'pandemic' fuelled by a pathetically-compliant medical system taking its orders from the tiny few at the top of their national hierarchy who answered to the World Health Organization which answers to Gates and the Cult. Doctors were told – ordered – to diagnose a particular set of symptoms 'Covid-19' and put that on the death certificate for any cause of death if the patient had tested positive with a test not testing for the virus or had 'Covid' symptoms like the flu. The United States even introduced big financial incentives to manipulate the figures with hospitals receiving £4,600 from the Medicare system for diagnosing someone with regular pneumonia, $13,000 if they made the diagnosis from the same symptoms 'Covid-19' pneumonia, and $39, 000 if they put a 'Covid' diagnosed patient on a ventilator that would almost certainly kill them. A few – painfully and pathetically few – medical whistleblowers revealed (before Cult-owned YouTube deleted their videos) that they had been instructed to 'let the patient crash' and put them straight on a ventilator instead of going through a series of far less intrusive and dangerous methods as they would have done before the pandemic hoax began and the financial incentives kicked in. We are talking cold-blooded murder given that ventilators are so damaging to respiratory systems they are usually the last step before heaven awaits. Renegade Minds never fall for the belief that people in white coats are all angels of mercy and cannot be full-on psychopaths. I have explained in detail in *The Answer* how what I am describing here played out across the world coordinated by the World Health Organization through the medical hierarchies in almost every country.

Medical scientist calls it

Information about the non-existence of the 'virus' began to emerge for me in late March, 2020, and mushroomed after that. I was sent an email by Sir Julian Rose, a writer, researcher, and organic farming promotor, from a medical scientist friend of his in the United States. Even at that early stage in March the scientist was able to explain how the 'Covid' hoax was being manipulated. He said there were no reliable tests for a specific 'Covid-19 virus' and nor were there any reliable agencies or media outlets for reporting numbers of actual 'Covid-19' cases. We have seen in the long period since then that he was absolutely right. 'Every action and reaction to Covid-19 is based on totally flawed data and we simply cannot make accurate assessments,' he said. Most people diagnosed with 'Covid-19' were showing nothing more than cold and flu-like symptoms 'because most coronavirus strains *are* nothing more than cold/flu-like symptoms'. We had farcical situations like an 84-year-old German man testing positive for 'Covid-19' and his nursing home ordered to quarantine only for him to be found to have a common cold. The scientist described back then why PCR tests and what he called the 'Mickey Mouse test kits' were useless for what they were claimed to be identifying. 'The idea these kits can isolate a specific virus like Covid-19 is nonsense,' he said. Significantly, he pointed out that 'if you want to create a totally false panic about a totally false pandemic – pick a coronavirus'. This is exactly what the Cult-owned Gates, World Economic Forum and Johns Hopkins University did with their Event 201 'simulation' followed by their real-life simulation called the 'pandemic'. The scientist said that all you had to do was select the sickest of people with respiratory-type diseases in a single location – 'say Wuhan' – and administer PCR tests to them. You can then claim that anyone showing 'viral sequences' similar to a coronavirus 'which will inevitably be quite a few' is suffering from a 'new' disease:

> Since you already selected the sickest flu cases a fairly high proportion of your sample will go on to die. You can then say this 'new' virus has a CFR [case fatality rate] higher than the flu and use this to infuse more concern and do more tests which will of course produce more 'cases', which expands the testing, which produces yet more 'cases' and so on and so on. Before long you have your 'pandemic', and all you have done is use a simple test kit trick to convert the worst flu and pneumonia cases into something new that doesn't ACTUALLY EXIST [my emphasis].

He said that you then 'just run the same scam in other countries' and make sure to keep the fear message running high 'so that people will feel panicky and less able to think critically'. The only problem to overcome was the fact *there is no* actual new deadly pathogen and only regular sick people. This meant that deaths from the 'new deadly pathogen' were going to be way too low for a real new deadly virus pandemic, but he said this could be overcome in the following ways – all of which would go on to happen:

1. You can claim this is just the beginning and more deaths are imminent [you underpin this with fantasy 'computer projections']. Use this as an excuse to quarantine everyone and then claim the quarantine prevented the expected millions of dead.

2. You can [say that people] 'minimizing' the dangers are irresponsible and bully them into not talking about numbers.

3. You can talk crap about made up numbers hoping to blind people with pseudoscience.

4. You can start testing well people (who, of course, will also likely have shreds of coronavirus [RNA] in them) and thus inflate your 'case figures' with 'asymptomatic carriers' (you will of course have to spin that to sound deadly even though any virologist knows the more symptom-less cases you have the less deadly is your pathogen).

The scientist said that if you take these simple steps 'you can have your own entirely manufactured pandemic up and running in weeks'. His analysis made so early in the hoax was brilliantly prophetic of what would actually unfold. Pulling all the information together in these recent chapters we have this is simple 1, 2, 3, of how you can delude virtually the entire human population into believing in a 'virus' that doesn't exist:

- A 'Covid case' is someone who tests positive with a test not testing for the 'virus'.

- A 'Covid death' is someone who dies of *any cause* within 28 days (or much longer) of testing positive with a test not testing for the 'virus'.

- Asymptomatic means there is nothing wrong with you, but they claim you can pass on what you don't have to justify locking down (quarantining) healthy people in totality.

The foundations of the hoax are that simple. A study involving ten million people in Wuhan, published in November, 2020, demolished the whole lie about those without symptoms passing on the 'virus'. They found '300 asymptomatic cases' and traced their contacts to find that not one of them was detected with the 'virus'. 'Asymptomatic' patients and their contacts were isolated for no less than two weeks and nothing changed. I know it's all crap, but if you are going to claim that those without symptoms can transmit 'the virus' then you must produce evidence for that and they never have. Even World Health Organization official Dr Maria Van Kerkhove, head of the emerging diseases and zoonosis unit, said as early as June, 2020, that she doubted the validity of asymptomatic transmission. She said that 'from the data we have, it still seems to be rare that an asymptomatic person actually transmits onward to a secondary individual' and by 'rare' she meant that she couldn't cite any case of asymptomatic transmission.

The Ferguson factor

The problem for the Cult as it headed into March, 2020, when the script had lockdown due to start, was that despite all the manipulation of the case and death figures they still did not have enough people alleged to have died from 'Covid' to justify mass house arrest. This was overcome in the way the scientist described: 'You can claim this is just the beginning and more deaths are imminent ... Use this as an excuse to quarantine everyone and then claim the quarantine prevented the expected millions of dead.' Enter one Professor Neil Ferguson, the Gates-funded 'epidemiologist' at the Gates-funded Imperial College in London. Ferguson is Britain's Christian Drosten in that he has a dire record of predicting health outcomes, but is still called upon to advise government on the next health outcome when another 'crisis' comes along. This may seem to be a strange and ridiculous thing to do. Why would you keep turning for policy guidance to people who have a history of being monumentally wrong? Ah, but it makes sense from the Cult point of view. These 'experts' keep on producing predictions that suit the Cult agenda for societal transformation and so it was with Neil Ferguson as he revealed his horrific (and clearly insane) computer model predictions that allowed lockdowns to be imposed in Britain, the United States and many other countries. Ferguson does not have even an A-level in biology and would appear to have no formal training in computer modelling, medicine or epidemiology, according to Derek Winton, an MSc in Computational Intelligence. He wrote an article somewhat aghast at what Ferguson did which included taking no account of respiratory disease 'seasonality' which means it is far worse in the winter months. Who would have thought that respiratory disease could be worse in the winter? Well, certainly not Ferguson.

The massively China-connected Imperial College and its bizarre professor provided the excuse for the long-incubated Chinese model of human control to travel westward at lightning speed. Imperial College confirms on its website that it collaborates with the Chinese Research Institute; publishes more than 600 research papers every year with Chinese research institutions; has 225 Chinese staff; 2,600 Chinese students – the biggest international group; 7,000 former students living in China which is the largest group outside the UK; and was selected for a tour by China's President Xi Jinping during his state visit to the UK in 2015. The college takes major donations from China and describes itself as the UK's number one university collaborator with Chinese research institutions. The China communist/fascist government did not appear phased by the woeful predictions of Ferguson and Imperial when during the lockdown that Ferguson induced the college signed a five-year collaboration deal with China tech giant Huawei that will have Huawei's indoor 5G network equipment installed at the college's West London tech campus along with an 'AI cloud platform'. The deal includes Chinese sponsorship of Imperial's Venture Catalyst entrepreneurship competition. Imperial is an example of the enormous influence the Chinese government has within British and North American universities and research centres – and further afield. Up to 200 academics from more than a dozen UK universities are being investigated on suspicion of 'unintentionally' helping the Chinese government build weapons of mass destruction by 'transferring world-leading research in advanced military technology such as aircraft, missile designs and cyberweapons'. Similar scandals have broken in the United States, but it's all a coincidence. Imperial College serves the agenda in many other ways including the promotion of every aspect of the United Nations Agenda 21/2030 (the Great Reset) and produced computer models to show that human-caused 'climate change' is happening when in the real world it isn't. Imperial College is driving the climate agenda as it drives the 'Covid' agenda (both Cult hoaxes) while Patrick Vallance, the UK government's Chief Scientific Adviser on 'Covid', was named Chief Scientific Adviser to the UN 'climate change' conference known as COP26 hosted by the government in Glasgow, Scotland. 'Covid' and 'climate' are fundamentally connected.

Professor Woeful

From Imperial's bosom came Neil Ferguson still advising government despite his previous disasters and it was announced early on that he and other key people like UK Chief Medical Adviser Chris Whitty had caught the 'virus' as the propaganda story was being sold. Somehow they managed to survive and we had Prime Minister Boris Johnson admitted to hospital with what was said to be a severe version of the 'virus' in this same period. His whole policy and demeanour changed when he returned to Downing Street. It's a small world with these government advisors – especially in their communal connections to Gates – and Ferguson had partnered with Whitty to write a paper called 'Infectious disease: Tough choices to reduce Ebola transmission' which involved another scare-story that didn't happen. Ferguson's 'models' predicted that up to150, 000 could die from 'mad cow disease', or BSE, and its version in sheep if it was transmitted to humans. BSE was not transmitted and instead triggered by an organophosphate pesticide used to treat a pest on cows. Fewer than 200 deaths followed from the human form. Models by Ferguson and his fellow incompetents led to the unnecessary culling of millions of pigs, cattle and sheep in the foot and mouth outbreak in 2001 which destroyed the lives and livelihoods of farmers and their families who had often spent decades building their herds and flocks. Vast numbers of these animals did not have foot and mouth and had no contact with the infection. Another 'expert' behind the cull was Professor Roy Anderson, a computer modeller at Imperial College specialising in the epidemiology of *human*, not animal, disease. Anderson has served on the Bill and Melinda Gates Grand Challenges in Global Health advisory board and chairs another Gates-funded organisation. Gates is everywhere.

In a precursor to the 'Covid' script Ferguson backed closing schools 'for prolonged periods' over the swine flu 'pandemic' in 2009 and said it would affect a third of the world population if it continued to spread at the speed he claimed to be happening. His mates at Imperial College said much the same and a news report said: 'One of the authors, the epidemiologist and disease modeller Neil Ferguson, who sits on the World Health Organisation's emergency committee for the outbreak, said the virus had "full pandemic potential".' Professor Liam Donaldson, the Chris Whitty of his day as Chief Medical Officer, said the worst case could see 30 percent of the British people infected by swine flu with 65,000 dying. Ferguson and Donaldson were indeed proved correct when at the end of the year the number of deaths attributed to swine flu was 392. The term 'expert' is rather liberally applied unfortunately, not least to complete idiots. Swine flu 'projections' were great for GlaxoSmithKline (GSK) as millions rolled in for its Pandemrix influenza vaccine which led to brain damage with children most affected. The British government (taxpayers) paid out more than £60 million in compensation after GSK was given immunity from prosecution. Yet another 'Covid' déjà vu. Swine flu was supposed to have broken out in Mexico, but Dr Wolfgang Wodarg, a German doctor, former member of parliament and critic of the 'Covid' hoax, observed 'the spread of swine flu' in Mexico City at the time. He said: 'What we experienced in Mexico City was a very mild flu which did not kill more than usual – which killed even fewer people than usual.' Hyping the fear against all the facts is not unique to 'Covid' and has happened many times before. Ferguson is reported to have over-estimated the projected death toll of bird flu (H5N1) by some three million-fold, but bird flu vaccine makers again made a killing from the scare. This is some of the background to the Neil Ferguson who produced the perfectly-timed computer models in early 2020 predicting that half a million people would die in Britain without draconian lockdown and 2.2 million in the United States. Politicians panicked, people panicked, and lockdowns of alleged short duration were instigated to 'flatten the curve' of cases gleaned from a test not testing for the 'virus'. I said at the time that the public could forget the 'short duration' bit. This was an agenda to destroy the livelihoods of the population and force them into mass control through dependency and there was going to be nothing 'short' about it. American researcher Daniel Horowitz described the consequences of the 'models' spewed out by Gates-funded Ferguson and Imperial College:

> What led our government and the governments of many other countries into panic was a single Imperial College of UK study, funded by global warming activists, that predicted 2.2 million deaths if we didn't lock down the country. In addition, the reported 8-9% death rate in Italy scared us into thinking there was some other mutation of this virus that they got, which might have come here.

> Together with the fact that we were finally testing and had the ability to actually report new cases, we thought we were headed for a death spiral. But again … we can't flatten a curve if we don't know when the curve started.

How about it *never* started?

Giving them what they want

An investigation by German news outlet *Welt Am Sonntag (World on Sunday)* revealed how in March, 2020, the German government gathered together 'leading scientists from several research institutes and universities' and 'together, they were to produce a [modelling] paper that would serve as legitimization for further tough political measures'. The Cult agenda was justified by computer modelling not based on evidence or reality; it was specifically constructed to justify the Cult demand for lockdowns all over the world to destroy the independent livelihoods of the global population. All these modellers and everyone responsible for the 'Covid' hoax have a date with a trial like those in Nuremberg after World War Two when Nazis faced the consequences of their war crimes. These corrupt-beyond-belief 'modellers' wrote the paper according to government instructions and it said that that if lockdown measures were lifted then up to one million Germans would die from 'Covid-19' adding that some would die 'agonizingly at home, gasping for breath' unable to be treated by hospitals that couldn't cope. All lies. No matter – it gave the Cult all that it wanted. What did long-time government 'modeller' Neil Ferguson say? If the UK and the United States didn't lockdown half a million would die in Britain and 2.2 million Americans. Anyone see a theme here? 'Modellers' are such a crucial part of the lockdown strategy that we should look into their background and follow the money. Researcher Rosemary Frei produced an excellent article headlined 'The Modelling-paper Mafiosi'. She highlights a guy called John Edmunds, a British epidemiologist, and professor in the Faculty of Epidemiology and Population Health at the London School of Hygiene & Tropical Medicine. He studied at Imperial College. Edmunds is a member of government 'Covid' advisory bodies which have been dictating policy, the New and Emerging Respiratory Virus Threats Advisory Group (NERVTAG) and the Scientific Advisory Group for Emergencies (SAGE).

Ferguson, another member of NERVTAG and SAGE, led the way with the original 'virus' and Edmunds has followed in the 'variant' stage and especially the so-called UK or Kent variant known as the 'Variant of Concern' (VOC) B.1.1.7. He said in a co-written report for the Centre for Mathematical modelling of Infectious Diseases at the London School of Hygiene and Tropical Medicine, with input from the Centre's 'Covid-19' Working Group, that there was 'a realistic possibility that VOC B.1.1.7 is associated with an increased risk of death compared to non-VOC viruses'. Fear, fear, fear, get the vaccine, fear, fear, fear, get the vaccine. Rosemary Frei reveals that almost all the paper's authors and members of the modelling centre's 'Covid-19' Working Group receive funding from the Bill and Melinda Gates Foundation and/or the associated Gates-funded Wellcome Trust. The paper was published by e-journal Medrχiv which only publishes papers not peer-reviewed and the journal was established by an organisation headed by Facebook's Mark Zuckerberg and his missus. What a small world it is. Frei discovered that Edmunds is on the Scientific Advisory Board of the Coalition for Epidemic Preparedness Innovations (CEPI) which was established by the Bill and Melinda Gates Foundation, Klaus Schwab's Davos World Economic Forum and Big Pharma giant Wellcome. CEPI was 'launched in Davos [in 2017] to develop vaccines to stop future epidemics', according to its website. 'Our mission is to accelerate the development of vaccines against emerging infectious diseases and enable equitable access to these vaccines for people during outbreaks.' What kind people they are. Rosemary Frei reveals that Public Health England (PHE) director Susan Hopkins is an author of her organisation's non-peer-reviewed reports on 'new variants'. Hopkins is a professor of infectious diseases at London's Imperial College which is gifted tens of millions of dollars a year by the Bill and Melinda Gates Foundation. Gates-funded modelling disaster Neil Ferguson also co-authors Public Health England reports and he spoke in December, 2020, about the potential danger of the B.1.1.7. 'UK variant' promoted by Gates-funded modeller John Edmunds. When I come to the 'Covid vaccines' the 'new variants' will be shown for what they are – bollocks.

Connections, connections

All these people and modellers are lockdown-obsessed or, put another way, they demand what the Cult demands. Edmunds said in January, 2021, that to ease lockdowns too soon would be a disaster and they had to 'vaccinate much, much, much more widely than the elderly'. Rosemary Frei highlights that Edmunds is married to Jeanne Pimenta who is described in a LinkedIn profile as director of epidemiology at GlaxoSmithKline (GSK) and she held shares in the company. Patrick Vallance, co-chair of SAGE and the government's Chief Scientific Adviser, is a former executive of GSK and has a deferred bonus of shares in the company worth £600,000. GSK has serious business connections with Bill Gates and is collaborating with mRNA-'vaccine' company CureVac to make 'vaccines' for the new variants that Edmunds is talking about. GSK is planning a 'Covid vaccine' with drug giant Sanofi. Puppet Prime Minister Boris Johnson announced in the spring of 2021 that up to 60 million vaccine doses were to be made at the GSK facility at Barnard Castle in the English North East. Barnard Castle, with a population of just 6,000, was famously visited in breach of lockdown rules in April, 2020, by Johnson aide Dominic Cummings who said that he drove there 'to test his eyesight' before driving back to London. Cummings would be better advised to test his integrity – not that it would take long. The GSK facility had nothing to do with his visit then although I'm sure Patrick Vallance would have been happy to arrange an introduction and some tea and biscuits. Ruthless psychopath Gates has made yet another fortune from vaccines in collaboration with Big Pharma companies and gushes at the phenomenal profits to be made from vaccines – more than a 20-to-1 return as he told one interviewer. Gates also tweeted in December, 2019, with the foreknowledge of what was coming: 'What's next for our foundation? I'm particularly excited about what the next year could mean for one of the best buys in global health: vaccines.'

Modeller John Edmunds is a big promotor of vaccines as all these people appear to be. He's the dean of the London School of Hygiene & Tropical Medicine's Faculty of Epidemiology and Population Health which is primarily funded by the Bill and Melinda Gates Foundation and the Gates-established and funded GAVI vaccine alliance which is the Gates vehicle to vaccinate the world. The organisation Doctors Without Borders has described GAVI as being 'aimed more at supporting drug-industry desires to promote new products than at finding the most efficient and sustainable means for fighting the diseases of poverty'. But then that's why the psychopath Gates created it. John Edmunds said in a video that the London School of Hygiene & Tropical Medicine is involved in every aspect of vaccine development including large-scale clinical trials. He contends that mathematical modelling can show that vaccines protect individuals and society. That's on the basis of shit in and shit out, I take it. Edmunds serves on the UK Vaccine Network as does Ferguson and the government's foremost 'Covid' adviser, the grim-faced, dark-eyed Chris Whitty. The Vaccine Network says it works 'to support the government to identify and shortlist targeted investment opportunities for the most promising vaccines and vaccine technologies that will help combat infectious diseases with epidemic potential, and to address structural issues related to the UK's broader vaccine infrastructure'. Ferguson is acting Director of the Imperial College Vaccine Impact Modelling Consortium which has funding from the Bill and Melina Gates Foundation and the Gates-created GAVI 'vaccine alliance'. Anyone wonder why these characters see vaccines as the answer to every problem? Ferguson is wildly enthusiastic in his support for GAVI's campaign to vaccine children en masse in poor countries. You would expect someone like Gates who has constantly talked about the need to reduce the population to want to fund vaccines to keep more people alive. I'm sure that's why he does it. The John Edmunds London School of Hygiene & Tropical Medicine (LSHTM) has a Vaccines Manufacturing Innovation Centre which develops, tests and commercialises vaccines. Rosemary Frei writes:

> The vaccines centre also performs affiliated activities like combating 'vaccine hesitancy'. The latter includes the Vaccine Confidence Project. The project's stated purpose is, among other things, 'to provide analysis and guidance for early response and engagement with the public to ensure sustained confidence in vaccines and immunisation'. The Vaccine Confidence Project's director is LSHTM professor Heidi Larson. For more than a decade she's been researching how to combat vaccine hesitancy.

How the bloody hell can blokes like John Edmunds and Neil Ferguson with those connections and financial ties model 'virus' case and death projections for the government and especially in a way that gives their paymasters like Gates exactly what they want? It's insane, but this is what you find throughout the world.

'Covid' is not dangerous, oops, wait, yes it is

Only days before Ferguson's nightmare scenario made Jackboot Johnson take Britain into a China-style lockdown to save us from a deadly 'virus' the UK government website gov.uk was reporting something very different to Ferguson on a page of official government guidance for 'high consequence infectious diseases (HCID)'. It said this about 'Covid-19':

As of 19 March 2020, COVID-19 *is no longer considered to be a high consequence infectious diseases (HCID) in the UK* [my emphasis]. The 4 nations public health HCID group made an interim recommendation in January 2020 to classify COVID-19 as an HCID. This was based on consideration of the UK HCID criteria about the virus and the disease with information available during the early stages of the outbreak.

Now that more is known about COVID-19, the public health bodies in the UK have reviewed the most up to date information about COVID-19 against the UK HCID criteria. They have determined that several features have now changed; in particular, more information is available about mortality rates (low overall), and there is now greater clinical awareness and a specific and sensitive laboratory test, the availability of which continues to increase. The Advisory Committee on Dangerous Pathogens (ACDP) is also of the opinion that COVID-19 should no longer be classified as an HCID.

Soon after the government had been exposed for downgrading the risk they upgraded it again and everyone was back to singing from the same Cult hymn book. Ferguson and his fellow Gates clones indicated that lockdowns and restrictions would have to continue until a Gates-funded vaccine was developed. Gates said the same because Ferguson and his like were repeating the Gates script which is the Cult script. 'Flatten the curve' became an ongoing nightmare of continuing lockdowns with periods in between of severe restrictions in pursuit of destroying independent incomes and had nothing to do with protecting health about which the Cult gives not a shit. Why wouldn't Ferguson be pushing a vaccine 'solution' when he's owned by vaccine-obsessive Gates who makes a fortune from them and when Ferguson heads the Vaccine Impact Modelling Consortium at Imperial College funded by the Gates Foundation and GAVI, the 'vaccine alliance', created by Gates as his personal vaccine promotion operation? To compound the human catastrophe that Ferguson's 'models' did so much to create he was later exposed for breaking his own lockdown rules by having sexual liaisons with his married girlfriend Antonia Staats at his home while she was living at another location with her husband and children. Staats was a 'climate' activist and senior campaigner at the Soros-funded Avaaz which I wouldn't trust to tell me that grass is green. Ferguson had to resign as a government advisor over this hypocrisy in May, 2020, but after a period of quiet he was back being quoted by the ridiculous media on the need for more lockdowns and a vaccine rollout. Other government-advising 'scientists' from Imperial College' held the fort in his absence and said lockdown could be indefinite until a vaccine was found. The Cult script was being sung by the payrolled choir. I said there was no intention of going back to 'normal' when the 'vaccine' came because the 'vaccine' is part of a very different agenda that I will discuss in Human 2.0. Why would the Cult want to let the world go back to normal when destroying that normal forever was the whole point of what was happening? House arrest, closing businesses and schools through lockdown, (un)social distancing and masks all followed the Ferguson fantasy models. Again as I predicted (these people are so predictable) when the 'vaccine' arrived we were told that house arrest, lockdown, (un)social distancing and masks would still have to continue. I will deal with the masks in the next chapter because they are of fundamental importance.

Where's the 'pandemic'?

Any mildly in-depth assessment of the figures revealed what was really going on. Cult-funded and controlled organisations still have genuine people working within them such is the number involved. So it is with Genevieve Briand, assistant program director of the Applied Economics master's degree program at Johns Hopkins University. She analysed the impact that 'Covid-19' had on deaths from *all* causes in the United States using official data from the CDC for the period from early February to early September, 2020. She found that allegedly 'Covid' *related*-deaths exceeded those from heart disease which she found strange with heart disease always the biggest cause of fatalities. Her research became even more significant when she noted the sudden decline in 2020 of *all* non-'Covid' deaths: 'This trend is completely contrary to the pattern observed in all previous years ... the total decrease in deaths by other causes almost exactly equals the increase in deaths by Covid-19.' This was such a game, set and match in terms of what was happening that Johns Hopkins University deleted the article on the grounds that it 'was being used to support false and dangerous inaccuracies about the impact of the pandemic'. No – because it exposed the scam from official CDC figures and this was confirmed when those figures were published in January, 2021. Here we can see the effect of people dying from heart attacks, cancer, road accidents and gunshot wounds – *anything* – having 'Covid-19' on the death certificate along with those diagnosed from 'symptoms' who had even not tested positive with a test not testing for the 'virus'. I am not kidding with the gunshot wounds, by the way. Brenda Bock, coroner in Grand County, Colorado, revealed that two gunshot victims tested positive for the 'virus' within the previous 30 days and were therefore classified as 'Covid deaths'. Bock said: 'These two people had tested positive for Covid, but that's not what killed them. A gunshot wound is what killed them.' She said she had not even finished her investigation when the state listed the gunshot victims as deaths due to the 'virus'. The death and case figures for 'Covid-19' are an absolute joke and yet they are repeated like parrots by the media, politicians and alleged medical 'experts'. The official Cult narrative is the only show in town.

Genevieve Briand found that deaths from all causes were not exceptional in 2020 compared with previous years and a Spanish magazine published figures that said the same about Spain which was a 'Covid' propaganda hotspot at one point. *Discovery Salud*, a health and medicine magazine, quoted government figures which showed how 17,000 *fewer* people died in Spain in 2020 than in 2019 and more than 26,000 fewer than in 2018. The age-standardised mortality rate for England and Wales when age distribution is taken into account was significantly lower in 2020 than the 1970s, 80s and 90s, and was only the ninth highest since 2000. Where is the 'pandemic'?

Post mortems and autopsies virtually disappeared for 'Covid' deaths amid claims that 'virus-infected' bodily fluids posed a risk to those carrying out the autopsy. This was rejected by renowned German pathologist and forensic doctor Klaus Püschel who said that he and his staff had by then done 150 autopsies on 'Covid' patients with no problems at all. He said they were needed to know why some 'Covid' patients suffered blood clots and not severe respiratory infections. The 'virus' is, after all, called SARS or 'severe acute respiratory syndrome'. I highlighted in the spring of 2020 this phenomenon and quoted New York intensive care doctor Cameron Kyle-Sidell who posted a soon deleted YouTube video to say that they had been told to prepare to treat an infectious disease called 'Covid-19', but that was not what they were dealing with. Instead he likened the lung condition of the most severely ill patients to what you would expect with cabin depressurisation in a plane at 30,000 feet or someone dropped on the top of Everest without oxygen or acclimatisation. I have never said this is not happening to a small minority of alleged 'Covid' patients – I am saying this is not caused by a phantom 'contagious virus'. Indeed Kyle-Sidell said that 'Covid-19' was not the disease they were told was coming their way. 'We are operating under a medical paradigm that is untrue,' he said, and he believed they were treating the wrong disease: 'These people are being slowly starved of oxygen.' Patients would take off their oxygen masks in a state of fear and stress and while they were blue in the face on the brink of death. They did not look like patients dying of pneumonia. You can see why they don't want autopsies when their virus doesn't exist and there is another condition in some people that they don't wish to be uncovered. I should add here that the 5G system of millimetre waves was being rapidly introduced around the world in 2020 and even more so now as they fire 5G at the Earth from satellites. At 60 gigahertz within the 5G range that frequency interacts with the oxygen molecule and stops people breathing in sufficient oxygen to be absorbed into the bloodstream. They are installing 5G in schools and hospitals. The world is not mad or anything. 5G can cause major changes to the lungs and blood as I detail in *The Answer* and these consequences are labelled 'Covid-19', the alleged symptoms of which can be caused by 5G and other electromagnetic frequencies as cells respond to radiation poisoning.

The 'Covid death' scam

Dr Scott Jensen, a Minnesota state senator and medical doctor, exposed 'Covid' Medicare payment incentives to hospitals and death certificate manipulation. He said he was sent a seven-page document by the US Department of Health 'coaching' him on how to fill out death certificates which had never happened before. The document said that he didn't need to have a laboratory test for 'Covid-19' to put that on the death certificate and that shocked him when death certificates are supposed to be about facts. Jensen described how doctors had been 'encouraged, if not pressured' to make a diagnosis of 'Covid-19' if they thought it was probable or *'presumed'*. No positive test was necessary – not that this would have mattered anyway. He said doctors were told to diagnose 'Covid' by symptoms when these were the same as colds, allergies, other respiratory problems, and certainly with influenza which 'disappeared' in the 'Covid' era. A common sniffle was enough to get the dreaded verdict. Ontario authorities decreed that a single care home resident with *one* symptom from a long list must lead to the isolation of the entire home. Other courageous doctors like Jensen made the same point about death figure manipulation and how deaths by other causes were falling while 'Covid-19 deaths' were rising at the same rate due to re-diagnosis. Their videos rarely survive long on YouTube with its Cult-supporting algorithms courtesy of CEO Susan Wojcicki and her bosses at Google. Figure-tampering was so glaring and ubiquitous that even officials were letting it slip or outright saying it. UK chief scientific adviser Patrick Vallance said on one occasion that 'Covid' on the death certificate doesn't mean 'Covid' was the cause of death (so why the hell is it there?) and we had the rare sight of a BBC reporter telling the truth when she said: 'Someone could be successfully treated for Covid, in say April, discharged, and then in June, get run over by a bus and die … That person would still be counted as a Covid death in England.' Yet the BBC and the rest of the world media went on repeating the case and death figures as if they were real. Illinois Public Health Director Dr Ngozi Ezike revealed the deceit while her bosses must have been clenching their buttocks:

> If you were in a hospice and given a few weeks to live and you were then found to have Covid that would be counted as a Covid death. [There might be] a clear alternate cause, but it is still listed as a Covid death. So everyone listed as a Covid death doesn't mean that was the cause of the death, but that they had Covid at the time of death.

Yes, a 'Covid virus' never shown to exist and tested for with a test not testing for the 'virus'. In the first period of the pandemic hoax through the spring of 2020 the process began of designating almost everything a 'Covid' death and this has continued ever since. I sat in a restaurant one night listening to a loud conversation on the next table where a family was discussing in bewilderment how a relative who had no symptoms of 'Covid', and had died of a long-term problem, could have been diagnosed a death by the 'virus'. I could understand their bewilderment. If they read this book they will know why this medical fraud has been perpetrated the world over.

Some media truth shock

The media ignored the evidence of death certificate fraud until eventually one columnist did speak out when she saw it first-hand. Bel Mooney is a long-time national newspaper journalist in Britain currently working for the *Daily Mail*. Her article on February 19th, 2021, carried this headline: 'My dad Ted passed three Covid tests and died of a chronic illness yet he's officially one of Britain's 120,000 victims of the virus and is far from alone ... so how many more are there?' She told how her 99-year-old father was in a care home with a long-standing chronic obstructive pulmonary disease and vascular dementia. Maybe, but he was still aware enough to tell her from the start that there was no 'virus' and he refused the 'vaccine' for that reason. His death was not unexpected given his chronic health problems and Mooney said she was shocked to find that 'Covid-19' was declared the cause of death on his death certificate. She said this was a 'bizarre and unacceptable untruth' for a man with long-time health problems who had tested negative twice at the home for the 'virus'. I was also shocked by this story although not by what she said. I had been highlighting the death certificate manipulation for ten months. It was the confirmation that a professional full-time journalist only realised this was going on when it affected her directly and neither did she know that whether her dad tested positive or negative was irrelevant with the test not testing for the 'virus'. Where had she been? She said she did not believe in 'conspiracy theories' without knowing I'm sure that this and 'conspiracy theorists' were terms put into widespread circulation by the CIA in the 1960s to discredit those who did not accept the ridiculous official story of the Kennedy assassination. A blanket statement of 'I don't believe in conspiracy theories' is always bizarre. The dictionary definition of the term alone means the world is drowning in conspiracies. What she said was even more daft when her dad had just been affected by the 'Covid' conspiracy. Why else does she think that 'Covid-19' was going on the death certificates of people who died of something else?

To be fair once she saw from personal experience what was happening she didn't mince words. Mooney was called by the care home on the morning of February 9th to be told her father had died in his sleep. When she asked for the official cause of death what came back was 'Covid-19'. Mooney challenged this and was told there had been deaths from Covid on the dementia floor (confirmed by a test not testing for the 'virus') so they considered it 'reasonable to assume'. 'But doctor,' Mooney rightly protested, 'an assumption isn't a diagnosis.' She said she didn't blame the perfectly decent and sympathetic doctor – 'he was just doing his job'. Sorry, but that's *bullshit*. He wasn't doing his job at all. He was putting a false cause of death on the death certificate and that is a criminal offence for which he should be brought to account and the same with the millions of doctors worldwide who have done the same. They were not doing their job they were following orders and that must not wash at new Nuremberg trials any more than it did at the first ones. Mooney's doctor was 'assuming' (presuming) as he was told to, but 'just following orders' makes no difference to his actions. A doctor's job is to serve the patient and the truth, not follow orders, but that's what they have done all over the world and played a central part in making the 'Covid' hoax possible with all its catastrophic consequences for humanity. Shame on them and they must answer for their actions. Mooney said her disquiet worsened when she registered her father's death by telephone and was told by the registrar there had been very many other cases like hers where 'the deceased' had not tested positive for 'Covid' yet it was recorded as the cause of death. The test may not matter, but those involved at their level *think* it matters and it shows a callous disregard for accurate diagnosis. The pressure to do this is coming from the top of the national 'health' pyramids which in turn obey the World Health Organization which obeys Gates and the Cult. Mooney said the registrar agreed that this must distort the national figures adding that 'the strangest thing is that every winter we record countless deaths from flu, and this winter there have been none. Not one!' She asked if the registrar thought deaths from flu were being misdiagnosed and lumped together with 'Covid' deaths. The answer was a 'puzzled yes'. Mooney said that the funeral director said the same about 'Covid' deaths which had nothing to do with 'Covid'. They had lost count of the number of families upset by this and other funeral companies in different countries have had the same experience. Mooney wrote:

> The nightly shroud-waving and shocking close-ups of pain imposed on us by the TV news bewildered and terrified the population into eager compliance with lockdowns. We were invited to 'save the NHS' and to grieve for strangers – the real-life loved ones behind those shocking death counts. Why would the public imagine what I now fear, namely that the way Covid-19 death statistics are compiled might make the numbers seem greater than they are?

Oh, just a little bit – like 100 percent.

Do the maths

Mooney asked why a country would wish to skew its mortality figures by wrongly certifying deaths? What had been going on? Well, if you don't believe in conspiracies you will never find the answer which is that *it's a conspiracy*. She did, however, describe what she had discovered as a 'national scandal'. In reality it's a global scandal and happening everywhere. Pillars of this conspiracy were all put into place before the button was pressed with the Drosten PCR protocol and high amplifications to produce the cases and death certificate changes to secure illusory 'Covid' deaths. Mooney notes that normally two doctors were needed to certify a death, with one having to know the patient, and how the rules were changed in the spring of 2020 to allow one doctor to do this. In the same period 'Covid deaths' were decreed to be all cases where Covid-19 was put on the death certificate even without a positive test or any symptoms. Mooney asked: 'How many of the 30,851 (as of January 15) care home resident deaths with Covid-19 on the certificate (32.4 per cent of all deaths so far) were based on an assumption, like that of my father? And what has that done to our national psyche?'All of them is the answer to the first question and it has devastated and dismantled the national psyche, actually the global psyche, on a colossal scale. In the UK case and death data is compiled by organisations like Public Health England (PHE) and the Office for National Statistics (ONS). Mooney highlights the insane policy of counting a death from any cause as 'Covid-19' if this happens within 28 days of a positive test (with a test not testing for the 'virus') and she points out that ONS statistics reflect deaths 'involving Covid' 'or due to Covid' which meant in practice any death where 'Covid-19' was mentioned on the death certificate. She described the consequences of this fraud:

> Most people will accept the narrative they are fed, so panicky governments here and in Europe witnessed the harsh measures enacted in totalitarian China and jumped into lockdown. Headlines about Covid deaths tolled like

the knell that would bring doomsday to us all. Fear stalked our empty streets. Politicians parroted the frankly ridiculous aim of 'zero Covid' and shut down the economy, while most British people agreed that lockdown was essential and (astonishingly to me, as a patriotic Brit) even wanted more restrictions.

For what? Lies on death certificates? Never mind the grim toll of lives ruined, suicides, schools closed, rising inequality, depression, cancelled hospital treatments, cancer patients in a torture of waiting, poverty, economic devastation, loneliness, families kept apart, and so on. How many lives have been lost as a direct result of lockdown?

She said that we could join in a national chorus of shock and horror at reaching the 120,000 death toll which was surely certain to have been totally skewed all along, but what about the human cost of lockdown justified by these 'death figures'? *The British Medical Journal* had reported a 1,493 percent increase in cases of children taken to Great Ormond Street Hospital with abusive head injuries alone and then there was the effect on families:

Perhaps the most shocking thing about all this is that families have been kept apart – and obeyed the most irrational, changing rules at the whim of government – because they believed in the statistics. They succumbed to fear, which his generation rejected in that war fought for freedom. Dad (God rest his soul) would be angry. And so am I.

Another theme to watch is that in the winter months when there are more deaths from all causes they focus on 'Covid' deaths and in the summer when the British Lung Foundation says respiratory disease plummets by 80 percent they rage on about 'cases'. Either way fascism on population is always the answer.

Nazi eugenics in the 21st century

Elderly people in care homes have been isolated from their families month after lonely month with no contact with relatives and grandchildren who were banned from seeing them. We were told that lockdown fascism was to 'protect the vulnerable' like elderly people. At the same time Do Not Resuscitate (DNR) orders were placed on their medical files so that if they needed resuscitation it wasn't done and 'Covid-19' went on their death certificates. Old people were not being 'protected' they were being culled – murdered in truth. DNR orders were being decreed for disabled and young people with learning difficulties or psychological problems. The UK Care Quality Commission, a non-departmental body of the Department of Health and Social Care, found that 34 percent of those working in health and social care were pressured into placing 'do not attempt cardiopulmonary resuscitation' orders on 'Covid' patients who suffered from disabilities and learning difficulties without involving the patient or their families in the decision. UK judges ruled that an elderly woman with dementia should have the DNA-manipulating 'Covid vaccine' against her son's wishes and that a man with severe learning difficulties should have the jab despite his family's objections. Never mind that many had already died. The judiciary always supports doctors and government in fascist dictatorships. They wouldn't dare do otherwise. A horrific video was posted showing fascist officers from Los Angeles police forcibly giving the 'Covid' shot to women with special needs who were screaming that they didn't want it. The same fascists are seen giving the jab to a sleeping elderly woman in a care home. This is straight out of the Nazi playbook. Hitler's Nazis committed mass murder of the mentally ill and physically disabled throughout Germany and occupied territories in the programme that became known as Aktion T4, or just T4. Sabbatian-controlled Hitler and his grotesque crazies set out to kill those they considered useless and unnecessary. The Reich Committee for the Scientific Registering of Hereditary and Congenital Illnesses registered the births of babies identified by physicians to have 'defects'. By 1941 alone more than 5,000 children were murdered by the state and it is estimated that in total the number of innocent people killed in Aktion T4 was between 275,000 and 300,000. Parents were told their children had been sent away for 'special treatment' never to return. It is rather pathetic to see claims about plans for new extermination camps being dismissed today when the same force behind current events did precisely that 80 years ago. Margaret Sanger was a Cult operative who used 'birth control' to sanitise her programme of eugenics. Organisations she founded became what is now Planned Parenthood. Sanger proposed that 'the whole dysgenic population would have its choice of segregation or sterilization'. These included epileptics, 'feeble-minded', and prostitutes. Sanger opposed charity because it perpetuated 'human waste'. She reveals the Cult mentality and if anyone thinks that extermination camps are a 'conspiracy theory' their naivety is touching if breathtakingly stupid.

If you don't believe that doctors can act with callous disregard for their patients it is worth considering that doctors and medical staff agreed to put government-decreed DNR orders on medical files and do nothing when resuscitation is called for. I don't know what you call such people in your house. In mine they are Nazis from the Josef Mengele School of Medicine. Phenomenal numbers of old people have died worldwide from the effects of lockdown, depression, lack of treatment, the 'vaccine' (more later) and losing the will to live. A common response at the start of the manufactured pandemic was to remove old people from hospital beds and transfer them to nursing homes. The decision would result in a mass cull of elderly people in those homes through lack of treatment – *not* 'Covid'. Care home whistleblowers have told how once the 'Covid' era began doctors would not come to their homes to treat patients and they were begging for drugs like antibiotics that often never came. The most infamous example was ordered by New York governor Andrew Cuomo, brother of a moronic CNN host, who amazingly was given an Emmy Award for his handling of the 'Covid crisis' by the ridiculous Wokers that hand them out. Just how ridiculous could be seen in February, 2021, when a Department of Justice and FBI investigation began into how thousands of old people in New York died in nursing homes after being discharged from hospital to make way for 'Covid' patients on Cuomo's say-so – and how he and his staff covered up these facts. This couldn't have happened to a nicer psychopath. Even then there was a 'Covid' spin. Reports said that thousands of old people who tested positive for 'Covid' in hospital were transferred to nursing homes to both die of 'Covid' and transmit it to others. No – they were in hospital because they were ill and the fact that they tested positive with a test not testing for the 'virus' is irrelevant. They were ill often with respiratory diseases ubiquitous in old people near the end of their lives. Their transfer out of hospital meant that their treatment stopped and many would go on to die.

They're old. Who gives a damn?

I have exposed in the books for decades the Cult plan to cull the world's old people and even to introduce at some point what they call a 'demise pill' which at a certain age everyone would take and be out of here by law. In March, 2021, Spain legalised euthanasia and assisted suicide following the Netherlands, Belgium, Luxembourg and Canada on the Tiptoe to the demise pill. Treatment of old people by many 'care' homes has been a disgrace in the 'Covid' era. There are many, many, caring staff – I know some. There have, however, been legions of stories about callous treatment of old people and their families. Police were called when families came to take their loved ones home in the light of isolation that was killing them. They became prisoners of the state. Care home residents in insane, fascist Ontario, Canada, were not allowed to leave their *room* once the 'Covid' hoax began. UK staff have even wheeled elderly people away from windows where family members were talking with them. Oriana Criscuolo from Stockport in the English North West dropped off some things for her 80-year-old father who has Parkinson's disease and dementia and she wanted to wave to him through a ground-floor window. She was told that was 'illegal'. When she went anyway they closed the curtains in the middle of the day. Oriana said:

It's just unbelievable. I cannot understand how care home staff – people who are being paid to care – have become so uncaring. Their behaviour is inhumane and cruel. It's beyond belief.

She was right and this was not a one-off. What a way to end your life in such loveless circumstances. UK registered nurse Nicky Millen, a proper old school nurse for 40 years, said that when she started her career care was based on dignity, choice, compassion and empathy. Now she said 'the things that are important to me have gone out of the window.' She was appalled that people were dying without their loved ones and saying goodbye on iPads. Nicky described how a distressed 89-year-old lady stroked her face and asked her 'how many paracetamol would it take to finish me off'. Life was no longer worth living while not seeing her family. Nicky said she was humiliated in front of the ward staff and patients for letting the lady stroke her face and giving her a cuddle. Such is the dehumanisation that the 'Covid' hoax has brought to the surface. Nicky worked in care homes where patients told her they were being held prisoner. 'I want to live until I die', one said to her. 'I had a lady in tears because she hadn't seen her great-grandson.' Nicky was compassionate old school meeting psychopathic New Normal. She also said she had worked on a 'Covid' ward with no 'Covid' patients. Jewish writer Shai Held wrote an article in March, 2020, which was headlined 'The Staggering, Heartless Cruelty Toward the Elderly'. What he described was happening from the earliest days of lockdown. He said 'the elderly' were considered a group and not unique individuals (the way of the Woke). Shai Held said:

> Notice how the all-too-familiar rhetoric of dehumanization works: 'The elderly' are bunched together as a faceless mass, all of them considered culprits and thus effectively deserving of the suffering the pandemic will inflict upon them. Lost entirely is the fact that the elderly are individual human beings, each with a distinctive face and voice, each with hopes and dreams, memories and regrets, friendships and marriages, loves lost and loves sustained.

'The elderly' have become another dehumanised group for which anything goes and for many that has resulted in cold disregard for their rights and their life. The distinctive face that Held talks about is designed to be deleted by masks until everyone is part of a faceless mass.

'War-zone' hospitals myth
Again and again medical professionals have told me what was really

going on and how hospitals 'overrun like war zones' according to the media were virtually empty. The mantra from medical whistleblowers was please don't use my name or my career is over. Citizen journalists around the world sneaked into hospitals to film evidence exposing the 'war-zone' lie. They really *were* largely empty with closed wards and operating theatres. I met a hospital worker in my town on the Isle of Wight during the first lockdown in 2020 who said the only island hospital had never been so quiet. Lockdown was justified by the psychopaths to stop hospitals being overrun. At the same time that the island hospital was near-empty the military arrived here to provide *extra beds*. It was all propaganda to ramp up the fear to ensure compliance with fascism as were never-used temporary hospitals with thousands of beds known as Nightingales and never-used make-shift mortuaries opened by the criminal UK government. A man who helped to install those extra island beds attributed to the army said they were never used and the hospital was empty. Doctors and nurses 'stood around talking or on their phones, wandering down to us to see what we were doing'. There were no masks or social distancing. He accused the useless local island paper, the *County Press*, of 'pumping the fear as if our hospital was overrun and we only have one so it should have been'. He described ambulances parked up with crews outside in deck chairs. When his brother called an ambulance he was told there was a two-hour backlog which he called 'bullshit'. An old lady on the island fell 'and was in a bad way', but a caller who rang for an ambulance was told the situation wasn't urgent enough. Ambulance stations were working under capacity while people would hear ambulances with sirens blaring driving through the streets. When those living near the stations realised what was going on they would follow them as they left, circulated around an urban area with the sirens going, and then came back without stopping. All this was to increase levels of fear and the same goes for the 'ventilator shortage crisis' that cost tens of millions for hastily produced ventilators never to be used. Ambulance crews that agreed to be exploited in this way for fear propaganda might find themselves a mirror. I wish them well with that. Empty hospitals were the obvious consequence of treatment and diagnoses of non-'Covid' conditions cancelled and those involved handed a death sentence. People have been dying at home from undiagnosed and untreated cancer, heart disease and other life-threatening conditions to allow empty hospitals to deal with a 'pandemic' that wasn't happening.

Death of the innocent

'War-zones' have been laying off nursing staff, even doctors where they can. There was no work for them. Lockdown was justified by saving lives and protecting the vulnerable they were actually killing with DNR orders and preventing empty hospitals being 'overrun'. In Britain the mantra of stay at home to 'save the NHS' was everywhere and across the world the same story was being sold when it was all lies. Two California doctors, Dan Erickson and Artin Massihi at Accelerated Urgent Care in Bakersfield, held a news conference in April, 2020, to say that intensive care units in California were 'empty, essentially', with hospitals shutting floors, not treating patients and laying off doctors. The California health system was working at minimum capacity 'getting rid of doctors because we just don't have the volume'. They said that people with conditions such as heart disease and cancer were not coming to hospital out of fear of 'Covid-19'. Their video was deleted by Susan Wojcicki's Cult-owned YouTube after reaching five million views. Florida governor Ron Desantis, who rejected the severe lockdowns of other states and is being targeted for doing so, said that in March, 2020, every US governor was given models claiming they would run out of hospital beds in days. That was never going to happen and the 'modellers' knew it. Deceit can be found at every level of the system. Urgent children's operations were cancelled including fracture repairs and biopsies to spot cancer. Eric Nicholls, a consultant paediatrician, said 'this is obviously concerning and we need to return to normal operating and to increase capacity as soon as possible'. Psychopaths in power were rather less concerned *because* they are psychopaths. Deletion of urgent care and diagnosis has been happening all over the world and how many kids and others have died as a result of the actions of these cold and heartless lunatics dictating 'health' policy? The number must be stratospheric. Richard Sullivan, professor of cancer and global health at King's College London, said people feared 'Covid' more than cancer such was the campaign of fear. 'Years of lost life will be quite dramatic', Sullivan said, with 'a huge amount of avoidable mortality'. Sarah Woolnough, executive director for policy at Cancer Research UK, said there had been a 75 percent drop in urgent referrals to hospitals by family doctors of people with suspected cancer. Sullivan said that 'a lot of services have had to scale back – we've seen a dramatic decrease in the amount of elective cancer surgery'. Lockdown deaths worldwide has been absolutely fantastic with the *New York Post* reporting how data confirmed that 'lockdowns end more lives than they save':

> There was a sharp decline in visits to emergency rooms and an increase in fatal heart attacks because patients didn't receive prompt treatment. Many fewer people were screened for cancer. Social isolation contributed to excess deaths from dementia and Alzheimer's.

> Researchers predicted that the social and economic upheaval would lead to tens of thousands of "deaths of despair" from drug overdoses, alcoholism and

suicide. As unemployment surged and mental-health and substance-abuse treatment programs were interrupted, the reported levels of anxiety, depression and suicidal thoughts increased dramatically, as did alcohol sales and fatal drug overdoses.

This has been happening while nurses and other staff had so much time on their hands in the 'war-zones' that Tic-Tok dancing videos began appearing across the Internet with medical staff dancing around in empty wards and corridors as people died at home from causes that would normally have been treated in hospital.

Mentions in dispatches

One brave and truth-committed whistleblower was Louise Hampton, a call handler with the UK NHS who made a viral Internet video saying she had done 'fuck all' during the 'pandemic' which was 'a load of bollocks'. She said that 'Covid-19' was rebranded flu and of course she lost her job. This is what happens in the medical and endless other professions now when you tell the truth. Louise filmed inside 'war-zone' accident and emergency departments to show they were empty and I mean *empty* as in no one there. The mainstream media could have done the same and blown the gaff on the whole conspiracy. They haven't to their eternal shame. Not that most 'journalists' seem capable of manifesting shame as with the psychopaths they slavishly repeat without question. The relative few who were admitted with serious health problems were left to die alone with no loved ones allowed to see them because of 'Covid' rules and they included kids dying without the comfort of mum and dad at their bedside while the evil behind this couldn't give a damn. It was all good fun to them. A Scottish NHS staff nurse publicly quit in the spring of 2021 saying: 'I can no longer be part of the lies and the corruption by the government.' She said hospitals 'aren't full, the beds aren't full, beds have been shut, wards have been shut'. Hospitals were never busy throughout 'Covid'. The staff nurse said that Nicola Sturgeon, tragically the leader of the Scottish government, was on television saying save the hospitals and the NHS – 'but the beds are empty' and 'we've not seen flu, we always see flu every year'. She wrote to government and spoke with her union Unison (the unions are Cult-compromised and *useless*, but nothing changed. Many of her colleagues were scared of losing their jobs if they spoke out as they wanted to. She said nursing staff were being affected by wearing masks all day and 'my head is splitting every shift from wearing a mask'. The NHS is part of the fascist tyranny and must be dismantled so we can start again with human beings in charge. (Ironically, hospitals were reported to be busier again when official 'Covid' cases *fell* in spring/summer of 2021 and many other conditions required treatment at the same time as *the fake vaccine rollout*.)

I will cover the 'Covid vaccine' scam in detail later, but it is another indicator of the sickening disregard for human life that I am highlighting here. The DNA-manipulating concoctions do not fulfil the definition of a 'vaccine', have never been used on humans before and were given only emergency approval because trials were not completed and they continued using the unknowing public. The result was what a NHS senior nurse with responsibility for 'vaccine' procedure said was 'genocide'. She said the 'vaccines' were not 'vaccines'. They had not been shown to be safe and claims about their effectiveness by drug companies were 'poetic licence'. She described what was happening as a 'horrid act of human annihilation'. The nurse said that management had instigated a policy of not providing a Patient Information Leaflet (PIL) before people were 'vaccinated' even though health care professionals are supposed to do this according to protocol. Patients should also be told that they are taking part in an ongoing clinical trial. Her challenges to what is happening had seen her excluded from meetings and ridiculed in others. She said she was told to 'watch my step … or I would find myself surplus to requirements'. The nurse, who spoke anonymously in fear of her career, said she asked her NHS manager why he/she was content with taking part in genocide against those having the 'vaccines'. The reply was that everyone had to play their part and to 'put up, shut up, and get it done'. Government was 'leaning heavily' on NHS management which was clearly leaning heavily on staff. This is how the global 'medical' hierarchy operates and it starts with the Cult and its World Health Organization.

She told the story of a doctor who had the Pfizer jab and when questioned had no idea what was in it. The doctor had never read the literature. We have to stop treating doctors as intellectual giants when so many are moral and medical pygmies. The doctor did not even know that the 'vaccines' were not fully approved or that their trials were ongoing. They were, however, asking their patients if they minded taking part in follow-ups for research purposes – yes, the *ongoing clinical trial*. The nurse said the doctor's ignorance was not rare and she had spoken to a hospital consultant who had the jab without any idea of the background or that the 'trials' had not been completed. Nurses and pharmacists had shown the same ignorance. 'My NHS colleagues have forsaken their duty of care, broken their code of conduct – Hippocratic Oath – and have been brainwashed just the same as the majority of the UK public through propaganda …' She said she had not been able to recruit a single NHS colleague, doctor, nurse or pharmacist to stand with her and speak out. Her union had refused to help. She said that if the genocide came to light she would not hesitate to give evidence at a Nuremberg-type trial against those in power who could have affected the outcomes but didn't.

And all for what?

To put the nonsense into perspective let's say the 'virus' does exist and let's go completely crazy and accept that the official manipulated figures for cases and deaths are accurate. *Even then* a study by Stanford University epidemiologist Dr John Ioannidis published on the World Health Organization website produced an average infection to fatality rate of … *0.23 percent!* Ioannidis said: 'If one could sample equally from all locations globally, the median infection fatality rate might even be substantially lower than the 0.23% observed in my analysis.' For healthy people under 70 it was … *0.05 percent!* This compares with the 3.4 percent claimed by the Cult-owned World Health Organization when the hoax was first played and maximum fear needed to be generated. An updated Stanford study in April, 2021, put the 'infection' to 'fatality' rate at just 0.15 percent. Another team of scientists led by Megan O'Driscoll and Henrik Salje studied data from 45 countries and published their findings on the Nature website. For children and young people the figure is so small it virtually does not register although authorities will be hyping dangers to the young when they introduce DNA-manipulating 'vaccines' for children. The O'Driscoll study produced an average infection-fatality figure of 0.003 for children from birth to four; 0.001 for 5 to 14; 0.003 for 15 to 19; and it was still only 0.456 up to 64. To claim that children must be 'vaccinated' to protect them from 'Covid' is an obvious lie and so there must be another reason and there is. What's more the average age of a 'Covid' death is akin to the average age that people die in general. The average age of death in England is about 80 for men and 83 for women. The average age of death from alleged 'Covid' is between 82 and 83. California doctors, Dan Erickson and Artin Massihi, said at their April media conference that projection models of millions of deaths had been 'woefully inaccurate'. They produced detailed figures showing that Californians had a 0.03 chance of dying from 'Covid' based on the number of people who tested positive (with a test not testing for the 'virus'). Erickson said there was a 0.1 percent chance of dying from 'Covid' in the *state* of New York, not just the city, and a 0.05 percent chance in Spain, a centre of 'Covid-19' hysteria at one stage. The Stanford studies supported the doctors' data with fatality rate estimates of 0.23 and 0.15 percent. How close are these figures to my estimate of *zero*? Death-rate figures claimed by the World Health Organization at the start of the hoax were some 15 times higher. The California doctors said there was no justification for lockdowns and the economic devastation they caused. Everything they had ever learned about quarantine was that you quarantine the *sick* and not the healthy. They had never seen this before and it made no medical sense.

Why in the in the light of all this would governments and medical systems the world over say that billions must go under house arrest; lose their livelihood; in many cases lose their mind, their health and their life; force people to wear masks dangerous to health and psychology; make human interaction and even family interaction a criminal offence; ban travel; close restaurants, bars, watching live sport, concerts, theatre, and any activity involving human togetherness and discourse; and closing schools to isolate children from their friends and cause many to commit suicide in acts of hopelessness and despair? The California doctors said lockdown consequences included increased child abuse, partner abuse, alcoholism, depression, and other impacts they were seeing every day. Who would do that to the entire human race if not mentally-ill psychopaths of almost unimaginable extremes like Bill Gates? We must face the reality of what we are dealing with and come out of denial. Fascism and tyranny are made possible only by the target population submitting and acquiescing to fascism and tyranny. The whole of human history shows that to be true. Most people naively and unquestioning believed what they were told about a 'deadly virus' and meekly and weakly submitted to house arrest. Those who didn't believe it – at least in total – still submitted in fear of the consequences of not doing so. For the rest who wouldn't submit draconian fines have been imposed, brutal policing by psychopaths *for* psychopaths, and condemnation from the meek and weak who condemn the Pushbackers on behalf of the very force that has them, too, in its gunsights. 'Pathetic' does not even begin to suffice. Britain's brainless 'Health' Secretary Matt Hancock warned anyone lying to border officials about returning from a list of 'hotspot' countries could face a jail sentence of up to ten years which is more than for racially-aggravated assault, incest and attempting to have sex with a child under 13. Hancock is a lunatic, but he has the state apparatus behind him in a Cult-led chain reaction and the same with UK 'Vaccine Minister' Nadhim Zahawi, a prominent member of the mega-Cult secret society, Le Cercle, which featured in my earlier books. The Cult enforces its will on governments and medical systems; government and medical systems enforce their will on business and police; business enforces its will on staff who enforce it on customers; police enforce the will of the Cult on the population and play their essential part in creating a world of fascist control that their own children and grandchildren will have to live in their entire lives. It is a hierarchical pyramid of imposition and acquiescence and, yes indeedy, of clinical insanity.

Does anyone bright enough to read this book have to ask what the answer is? I think not, but I will reveal it anyway in the fewest of syllables: Tell the psychos and their moronic lackeys to fuck off and let's get on with our lives. We are many – They are few.

CHAPTER SEVEN

War on your mind

One believes things because one has been conditioned to believe them
Aldous Huxley, *Brave New World*

I have described the 'Covid' hoax as a 'Psyop' and that is true in every sense and on every level in accordance with the definition of that term which is psychological warfare. Break down the 'Covid pandemic' to the foundation themes and it is psychological warfare on the human individual and collective mind.

The same can be said for the entire human belief system involving every subject you can imagine. Huxley was right in his contention that people believe what they are conditioned to believe and this comes from the repetition throughout their lives of the same falsehoods. They spew from government, corporations, media and endless streams of 'experts' telling you what the Cult wants you to believe and often believing it themselves (although *far* from always). 'Experts' are rewarded with 'prestigious' jobs and titles and as agents of perceptual programming with regular access to the media. The Cult has to control the narrative – control *information* – or they lose control of the vital, crucial, without-which-they-cannot-prevail public perception of reality. The foundation of that control today is the Internet made possible by the Defense Advanced Research Projects Agency (DARPA), the incredibly sinister technological arm of the Pentagon. The Internet is the result of military technology. DARPA openly brags about establishing the Internet which has been a long-term project to lasso the minds of the global population. I have said for decades the plan is to control information to such an extreme that eventually no one would see or hear anything that the Cult does not approve. We are closing in on that end with ferocious censorship since the 'Covid' hoax began and in my case it started back in the 1990s in terms of books and speaking venues. I had to create my own publishing company in 1995 precisely because no one else would publish my books even then. I think they're all still running.

Cult Internet

To secure total control of information they needed the Internet in which pre-programmed algorithms can seek out 'unclean' content for deletion and even stop it being posted in the first place. The Cult had to dismantle print and non-Internet broadcast media to ensure the transfer of information to the appropriate-named 'Web' – a critical expression of the *Cult* web. We've seen the ever-quickening demise of traditional media and control of what is left by a tiny number of corporations operating worldwide. Independent journalism in the mainstream is already dead and never was that more obvious than since the turn of 2020. The Cult wants all information communicated via the Internet to globally censor and allow the plug to be pulled any time. Lockdowns and forced isolation has meant that communication between people has been through electronic means and no longer through face-to-face discourse and discussion. Cult psychopaths have targeted the bars, restaurants, sport, venues and meeting places in general for this reason. None of this is by chance and it's to stop people gathering in any kind of privacy or number while being able to track and monitor all Internet communications and block them as necessary. Even private messages between individuals have been censored by these fascists that control Cult fronts like Facebook, Twitter, Google and YouTube which are all officially run by Sabbatian place-people and from the background by higher-level Sabbatian place people. Facebook, Google, Amazon and their like were seed-funded and supported into existence with money-no-object infusions of funds either directly or indirectly from DARPA and CIA technology arm In-Q-Tel. The Cult plays the long game and prepares very carefully for big plays like 'Covid'. Amazon is another front in the psychological war and pretty much controls the global market in book sales and increasingly publishing. Amazon's limitless funds have deleted fantastic numbers of independent publishers to seize global domination on the way to deciding which books can be sold and circulated and which cannot. Moves in that direction are already happening. Amazon's leading light Jeff Bezos is the grandson of Lawrence Preston Gise who worked with DARPA predecessor ARPA. Amazon has big connections to the CIA and the Pentagon. The plan I have long described went like this:

1. Employ military technology to establish the Internet.

2. Sell the Internet as a place where people can freely communicate without censorship and allow that to happen until the Net becomes the central and irreversible pillar of human society. If the Internet had been highly censored from the start many would have rejected it.

3. Fund and manipulate major corporations into being to control the circulation of information on your Internet using cover stories about

geeks in garages to explain how they came about. Give them unlimited funds to expand rapidly with no need to make a profit for years while non-Cult companies who need to balance the books cannot compete. You know that in these circumstances your Googles, YouTubes, Facebooks and Amazons are going to secure near monopolies by either crushing or buying up the opposition.

4. Allow freedom of expression on both the Internet and communication platforms to draw people in until the Internet is the central and irreversible pillar of human society and your communication corporations have reached a stage of near monopoly domination.

5. Then unleash your always-planned frenzy of censorship on the basis of 'where else are you going to go?' and continue to expand that until nothing remains that the Cult does not want its human targets to see.

The process was timed to hit the 'Covid' hoax to ensure the best chance possible of controlling the narrative which they knew they had to do at all costs. They were, after all, about to unleash a 'deadly virus' that didn't really exist. If you do that in an environment of free-flowing information and opinion you would be dead in the water before you could say Gates is a psychopath. The network was in place through which the Cult-created-and-owned World Health Organization could dictate the 'Covid' narrative and response policy slavishly supported by Cult-owned Internet communication giants and mainstream media while those telling a different story were censored. Google, YouTube, Facebook and Twitter openly announced that they would do this. What else would we expect from Cult-owned operations like Facebook which former executives have confirmed set out to make the platform more addictive than cigarettes and coldly manipulates emotions of its users to sow division between people and groups and scramble the minds of the young? If Zuckerberg lives out the rest of his life without going to jail for crimes against humanity, and most emphatically against the young, it will be a travesty of justice. Still, no matter, cause and effect will catch up with him eventually and the same with Sergey Brin and Larry Page at Google with its CEO Sundar Pichai who fix the Google search results to promote Cult narratives and hide the opposition. Put the same key words into Google and other search engines like DuckDuckGo and you will see how different results can be. Wikipedia is another intensely biased 'encyclopaedia' which skews its content to the Cult agenda. YouTube links to Wikipedia's version of 'Covid' and 'climate change' on video pages in which experts in their field offer a different opinion (even that is increasingly rare with Wojcicki censorship). Into this 'Covid' silence-them network must be added government media censors, sorry 'regulators', such as Ofcom in the UK which imposed tyrannical restrictions on British broadcasters that had the effect of banning me from ever appearing. Just to debate with me about my evidence and views on 'Covid' would mean breaking the fascistic impositions of Ofcom and its CEO career government bureaucrat Melanie Dawes. Gutless British broadcasters tremble at the very thought of fascist Ofcom.

Psychos behind 'Covid'

The reason for the 'Covid' catastrophe in all its facets and forms can be seen by whom and what is driving the policies worldwide in such a coordinated way. Decisions are not being made to protect health, but to target psychology. The dominant group guiding and 'advising' government policy are not medical professionals. They are psychologists and behavioural scientists. Every major country has its own version of this phenomenon and I'll use the British example to show how it works. In many ways the British version has been affecting the wider world in the form of the huge behaviour manipulation network in the UK which operates in other countries. The network involves private companies, government, intelligence and military. The Cabinet Office is at the centre of the government 'Covid' Psyop and part-owns, with 'innovation charity' Nesta, the Behavioural Insights Team (BIT) which claims to be independent of government but patently isn't. The BIT was established in 2010 and its job is to manipulate the psyche of the population to acquiesce to government demands and so much more. It is also known as the 'Nudge Unit', a name inspired by the 2009 book by two ultra-Zionists, Cass Sunstein and Richard Thaler, called *Nudge: Improving Decisions About Health, Wealth, and Happiness*. The book, as with the Behavioural Insights Team, seeks to 'nudge' behaviour (manipulate it) to make the public follow patterns of action and perception that suit those in authority (the Cult). Sunstein is so skilled at this that he advises the World Health Organization and the UK Behavioural Insights Team and was Administrator of the White House Office of Information and Regulatory Affairs in the Obama administration. Biden appointed him to the Department of Homeland Security – another ultra-Zionist in the fold to oversee new immigration laws which is another policy the Cult wants to control. Sunstein is desperate to silence anyone exposing conspiracies and co-authored a 2008 report on the subject in which suggestions were offered to ban 'conspiracy theorizing' or impose 'some kind of tax, financial or otherwise, on those who disseminate such theories'. I guess a psychiatrist's chair is out of the question?

Sunstein's mate Richard Thaler, an 'academic affiliate' of the UK

Behavioural Insights Team, is a proponent of 'behavioural economics' which is defined as the study of 'the effects of psychological, cognitive, emotional, cultural and social factors on the decisions of individuals and institutions'. Study the effects so they can be manipulated to be what you want them to be. Other leading names in the development of behavioural economics are ultra-Zionists Daniel Kahneman and Robert J. Shiller and they, with Thaler, won the Nobel Memorial Prize in Economic Sciences for their work in this field. The Behavioural Insights Team is operating at the heart of the UK government and has expanded globally through partnerships with several universities including Harvard, Oxford, Cambridge, University College London (UCL) and Pennsylvania. They claim to have 'trained' (reframed) 20,000 civil servants and run more than 750 projects involving 400 randomised controlled trials in dozens of countries' as another version of mind reframers Common Purpose. BIT works from its office in New York with cities and their agencies, as well as other partners, across the United States and Canada – this is a company part-owned by the British government Cabinet Office. An executive order by President Cult-servant Obama established a US Social and Behavioral Sciences Team in 2015. They all have the same reason for being and that's to brainwash the population directly and by brainwashing those in positions of authority.

'Covid' mind game

Another prime aspect of the UK mind-control network is the 'independent' [joke] Scientific Pandemic Insights Group on Behaviours (SPI-B) which 'provides behavioural science advice aimed at anticipating and helping people adhere to interventions that are recommended by medical or epidemiological experts'. That means manipulating public perception and behaviour to do whatever government tells them to do. It's disgusting and if they really want the public to be 'safe' this lot should all be under lock and key. According to the government website SPI-B consists of 'behavioural scientists, health and social psychologists, anthropologists and historians' and advises the Whitty-Vallance-led Scientific Advisory Group for Emergencies (SAGE) which in turn advises the government on 'the science' (it doesn't) and 'Covid' policy. When politicians say they are being guided by 'the science' this is the rabble in each country they are talking about and that 'science' is dominated by behaviour manipulators to enforce government fascism through public compliance. The Behaviour Insight Team is headed by psychologist David Solomon Halpern, a visiting professor at King's College London, and connects with a national and global web of other civilian and military organisations as the Cult moves towards its goal of fusing them into one fascistic whole in every country through its 'Fusion

Doctrine'. The behaviour manipulation network involves, but is not confined to, the Foreign Office; National Security Council; government communications headquarters (GCHQ); MI5; MI6; the Cabinet Office-based Media Monitoring Unit; and the Rapid Response Unit which 'monitors digital trends to spot emerging issues; including misinformation and disinformation; and identifies the best way to respond'.

There is also the 77th Brigade of the UK military which operates like the notorious Israeli military's Unit 8200 in manipulating information and discussion on the Internet by posing as members of the public to promote the narrative and discredit those who challenge it. Here we have the military seeking to manipulate *domestic* public opinion while the Nazis in government are fine with that. Conservative Member of Parliament Tobias Ellwood, an advocate of lockdown and control through 'vaccine passports', is a Lieutenant Colonel reservist in the 77th Brigade which connects with the military operation jHub, the 'innovation centre' for the Ministry of Defence and Strategic Command. jHub has also been involved with the civilian National Health Service (NHS) in 'symptom tracing' the population. The NHS is a key part of this mind control network and produced a document in December, 2020, explaining to staff how to use psychological manipulation with different groups and ages to get them to have the DNA-manipulating 'Covid vaccine' that's designed to cumulatively rewrite human genetics. The document, called 'Optimising Vaccination Roll Out – Do's and Dont's for all messaging, documents and "communications" in the widest sense', was published by NHS England and the NHS Improvement *Behaviour Change Unit* in partnership with Public Health England and Warwick Business School. I hear the mantra about 'save the NHS' and 'protect the NHS' when we need to scrap the NHS and start again. The current version is far too corrupt, far too anti-human and totally compromised by Cult operatives and their assets. UK government broadcast media censor Ofcom will connect into this web – as will the BBC with its tremendous Ofcom influence – to control what the public see and hear and dictate mass perception. Nuremberg trials must include personnel from all these organisations.

The fear factor

The 'Covid' hoax has led to the creation of the UK Cabinet Office-connected Joint Biosecurity Centre (JBC) which is officially described as providing 'expert advice on pandemics' using its independent [all Cult operations are 'independent'] analytical function to provide real-time analysis about infection outbreaks to identify and respond to outbreaks of Covid-19'. Another role is to advise the government on a response to spikes in infections – 'for example by closing schools or workplaces in local areas where infection levels have risen'. Put another way, promoting the Cult agenda. The Joint Biosecurity Centre is modelled on the Joint Terrorism Analysis Centre which analyses intelligence to set 'terrorism threat levels' and here again you see the fusion of civilian and military operations and intelligence that has led to military intelligence producing documents about 'vaccine hesitancy' and how it can be combated. Domestic civilian matters and opinions should not be the business of the military. The Joint Biosecurity Centre is headed by Tom Hurd, director general of the Office for Security and Counter-Terrorism from the establishment-to-its-fingertips Hurd family. His father is former Foreign Secretary Douglas Hurd. How coincidental that Tom Hurd went to the elite Eton College and Oxford University with Boris Johnson. Imperial College with its ridiculous computer modeller Neil Ferguson will connect with this gigantic web that will itself interconnect with similar set-ups in other major and not so major countries. Compared with this Cult network the politicians, be they Boris Johnson, Donald Trump or Joe Biden, are bit-part players 'following the science'. The network of psychologists was on the 'Covid' case from the start with the aim of generating maximum fear of the 'virus' to ensure compliance by the population. A government behavioural science group known as SPI-B produced a paper in March, 2020, for discussion by the main government science advisory group known as SAGE. It was headed 'Options for increasing adherence to social distancing measures' and it said the following in a section headed 'Persuasion':

- A substantial number of people still do not feel sufficiently personally threatened; it could be that they are reassured by the low death rate in their demographic group, although levels of concern may be rising. Having a good understanding of the risk has been found to be positively associated with adoption of COVID-19 social distancing measures in Hong Kong.

- The perceived level of personal threat needs to be increased among those who are complacent, using hard-hitting evaluation of options for increasing social distancing emotional messaging. To be effective this must also empower people by making clear the actions they can take to reduce the threat.

- Responsibility to others: There seems to be insufficient understanding of, or feelings of responsibility about, people's role in transmitting the infection to others … Messaging about actions need to be framed positively in terms of protecting oneself and the community, and increase confidence that they will be effective.

- Some people will be more persuaded by appeals to play by the rules, some by duty to the community, and some to personal risk. All these different approaches are needed. The messaging also needs to take account of the realities of different people's lives. Messaging needs to take account of the different motivational levers and circumstances of different people.

All this could be achieved the SPI-B psychologists said by *using the media to increase the sense of personal threat* which translates as terrify the shit out of the population, including children, so they all do what we want. That's not happened has it? Those excuses for 'journalists' who wouldn't know journalism if it bit them on the arse (the great majority) have played their crucial part in serving this Cult-government Psyop to enslave their own kids and grandkids. How they live with themselves I have no idea. The psychological war has been underpinned by constant government 'Covid' propaganda in almost every television and radio ad break, plus the Internet and print media, which has pounded out the fear with taxpayers footing the bill for their own programming. The result has been people terrified of a 'virus' that doesn't exist or one with a tiny fatality rate even if you believe it does. People walk down the street and around the shops wearing face-nappies damaging their health and psychology while others report those who refuse to be that naïve to the police who turn up in their own face-nappies. I had a cameraman come to my flat and he was so frightened of 'Covid' he came in wearing a mask and refused to shake my hand in case he caught something. He had – naïveitis – and the thought that he worked in the mainstream media was both depressing and made his behaviour perfectly explainable. The fear which has gripped the minds of so many and frozen them into compliance has been carefully cultivated by these psychologists who are really psychopaths. If lives get destroyed and a lot of young people commit suicide it shows our plan is working. SPI-B then turned to compulsion on the public to comply. 'With adequate preparation, rapid change can be achieved', it said. Some countries had introduced mandatory self-isolation on a wide scale without evidence of major public unrest and a large majority of the UK's population appeared to be supportive of more coercive measures with 64 percent of adults saying they would support putting London under a lockdown (watch the 'polls' which are designed to make people believe that public opinion is in favour or against whatever the subject in hand).

For 'aggressive protective measures' to be effective, the SPI-B paper said, special attention should be devoted to those population groups that are more at risk. Translated from the Orwellian this means making the rest of population feel guilty for not protecting the 'vulnerable' such as old people which the Cult and its agencies were about to kill on an industrial scale with lockdown, lack of treatment and the Gates 'vaccine'. Psychopath psychologists sold their guilt-trip so comprehensively that Los Angeles County Supervisor Hilda Solis reported that children were apologising (from a distance) to their parents and grandparents for bringing 'Covid' into their homes and getting them sick. '… These apologies are just some of the last words that loved ones will ever hear as they die alone,' she said. Gut-wrenchingly Solis then used this childhood tragedy to tell children to stay at home and 'keep your loved ones alive'. Imagine heaping such potentially life-long guilt on a kid when it has absolutely nothing to do with them. These people are deeply disturbed and the psychologists behind this even more so.

Uncivil war – divide and rule

Professional mind-controllers at SPI-B wanted the media to increase a sense of responsibility to others (do as you're told) and promote 'positive messaging' for those actions while in contrast to invoke 'social disapproval' by the unquestioning, obedient, community of anyone with a mind of their own. Again the compliant Goebbels-like media obliged. This is an old, old, trick employed by tyrannies the world over throughout human history. You get the target population to keep the target population in line – *your* line. SPI-B said this could 'play an important role in preventing anti-social behaviour or discouraging failure to enact pro-social behaviour'. For 'anti-social' in the Orwellian parlance of SPI-B see any behaviour that government doesn't approve. SPI-B recommendations said that 'social disapproval' should be accompanied by clear messaging and promotion of strong collective identity – hence the government and celebrity mantra of 'we're all in this together'. Sure we are. The mind doctors have such contempt for their targets that they think some clueless comedian, actor or singer telling them to do what the government wants will be enough to win them over. We have had UK comedian Lenny Henry, actor Michael Caine and singer Elton John wheeled out to serve the propagandists by urging people to have the DNA-manipulating 'Covid' non-'vaccine'. The role of Henry and fellow black celebrities in seeking to coax a 'vaccine' reluctant black community into doing the government's will was especially stomach-turning. An emotion-manipulating script and carefully edited video featuring these black 'celebs' was such an insult to the intelligence of black people and where's the self-respect of those involved selling their souls to a fascist government agenda? Henry said he heard black people's 'legitimate worries and concerns', but people must 'trust the facts' when they were doing exactly that by not having the 'vaccine'. They had to include the obligatory reference to Black Lives Matter with the line … 'Don't let coronavirus cost even more black lives – because we matter'. My god, it was pathetic. 'I know the vaccine is safe and what it does.' How? 'I'm a comedian and it says so in my script.'

SPI-B said social disapproval needed to be carefully managed to avoid victimisation, scapegoating and misdirected criticism, but they knew that their 'recommendations' would lead to exactly that and the media were specifically used to stir-up the divide-and-conquer hostility. Those who conform like good little baa, baas, are praised while those who have seen through the tidal wave of lies are 'Covidiots'. The awake have been abused by the fast asleep for not conforming to fascism and impositions that the awake know are designed to endanger their health, dehumanise them, and tear asunder the very fabric of human society. We have had the curtain-twitchers and morons reporting neighbours and others to the face-nappied police for breaking 'Covid rules' with fascist police delighting in posting links and phone numbers where this could be done. The Cult cannot impose its will without a compliant police and military or a compliant population willing to play their part in enslaving themselves and their kids. The words of a pastor in Nazi Germany are so appropriate today:

> First they came for the socialists and I did not speak out because I was not a socialist.
>
> Then they came for the trade unionists and I did not speak out because I was not a trade unionist.
>
> Then they came for the Jews and I did not speak out because I was not a Jew.
>
> Then they came for me and there was no one left to speak for me.

Those who don't learn from history are destined to repeat it and so many are.

'Covid' rules: Rewiring the mind

With the background laid out to this gigantic national and global web of psychological manipulation we can put 'Covid' rules into a clear and sinister perspective. Forget the claims about protecting health. 'Covid' rules are about dismantling the human mind, breaking the human spirit, destroying self-respect, and then putting Humpty Dumpty together again as a servile, submissive slave. Social isolation through lockdown and distancing have devastating effects on the human psyche as the psychological psychopaths well know and that's the real reason for them. Humans need contact with each other, discourse, closeness and touch, or they eventually, and literarily, go crazy. Masks, which I will address at some length, fundamentally add to the effects of isolation and the Cult agenda to dehumanise and de-individualise the population. To do this while knowing – in fact *seeking* – this outcome is the very epitome of evil and psychologists involved in this *are* the epitome of evil. They must like all the rest of the Cult demons and their assets stand trial for crimes against humanity on a scale that defies the imagination. Psychopaths in uniform use isolation to break enemy troops and agents and make them subservient and submissive to tell what they know. The technique is rightly considered a form of torture and torture is most certainly what has been imposed on the human population.

Clinically-insane American psychologist Harry Harlow became famous for his isolation experiments in the 1950s in which he separated baby monkeys from their mothers and imprisoned them for months on end in a metal container or 'pit of despair'. They soon began to show mental distress and depression as any idiot could have predicted. Harlow put other monkeys in steel chambers for three, six or twelve months while denying them any contact with animals or humans. He said that the effects of total social isolation for six months were 'so devastating and debilitating that we had assumed initially that twelve months of isolation would not produce any additional decrement'; but twelve months of isolation 'almost obliterated the animals socially'. This is what the Cult and its psychopaths are doing to you and your children. Even monkeys in partial isolation in which they were not allowed to form relationships with other monkeys became 'aggressive and hostile, not only to others, but also towards their own bodies'. We have seen this in the young as a consequence of lockdown. UK government psychopaths launched a public relations campaign telling people not to hug each other even after they received the 'Covid-19 vaccine' which we were told with more lies would allow a return to 'normal life'. A government source told *The Telegraph*: 'It will be along the lines that it is great that you have been vaccinated, but if you are going to visit your family and hug your grandchildren there is a chance you are going to infect people you love.' The source was apparently speaking from a secure psychiatric facility. Janet Lord, director of Birmingham University's Institute of Inflammation and Ageing, said that parents and grandparents should avoid hugging their children. Well, how can I put it, Ms Lord? Fuck off. Yep, that'll do.

Destroying the kids – where are the parents?

Observe what has happened to people enslaved and isolated by lockdown as suicide and self-harm has soared worldwide, particularly among the young denied the freedom to associate with their friends. A study of 49,000 people in English-speaking countries concluded that almost half of young adults are at clinical risk of mental health disorders. A national survey in America of 1,000 currently enrolled high school and college students found that 5 percent reported attempting suicide during the pandemic. Data from the US CDC's National Syndromic Surveillance Program from January 1st to October 17th, 2020, revealed a *31 percent* increase in mental health issues among adolescents aged 12 to 17 compared with 2019. The CDC reported that America in general suffered the biggest drop in life expectancy since World War Two as it fell by a year in the first half of 2020 as a result of 'deaths of despair' – overdoses and suicides. Deaths of despair have leapt by more than 20 percent during lockdown and include the highest number of fatal overdoses ever recorded in a single year – 81,000. Internet addiction is another consequence of being isolated at home which lowers interest in physical activities as kids fall into inertia and what's the point? Children and young people are losing hope and giving up on life, sometimes literally. A 14-year-old boy killed himself in Maryland because he had 'given up' when his school district didn't reopen; an 11-year-old boy shot himself during a zoom class; a teenager in Maine succumbed to the isolation of the 'pandemic' when he ended his life after experiencing a disrupted senior year at school. Children as young as nine have taken their life and all these stories can be repeated around the world. Careers are being destroyed before they start and that includes those in sport in which promising youngsters have not been able to take part. The plan of the psycho-psychologists is working all right. Researchers at Cambridge University found that lockdowns cause significant harm to children's mental health. Their study was published in the *Archives of Disease in Childhood*, and followed 168 children aged between 7 and 11. The researchers concluded:

> During the UK lockdown, children's depression symptoms have increased substantially, relative to before lockdown. The scale of this effect has direct relevance for the continuation of different elements of lockdown policy, such as complete or partial school closures …

> … Specifically, we observed a statistically significant increase in ratings of depression, with a medium-to-large effect size. Our findings emphasise the need to incorporate the potential impact of lockdown on child mental health in planning the ongoing response to the global pandemic and the recovery from it.

Not a chance when the Cult's psycho-psychologists were getting exactly what they wanted. The UK's Royal College of Paediatrics and Child Health has urged parents to look for signs of eating disorders in children and young people after a three to four fold increase. Specialists say the 'pandemic' is a major reason behind the rise. You don't say. The College said isolation from friends during school closures, exam cancellations, loss of extra-curricular activities like sport, and an increased use of social media were all contributory factors along with fears about the virus (psycho-psychologists again), family finances, and students being forced to quarantine. Doctors said young people were becoming severely ill by the time they were seen with 'Covid' regulations reducing face-to-face consultations. Nor is it only the young that have been devastated by the psychopaths. Like all bullies and cowards the Cult is targeting the young, elderly, weak and infirm. A typical story was told by a British lady called Lynn Parker who was not allowed to visit her husband in 2020 for the last ten and half months of his life 'when he needed me most' between March 20th and when he died on December 19th. This vacates the criminal and enters the territory of evil. The emotional impact on the immune system alone is immense as are the number of people of all ages worldwide who have died as a result of Cult-demanded, Gates-demanded, lockdowns.

Isolation is torture

The experience of imposing solitary confinement on millions of prisoners around the world has shown how a large percentage become 'actively psychotic and/or acutely suicidal'. Social isolation has been found to trigger 'a specific psychiatric syndrome, characterized by hallucinations; panic attacks; overt paranoia; diminished impulse control; hypersensitivity to external stimuli; and difficulties with thinking, concentration and memory'. Juan Mendez, a United Nations rapporteur (investigator), said that isolation is a form of torture. Research has shown that even after isolation prisoners find it far more difficult to make social connections and I remember chatting to a shop assistant after one lockdown who told me that when her young son met another child again he had no idea how to act or what to do. Hannah Flanagan, Director of Emergency Services at Journey Mental Health Center in Dane County, Wisconsin, said: 'The specificity about Covid social distancing and isolation that we've come across as contributing factors to the suicides are really new to us this year.' But they are not new to those that devised them. They are getting the effect they want as the population is psychologically dismantled to be rebuilt in a totally different way. Children and the young are particularly targeted. They will be the adults when the full-on fascist AI-controlled technocracy is planned to be imposed and they are being prepared to meekly submit. At the same time older people who still have a memory of what life was like before – and how fascist the new normal really is – are being deleted. You are going to see efforts to turn the young against the old to support this geriatric genocide. Hannah Flanagan said the big increase in suicide in her county proved that social isolation is not only harmful, but deadly. Studies have shown that isolation from others is one of the main risk factors in suicide and even more so with women. Warnings that lockdown could create a 'perfect storm' for suicide were ignored. After all this was one of the *reasons* for lockdown. Suicide, however, is only the most extreme of isolation consequences. There are many others. Dr Dhruv Khullar, assistant professor of healthcare policy at Weill Cornell Medical College, said in a *New York Times* article in 2016 long before the fake 'pandemic':

A wave of new research suggests social separation is bad for us. Individuals with less social connection have disrupted sleep patterns, altered immune systems, more inflammation and higher levels of stress hormones. One recent study found that isolation increases the risk of heart disease by 29 percent and stroke by 32 percent. Another analysis that pooled data from 70 studies and 3.4 million people found that socially isolated individuals had a 30 percent higher risk of dying in the next seven years, and that this effect was largest in middle age.

Loneliness can accelerate cognitive decline in older adults, and isolated individuals are twice as likely to die prematurely as those with more robust social interactions. These effects start early: Socially isolated children have significantly poorer health 20 years later, even after controlling for other factors. All told, loneliness is as important a risk factor for early death as obesity and smoking.

There you have proof from that one article alone four years before 2020 that those who have enforced lockdown, social distancing and isolation knew what the effect would be and that is even more so with professional psychologists that have been driving the policy across the globe. We can go back even further to the years 2000 and 2003 and the start of a major study on the effects of isolation on health by Dr Janine Gronewold and Professor Dirk M. Hermann at the University Hospital in Essen, Germany, who analysed data on 4,316 people with an average age of 59 who were recruited for the long-term research project. They found that socially isolated people are more than 40 percent more likely to have a heart attack, stroke, or other major cardiovascular event and nearly 50 percent more likely to die from any cause. Given the financial Armageddon unleashed by lockdown we should note that the study found a relationship between increased cardiovascular risk and lack of financial support. After excluding other factors social isolation was still connected to a 44 percent increased risk of cardiovascular problems and a 47 percent increased risk of death by any cause. Lack of financial support was associated with a 30 percent increase in the risk of cardiovascular health events. Dr Gronewold said it had been known for some time that feeling lonely or lacking contact with close friends and family can have an impact on physical health and the study had shown that having strong social relationships is of high importance for heart health. Gronewold said they didn't understand yet why people who are socially isolated have such poor health outcomes, but this was obviously a worrying finding, particularly during these times of prolonged social distancing. Well, it can be explained on many levels. You only have to identify the point in the body where people feel loneliness and missing people they are parted from – it's in the centre of the chest where they feel the ache of loneliness and the ache of missing people. 'My heart aches for you' … 'My heart aches for some company.' I will explain this more in the chapter Escaping Wetiko, but when you realise that the body is the mind – they are expressions of each other – the reason why state of the mind dictates state of the body becomes clear.

American psychologist Ranjit Powar was highlighting the effects of lockdown isolation as early as April, 2020. She said humans have evolved to be social creatures and are wired to live in interactive groups. Being isolated from family, friends and colleagues could be unbalancing and traumatic for most people and could result in short or even long-term psychological and physical health problems. An increase in levels of anxiety, aggression, depression, forgetfulness and hallucinations were possible psychological effects of isolation. 'Mental conditions may be precipitated for those with underlying pre-existing susceptibilities and show up in many others without any pre-condition.' Powar said personal relationships helped us cope with stress and if we lost this outlet for letting off steam the result can be a big emotional void which, for an average person, was difficult to deal with. 'Just a few days of isolation can cause increased levels of anxiety and depression' – so what the hell has been the effect on the global population of *18 months* of this at the time of writing? Powar said: 'Add to it the looming threat of a dreadful disease being repeatedly hammered in through the media and you have a recipe for many shades of mental and physical distress.' For those with a house and a garden it is easy to forget that billions have had to endure lockdown isolation in tiny overcrowded flats and apartments with nowhere to go outside. The psychological and physical consequences of this are unimaginable and with lunatic and abusive partners and parents the consequences have led to tremendous increases in domestic and child abuse and alcoholism as people seek to shut out the horror. Ranjit Powar said:

Staying in a confined space with family is not all a rosy picture for everyone. It can be extremely oppressive and claustrophobic for large low-income families huddled together in small single-room houses. Children here are not lucky enough to have many board/electronic games or books to keep them occupied.

Add to it the deep insecurity of running out of funds for food and basic necessities. On the other hand, there are people with dysfunctional family dynamics, such as domineering, abusive or alcoholic partners, siblings or parents which makes staying home a period of trial. Incidence of suicide and physical abuse against women has shown a worldwide increase. Heightened anxiety and depression also affect a person's immune system, making them more susceptible to illness.

To think that Powar's article was published on April 11th, 2020.

Six-feet fantasy

Social (unsocial) distancing demanded that people stay six feet or two metres apart. UK government advisor Robert Dingwall from the New and Emerging Respiratory Virus Threats Advisory Group said in a radio interview that the two-metre rule was 'conjured up out of nowhere' and was not based on science. No, it was not based on *medical* science, but it didn't come out of nowhere. The distance related to *psychological* science. Six feet/two metres was adopted in many countries and we were told by people like the criminal Anthony Fauci and his ilk that it was founded on science. Many schools could not reopen because they did not have the space for six-feet distancing. Then in March, 2021, after a year of six-feet 'science', a study published in the *Journal of Infectious Diseases* involving more than 500,000 students and almost 100,000 staff over 16 weeks revealed no significant difference in 'Covid' cases between six feet and three feet and Fauci changed his tune. Now three feet was okay. There is no difference between six feet and three *inches* when there is no 'virus' and they got away with six feet for psychological reasons for as long as they could. I hear journalists and others talk about 'unintended consequences' of lockdown. They are not *unintended* at all; they have been coldly-calculated for a specific outcome of human control and that's why super-psychopaths like Gates have called for them so vehemently. Super-psychopath psychologists have demanded them and psychopathic or clueless, spineless, politicians have gone along with them by 'following the science'. But it's not science at all. 'Science' is not what is; it's only what people can be manipulated to believe it is. The whole 'Covid' catastrophe is founded on mind control. Three word or three statement mantras issued by the UK government are a well-known mind control technique and so we've had 'Stay home/protect the NHS/save lives', 'Stay alert/control the virus/save lives' and 'hands/face/space'. One of the most vocal proponents of extreme 'Covid' rules in the UK has been Professor Susan Michie, a member of the British Communist Party, who is not a medical professional. Michie is the director of the Centre for Behaviour Change at University College London. She is a *behavioural psychologist* and another filthy rich 'Marxist' who praised China's draconian lockdown. She was known by fellow students at Oxford University as 'Stalin's nanny' for her extreme Marxism. Michie is an influential member of the UK government's Scientific Advisory Group for Emergencies (SAGE) and behavioural manipulation groups which have dominated 'Covid' policy. She is a consultant adviser to the World Health Organization on 'Covid-19' and behaviour. Why the hell are lockdowns anything to do with her when they are claimed to be about health? Why does a behavioural psychologist from a group charged with changing the behaviour of the public want lockdown, human isolation and mandatory masks? Does that question really need an answer? Michie *absolutely* has to explain herself before a Nuremberg court when humanity takes back its world again and even more so when you see the consequences of masks that she demands are compulsory. This is a Michie classic:

> The benefits of getting primary school children to wear masks is that regardless of what little degree of transmission is occurring in those age groups it could help normalise the practice. Young children wearing masks may be more likely to get their families to accept masks.

Those words alone should carry a prison sentence when you ponder on the callous disregard for children involved and what a statement it makes about the mind and motivations of Susan Michie. What a lovely lady and what she said there encapsulates the mentality of the psychopaths behind the 'Covid' horror. Let us compare what Michie said with a countrywide study in Germany published at researchsquare.com involving 25,000 school children and 17,854 health complaints submitted by parents. Researchers found that masks are harming children physically, psychologically, and behaviourally with 24 health issues associated with mask wearing. They include: shortness of breath (29.7%); dizziness (26.4%); increased headaches (53%); difficulty concentrating (50%); drowsiness or fatigue (37%); and malaise (42%). Nearly a third of children experienced more sleep issues than before and a quarter developed new fears. Researchers found health issues and other impairments in 68 percent of masked children covering their faces for an average of 4.5 hours a day. Hundreds of those taking part experienced accelerated respiration, tightness in the chest, weakness, and short-term impairment of consciousness. A reminder of what Michie said again:

> The benefits of getting primary school children to wear masks is that regardless of what little degree of transmission is occurring in those age groups it could help normalise the practice. Young children wearing masks may be more likely to get their families to accept masks.

Psychopaths in government and psychology now have children and
young people – plus all the adults – wearing masks for hours on end
while clueless teachers impose the will of the psychopaths on the young
they should be protecting. What the hell are parents doing?

Cult lab rats

We have some schools already imposing on students microchipped
buzzers that activate when they get 'too close' to their pals in the way
they do with lab rats. How apt. To the Cult and its brain-dead servants
our children *are* lab rats being conditioned to be unquestioning,
dehumanised slaves for the rest of their lives. Children and young
people are being weaned and frightened away from the most natural
human instincts including closeness and touch. I have tracked in the
books over the years how schools were banning pupils from greeting
each other with a hug and the whole Cult-induced MeToo movement
has terrified men and boys from a relaxed and natural interaction with
female friends and work colleagues to the point where many men try
never to be in a room alone with a woman that's not their partner.
Airhead celebrities have as always played their virtue-signalling part in
making this happen with their gross exaggeration. For every monster
like Harvey Weinstein there are at least tens of thousands of men that
don't treat women like that; but everyone must be branded the same and
policy changed for them as well as the monster. I am going to be using
the word 'dehumanise' many times in this chapter because that is what
the Cult is seeking to do and it goes very deep as we shall see. Don't let
them kid you that social distancing is planned to end one day. That's not
the idea. We are seeing more governments and companies funding and
producing wearable gadgets to keep people apart and they would not be
doing that if this was meant to be short-term. A tech start-up company
backed by GCHQ, the British Intelligence and military surveillance
headquarters, has created a social distancing wrist sensor that alerts
people when they get too close to others. The CIA has also supported
tech companies developing similar devices. The wearable sensor was
developed by Tended, one of a number of start-up companies supported
by GCHQ (see the CIA and DARPA). The device can be worn on the
wrist or as a tag on the waistband and will vibrate whenever someone
wearing the device breaches social distancing and gets anywhere near
natural human contact. The company had a lucky break in that it was
developing a distancing sensor when the 'Covid' hoax arrived which
immediately provided a potentially enormous market. How fortunate.
The government in big-time Cult-controlled Ontario in Canada is
investing $2.5 million in wearable contact tracing technology that 'will
alert users if they may have been exposed to the Covid-19 in the

workplace and will beep or vibrate if they are within six feet of another person'. Facedrive Inc., the technology company behind this, was founded in 2016 with funding from the Ontario Together Fund and obviously they, too, had a prophet on the board of directors. The human surveillance and control technology is called TraceSCAN and would be worn by the human cyborgs in places such as airports, workplaces, construction sites, care homes and ... *schools.*

I emphasise schools with children and young people the prime targets. You know what is planned for society as a whole if you keep your eyes on the schools. They have always been places where the state program the next generation of slaves to be its compliant worker-ants – or Woker-ants these days; but in the mist of the 'Covid' madness they have been transformed into mind laboratories on a scale never seen before. Teachers and head teachers are just as programmed as the kids – often more so. Children are kept apart from human interaction by walk lanes, classroom distancing, staggered meal times, masks, and the rolling-out of buzzer systems. Schools are now physically laid out as a laboratory maze for lab-rats. Lunatics at a school in Anchorage, Alaska, who should be prosecuted for child abuse, took away desks and forced children to kneel (know your place) on a mat for five hours a day while wearing a mask and using their chairs as a desk. How this was supposed to impact on a 'virus' only these clinically insane people can tell you and even then it would be clap-trap. The school banned recess (interaction), art classes (creativity), and physical exercise (getting body and mind moving out of inertia). Everyone behind this outrage should be in jail or better still a mental institution. The behavioural manipulators are all for this dystopian approach to schools. Professor Susan Michie, the mind-doctor and British Communist Party member, said it was wrong to say that schools were safe. They had to be made so by 'distancing', masks and ventilation (sitting all day in the cold). I must ask this lady round for dinner on a night I know I am going to be out and not back for weeks. She probably wouldn't be able to make it, anyway, with all the visits to her own psychologist she must have block-booked.

Masking identity

I know how shocking it must be for you that a behaviour manipulator like Michie wants everyone to wear masks which have long been a feature of mind-control programs like the infamous MKUltra in the United States, but, there we are. We live and learn. I spent many years from 1996 to right across the millennium researching mind control in detail on both sides of the Atlantic and elsewhere. I met a large number of mind-control survivors and many had been held captive in body and mind by MKUltra. MK stands for mind-control, but employs the

German spelling in deference to the Nazis spirited out of Germany at the end of World War Two by Operation Paperclip in which the US authorities, with help from the Vatican, transported Nazi mind-controllers and engineers to America to continue their work. Many of them were behind the creation of NASA and they included Nazi scientist and SS officer Wernher von Braun who swapped designing V-2 rockets to bombard London with designing the Saturn V rockets that powered the NASA moon programme's Apollo craft. I think I may have mentioned that the Cult has no borders. Among Paperclip escapees was Josef Mengele, the Angel of Death in the Nazi concentration camps where he conducted mind and genetic experiments on children often using twins to provide a control twin to measure the impact of his 'work' on the other. If you want to observe the Cult mentality in all its extremes of evil then look into the life of Mengele. I have met many people who suffered mercilessly under Mengele in the United States where he operated under the name Dr Greene and became a stalwart of MKUltra programming and torture. Among his locations was the underground facility in the Mojave Desert in California called the China Lake Naval Weapons Station which is almost entirely below the surface. My books *The Biggest Secret*, *Children of the Matrix* and *The Perception Deception* have the detailed background to MKUltra.

The best-known MKUltra survivor is American Cathy O'Brien. I first met her and her late partner Mark Phillips at a conference in Colorado in 1996. Mark helped her escape and deprogram from decades of captivity in an offshoot of MKUltra known as Project Monarch in which 'sex slaves' were provided for the rich and famous including Father George Bush, Dick Cheney and the Clintons. Read Cathy and Mark's book *Trance-Formation of America* and if you are new to this you will be shocked to the core. I read it in 1996 shortly before, with the usual synchronicity of my life, I found myself given a book table at the conference right next to hers. MKUltra never ended despite being very publicly exposed (only a small part of it) in the 1970s and continues in other guises. I am still in touch with Cathy. She contacted me during 2020 after masks became compulsory in many countries to tell me how they were used as part of MKUltra programming. I had been observing 'Covid regulations' and the relationship between authority and public for months. I saw techniques that I knew were employed on individuals in MKUltra being used on the global population. I had read many books and manuals on mind control including one called *Silent Weapons for Quiet Wars* which came to light in the 1980s and was a guide on how to perceptually program on a mass scale. 'Silent Weapons' refers to mind-control. I remembered a line from the manual as governments, medical authorities and law enforcement agencies have so obviously talked to – or rather at – the adult population since the 'Covid' hoax began as if they are children. The document said:

> If a person is spoken to by a T.V. advertiser as if he were a twelve-year-old, then, due to suggestibility, he will, with a certain probability, respond or react to that suggestion with the uncritical response of a twelve-year-old and will reach in to his economic reservoir and deliver its energy to buy that product on impulse when he passes it in the store.

That's why authority has spoken to adults like children since all this began.

Why did Michael Jackson wear masks?

Every aspect of the 'Covid' narrative has mind-control as its central theme. Cathy O'Brien wrote an article for davidicke.com about the connection between masks and mind control. Her daughter Kelly who I first met in the 1990s was born while Cathy was still held captive in MKUltra. Kelly was forced to wear a mask as part of her programming from the age of *two* to dehumanise her, target her sense of individuality and reduce the amount of oxygen her brain and body received. *Bingo.* This is the real reason for compulsory masks, why they have been enforced en masse, and why they seek to increase the number they demand you wear. First one, then two, with one disgraceful alleged 'doctor' recommending four which is nothing less than a death sentence. Where and how often they must be worn is being expanded for the purpose of mass mind control and damaging respiratory health which they can call 'Covid-19'. Canada's government headed by the man-child Justin Trudeau, says it's fine for children of two and older to wear masks. An insane 'study' in Italy involving just 47 children concluded there was no problem for babies as young as *four months* wearing them. Even after people were 'vaccinated' they were still told to wear masks by the criminal that is Anthony Fauci. Cathy wrote that mandating masks is allowing the authorities literally to control the air we breathe which is what was done in MKUltra. You might recall how the singer Michael Jackson wore masks and there is a reason for that. He was subjected to MKUltra mind control through Project Monarch and his psyche was scrambled by these simpletons. Cathy wrote:

> In MKUltra Project Monarch mind control, Michael Jackson had to wear a mask to silence his voice so he could not reach out for help. Remember how he developed that whisper voice when he wasn't singing? Masks control the mind from the outside in, like the redefining of words is doing. By controlling what we can and cannot say for fear of being labeled racist or beaten, for example, it ultimately controls thought that drives our words and ultimately actions (or lack thereof).

Likewise, a mask muffles our speech so that we are not heard, which controls voice … words … mind. This is Mind Control. Masks are an obvious mind control device, and I am disturbed so many people are complying on a global scale. Masks depersonalize while making a person feel as though they have no voice. It is a barrier to others. People who would never choose to comply but are forced to wear a mask in order to keep their job, and ultimately their family fed, are compromised. They often feel shame and are subdued. People have stopped talking with each other while media controls the narrative.

The 'no voice' theme has often become literal with train passengers told not to speak to each other in case they pass on the 'virus', singing banned for the same reason and bonkers California officials telling people riding roller coasters that they cannot shout and scream. Cathy said she heard every day from healed MKUltra survivors who cannot wear a mask without flashing back on ways their breathing was controlled – 'from ball gags and penises to water boarding'. She said that through the years when she saw images of people in China wearing masks 'due to pollution' that it was really to control their oxygen levels. 'I knew it was as much of a population control mechanism of depersonalisation as are burkas', she said. Masks are another Chinese communist/fascist method of control that has been swept across the West as the West becomes China at lightning speed since we entered 2020.

Mask-19

There are other reasons for mandatory masks and these include destroying respiratory health to call it 'Covid-19' and stunting brain development of children and the young. Dr Margarite Griesz-Brisson MD, PhD, is a Consultant Neurologist and Neurophysiologist and the Founder and Medical Director of the London Neurology and Pain Clinic. Her CV goes down the street and round the corner. She is clearly someone who cares about people and won't parrot the propaganda. Griesz-Brisson has a PhD in pharmacology, with special interest in neurotoxicology, environmental medicine, neuroregeneration and neuroplasticity (the way the brain can change in the light of information received). She went public in October, 2020, with a passionate warning about the effects of mask-wearing laws:

The reinhalation of our exhaled air will without a doubt create oxygen deficiency and a flooding of carbon dioxide. We know that the human brain is very sensitive to oxygen deprivation. There are nerve cells for example in the hippocampus that can't be longer than 3 minutes without oxygen – they cannot survive. The acute warning symptoms are headaches, drowsiness, dizziness, issues in concentration, slowing down of reaction time – reactions of the cognitive system.

Oh, I know, let's tell bus, truck and taxi drivers to wear them and people working machinery. How about pilots, doctors and police? Griesz-Brisson makes the important point that while the symptoms she mentions may fade as the body readjusts this does not alter the fact that people continue to operate in oxygen deficit with long list of potential consequences. She said it was well known that neurodegenerative diseases take years or decades to develop. 'If today you forget your phone number, the breakdown in your brain would have already started 20 or 30 years ago.' She said degenerative processes in your brain are getting amplified as your oxygen deprivation continues through wearing a mask. Nerve cells in the brain are unable to divide themselves normally in these circumstances and lost nerve cells will no longer be regenerated. 'What is gone is gone.' Now consider that people like shop workers and *schoolchildren* are wearing masks for hours every day. What in the name of sanity is going to be happening to them? 'I do not wear a mask, I need my brain to think', Griesz-Brisson said, 'I want to have a clear head when I deal with my patients and not be in a carbon dioxide-induced anaesthesia'. If you are told to wear a mask anywhere ask the organisation, police, store, whatever, for their risk assessment on the dangers and negative effects on mind and body of enforcing mask-wearing. They won't have one because it has never been done not even by government. All of them must be subject to class-action lawsuits as the consequences come to light. They don't do mask risk assessments for an obvious reason. They know what the conclusions would be and independent scientific studies that *have* been done tell a horror story of consequences.

'Masks are criminal'

Dr Griesz-Brisson said that for children and adolescents, masks are an absolute no-no. They had an extremely active and adaptive immune system and their brain was incredibly active with so much to learn. 'The child's brain, or the youth's brain, is thirsting for oxygen.' The more metabolically active an organ was, the more oxygen it required; and in children and adolescents every organ was metabolically active. Griesz-Brisson said that to deprive a child's or adolescent's brain of oxygen, or to restrict it in any way, was not only dangerous to their health, it was absolutely criminal. 'Oxygen deficiency inhibits the development of the brain, and the damage that has taken place as a result CANNOT be reversed.' Mind manipulators of MKUltra put masks on two-year-olds they wanted to neurologically rewire and you can see why. Griesz-Brisson said a child needs the brain to learn and the brain needs oxygen to function. 'We don't need a clinical study for that. This is simple, indisputable physiology.' Consciously and purposely induced oxygen deficiency was an absolutely deliberate health hazard, and an absolute medical contraindication which means that 'this drug, this therapy, this method or measure should not be used, and is not allowed to be used'. To coerce an entire population to use an absolute medical contraindication by force, she said, there had to be definite and serious reasons and the reasons must be presented to competent interdisciplinary and independent bodies to be verified and authorised. She had this warning of the consequences that were coming if mask wearing continued:

> When, in ten years, dementia is going to increase exponentially, and the younger generations couldn't reach their god-given potential, it won't help to say 'we didn't need the masks'. I know how damaging oxygen deprivation is for the brain, cardiologists know how damaging it is for the heart, pulmonologists know how damaging it is for the lungs. Oxygen deprivation damages every single organ. Where are our health departments, our health insurance, our medical associations? It would have been their duty to be vehemently against the lockdown and to stop it and stop it from the very beginning.

> Why do the medical boards issue punishments to doctors who give people exemptions? Does the person or the doctor seriously have to prove that oxygen deprivation harms people? What kind of medicine are our doctors and medical associations representing? Who is responsible for this crime? The ones who want to enforce it? The ones who let it happen and play along, or the ones who don't prevent it?

All of the organisations and people she mentions there either answer directly to the Cult or do whatever hierarchical levels above them tell them to do. The outcome of both is the same. 'It's not about masks, it's not about viruses, it's certainly not about your health', Griesz-Brisson said. 'It is about much, much more. I am not participating. I am not afraid.' They were taking our air to breathe and there was no unfounded medical exemption from face masks. Oxygen deprivation was dangerous for every single brain. It had to be the free decision of every human being whether they want to wear a mask that was absolutely ineffective to protect themselves from a virus. She ended by rightly identifying where the responsibility lies for all this:

> The imperative of the hour is personal responsibility. We are responsible for what we think, not the media. We are responsible for what we do, not our superiors. We are responsible for our health, not the World Health

Organization. And we are responsible for what happens in our country, not the government.

Halle-bloody-lujah.

But surgeons wear masks, right?

Independent studies of mask-wearing have produced a long list of reports detailing mental, emotional and physical dangers. What a definition of insanity to see police officers imposing mask-wearing on the public which will cumulatively damage their health while the police themselves wear masks that will cumulatively damage *their* health. It's utter madness and both public and police do this because 'the government says so' – yes a government of brain-donor idiots like UK Health Secretary Matt Hancock reading the 'follow the science' scripts of psychopathic, lunatic psychologists. The response you get from Stockholm syndrome sufferers defending the very authorities that are destroying them and their families is that 'surgeons wear masks'. This is considered the game, set and match that they must work and don't cause oxygen deficit. Well, actually, scientific studies have shown that they *do* and oxygen levels are monitored in operating theatres to compensate. Surgeons wear masks to stop spittle and such like dropping into open wounds – not to stop 'viral particles' which are so miniscule they can only be seen through an electron microscope. Holes in the masks are significantly bigger than 'viral particles' and if you sneeze or cough they will breach the mask. I watched an incredibly disingenuous 'experiment' that claimed to prove that masks work in catching 'virus' material from the mouth and nose. They did this with a slow motion camera and the mask did block big stuff which stayed inside the mask and against the face to be breathed in or cause infections on the face as we have seen with many children. 'Viral particles', however, would never have been picked up by the camera as they came through the mask when they are far too small to be seen. The 'experiment' was therefore disingenuous *and* useless.

Studies have concluded that wearing masks in operating theatres (and thus elsewhere) make no difference to preventing infection while the opposite is true with toxic shite building up in the mask and this had led to an explosion in tooth decay and gum disease dubbed by dentists 'mask mouth'. You might have seen the Internet video of a furious American doctor urging people to take off their masks after a four-year-old patient had been rushed to hospital the night before and nearly died with a lung infection that doctors sourced to mask wearing. A study in the journal *Cancer Discovery* found that inhalation of harmful microbes can contribute to advanced stage lung cancer in adults and long-term use of masks can help breed dangerous pathogens. Microbiologists have said frequent mask wearing creates a moist environment in which microbes can grow and proliferate before entering the lungs. The Canadian Agency for Drugs and Technologies in Health, or CADTH, a Canadian national organisation that provides research and analysis to healthcare decision-makers, said this as long ago as 2013 in a report entitled 'Use of Surgical Masks in the Operating Room: A Review of the Clinical Effectiveness and Guidelines'. It said:

- No evidence was found to support the use of surgical face masks to reduce the frequency of surgical site infections
- No evidence was found on the effectiveness of wearing surgical face masks to protect staff from infectious material in the operating room.
- Guidelines recommend the use of surgical face masks by staff in the operating room to protect both operating room staff and patients (despite the lack of evidence).

We were told that the world could go back to 'normal' with the arrival of the 'vaccines'. When they came, fraudulent as they are, the story changed as I knew that it would. We are in the midst of transforming 'normal', not going back to it. Mary Ramsay, head of immunisation at Public Health England, echoed the words of US criminal Anthony Fauci who said masks and other regulations must stay no matter if people are vaccinated. The Fauci idiot continued to wear two masks – different colours so both could be clearly seen – after he *claimed* to have been vaccinated. Senator Rand Paul told Fauci in one exchange that his double-masks were 'theatre' and he was right. It's all theatre. Mary Ramsay back-tracked on the vaccine-return-to-normal theme when she said the public may need to wear masks and social-distance for years despite the jabs. 'People have got used to those lower-level restrictions now, and [they] can live with them', she said telling us what the idea has been all along. 'The vaccine does not give you a pass, even if you have had it, you must continue to follow all the guidelines' said a Public Health England statement which reneged on what we had been told before and made having the 'vaccine' irrelevant to 'normality' even by the official story. Spain's fascist government trumped everyone by passing a law mandating the wearing of masks on the beach and even when swimming in the sea. The move would have devastated what's left of the Spanish tourist industry, posed potential breathing dangers to swimmers and had Northern European sunbathers walking around with their forehead brown and the rest of their face white as a sheet. The ruling was so crazy that it had to be retracted after pressure from public and tourist industry, but it confirmed where the Cult wants to go with masks and how clinically insane authority has become. The determination to make masks permanent and hide the serious dangers to body and mind can be seen in the censorship of scientist Professor Denis Rancourt by Bill Gates-funded academic publishing website ResearchGate over his papers exposing the dangers and uselessness of masks. Rancourt said:

> ResearchGate today has permanently locked my account, which I have had since 2015. Their reasons graphically show the nature of their attack against democracy, and their corruption of science … By their obscene non-logic, a scientific review of science articles reporting on harms caused by face masks has a 'potential to cause harm'. No criticism of the psychological device (face masks) is tolerated, if the said criticism shows potential to influence public policy.

This is what happens in a fascist world.

Where are the 'greens' (again)?

Other dangers of wearing masks especially regularly relate to the inhalation of minute plastic fibres into the lungs and the deluge of discarded masks in the environment and oceans. Estimates predicted that more than 1.5 billion disposable masks will end up in the world's oceans every year polluting the water with tons of plastic and endangering marine wildlife. Studies project that humans are using 129 billion face masks each month worldwide – about three million a minute. Most are disposable and made from plastic, non-biodegradable microfibers that break down into smaller plastic particles that become widespread in ecosystems. They are littering cities, clogging sewage channels and turning up in bodies of water. I have written in other books about the immense amounts of microplastics from endless sources now being absorbed into the body. Rolf Halden, director of the Arizona State University (ASU) Biodesign Center for Environmental Health Engineering, was the senior researcher in a 2020 study that analysed 47 human tissue samples and found microplastics in all of them. 'We have detected these chemicals of plastics in every single organ that we have investigated', he said. I wrote in *The Answer* about the world being deluged with microplastics. A study by the Worldwide Fund for Nature (WWF) found that people are consuming on average every week some 2,000 tiny pieces of plastic mostly through water and also through marine life and the air. Every year humans are ingesting enough microplastics to fill a heaped dinner plate and in a life-time of 79 years it is enough to fill two large waste bins. Marco Lambertini, WWF International director general said: 'Not only are plastics polluting our oceans and waterways and killing marine life – it's in all of us and we can't escape consuming plastics,' American geologists found tiny plastic fibres, beads and shards in rainwater samples collected from the remote slopes of the Rocky Mountain National Park near Denver, Colorado. Their report was headed: 'It is raining plastic.' Rachel Adams, senior lecturer in Biomedical Science at Cardiff Metropolitan University, said that among health consequences are internal inflammation and immune responses to a 'foreign body'. She further pointed out that microplastics become carriers of toxins including mercury, pesticides and dioxins (a known cause of cancer and reproductive and developmental problems). These toxins accumulate in the fatty tissues once they enter the body through microplastics. Now this is being compounded massively by people putting plastic on their face and throwing it away.

Workers exposed to polypropylene plastic fibres known as 'flock' have developed 'flock worker's lung' from inhaling small pieces of the flock fibres which can damage lung tissue, reduce breathing capacity and exacerbate other respiratory problems. *Now* ... commonly used surgical masks have three layers of melt-blown textiles made of ... polypropylene. We have billions of people putting these microplastics against their mouth, nose and face for hours at a time day after day in the form of masks. How does anyone think that will work out? I mean – what could possibly go wrong? We posted a number of scientific studies on this at davidicke.com, but when I went back to them as I was writing this book the links to the science research website where they were hosted were dead. Anything that challenges the official narrative in any way is either censored or vilified. The official narrative is so unsupportable by the evidence that only deleting the truth can protect it. A study by Chinese scientists still survived – with the usual twist which it why it was still active, I guess. Yes, they found that virtually all the masks they tested increased the daily intake of microplastic fibres, but people should still wear them because the danger from the 'virus' was worse said the crazy 'team' from the Institute of Hydrobiology in Wuhan. Scientists first discovered microplastics in lung tissue of some patients who died of lung cancer in the 1990s. Subsequent studies have confirmed the potential health damage with the plastic degrading slowly and remaining in the lungs to accumulate in volume. Wuhan researchers used a machine simulating human breathing to establish that masks shed up to nearly 4,000 microplastic fibres in a month with reused masks producing more. Scientists said some masks are laced with toxic chemicals and a variety of compounds seriously restricted for both health and environmental reasons. They include cobalt (used in blue dye) and formaldehyde known to cause watery eyes, burning sensations in the eyes, nose, and throat, plus coughing, wheezing and nausea. No – that must be 'Covid-19'.

Mask 'worms'

There is another and potentially even more sinister content of masks.

Mostly new masks of different makes filmed under a microscope around the world have been found to contain strange black fibres or 'worms' that appear to move or 'crawl' by themselves and react to heat and water. The nearest I have seen to them are the self-replicating fibres that are pulled out through the skin of those suffering from Morgellons disease which has been connected to the phenomena of 'chemtrails' which I will bring into the story later on. Morgellons fibres continue to grow outside the body and have a form of artificial intelligence. Black 'worm' fibres in masks have that kind of feel to them and there is a nanotechnology technique called 'worm micelles' which carry and release drugs or anything else you want to deliver to the body. For sure the suppression of humanity by mind altering drugs is the Cult agenda big time and the more excuses they can find to gain access to the body the more opportunities there are to make that happen whether through 'vaccines' or masks pushed against the mouth and nose for hours on end.

So let us summarise the pros and cons of masks:

Against masks: Breathing in your own carbon dioxide; depriving the body and brain of sufficient oxygen; build-up of toxins in the mask that can be breathed into the lungs and cause rashes on the face and 'mask-mouth'; breathing microplastic fibres and toxic chemicals into the lungs; dehumanisation and deleting individualisation by literally making people faceless; destroying human emotional interaction through facial expression and deleting parental connection with their babies which look for guidance to their facial expression.

For masks: They don't protect you from a 'virus' that doesn't exist and even if it did 'viral' particles are so minute they are smaller than the holes in the mask.

Governments, police, supermarkets, businesses, transport companies, and all the rest who seek to impose masks have done no risk assessment on their consequences for health and psychology and are now open to group lawsuits when the impact becomes clear with a cumulative epidemic of respiratory and other disease. Authorities will try to exploit these effects and hide the real cause by dubbing them 'Covid-19'. Can you imagine setting out to force the population to wear health-destroying masks without doing any assessment of the risks? It is criminal and it is evil, but then how many people targeted in this way, who see their children told to wear them all day at school, have asked for a risk assessment? Billions can't be imposed upon by the few unless the billions allow it. Oh, yes, with just a tinge of irony, 85 percent of all masks made worldwide come from *China*.

Wash your hands in toxic shite

'Covid' rules include the use of toxic sanitisers and again the health consequences of constantly applying toxins to be absorbed through the skin is obvious to any level of Renegade Mind. America's Food and Drug Administration (FDA) said that sanitisers are drugs and issued a warning about 75 dangerous brands which contain methanol used in antifreeze and can cause death, kidney damage and blindness. The FDA circulated the following warning even for those brands that it claims to be safe:

> Store hand sanitizer out of the reach of pets and children, and children should use it only with adult supervision. Do not drink hand sanitizer. This is particularly important for young children, especially toddlers, who may be attracted by the pleasant smell or brightly colored bottles of hand sanitizer.

> Drinking even a small amount of hand sanitizer can cause alcohol poisoning in children. (However, there is no need to be concerned if your children eat with or lick their hands after using hand sanitizer.) During this coronavirus pandemic, poison control centers have had an increase in calls about accidental ingestion of hand sanitizer, so it is important that adults monitor young children's use.

> Do not allow pets to swallow hand sanitizer. If you think your pet has eaten something potentially dangerous, call your veterinarian or a pet poison control center right away. Hand sanitizer is flammable and should be stored away from heat and flames. When using hand sanitizer, rub your hands until they feel completely dry before performing activities that may involve heat, sparks, static electricity, or open flames.

There you go, perfectly safe, then, and that's without even a mention of the toxins absorbed through the skin. Come on kids – sanitise your hands everywhere you go. It will save you from the 'virus'. Put all these elements together of the 'Covid' normal and see how much health and psychology is being cumulatively damaged, even devastated, to 'protect your health'. Makes sense, right? They are only imposing these things because they care, right? *Right?*

Submitting to insanity

Psychological reframing of the population goes very deep and is done in many less obvious ways. I hear people say how contradictory and crazy 'Covid' rules are and how they are ever changing. This is explained away by dismissing those involved as idiots. It is a big mistake. The Cult is delighted if its cold calculation is perceived as incompetence and idiocy when it is anything but. Oh, yes, there are idiots within the system – lots of them – but they are *administering* the Cult agenda, mostly unknowingly. They are not deciding and dictating it. The bulwark against tyranny is self-respect, always has been, always will be. It is self-respect that has broken every tyranny in history. By its very nature self-respect will not bow to oppression and its perpetrators. There is so little self-respect that it's always the few that overturn dictators. Many may eventually follow, but the few with the iron spines (self-respect) kick it off and generate the momentum. The Cult targets self-respect in the knowledge that once this has gone only submission remains. Crazy, contradictory, ever-changing 'Covid' rules are systematically applied by psychologists to delete self-respect. They *want* you to see that the rules make no sense. It is one thing to decide to do something when *you* have made the choice based on evidence and logic. You still retain your self-respect. It is quite another when you can see what you are being told to do is insane, ridiculous and makes no sense, and *yet you still do it*. Your self-respect is extinguished and this has been happening as ever more obviously stupid and nonsensical things have been demanded and the great majority have complied even when they can see they are stupid and nonsensical.

People walk around in face-nappies knowing they are damaging their health and make no difference to a 'virus'. They do it in fear of not doing it. I know it's daft, but I'll do it anyway. When that happens something dies inside of you and submissive reframing has begun. Next there's a need to hide from yourself that you have conceded your self-respect and you convince yourself that you have not really submitted to fear and intimidation. You begin to believe that you are complying with craziness because it's the right thing to do. When first you concede your self-respect of 2+2 = 4 to 2+2 = 5 you *know* you are compromising your self-respect. Gradually to avoid facing that fact you begin to *believe* that 2+2=5. You have been reframed and I have been watching this process happening in the human psyche on an industrial scale. The Cult is working to break your spirit and one of its major tools in that war is humiliation. I read how former American soldier Bradley Manning (later Chelsea Manning after a sex-change) was treated after being jailed for supplying WikiLeaks with documents exposing the enormity of government and elite mendacity. Manning was isolated in solitary confinement for eight months, put under 24-hour surveillance, forced to hand over clothing before going to bed, and stand naked for every roll call. This is systematic humiliation. The introduction of anal swab 'Covid' tests in China has been done for the same reason to delete self-respect and induce compliant submission. Anal swabs are mandatory for incoming passengers in parts of China and American diplomats have said they were forced to undergo the indignity which would have been calculated humiliation by the Cult-owned Chinese government that has America in its sights.

Government-people: An abusive relationship

Spirit-breaking psychological techniques include giving people hope and apparent respite from tyranny only to take it away again. This happened in the UK during Christmas, 2020, when the psycho-psychologists and their political lackeys announced an easing of restrictions over the holiday only to reimpose them almost immediately on the basis of yet another lie. There is a big psychological difference between getting used to oppression and being given hope of relief only to have that dashed. Psychologists know this and we have seen the technique used repeatedly. Then there is traumatising people before you introduce more extreme regulations that require compliance. A perfect case was the announcement by the dark and sinister Whitty and Vallance in the UK that 'new data' predicted that 4,000 could die every day over the winter of 2020/2021 if we did not lockdown again. I think they call it lying and after traumatising people with that claim out came Jackboot Johnson the next day with new curbs on human freedom. Psychologists know that a frightened and traumatised mind becomes suggestable to submission and behaviour reframing. Underpinning all this has been to make people fearful and suspicious of each other and see themselves as a potential danger to others. In league with deleted self-respect you have the perfect psychological recipe for self-loathing. The relationship between authority and public is now demonstrably the same as that of subservience to an abusive partner. These are signs of an abusive relationship explained by psychologist Leslie Becker-Phelps:

Psychological and emotional abuse: Undermining a partner's self-worth with verbal attacks, name-calling, and belittling. Humiliating the partner in public, unjustly accusing them of having an affair, or interrogating them about their every behavior. Keeping partner confused or off balance by saying they were just kidding or blaming the partner for 'making' them act this way … Feigning in public that they care while turning against them in private. This leads to victims frequently feeling confused, incompetent, unworthy, hopeless, and chronically self-doubting. [Apply these techniques to how governments have treated the population since New Year, 2020, and the parallels are obvious.]

Physical abuse: The abuser might physically harm their partner in a range of ways, such as grabbing, hitting, punching, or shoving them. They might throw objects at them or harm them with a weapon. [Observe the physical harm imposed by masks, lockdown, and so on.]

Threats and intimidation: One way abusers keep their partners in line is by instilling fear. They might be verbally threatening, or give threatening looks or gestures. Abusers often make it known that they are tracking their partner's every move. They might destroy their partner's possessions, threaten to harm them, or threaten to harm their family members. Not surprisingly, victims of this abuse often feel anxiety, fear, and panic. [No words necessary.]

Isolation: Abusers often limit their partner's activities, forbidding them to talk or interact with friends or family. They might limit access to a car or even turn off their phone. All of this might be done by physically holding them against their will, but is often accomplished through psychological abuse and intimidation. The more isolated a person feels, the fewer resources they have to help gain perspective on their situation and to escape from it. [No words necessary.]

Economic abuse: Abusers often make their partners beholden to them for money by controlling access to funds of any kind. They might prevent their partner from getting a job or withhold access to money they earn from a job. This creates financial dependency that makes leaving the relationship very difficult. [See destruction of livelihoods and the proposed meagre 'guaranteed income' so long as you do whatever you are told.]

Using children: An abuser might disparage their partner's parenting skills, tell their children lies about their partner, threaten to take custody of their children, or threaten to harm their children. These tactics instil fear and often elicit compliance. [See reframed social service mafia and how children are being mercilessly abused by the state over 'Covid' while their parents look on too frightened to do anything.]

A further recurring trait in an abusive relationship is the abused blaming themselves for their abuse and making excuses for the abuser. We have the public blaming each other for lockdown abuse by government and many making excuses for the government while attacking those who challenge the government. How often we have heard authorities say that rules are being imposed or reimposed only because people have refused to 'behave' and follow the rules. We don't want to do it – it's *you*.

Renegade Minds are an antidote to all of these things. They will never concede their self-respect no matter what the circumstances. Even when apparent humiliation is heaped upon them they laugh in its face and reflect back the humiliation on the abuser where it belongs. Renegade Minds will never wear masks they know are only imposed to humiliate, suppress and damage both physically and psychologically. Consequences will take care of themselves and they will never break their spirit or cause them to concede to tyranny. UK newspaper columnist Peter Hitchens was one of the few in the mainstream media to speak out against lockdowns and forced vaccinations. He then announced he had taken the jab. He wanted to see family members abroad and he believed vaccine passports were inevitable even though they had not yet been introduced. Hitchens has a questioning and critical mind, but not a Renegade one. If he had no amount of pressure would have made him concede. Hitchens excused his action by saying that the battle has been lost. Renegade Minds never accept defeat when freedom is at stake and even if they are the last one standing the self-respect of not submitting to tyranny is more important than any outcome or any consequence.

That's why Renegade Minds are the only minds that ever changed anything worth changing.

CHAPTER EIGHT

'Reframing' insanity

Insanity is relative. It depends on who has who locked in what cage
Ray Bradbury

'Reframing' a mind means simply to change its perception and behaviour. This can be done subconsciously to such an extent that subjects have no idea they have been 'reframed' while to any observer changes in behaviour and attitudes are obvious.

Human society is being reframed on a ginormous scale since the start of 2020 and here we have the reason why psychologists rather than doctors have been calling the shots. Ask most people who have succumbed to 'Covid' reframing if they have changed and most will say 'no'; but they *have* and fundamentally. The Cult's long-game has been preparing for these times since way back and crucial to that has been to prepare both population and officialdom mentally and emotionally. To use the mind-control parlance they had to reframe the population with a mentality that would submit to fascism and reframe those in government and law enforcement to impose fascism or at least go along with it. The result has been the fact-deleted mindlessness of 'Wokeness' and officialdom that has either enthusiastically or unquestioningly imposed global tyranny demanded by reframed politicians on behalf of psychopathic and deeply evil cultists. 'Cognitive reframing' identifies and challenges the way someone sees the world in the form of situations, experiences and emotions and then restructures those perceptions to view the same set of circumstances in a different way. This can have benefits if the attitudes are personally destructive while on the other side it has the potential for individual and collective mind control which the subject has no idea has even happened.

Cognitive therapy was developed in the 1960s by Aaron T. Beck who was born in Rhode Island in 1921 as the son of Jewish immigrants from the Ukraine. He became interested in the techniques as a treatment for depression. Beck's daughter Judith S. Beck is prominent in the same field and they founded the Beck Institute for Cognitive Behavior Therapy in Philadelphia in 1994. Cognitive reframing, however, began to be used worldwide by those with a very dark agenda. The Cult reframes politicians to change their attitudes and actions until they are completely at odds with what they once appeared to stand for. The same has been happening to government administrators at all levels, law enforcement, military and the human population. Cultists love mind control for two main reasons: It allows them to control what people think, do and say to secure agenda advancement and, by definition, it calms their legendary insecurity and fear of the unexpected. I have studied mind control since the time I travelled America in 1996. I may have been talking to next to no one in terms of an audience in those years, but my goodness did I gather a phenomenal amount of information and knowledge about so many things including the techniques of mind control. I have described this in detail in other books going back to *The Biggest Secret* in 1998. I met a very large number of people recovering from MKUltra and its offshoots and successors and I began to see how these same techniques were being used on the population in general. This was never more obvious than since the 'Covid' hoax began.

Reframing the enforcers

I have observed over the last two decades and more the very clear transformation in the dynamic between the police, officialdom and the public. I tracked this in the books as the relationship mutated from one of serving the public to seeing them as almost the enemy and certainly a lower caste. There has always been a class divide based on income and always been some psychopathic, corrupt, and big-I-am police officers. This was different. Wholesale change was unfolding in the collective dynamic; it was less about money and far more about position and perceived power. An us-and-them was emerging. Noses were lifted skyward by government administration and law enforcement and their attitude to the public they were *supposed* to be serving changed to one of increasing contempt, superiority and control. The transformation was so clear and widespread that it had to be planned. Collective attitudes and dynamics do not change naturally and organically that quickly on that scale. I then came across an organisation in Britain called Common Purpose created in the late 1980s by Julia Middleton who would work in the office of Deputy Prime Minister John Prescott during the long and disastrous premiership of war criminal Tony Blair. When Blair speaks the Cult is speaking and the man should have been in jail a long time ago. Common Purpose proclaims itself to be one of the biggest 'leadership development' organisations in the world while functioning as a *charity* with all the financial benefits which come from that. It hosts 'leadership development' courses and programmes all over the world and claims to have 'brought together' what it calls 'leaders' from more than 100 countries on six continents. The modus operandi of Common Purpose can be compared with the work of the UK government's reframing network that includes the Behavioural Insights Team 'nudge unit' and 'Covid' reframing specialists at SPI-B. WikiLeaks described Common Purpose long ago as 'a hidden virus in our government and schools' which is unknown to the general public: 'It recruits and trains "leaders" to be loyal to the directives of Common Purpose and the EU, instead of to their own departments, which they then undermine or subvert, the NHS [National Health Service] being an example.' This is a vital point to understand the 'Covid' hoax. The NHS, and its equivalent around the world, has been utterly reframed in terms of administrators and much of the medical personnel with the transformation underpinned by recruitment policies. The outcome has been the criminal and psychopathic behaviour of the NHS over 'Covid' and we have seen the same in every other major country. WikiLeaks said Common Purpose trainees are 'learning to rule without regard to democracy' and to usher in a police state (current events explained). Common Purpose operated like a 'glue' and had members in the NHS, BBC, police, legal profession, church, many of Britain's 7,000 quangos, local councils, the Civil Service, government ministries and Parliament, and controlled many RDA's (Regional Development Agencies). Here we have one answer for how and why British institutions and their like in other countries have changed so negatively in relation to the public. This further explains how and why the beyond-disgraceful reframed BBC has become a propaganda arm of 'Covid' fascism. They are all part of a network pursuing the same goal.

By 2019 Common Purpose was quoting a figure of 85,000 'leaders' that had attended its programmes. These 'students' of all ages are known as Common Purpose 'graduates' and they consist of government, state and local government officials and administrators, police chiefs and officers, and a whole range of others operating within the national, local and global establishment. Cressida Dick, Commissioner of the London Metropolitan Police, is the Common Purpose graduate who was the 'Gold Commander' that oversaw what can only be described as the murder of Brazilian electrician Jean Charles de Menezes in 2005. He was held down by psychopathic police and shot seven times in the head by a psychopathic lunatic after being mistaken for a terrorist when he was just a bloke going about his day. Dick authorised officers to pursue and keep surveillance on de Menezes and ordered that he be stopped from entering the underground train system. Police psychopaths took her at her word clearly. She was 'disciplined' for this outrage by being *promoted* – eventually to the top of the 'Met' police where she has been a disaster. Many Chief Constables controlling the police in different parts of the UK are and have been Common Purpose graduates. I have heard the 'graduate' network described as a sort of Mafia or secret society operating within the fabric of government at all levels pursuing a collective policy ingrained at Common Purpose training events. Founder Julia Middleton herself has said:

> Locally and internationally, Common Purpose graduates will be 'lighting small fires' to create change in their organisations and communities … The Common Purpose effect is best illustrated by the many stories of small changes brought about by leaders, who themselves have changed.

A Common Purpose mission statement declared:

> Common Purpose aims to improve the way society works by expanding the vision, decision-making ability and influence of all kinds of leaders. The organisation runs a variety of educational programmes for leaders of all ages, backgrounds and sectors, in order to provide them with the inspirational, information and opportunities they need to change the world.

Yes, but into what? Since 2020 the answer has become clear.

NLP and the Delphi technique

Common Purpose would seem to be a perfect name or would common programming be better? One of the foundation methods of reaching 'consensus' (group think) is by setting the agenda theme and then encouraging, cajoling or pressuring everyone to agree a 'consensus' in line with the core theme promoted by Common Purpose. The methodology involves the 'Delphi technique', or an adaption of it, in which opinions are expressed that are summarised by a 'facilitator or change agent' at each stage. Participants are 'encouraged' to modify their views in the light of what others have said. Stage by stage the former individual opinions are merged into group consensus which just happens to be what Common Purpose wants them to believe. A key part of this is to marginalise anyone refusing to concede to group think and turn the group against them to apply pressure to conform. We are seeing this very technique used on the general population to make 'Covid' group-thinkers hostile to those who have seen through the bullshit. People can be reframed by using perception manipulation methods such as Neuro-Linguistic Programming (NLP) in which you change perception with the use of carefully constructed language. An NLP website described the technique this way:

> … A method of influencing brain behaviour (the 'neuro' part of the phrase) through the use of language (the 'linguistic' part) and other types of communication to enable a person to 'recode' the way the brain responds to stimuli (that's the 'programming') and manifest new and better behaviours. Neuro-Linguistic Programming often incorporates hypnosis and self-hypnosis

to help achieve the change (or 'programming') that is wanted.

British alternative media operation UKColumn has done very detailed research into Common Purpose over a long period. I quoted co-founder and former naval officer Brian Gerrish in my book *Remember Who You Are*, published in 2011, as saying the following years before current times:

> It is interesting that many of the mothers who have had children taken by the State speak of the Social Services people being icily cool, emotionless and, as two ladies said in slightly different words, '… like little robots'. We know that NLP is cumulative, so people can be given small imperceptible doses of NLP in a course here, another in a few months, next year etc. In this way, major changes are accrued in their personality, but the day by day change is almost unnoticeable.

In these and other ways 'graduates' have had their perceptions uniformly reframed and they return to their roles in the institutions of government, law enforcement, legal profession, military, 'education', the UK National Health Service and the whole swathe of the establishment structure to pursue a common agenda preparing for the 'post-industrial', 'post-democratic' society. I say 'preparing' but we are now there. 'Post-industrial' is code for the Great Reset and 'post-democratic' is 'Covid' fascism. UKColumn has spoken to partners of those who have attended Common Purpose 'training'. They have described how personalities and attitudes of 'graduates' changed very noticeably for the worse by the time they had completed the course. They had been 'reframed' and told they are the 'leaders' – the special ones – who know better than the population. There has also been the very demonstrable recruitment of psychopaths and narcissists into government administration at all levels and law enforcement. If you want psychopathy hire psychopaths and you get a simple cause and effect. If you want administrators, police officers and 'leaders' to perceive the public as lesser beings who don't matter then employ narcissists. These personalities are identified using 'psychometrics' that identifies knowledge, abilities, attitudes and personality traits, mostly through carefully-designed questionnaires and tests. As this policy has passed through the decades we have had power-crazy, power-trippers appointed into law enforcement, security and government administration in preparation for current times and the dynamic between public and law enforcement/officialdom has been transformed. UKColumn's Brian Gerrish said of the narcissistic personality:

> Their love of themselves and power automatically means that they will crush

others who get in their way. I received a major piece of the puzzle when a friend pointed out that when they made public officials re-apply for their own jobs several years ago they were also required to do psychometric tests. This was undoubtedly the start of the screening process to get 'their' sort of people in post.

How obvious that has been since 2020 although it was clear what was happening long before if people paid attention to the changing public-establishment dynamic.

Change agents

At the centre of events in 'Covid' Britain is the National Health Service (NHS) which has behaved disgracefully in slavishly following the Cult agenda. The NHS management structure is awash with Common Purpose graduates or 'change agents' working to a common cause. Helen Bevan, a Chief of Service Transformation at the NHS Institute for Innovation and Improvement, co-authored a document called 'Towards a million change agents, a review of the social movements literature: implications for large scale change in the NHS'. The document compared a project management approach to that of change and social movements where 'people change themselves and each other – peer to peer'. Two definitions given for a 'social movement' were:

A group of people who consciously attempt to build a radically new social order; involves people of a broad range of social backgrounds; and deploys politically confrontational and socially disruptive tactics – Cyrus Zirakzadeh 1997

Collective challenges, based on common purposes and social solidarities, in sustained interaction with elites, opponents, and authorities – Sidney Tarrow 1994

Helen Bevan wrote another NHS document in which she defined 'framing' as 'the process by which leaders construct, articulate and put across their message in a powerful and compelling way in order to win people to their cause and call them to action'. I think I could come up with another definition that would be rather more accurate. The National Health Service and institutions of Britain and the wider world have been taken over by reframed 'change agents' and that includes everything from the United Nations to national governments, local councils and social services which have been kidnapping children from loving parents on an extraordinary and gathering scale on the road to the end of parenthood altogether. Children from loving homes are stolen and kidnapped by the state and put into the 'care' (inversion) of the local authority through council homes, foster parents and forced adoption. At the same time children are allowed to be abused without response while many are under council 'care'. UKColumn highlighted the Common Purpose connection between South Yorkshire Police and Rotherham council officers in the case of the scandal in that area of the sexual exploitation of children to which the authorities turned not one blind eye, but both:

> We were alarmed to discover that the Chief Executive, the Strategic Director of Children and Young People's Services, the Manager for the Local Strategic Partnership, the Community Cohesion Manager, the Cabinet Member for Cohesion, the Chief Constable and his predecessor had all attended Leadership training courses provided by the pseudo-charity Common Purpose.

Once 'change agents' have secured positions of hire and fire within any organisation things start to move very quickly. Personnel are then hired and fired on the basis of whether they will work towards the agenda the change agent represents. If they do they are rapidly promoted even though they may be incompetent. Those more qualified and skilled who are pre-Common Purpose 'old school' see their careers stall and even disappear. This has been happening for decades in every institution of state, police, 'health' and social services and all of them have been transformed as a result in their attitudes to their jobs and the public. Medical professions, including nursing, which were once vocations for the caring now employ many cold, callous and couldn't give a shit personality types. The UKColumn investigation concluded:

> By blurring the boundaries between people, professions, public and private sectors, responsibility and accountability, Common Purpose encourages 'graduates' to believe that as new selected leaders, they can work together, outside of the established political and social structures, to achieve a paradigm shift or CHANGE – so called 'Leading Beyond Authority'. In doing so, the allegiance of the individual becomes 'reframed' on CP colleagues and their NETWORK.

Reframing the Face-Nappies

Nowhere has this process been more obvious than in the police where recruitment of psychopaths and development of unquestioning mind-controlled group-thinkers have transformed law enforcement into a politically-correct 'Woke' joke and a travesty of what should be public service. Today they wear their face-nappies like good little gofers and enforce 'Covid' rules which are fascism under another name. Alongside the specifically-recruited psychopaths we have software minds incapable of free thought. Brian Gerrish again:

An example is the policeman who would not get on a bike for a press photo because he had not done the cycling proficiency course. Normal people say this is political correctness gone mad. Nothing could be further from the truth. The policeman has been reframed, and in his reality it is perfect common sense not to get on the bike 'because he hasn't done the cycling course'.

Another example of this is where the police would not rescue a boy from a pond until they had taken advice from above on the 'risk assessment'. A normal person would have arrived, perhaps thought of the risk for a moment, and dived in. To the police now 'reframed', they followed 'normal' procedure.

There are shocking cases of reframed ambulance crews doing the same. Sheer unthinking stupidity of London Face-Nappies headed by Common Purpose graduate Cressida Dick can be seen in their behaviour at a vigil in March, 2021, for a murdered woman, Sarah Everard. A police officer had been charged with the crime. Anyone with a brain would have left the vigil alone in the circumstances. Instead they 'manhandled' women to stop them breaking 'Covid rules' to betray classic reframing. Minds in the thrall of perception control have no capacity for seeing a situation on its merits and acting accordingly. 'Rules is rules' is their only mind-set. My father used to say that rules and regulations are for the guidance of the intelligent and the blind obedience of the idiot. Most of the intelligent, decent, coppers have gone leaving only the other kind and a few old school for whom the job must be a daily nightmare. The combination of psychopaths and rule-book software minds has been clearly on public display in the 'Covid' era with automaton robots in uniform imposing fascistic 'Covid' regulations on the population without any personal initiative or judging situations on their merits. There are thousands of examples around the world, but I'll make my point with the infamous Derbyshire police in the English East Midlands – the ones who think pouring dye into beauty spots and using drones to track people walking in the countryside away from anyone is called 'policing'. To them there are rules decreed by the government which they have to enforce and in their bewildered state a group gathering in a closed space and someone walking alone in the countryside are the same thing. It is beyond idiocy and enters the realm of clinical insanity.

Police officers in Derbyshire said they were 'horrified' – *horrified* – to find 15 to 20 'irresponsible' kids playing a football match at a closed leisure centre 'in breach of coronavirus restrictions'. When they saw the police the kids ran away leaving their belongings behind and the reframed men and women of Derbyshire police were seeking to establish their identities with a view to fining their parents. The most natural thing for youngsters to do – kicking a ball about – is turned into a criminal activity and enforced by the moronic software programs of Derbyshire police. You find the same mentality in every country. These barely conscious 'horrified' officers said they had to take action because 'we need to ensure these rules are being followed' and 'it is of the utmost importance that you ensure your children are following the rules and regulations for Covid-19'. Had any of them done ten seconds of research to see if this parroting of their masters' script could be supported by any evidence? Nope. Reframed people don't think – others think for them and that's the whole idea of reframing. I have seen police officers one after the other repeating without question word for word what officialdom tells them just as I have seen great swathes of the public doing the same. Ask either for 'their' opinion and out spews what they have been told to think by the official narrative. Police and public may seem to be in different groups, but their mentality is the same. Most people do whatever they are told in fear not doing so or because they believe what officialdom tells them; almost the entirety of the police do what they are told for the same reason. Ultimately it's the tiny inner core of the global Cult that's telling both what to do.

So Derbyshire police were 'horrified'. Oh, really? Why did they think those kids were playing football? It was to relieve the psychological consequences of lockdown and being denied human contact with their friends and interaction, touch and discourse vital to human psychological health. Being denied this month after month has dismantled the psyche of many children and young people as depression and suicide have exploded. Were Derbyshire police *horrified by that*? Are you kidding? Reframed people don't have those mental and emotional processes that can see how the impact on the psychological health of youngsters is far more dangerous than any 'virus' even if you take the mendacious official figures to be true. The reframed are told (programmed) how to act and so they do. The Derbyshire Chief Constable in the first period of lockdown when the black dye and drones nonsense was going on was Peter Goodman. He was the man who severed the connection between his force and the Derbyshire Constabulary *Male Voice* Choir when he decided that it was not inclusive enough to allow women to join. The fact it was a male voice choir making a particular sound produced by male voices seemed to elude a guy who terrifyingly ran policing in Derbyshire. He retired weeks after his force was condemned as disgraceful by former Supreme Court Justice Jonathan Sumption for their behaviour over extreme lockdown impositions. Goodman was replaced by his deputy Rachel Swann who was in charge when her officers were 'horrified'. The police statement over the boys committing the hanging-offence of playing football included the line about the youngsters being 'irresponsible in the times we are all living through' missing the point that the real relevance of the 'times we are all living through' is the imposition of fascism enforced by psychopaths and reframed minds of police officers playing such a vital part in establishing the fascist tyranny that their own children and grandchildren will have to live in their entire lives. As a definition of insanity that is hard to beat although it might be run close by imposing masks on people that can have a serious effect on their health while wearing a face nappy all day themselves. Once again public and police do it for the same reason – the authorities tell them to and who are they to have the self-respect to say no?

Wokers in uniform

How reframed do you have to be to arrest a *six-year-old* and take him to court for *picking a flower* while waiting for a bus? Brain dead police and officialdom did just that in North Carolina where criminal proceedings happen regularly for children under nine. Attorney Julie Boyer gave the six-year-old crayons and a colouring book during the 'flower' hearing while the 'adults' decided his fate. County Chief District Court Judge Jay Corpening asked: 'Should a child that believes in Santa Claus, the Easter Bunny and the tooth fairy be making life-altering decisions?' Well, of course not, but common sense has no meaning when you have a common purpose and a reframed mind. Treating children in this way, and police operating in American schools, is all part of the psychological preparation for children to accept a police state as normal all their adult lives. The same goes for all the cameras and biometric tracking technology in schools. Police training is focused on reframing them as snowflake Wokers and this is happening in the military. Pentagon top brass said that 'training sessions on extremism' were needed for troops who asked why they were so focused on the Capitol Building riot when Black Lives Matter riots were ignored. What's the difference between them some apparently and rightly asked. Actually, there is a difference. Five people died in the Capitol riot, only one through violence, and that was a police officer shooting an unarmed protestor. BLM riots killed at least 25 people and cost billions. Asking the question prompted the psychopaths and reframed minds that run the Pentagon to say that more 'education' (programming) was needed. Troop training is all based on psychological programming to make them fodder for the Cult – 'Military men are just dumb, stupid animals to be used as pawns in foreign policy' as Cult-to-his-DNA former Secretary of State Henry Kissinger famously said. Governments see the police in similar terms and it's time for those among them who can see this to defend the people and stop being enforcers of the Cult agenda upon the people.

The US military, like the country itself, is being targeted for destruction through a long list of Woke impositions. Cult-owned gaga

'President' Biden signed an executive order when he took office to allow taxpayer money to pay for transgender surgery for active military personnel and veterans. Are you a man soldier? No, I'm a LGBTQIA+ with a hint of Skoliosexual and Spectrasexual. Oh, good man. Bad choice of words you bigot. The Pentagon announced in March, 2021, the appointment of the first 'diversity and inclusion officer' for US Special Forces. Richard Torres-Estrada arrived with the publication of a 'D&I Strategic Plan which will guide the enterprise-wide effort to institutionalize and sustain D&I'. If you think a Special Forces 'Strategic Plan' should have something to do with defending America you haven't been paying attention. Defending Woke is now the military's new role. Torres-Estrada has posted images comparing Donald Trump with Adolf Hitler and we can expect no bias from him as a representative of the supposedly non-political Pentagon. Cable news host Tucker Carlson said: 'The Pentagon is now the Yale faculty lounge but with cruise missiles.' Meanwhile Secretary of Defense Lloyd Austin, a board member of weapons-maker Raytheon with stock and compensation interests in October, 2020, worth $1.4 million, said he was purging the military of the 'enemy within' – anyone who isn't Woke and supports Donald Trump. Austin refers to his targets as 'racist extremists' while in true Woke fashion being himself a racist extremist. Pentagon documents pledge to 'eradicate, eliminate and conquer all forms of racism, sexism and homophobia'. The definitions of these are decided by 'diversity and inclusion committees' peopled by those who see racism, sexism and homophobia in every situation and opinion. Woke (the Cult) is dismantling the US military and purging testosterone as China expands its military and gives its troops 'masculinity training'. How do we think that is going to end when this is all Cult coordinated? The US military, like the British military, is controlled by Woke and spineless top brass who just go along with it out of personal career interests.

'Woke' means fast asleep

Mind control and perception manipulation techniques used on individuals to create group-think have been unleashed on the global population in general. As a result many have no capacity to see the obvious fascist agenda being installed all around them or what 'Covid' is really all about. Their brains are firewalled like a computer system not to process certain concepts, thoughts and realisations that are bad for the Cult. The young are most targeted as the adults they will be when the whole fascist global state is planned to be fully implemented. They need to be prepared for total compliance to eliminate all pushback from entire generations. The Cult has been pouring billions into taking complete control of 'education' from schools to universities via its operatives and corporations and not least Bill Gates as always. The plan has been to transform 'education' institutions into programming centres for the mentality of 'Woke'. James McConnell, professor of psychology at the University of Michigan, wrote in *Psychology Today* in 1970:

> The day has come when we can combine sensory deprivation with drugs, hypnosis, and astute manipulation of reward and punishment, to gain almost absolute control over an individual's behaviour. It should then be possible to achieve a very rapid and highly effective type of brainwashing that would allow us to make dramatic changes in a person's behaviour and personality ...
>
> ... We should reshape society so that we all would be trained from birth to want to do what society wants us to do. We have the techniques to do it... no-one owns his own personality you acquired, and there's no reason to believe you should have the right to refuse to acquire a new personality if your old one is anti-social.

This was the potential for mass brainwashing in 1970 and the mentality there displayed captures the arrogant psychopathy that drives it forward. I emphasise that not all young people have succumbed to Woke programming and those that haven't are incredibly impressive people given that today's young are the most perceptually-targeted generations in history with all the technology now involved. Vast swathes of the young generations, however, have fallen into the spell – and that's what it is – of Woke. The Woke mentality and perceptual program is founded on *inversion* and you will appreciate later why that is so significant. Everything with Woke is inverted and the opposite of what it is claimed to be. Woke was a term used in African-American culture from the 1900s and referred to an awareness of social and racial justice. This is not the meaning of the modern version or 'New Woke' as I call it in *The Answer*. Oh, no, Woke today means something very different no matter how much Wokers may seek to hide that and insist Old Woke and New Woke are the same. See if you find any 'awareness of social justice' here in the modern variety:

- Woke demands 'inclusivity' while excluding anyone with a different opinion and calls for mass censorship to silence other views.

- Woke claims to stand against oppression when imposing oppression is the foundation of all that it does. It is the driver of political correctness which is nothing more than a Cult invention to manipulate the population to silence itself.

- Woke believes itself to be 'liberal' while pursuing a global society that can only be described as fascist (see 'anti-fascist' fascist Antifa).

- Woke calls for 'social justice' while spreading injustice wherever it goes against the common 'enemy' which can be easily identified as a differing view.

- Woke is supposed to be a metaphor for 'awake' when it is solid-gold asleep and deep in a Cult-induced coma that meets the criteria for 'off with the fairies'.

I state these points as obvious facts if people only care to look. I don't do this with a sense of condemnation. We need to appreciate that the onslaught of perceptual programming on the young has been incessant and merciless. I can understand why so many have been reframed, or, given their youth, framed from the start to see the world as the Cult demands. The Cult has had access to their minds day after day in its 'education' system for their entire formative years. Perception is formed from information received and the Cult-created system is a life-long download of information delivered to elicit a particular perception, thus behaviour. The more this has expanded into still new extremes in recent decades and ever-increasing censorship has deleted other opinions and information why wouldn't that lead to a perceptual reframing on a mass scale? I have described already cradle-to-grave programming and in more recent times the targeting of young minds from birth to adulthood has entered the stratosphere. This has taken the form of skewing what is 'taught' to fit the Cult agenda and the omnipresent techniques of group-think to isolate non-believers and pressure them into line. There has always been a tendency to follow the herd, but we really are in a new world now in relation to that. We have parents who can see the 'Covid' hoax told by their children not to stop them wearing masks at school, being 'Covid' tested or having the 'vaccine' in fear of the peer-pressure consequences of being different. What is 'peer-pressure' if not pressure to conform to group-think? Renegade Minds never group-think and always retain a set of perceptions that are unique to them. Group-think is always underpinned by consequences for not group-thinking. Abuse now aimed at those refusing DNA-manipulating 'Covid vaccines' are a potent example of this. The biggest pressure to conform comes from the very group which is itself being manipulated. 'I am programmed to be part of a hive mind and so you must be.'

Woke control structures in 'education' now apply to every mainstream organisation. Those at the top of the 'education' hierarchy (the Cult) decide the policy. This is imposed on governments through the Cult network; governments impose it on schools, colleges and universities; their leadership impose the policy on teachers and academics and they impose it on children and students. At any level where there is resistance, perhaps from a teacher or university lecturer, they are targeted by the authorities and often fired. Students themselves regularly demand the dismissal of academics (increasingly few) at odds with the narrative that the students have been programmed to believe in. It is quite a thought that students who are being targeted by the Cult become so consumed by programmed group-think that they launch protests and demand the removal of those who are trying to push back against those targeting the students. Such is the scale of perceptual inversion. We see this with 'Covid' programming as the Cult imposes the rules via psycho-psychologists and governments on shops, transport companies and businesses which impose them on their staff who impose them on their customers who pressure Pushbackers to conform to the will of the Cult which is in the process of destroying them and their families. Scan all aspects of society and you will see the same sequence every time.

Fact free Woke and hijacking the 'left'

There is no more potent example of this than 'Woke', a mentality only made possible by the deletion of factual evidence by an 'education' system seeking to produce an ever more uniform society. Why would you bother with facts when you don't know any? Deletion of credible history both in volume and type is highly relevant. Orwell said: 'Who controls the past controls the future: who controls the present controls the past.' They who control the perception of the past control the perception of the future and they who control the present control the perception of the past through the writing and deleting of history. Why would you oppose the imposition of Marxism in the name of Wokeism when you don't know that Marxism cost at least 100 million lives in the 20th century alone? Watch videos and read reports in which Woker generations are asked basic historical questions – it's mind-blowing. A survey of 2,000 people found that six percent of millennials (born approximately early1980s to early 2000s) believed the Second World War (1939-1945) broke out with the assassination of President Kennedy (in 1963) and one in ten thought Margaret Thatcher was British Prime Minister at the time. She was in office between 1979 and 1990. We are in a post-fact society. Provable facts are no defence against the fascism of political correctness or Silicon Valley censorship. Facts don't matter anymore as we have witnessed with the 'Covid' hoax. Sacrificing uniqueness to the Woke group-think religion is all you are required to do and that means thinking for yourself is the biggest Woke no, no. All religions are an expression of group-think and censorship and Woke is just another religion with an orthodoxy defended by group-think and censorship. Burned at the stake becomes burned on Twitter which leads back eventually to burned at the stake as Woke humanity regresses to ages past.

The biggest Woke inversion of all is its creators and funders. I grew up in a traditional left of centre political household on a council estate in Leicester in the 1950s and 60s – you know, the left that challenged the power of wealth-hoarding elites and threats to freedom of speech and opinion. In those days students went on marches defending freedom of speech while today's Wokers march for its deletion. What on earth could have happened? Those very elites (collectively the Cult) that we opposed in my youth and early life have funded into existence the antithesis of that former left and hijacked the 'brand' while inverting everything it ever stood for. We have a mentality that calls itself 'liberal' and 'progressive' while acting like fascists. Cult billionaires and their corporations have funded themselves into control of 'education' to ensure that Woke programming is unceasing throughout the formative years of children and young people and that non-Wokers are isolated (that word again) whether they be students, teachers or college professors. The Cult has funded into existence the now colossal global network of Woke organisations that have spawned and promoted all the 'causes' on the Cult wish-list for global transformation and turned Wokers into demanders of them. Does anyone really think it's a coincidence that the Cult agenda for humanity is a carbon (sorry) copy of the societal transformations desired by Woke?? These are only some of them:

Political correctness: The means by which the Cult deletes all public debates that it knows it cannot win if we had the free-flow of information and evidence.

Human-caused 'climate change': The means by which the Cult seeks to transform society into a globally-controlled dictatorship imposing its will over the fine detail of everyone's lives 'to save the planet' which doesn't actually need saving.

Transgender obsession: Preparing collective perception to accept the 'new human' which would not have genders because it would be created technologically and not through procreation. I'll have much more on this in Human 2.0.

Race obsession: The means by which the Cult seeks to divide and rule the population by triggering racial division through the perception that society is more racist than ever when the opposite is the case. Is it perfect in that regard? No. But to compare today with the racism of apartheid and segregation brought to an end by the civil rights movement in the 1960s is to insult the memory of that movement and inspirations like

Martin Luther King. Why is the 'anti-racism' industry (which it is) so dominated by privileged white people?

White supremacy: This is a label used by privileged white people to demonise poor and deprived white people pushing back on tyranny to marginalise and destroy them. White people are being especially targeted as the dominant race by number within Western society which the Cult seeks to transform in its image. If you want to change a society you must weaken and undermine its biggest group and once you have done that by using the other groups you next turn on them to do the same … 'Then they came for the Jews and I was not a Jew so I did nothing.'

Mass migration: The mass movement of people from the Middle East, Africa and Asia into Europe, from the south into the United States and from Asia into Australia are another way the Cult seeks to dilute the racial, cultural and political influence of white people on Western society. White people ask why their governments appear to be working against them while being politically and culturally biased towards incoming cultures. Well, here's your answer. In the same way sexually 'straight' people, men and women, ask why the authorities are biased against them in favour of other sexualities. The answer is the same – that's the way the Cult wants it to be for very sinister motives.

These are all central parts of the Cult agenda and central parts of the Woke agenda and Woke was created and continues to be funded to an immense degree by Cult billionaires and corporations. If anyone begins to say 'coincidence' the syllables should stick in their throat.

Billionaire 'social justice warriors'

Joe Biden is a 100 percent-owned asset of the Cult and the Wokers' man in the White House whenever he can remember his name and for however long he lasts with his rapidly diminishing cognitive function. Even walking up the steps of an aircraft without falling on his arse would appear to be a challenge. He's not an empty-shell puppet or anything. From the minute Biden took office (or the Cult did) he began his executive orders promoting the Woke wish-list. You will see the Woke agenda imposed ever more severely because it's really the *Cult* agenda. Woke organisations and activist networks spawned by the Cult are funded to the extreme so long as they promote what the Cult wants to happen. Woke is funded to promote 'social justice' by billionaires who become billionaires by destroying social justice. The social justice mantra is only a cover for dismantling social justice and funded by billionaires that couldn't give a damn about social justice. Everything makes sense when you see that. One of Woke's premier funders is Cult billionaire financier George Soros who said: 'I am basically there to make money, I cannot and do not look at the social consequences of what I do.' This is the same Soros who has given more than $32 billion to his Open Society Foundations global Woke network and funded Black Lives Matter, mass immigration into Europe and the United States, transgender activism, climate change activism, political correctness and groups targeting 'white supremacy' in the form of privileged white thugs that dominate Antifa. What a scam it all is and when you are dealing with the unquestioning fact-free zone of Woke scamming them is child's play. All you need to pull it off in all these organisations are a few in-the-know agents of the Cult and an army of naïve, reframed, uninformed, narcissistic, know-nothings convinced of their own self-righteousness, self-purity and virtue.

Soros and fellow billionaires and billionaire corporations have poured hundreds of millions into Black Lives Matter and connected groups and promoted them to a global audience. None of this is motivated by caring about black people. These are the billionaires that have controlled and exploited a system that leaves millions of black people in abject poverty and deprivation which they do absolutely nothing to address. The same Cult networks funding BLM were behind the *slave trade!* Black Lives Matter hijacked a phrase that few would challenge and they have turned this laudable concept into a political weapon to divide society. You know that BLM is a fraud when it claims that *All* Lives Matter, the most inclusive statement of all, is 'racist'. BLM and its Cult masters don't want to end racism. To them it's a means to an end to control all of humanity never mind the colour, creed, culture or background. What has destroying the nuclear family got to do with ending racism? Nothing – but that is one of the goals of BLM and also happens to be a goal of the Cult as I have been exposing in my books for decades. Stealing children from loving parents and giving schools ever more power to override parents is part of that same agenda. BLM is a Marxist organisation and why would that not be the case when the Cult created Marxism *and* BLM? Patrisse Cullors, a BLM co-founder, said in a 2015 video that she and her fellow organisers, including co-founder Alicia Garza, are 'trained Marxists'. The lady known after marriage as Patrisse Khan-Cullors bought a $1.4 million home in 2021 in one of the whitest areas of California with a black population of just 1.6 per cent and has so far bought *four* high-end homes for a total of $3.2 million. How very Marxist. There must be a bit of spare in the BLM coffers, however, when Cult corporations and billionaires have handed over the best part of $100 million. Many black people can see that Black Lives Matter is not working for them, but against them, and this is still more confirmation. Black journalist Jason Whitlock, who had his account suspended by Twitter for simply linking to the story about the 'Marxist's' home buying spree, said that BLM leaders are 'making millions of dollars off the backs of these dead black men who they wouldn't spit on if they were on fire and alive'.

Black Lies Matter

Cult assets and agencies came together to promote BLM in the wake of the death of career criminal George Floyd who had been jailed a number of times including for forcing his way into the home of a black woman with others in a raid in which a gun was pointed at her stomach. Floyd was filmed being held in a Minneapolis street in 2020 with the knee of a police officer on his neck and he subsequently died. It was an appalling thing for the officer to do, but the same technique has been used by police on peaceful protestors of lockdown without any outcry from the Woke brigade. As unquestioning supporters of the Cult agenda Wokers have supported lockdown and all the 'Covid' claptrap while attacking anyone standing up to the tyranny imposed in its name. Court documents would later include details of an autopsy on Floyd by County Medical Examiner Dr Andrew Baker who concluded that Floyd had taken a fatal level of the drug fentanyl. None of this mattered to fact-free, question-free, Woke. Floyd's death was followed by worldwide protests against police brutality amid calls to defund the police. Throwing babies out with the bathwater is a Woke speciality. In the wake of the murder of British woman Sarah Everard a Green Party member of the House of Lords, Baroness Jones of Moulescoomb (Nincompoopia would have been better), called for a 6pm curfew for all men. This would be in breach of the Geneva Conventions on war crimes which ban collective punishment, but that would never have crossed the black and white Woke mind of Baroness Nincompoopia who would have been far too convinced of her own self-righteousness to compute such details. Many American cities did defund the police in the face of Floyd riots and after $15 million was deleted from the police budget in Washington DC under useless Woke mayor Muriel Bowser car-jacking alone rose by 300 percent and within six months the US capital recorded its highest murder rate in 15 years. The same happened in Chicago and other cities in line with the Cult/Soros plan to bring fear to streets and neighbourhoods by reducing the police, releasing violent criminals and not prosecuting crime. This is the mob-rule agenda that I have warned in the books was coming for so long. Shootings in the area of Minneapolis where Floyd was arrested increased by 2,500 percent compared with the year before. Defunding the police over George Floyd has led to a big increase in dead people with many of them black. Police protection for politicians making these decisions stayed the same or increased as you would expect from professional hypocrites. The Cult doesn't actually want to abolish the police. It wants to abolish local control over the police and hand it to federal government as the psychopaths advance the Hunger Games Society. Many George Floyd protests turned into violent riots with black stores and businesses destroyed by fire and looting across America fuelled by Black Lives Matter. Woke doesn't do irony. If you want civil rights you must loot the liquor store and the supermarket and make off with a smart TV. It's the only way.

It's not a race war – it's a class war

Black people are patronised by privileged blacks and whites alike and told they are victims of white supremacy. I find it extraordinary to watch privileged blacks supporting the very system and bloodline networks behind the slave trade and parroting the same Cult-serving manipulative crap of their privileged white, often billionaire, associates. It is indeed not a race war but a class war and colour is just a diversion. Black Senator Cory Booker and black Congresswoman Maxine Waters, more residents of Nincompoopia, personify this. Once you tell people they are victims of someone else you devalue both their own responsibility for their plight and the power they have to impact on their reality and experience. Instead we have: 'You are only in your situation because of whitey – turn on them and everything will change.' It won't change. Nothing changes in our lives unless *we* change it. Crucial to that is never seeing yourself as a victim and always as the creator of your reality. Life is a simple sequence of choice and consequence. Make different choices and you create different consequences. *You* have to make those choices – not Black Lives Matter, the Woke Mafia and anyone else that seeks to dictate your life. Who are they these Wokers, an emotional and psychological road traffic accident, to tell you what to do? Personal empowerment is the last thing the Cult and its Black Lives Matter want black people or anyone else to have. They claim to be defending the underdog while *creating* and perpetuating the underdog. The Cult's worst nightmare is human unity and if they are going to keep blacks, whites and every other race under economic servitude and control then the focus must be diverted from what they have in common to what they can be manipulated to believe divides them. Blacks have to be told that their poverty and plight is the fault of the white bloke living on the street in the same poverty and with the same plight they are experiencing. The difference is that your plight black people is due to him, a white supremacist with 'white privilege' living on the street. Don't unite as one human family against your mutual oppressors and suppressors – fight the oppressor with the white face who is as financially deprived as you are. The Cult knows that as its 'Covid' agenda moves into still new levels of extremism people are going to respond and it has been spreading the seeds of disunity everywhere to stop a united response to the evil that targets *all of us*.

Racist attacks on 'whiteness' are getting ever more outrageous and especially through the American Democratic Party which has an appalling history for anti-black racism. Barack Obama, Joe Biden, Hillary Clinton and Nancy Pelosi all eulogised about Senator Robert Byrd at his funeral in 2010 after a nearly 60-year career in Congress. Byrd was a brutal Ku Klux Klan racist and a violent abuser of Cathy O'Brien in MKUltra. He said he would never fight in the military 'with a negro by my side' and 'rather I should die a thousand times, and see Old Glory trampled in the dirt never to rise again, than to see this beloved land of ours become degraded by race mongrels, a throwback to the blackest specimen from the wilds'. Biden called Byrd a 'very close friend and mentor'. These 'Woke' hypocrites are not anti-racist they are anti-poor and anti-people not of their perceived class. Here is an illustration of the scale of anti-white racism to which we have now descended. Seriously Woke and moronic *New York Times* contributor Damon Young described whiteness as a 'virus' that 'like other viruses will not die until there are no bodies left for it to infect'. He went on: '… the only way to stop it is to locate it, isolate it, extract it, and kill it.' Young can say that as a black man with no consequences when a white man saying the same in reverse would be facing a jail sentence. *That's* racism. We had super-Woke numbskull senators Tammy Duckworth and Mazie Hirono saying they would object to future Biden Cabinet appointments if he did not nominate more Asian Americans and Pacific Islanders. Never mind the ability of the candidate what do they look like? Duckworth said: 'I will vote for racial minorities and I will vote for LGBTQ, but anyone else I'm not voting for.' Appointing people on the grounds of race is illegal, but that was not a problem for this ludicrous pair. They were on-message and that's a free pass in any situation.

Critical race racism

White children are told at school they are intrinsically racist as they are taught the divisive 'critical race theory'. This claims that the law and legal institutions are inherently racist and that race is a socially constructed concept used by white people to further their economic and political interests at the expense of people of colour. White is a 'virus' as we've seen. Racial inequality results from 'social, economic, and legal differences that white people create between races to maintain white interests which leads to poverty and criminality in minority communities'. I must tell that to the white guy sleeping on the street. The principal of East Side Community School in New York sent white parents a manifesto that called on them to become 'white traitors' and advocate for full 'white abolition'. These people are teaching your kids when they urgently need a psychiatrist. The 'school' included a chart with 'eight white identities' that ranged from 'white supremacist' to 'white abolition' and defined the behaviour white people must follow to end 'the regime of whiteness'. Woke blacks and their privileged white associates are acting exactly like the slave owners of old and Ku Klux Klan racists like Robert Byrd. They are too full of their own self-purity to see that, but it's true. Racism is not a body type; it's a state of mind that can manifest through any colour, creed or culture.

Another racial fraud is *'equity'*. Not equality of treatment and opportunity – equity. It's a term spun as equality when it means something very different. Equality in its true sense is a raising up while 'equity' is a race to the bottom. Everyone in the same level of poverty is 'equity'. Keep everyone down – that's equity. The Cult doesn't want anyone in the human family to be empowered and BLM leaders, like all these 'anti-racist' organisations, continue their privileged, pampered existence by perpetuating the perception of gathering racism. When is the last time you heard an 'anti-racist' or 'anti-Semitism' organisation say that acts of racism and discrimination have *fallen?* It's not in the interests of their fund-raising and power to influence and the same goes for the professional soccer anti-racism operation, Kick It Out. Two things confirmed that the Black Lives Matter riots in the summer of 2020 were Cult creations. One was that while anti-lockdown protests were condemned in this same period for 'transmitting 'Covid' the authorities supported mass gatherings of Black Lives Matter supporters. I even saw self-deluding people claiming to be doctors say the two types of protest were not the same. No – the non-existent 'Covid' was in favour of lockdowns and attacked those that protested against them while 'Covid' supported Black Lives Matter and kept well away from its protests. The whole thing was a joke and as lockdown protestors were arrested, often brutally, by reframed Face-Nappies we had the grotesque sight of police officers taking the knee to Black Lives Matter, a Cult-funded Marxist organisation that supports violent riots and wants to destroy the nuclear family and white people.

He's not white? Shucks!

Woke obsession with race was on display again when ten people were shot dead in Boulder, Colorado, in March, 2021. Cult-owned Woke TV channels like CNN said the shooter appeared to be a white man and Wokers were on Twitter condemning 'violent white men' with the usual mantras. Then the shooter's name was released as Ahmad Al Aliwi Alissa, an anti-Trump Arab-American, and the sigh of disappointment could be heard five miles away. Never mind that ten people were dead and what that meant for their families. Race baiting was all that mattered to these sick Cult-serving people like Barack Obama who exploited the deaths to further divide America on racial grounds which is his job for the Cult. This is the man that 'racist' white Americans made the first black president of the United States and then gave him a second term. Not-very-bright Obama has become filthy rich on the back of that and today appears to have a big influence on the Biden administration. Even so he's still a downtrodden black man and a victim of white supremacy. This disingenuous fraud reveals the contempt he has for black people when he puts on a Deep South Alabama accent whenever he talks to them, no, *at* them.

Another BLM red flag was how the now fully-Woke (fully-Cult) and fully-virtue-signalled professional soccer authorities had their teams taking the knee before every match in support of Marxist Black Lives Matter. Soccer authorities and clubs displayed 'Black Lives Matter' on the players' shirts and flashed the name on electronic billboards around the pitch. Any fans that condemned what is a Freemasonic taking-the-knee ritual were widely condemned as you would expect from the Woke virtue-signallers of professional sport and the now fully-Woke media. We have reverse racism in which you are banned from criticising any race or culture except for white people for whom anything goes – say what you like, no problem. What has this got to do with racial harmony and equality? We've had black supremacists from Black Lives Matter telling white people to fall to their knees in the street and apologise for their white supremacy. Black supremacists acting like white supremacist slave owners of the past couldn't breach their self-obsessed, race-obsessed sense of self-purity. Joe Biden appointed a race-obsessed black supremacist Kristen Clarke to head the Justice Department Civil Rights Division. Clarke claimed that blacks are endowed with 'greater mental, physical and spiritual abilities' than whites. If anyone reversed that statement they would be vilified. Clarke is on-message so no problem. She's never seen a black-white situation in which the black figure is anything but a virtuous victim and she heads the Civil Rights Division which should treat everyone the same or it isn't civil rights. Another perception of the Renegade Mind: If something or someone is part of the Cult agenda they will be supported by Woke governments and media no matter what. If they're not, they will be condemned and censored. It really is that simple and so racist Clarke prospers despite (make that because of) her racism.

The end of culture

Biden's administration is full of such racial, cultural and economic bias as the Cult requires the human family to be divided into warring factions. We are now seeing racially-segregated graduations and everything, but everything, is defined through the lens of perceived 'racism. We have 'racist' mathematics, 'racist' food and even 'racist' *plants*. World famous Kew Gardens in London said it was changing labels on plants and flowers to tell its pre-'Covid' more than two million visitors a year how racist they are. Kew director Richard Deverell said this was part of an effort to 'move quickly to decolonise collections' after they were approached by one Ajay Chhabra 'an actor with an insight into how sugar cane was linked to slavery'. They are *plants* you idiots. 'Decolonisation' in the Woke manual really means colonisation of society with its mentality and by extension colonisation by the Cult. We are witnessing a new Chinese-style 'Cultural Revolution' so essential to the success of all Marxist takeovers. Our cultural past and traditions have to be swept away to allow a new culture to be built-back-better. Woke targeting of long-standing Western cultural pillars including historical monuments and cancelling of historical figures is what happened in the Mao revolution in China which 'purged remnants of capitalist and traditional elements from Chinese society' and installed Maoism as the dominant ideology'. For China see the Western world today and for 'dominant ideology' see Woke. Better still see Marxism or Maoism. The 'Covid' hoax has specifically sought to destroy the arts and all elements of Western culture from people meeting in a pub or restaurant to closing theatres, music venues, sports stadiums, places of worship and even banning *singing*. Destruction of Western society is also why criticism of any religion is banned except for Christianity which again is the dominant religion as white is the numerically-dominant race. Christianity may be fading rapidly, but its history and traditions are weaved through the fabric of Western society. Delete the pillars and other structures will follow until the whole thing collapses. I am not a Christian defending that religion when I say that. I have no religion. It's just a fact. To this end Christianity has itself been turned Woke to usher its own downfall and its ranks are awash with 'change agents' – knowing and unknowing – at every level including Pope Francis (*definitely* knowing) and the clueless Archbishop of Canterbury Justin Welby (possibly not, but who can be sure?). Woke seeks to coordinate attacks on Western culture, traditions, and ways of life through 'intersectionality' defined as 'the complex, cumulative way in which the effects of multiple forms of discrimination (such as racism, sexism, and classism) combine, overlap, or intersect especially in the experiences of marginalised individuals or groups'. Wade through the Orwellian Woke-speak and this means coordinating disparate groups in a common cause to overthrow freedom and liberal values.

The entire structure of public institutions has been infested with Woke – government at all levels, political parties, police, military, schools, universities, advertising, media and trade unions. This abomination has been achieved through the Cult web by appointing Wokers to positions of power and battering non-Wokers into line through intimidation, isolation and threats to their job. Many have been fired in the wake of the empathy-deleted, vicious hostility of 'social justice' Wokers and the desire of gutless, spineless employers to virtue-signal their Wokeness. Corporations are filled with Wokers today, most notably those in Silicon Valley. Ironically at the top they are not Woke at all. They are only exploiting the mentality their Cult masters have created and funded to censor and enslave while the Wokers cheer them on until it's their turn. Thus the Woke 'liberal left' is an inversion of the traditional liberal left. Campaigning for justice on the grounds of power and wealth distribution has been replaced by campaigning for identity politics. The genuine traditional left would never have taken money from today's billionaire abusers of fairness and justice and nor would the billionaires have wanted to fund that genuine left. It would not have been in their interests to do so. The division of opinion in those days was between the haves and have nots. This all changed with Cult manipulated and funded identity politics. The division of opinion today is between Wokers and non-Wokers and not income brackets. Cult corporations and their billionaires may have taken wealth disparity to cataclysmic levels of injustice, but as long as they speak the language of Woke, hand out the dosh to the Woke network and censor the enemy they are 'one of us'. Billionaires who don't give a damn about injustice are laughing at them till their bellies hurt. Wokers are not even close to self-aware enough to see that. The transformed 'left' dynamic means that Wokers who drone on about 'social justice' are funded by billionaires that have destroyed social justice the world over. It's *why* they are billionaires.

The climate con

Nothing encapsulates what I have said more comprehensively than the hoax of human-caused global warming. I have detailed in my books over the years how Cult operatives and organisations were the pump-primers from the start of the climate con. A purpose-built vehicle for this is the Club of Rome established by the Cult in 1968 with the Rockefellers and Rothschilds centrally involved all along. Their gofer frontman Maurice Strong, a Canadian oil millionaire, hosted the Earth Summit in Rio de Janeiro, Brazil, in 1992 where the global 'green movement' really expanded in earnest under the guiding hand of the Cult. The Earth Summit established Agenda 21 through the Cult-created-and-owned United Nations to use the illusion of human-caused climate change to justify the transformation of global society to save the world from climate disaster. It is a No-Problem-Reaction-Solution sold through governments, media, schools and universities as whole generations have been terrified into believing that the world was going to end in their lifetimes unless what old people had inflicted upon them was stopped by a complete restructuring of how everything is done. Chill, kids, it's all a hoax. Such restructuring is precisely what the Cult agenda demands (purely by coincidence of course). Today this has been given the codename of the Great Reset which is only an updated term for Agenda 21 and its associated Agenda 2030. The latter, too, is administered through the UN and was voted into being by the General Assembly in 2015. Both 21 and 2030 seek centralised control of all resources and food right down to the raindrops falling on your own land. These are some of the demands of Agenda 21 established in 1992. See if you recognise this society emerging today:

- End national sovereignty
- State planning and management of all land resources, ecosystems, deserts, forests, mountains, oceans and fresh water; agriculture; rural development; biotechnology; and ensuring *'equity'*
- The state to 'define the role' of business and financial resources
- Abolition of private property
- 'Restructuring' the family unit (see BLM)
- Children raised by the state
- People told what their job will be
- Major restrictions on movement
- Creation of 'human settlement zones'
- Mass resettlement as people are forced to vacate land where they live
- Dumbing down education
- Mass global depopulation in pursuit of all the above

The United Nations was created as a Trojan horse for world government. With the climate con of critical importance to promoting that outcome you would expect the UN to be involved. Oh, it's involved all right. The UN is promoting Agenda 21 and Agenda 2030 justified by 'climate change' while also driving the climate hoax through its Intergovernmental Panel on Climate Change (IPCC), one of the world's most corrupt organisations. The IPCC has been lying ferociously and constantly since the day it opened its doors with the global media hanging unquestioningly on its every mendacious word. The Green movement is entirely Woke and has long lost its original environmental focus since it was co-opted by the Cult. An obsession with 'global warming' has deleted its values and scrambled its head. I experienced a small example of what I mean on a beautiful country walk that I have enjoyed several times a week for many years. The path merged into the fields and forests and you felt at one with the natural world. Then a 'Green' organisation, the Hampshire and Isle of Wight Wildlife Trust, took over part of the land and proceeded to cut down a large number of trees, including mature ones, to install a horrible big, bright steel 'this-is-

ours-stay-out' fence that destroyed the whole atmosphere of this
beautiful place. No one with a feel for nature would do that. Day after
day I walked to the sound of chainsaws and a magnificent mature
weeping willow tree that I so admired was cut down at the base of the
trunk. When I challenged a Woke young girl in a green shirt (of course)
about this vandalism she replied: 'It's a weeping willow – it will grow
back.' This is what people are paying for when they donate to the
Hampshire and Isle of Wight Wildlife Trust and many other 'green'
organisations today. It is not the environmental movement that I knew
and instead has become a support-system – as with Extinction Rebellion
– for a very dark agenda.

Private jets for climate justice

The Cult-owned, Gates-funded, World Economic Forum and its founder
Klaus Schwab were behind the emergence of Greta Thunberg to harness
the young behind the climate agenda and she was invited to speak to the
world at … the UN. Schwab published a book, *Covid-19: The Great Reset*
in 2020 in which he used the 'Covid' hoax and the climate hoax to lay
out a new society straight out of Agenda 21 and Agenda 2030. Bill Gates
followed in early 2021 when he took time out from destroying the world
to produce a book in his name about the way to save it. Gates flies across
the world in private jets and admitted that 'I probably have one of the
highest greenhouse gas footprints of anyone on the planet … my
personal flying alone is gigantic.' He has also bid for the planet's biggest
private jet operator. Other climate change saviours who fly in private
jets include John Kerry, the US Special Presidential Envoy for Climate,
and actor Leonardo DiCaprio, a 'UN Messenger of Peace with special
focus on climate change'. These people are so full of bullshit they could
corner the market in manure. We mustn't be sceptical, though, because
the Gates book, *How to Avoid a Climate Disaster: The Solutions We Have
and the Breakthroughs We Need,* is a genuine attempt to protect the world
and not an obvious pile of excrement attributed to a mega-psychopath
aimed at selling his masters' plans for humanity. The Gates book and the
other shite-pile by Klaus Schwab could have been written by the same
person and may well have been. Both use 'climate change' and 'Covid'
as the excuses for their new society and by coincidence the Cult's World
Economic Forum and Bill and Melinda Gates Foundation promote the
climate hoax and hosted Event 201 which pre-empted with a
'simulation' the very 'coronavirus' hoax that would be simulated for real
on humanity within weeks. The British 'royal' family is promoting the
'Reset' as you would expect through Prince 'climate change caused the
war in Syria' Charles and his hapless son Prince William who said that
we must 'reset our relationship with nature and our trajectory as a
species' to avoid a climate disaster. Amazing how many promotors of

the 'Covid' and 'climate change' control systems are connected to Gates and the World Economic Forum. A 'study' in early 2021 claimed that carbon dioxide emissions must fall by the equivalent of a global lockdown roughly every two years for the next decade to save the planet. The 'study' appeared in the same period that the Schwab mob claimed in a video that lockdowns destroying the lives of billions are good because they make the earth 'quieter' with less 'ambient noise'. They took down the video amid a public backlash for such arrogant, empathy-deleted stupidity You see, however, where they are going with this. Corinne Le Quéré, a professor at the Tyndall Centre for Climate Change Research, University of East Anglia, was lead author of the climate lockdown study, and she writes for … the World Economic Forum. Gates calls in 'his' book for changing 'every aspect of the economy' (long-time Cult agenda) and for humans to eat synthetic 'meat' (predicted in my books) while cows and other farm animals are eliminated. Australian TV host and commentator Alan Jones described what carbon emission targets would mean for farm animals in Australia alone if emissions were reduced as demanded by 35 percent by 2030 and zero by 2050:

> Well, let's take agriculture, the total emissions from agriculture are about 75 million tonnes of carbon dioxide, equivalent. Now reduce that by 35 percent and you have to come down to 50 million tonnes, I've done the maths. So if you take for example 1.5 million cows, you're going to have to reduce the herd by 525,000 [by] 2030, nine years, that's 58,000 cows a year. The beef herd's 30 million, reduce that by 35 percent, that's 10.5 million, which means 1.2 million cattle have to go every year between now and 2030. This is insanity!
>
> There are 75 million sheep. Reduce that by 35 percent, that's 26 million sheep, that's almost 3 million a year. So under the Paris Agreement over 30 million beasts. dairy cows, cattle, pigs and sheep would go. More than 8,000 every minute of every hour for the next decade, do these people know what they're talking about?

Clearly they don't at the level of campaigners, politicians and administrators. The Cult *does* know; that's the outcome it wants. We are faced with not just a war on humanity. Animals and the natural world are being targeted and I have been saying since the 'Covid' hoax began that the plan eventually was to claim that the 'deadly virus' is able to jump from animals, including farm animals and domestic pets, to humans. Just before this book went into production came this story: 'Russia registers world's first Covid-19 vaccine for cats & dogs as makers of Sputnik V warn pets & farm animals could spread virus'. The report said 'top scientists warned that the deadly pathogen could soon begin spreading through homes and farms' and 'the next stage is the infection of farm and domestic animals'. Know the outcome and you'll see the journey. Think what that would mean for animals and keep your eye on a term called zoonosis or zoonotic diseases which transmit between animals and humans. The Cult wants to break the connection between animals and people as it does between people and people. Farm animals fit with the Cult agenda to transform food from natural to synthetic.

The gas of life is killing us

There can be few greater examples of Cult inversion than the condemnation of carbon dioxide as a dangerous pollutant when it is the gas of life. Without it the natural world would be dead and so we would all be dead. We breathe in oxygen and breathe out carbon dioxide while plants produce oxygen and absorb carbon dioxide. It is a perfect symbiotic relationship that the Cult wants to dismantle for reasons I will come to in the final two chapters. Gates, Schwab, other Cult operatives and mindless repeaters, want the world to be 'carbon neutral' by at least 2050 and the earlier the better. 'Zero carbon' is the cry echoed by lunatics calling for 'Zero Covid' when we already have it. These carbon emission targets will deindustrialise the world in accordance with Cult plans – the post-industrial, post-democratic society – and with so-called renewables like solar and wind not coming even close to meeting human energy needs blackouts and cold are inevitable. Texans got the picture in the winter of 2021 when a snow storm stopped wind turbines and solar panels from working and the lights went down along with water which relies on electricity for its supply system. Gates wants everything to be powered by electricity to ensure that his masters have the kill switch to stop all human activity, movement, cooking, water and warmth any time they like. The climate lie is so stupendously inverted that it claims we must urgently reduce carbon dioxide when we *don't have enough*.

Co2 in the atmosphere is a little above 400 parts per million when the optimum for plant growth is 2,000 ppm and when it falls anywhere near 150 ppm the natural world starts to die and so do we. It fell to as low as 280 ppm in an 1880 measurement in Hawaii and rose to 413 ppm in 2019 with industrialisation which is why the planet has become *greener* in the industrial period. How insane then that psychopathic madman Gates is not satisfied only with blocking the rise of Co2. He's funding technology to suck it out of the atmosphere. The reason why will become clear. The industrial era is not destroying the world through Co2 and has instead turned around a potentially disastrous ongoing fall in Co2. Greenpeace co-founder and scientist Patrick Moore walked away from Greenpeace in 1986 and has exposed the green movement for fear-mongering and lies. He said that 500 million years ago there was *17 times* more Co2 in the atmosphere than we have today and levels have been falling for hundreds of millions of years. In the last 150 million years Co2 levels in Earth's atmosphere had reduced by *90 percent*. Moore said that by the time humanity began to unlock carbon dioxide from fossil fuels we were at '38 seconds to midnight' and in that sense: 'Humans are [the Earth's] salvation.' Moore made the point that only half the Co2 emitted by fossil fuels stays in the atmosphere and we should remember that all pollution pouring from chimneys that we are told is carbon dioxide is in fact nothing of the kind. It's pollution. Carbon dioxide is an invisible gas.

William Happer, Professor of Physics at Princeton University and long-time government adviser on climate, has emphasised the Co2 deficiency for maximum growth and food production. Greenhouse growers don't add carbon dioxide for a bit of fun. He said that most of the warming in the last 100 years, after the earth emerged from the super-cold period of the 'Little Ice Age' into a natural warming cycle, was over by 1940. Happer said that a peak year for warming in 1988 can be explained by a 'monster El Nino' which is a natural and cyclical warming of the Pacific that has nothing to do with 'climate change'. He said the effect of Co2 could be compared to painting a wall with red paint in that once two or three coats have been applied it didn't matter how much more you slapped on because the wall will not get much redder. Almost all the effect of the rise in Co2 has already happened, he said, and the volume in the atmosphere would now have to *double* to increase temperature by a single degree. Climate hoaxers know this and they have invented the most ridiculously complicated series of 'feedback' loops to try to overcome this rather devastating fact. You hear puppet Greta going on cluelessly about feedback loops and this is why.

The Sun affects temperature? No you *climate denier*

Some other nonsense to contemplate: Climate graphs show that rises in temperature do not follow rises in Co2 – *it's the other way round* with a lag between the two of some 800 years. If we go back 800 years from present time we hit the Medieval Warm Period when temperatures were higher than now without any industrialisation and this was followed by the Little Ice Age when temperatures plummeted. The world was still emerging from these centuries of serious cold when many climate records began which makes the ever-repeated line of the 'hottest year since records began' meaningless when you are not comparing like with like. The coldest period of the Little Ice Age corresponded with the lowest period of sunspot activity when the Sun was at its least active. Proper scientists will not be at all surprised by this when it confirms the obvious fact that earth temperature is affected by the scale of Sun activity and the energetic power that it subsequently emits; but when is

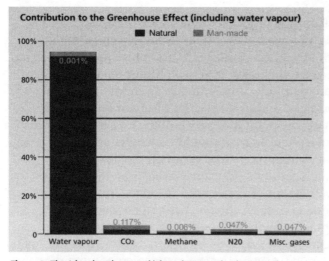

Figure 9: The idea that the gas of life is disastrously changing the climate is an insult to brain cell activity.

the last time you heard a climate hoaxer talking about the Sun as a source of earth temperature?? Everything has to be focussed on Co2 which makes up just 0.117 percent of so-called greenhouse gases and only a fraction of even that is generated by human activity. The rest is natural. More than *90 percent* of those greenhouse gases are water vapour and clouds (Fig 9). Ban moisture I say. Have you noticed that the climate hoaxers no longer use the polar bear as their promotion image? That's because far from becoming extinct polar bear communities are stable or thriving. Joe Bastardi, American meteorologist, weather forecaster and outspoken critic of the climate lie, documents in his book *The Climate Chronicles* how weather patterns and events claimed to be evidence of climate change have been happening since long before industrialisation: 'What happened before naturally is happening again, as is to be expected given the cyclical nature of the climate due to the design of the planet.' If you read the detailed background to the climate hoax in my other books you will shake your head and wonder how anyone could believe the crap which has spawned a multi-trillion dollar industry based on absolute garbage (see HIV causes AIDs and Sars-Cov-2 causes 'Covid-19'). Climate and 'Covid' have much in common given they have the same source. They both have the contradictory *everything* factor in which everything is explained by reference to them. It's hot – 'it's climate change'. It's cold – 'it's climate change'. I got a sniffle – 'it's Covid'. I haven't got a sniffle – 'it's Covid'. Not having a sniffle has to be a symptom of 'Covid'. Everything is and not having a sniffle is especially dangerous if you are a slow walker. For sheer audacity I offer you a Cambridge University 'study' that actually linked 'Covid' to 'climate change'. It had to happen eventually. They concluded that climate change played a role in 'Covid-19' spreading from animals to humans because ... wait for it ... I kid you not ... *the two groups were forced closer together as populations grow.* Er, that's it. The whole foundation on which this depended was that 'Bats are the likely zoonotic origin of SARS-CoV-1 and SARS-CoV-2'. Well, they are not. They are nothing to do with it. Apart from bats not being the origin and therefore 'climate change' effects on bats being irrelevant I am in awe of their academic insight. Where would we be without them? Not where we are that's for sure.

One other point about the weather is that climate modification is now well advanced and not every major weather event is natural – or earthquake come to that. I cover this subject at some length in other books. China is openly planning a rapid expansion of its weather modification programme which includes changing the climate in an area more than one and a half times the size of India. China used weather manipulation to ensure clear skies during the 2008 Olympics in Beijing. I have quoted from US military documents detailing how to employ weather manipulation as a weapon of war and they did that in the 1960s and 70s during the conflict in Vietnam with Operation Popeye manipulating monsoon rains for military purposes. Why would there be international treaties on weather modification if it wasn't possible? Of course it is. Weather is energetic information and it can be changed.

How was the climate hoax pulled off? See 'Covid'

If you can get billions to believe in a 'virus' that doesn't exist you can get them to believe in human-caused climate change that doesn't exist. Both are being used by the Cult to transform global society in the way it has long planned. Both hoaxes have been achieved in pretty much the same way. First you declare a lie is a fact. There's a 'virus' you call SARS-Cov-2 or humans are warming the planet with their behaviour. Next this becomes, via Cult networks, the foundation of government, academic and science policy and belief. Those who parrot the mantra are given big grants to produce research that confirms the narrative is true and ever more 'symptoms' are added to make the 'virus'/'climate change' sound even more scary. Scientists and researchers who challenge the narrative have their grants withdrawn and their careers destroyed. The media promote the lie as the unquestionable truth and censor those with an alternative view or evidence. A great percentage of the population believe what they are told as the lie becomes an everybody-knows-that and the believing-masses turn on those with a mind of their own. The technique has been used endlessly throughout human history. Wokers are the biggest promotors of the climate lie *and* 'Covid' fascism because their minds are owned by the Cult; their sense of self-righteous self-purity knows no bounds; and they exist in a bubble of reality in which facts are irrelevant and only get in the way of looking without seeing.

Running through all of this like veins in a blue cheese is control of information, which means control of perception, which means control of behaviour, which collectively means control of human society. The Cult owns the global media and Silicon Valley fascists for the simple reason that it *has* to. Without control of information it can't control perception and through that human society. Examine every facet of the Cult agenda and you will see that anything supporting its introduction is never censored while anything pushing back is always censored. I say again: Psychopaths that know why they are doing this must go before Nuremberg trials and those that follow their orders must trot along behind them into the same dock. 'I was just following orders' didn't work the first time and it must not work now. Nuremberg trials must be held all over the world before public juries for politicians, government officials, police, compliant doctors, scientists and virologists, and all Cult operatives such as Gates, Tedros, Fauci, Vallance, Whitty, Ferguson, Zuckerberg, Wojcicki, Brin, Page, Dorsey, the whole damn lot of them – including, no *especially*, the psychopath psychologists. Without them and the brainless, gutless excuses for journalists that have repeated their lies, none of this could be happening. Nobody can be allowed to escape justice for the psychological and economic Armageddon they are all responsible for visiting upon the human race.

As for the compliant, unquestioning, swathes of humanity, and the self-obsessed, all-knowing ignorance of the Wokers … don't start me. God help their kids. God help their grandkids. God *help them*.

CHAPTER NINE

We must have it?
So what is it?

Well I won't back down. No, I won't back down. You can stand me up
at the Gates of Hell. But I won't back down
Tom Petty

I will now focus on the genetically-manipulating 'Covid vaccines' which do not meet this official definition of a vaccine by the US Centers for Disease Control (CDC): 'A product that stimulates a person's immune system to produce immunity to a specific disease, protecting the person from that disease.' On that basis 'Covid vaccines' are not a vaccine in that the makers don't even claim they stop infection or transmission.

They are instead part of a multi-levelled conspiracy to change the nature of the human body and what it means to be 'human' and to depopulate an enormous swathe of humanity. What I shall call Human 1.0 is on the cusp of becoming Human 2.0 and for very sinister reasons. Before I get to the 'Covid vaccine' in detail here's some background to vaccines in general. Government regulators do not test vaccines – the makers do – and the makers control which data is revealed and which isn't. Children in America are given 50 vaccine doses by age six and 69 by age 19 and the effect of the whole combined schedule has never been tested. Autoimmune diseases when the immune system attacks its own body have soared in the mass vaccine era and so has disease in general in children and the young. Why wouldn't this be the case when vaccines target the *immune system?* The US government gave Big Pharma drug companies immunity from prosecution for vaccine death and injury in the 1986 National Childhood Vaccine Injury Act (NCVIA) and since then the government (taxpayer) has been funding compensation for the consequences of Big Pharma vaccines. The criminal and satanic drug giants can't lose and the vaccine schedule has increased dramatically since 1986 for this reason. There is no incentive to make vaccines safe and a big incentive to make money by introducing ever more. Even against a ridiculously high bar to prove vaccine liability, and with the government controlling the hearing in which it is being challenged for compensation, the vaccine court has so far paid out more than $4 billion. These are the vaccines we are told are safe and psychopaths like Zuckerberg censor posts saying otherwise. The immunity law was even justified by a ruling that vaccines by their nature were 'unavoidably unsafe'.

Check out the ingredients of vaccines and you will be shocked if you are new to this. *They put that in children's bodies?? What??* Try aluminium, a brain toxin connected to dementia, aborted foetal tissue and formaldehyde which is used to embalm corpses. World-renowned aluminium expert Christopher Exley had his research into the health effect of aluminium in vaccines shut down by Keele University in the UK when it began taking funding from the Bill and Melinda Gates Foundation. Research when diseases 'eradicated' by vaccines began to decline and you will find the fall began long *before* the vaccine was introduced. Sometimes the fall even plateaued after the vaccine. Diseases like scarlet fever for which there was no vaccine declined in the same way because of environmental and other factors. A perfect case in point is the polio vaccine. Polio began when lead arsenate was first sprayed as an insecticide and residues remained in food products. Spraying started in 1892 and the first US polio epidemic came in Vermont in 1894. The simple answer was to stop spraying, but Rockefeller-created Big Pharma had a better idea. Polio was decreed to be caused by the *poliovirus* which 'spreads from person to person and can infect a person's spinal cord'. Lead arsenate was replaced by the lethal DDT which had the same effect of causing paralysis by damaging the brain and central nervous system. Polio plummeted when DDT was reduced and then banned, but the vaccine is still given the credit for something it didn't do. Today by far the biggest cause of polio is the vaccines promoted by Bill Gates. Vaccine justice campaigner Robert Kennedy Jr, son of assassinated (by the Cult) US Attorney General Robert Kennedy, wrote:

> In 2017, the World Health Organization (WHO) reluctantly admitted that the global explosion in polio is predominantly vaccine strain. The most frightening epidemics in Congo, Afghanistan, and the Philippines, are all linked to vaccines. In fact, by 2018, 70% of global polio cases were vaccine strain.

Vaccines make fortunes for Cult-owned Gates and Big Pharma while undermining the health and immune systems of the population. We had a glimpse of the mentality behind the Big Pharma cartel with a report on WION (World is One News), an international English language TV station based in India, which exposed the extraordinary behaviour of US drug company Pfizer over its 'Covid vaccine'. The WION report told how Pfizer had made fantastic demands of Argentina, Brazil and other countries in return for its 'vaccine'. These included immunity from prosecution, even for Pfizer negligence, government insurance to protect Pfizer from law suits and handing over as collateral sovereign assets of the country to include Argentina's bank reserves, military bases and embassy buildings. Pfizer demanded the same of Brazil in the form of waiving sovereignty of its assets abroad; exempting Pfizer from Brazilian laws; and giving Pfizer immunity from all civil liability. This is a 'vaccine' developed with government funding. Big Pharma is evil incarnate as a creation of the Cult and all must be handed tickets to Nuremberg.

Phantom 'vaccine' for a phantom 'disease'

I'll expose the 'Covid vaccine' fraud and then go on to the wider background of why the Cult has set out to 'vaccinate' every man, woman and child on the planet for an alleged 'new disease' with a survival rate of 99.77 percent (or more) even by the grotesquely-manipulated figures of the World Health Organization and Johns Hopkins University. The 'infection' to 'death' ratio is 0.23 to 0.15 percent according to Stanford epidemiologist Dr John Ioannidis and while estimates vary the danger remains tiny. I say that if the truth be told the fake infection to fake death ratio is zero. Never mind all the evidence I have presented here and in *The Answer* that there is no 'virus' let us just focus for a moment on that death-rate figure of say 0.23 percent. The figure includes all those worldwide who have tested positive with a test not testing for the 'virus' and then died within 28 days or even longer of any other cause – *any other cause*. Now subtract all those illusory 'Covid' deaths on the global data sheets from the 0.23 percent. What do you think you would be left with? *Zero*. A vaccination has never been successfully developed for a so-called coronavirus. They have all failed at the animal testing stage when they caused hypersensitivity to what they were claiming to protect against and made the impact of a disease far worse. Cult-owned vaccine corporations got around that problem this time by bypassing animal trials, going straight to humans and making the length of the 'trials' before the public rollout as short as they could get away with. Normally it takes five to ten years or more to develop vaccines that still cause demonstrable harm to many people and that's without including the long-term effects that are never officially connected to the vaccination. 'Covid' non-vaccines have been officially produced and approved in a matter of months from a standing start and part of the reason is that (a) they were developed before the 'Covid' hoax began and (b) they are based on computer programs and not

natural sources. Official non-trials were so short that government
agencies gave *emergency,* not full, approval. 'Trials' were not even
completed and full approval cannot be secured until they are. Public
'Covid vaccination' is actually a *continuation of the trial.* Drug company
'trials' are not scheduled to end until 2023 by which time a lot of people
are going to be dead. Data on which government agencies gave this
emergency approval was supplied by the Big Pharma corporations
themselves in the form of Pfizer/BioNTech, AstraZeneca, Moderna,
Johnson & Johnson, and others, and this is the case with all vaccines. By
its very nature *emergency* approval means drug companies do not have
to prove that the 'vaccine' is 'safe and effective'. How could they with
trials way short of complete? Government regulators only have to *believe*
that they *could* be safe and effective. It is criminal manipulation to get
products in circulation with no testing worth the name. Agencies giving
that approval are infested with Big Pharma-connected place-people and
they act in the interests of Big Pharma (the Cult) and not the public
about whom they do not give a damn.

More human lab rats

'Covid vaccines' produced in record time by Pfizer/BioNTech and
Moderna employ a technique *never approved before for use on humans.*
They are known as mRNA 'vaccines' and inject a synthetic version of
'viral' mRNA or 'messenger RNA'. The key is in the term 'messenger'.
The body works, or doesn't, on the basis of information messaging.
Communications are constantly passing between and within the genetic
system and the brain. Change those messages and you change the state
of the body and even its very nature and you can change psychology
and behaviour by the way the brain processes information. I think you
are going to see significant changes in personality and perception of
many people who have had the 'Covid vaccine' synthetic potions.
Insider Aldous Huxley predicted the following in 1961 and mRNA
'vaccines' can be included in the term 'pharmacological methods':

> There will be, in the next generation or so, a pharmacological method of
> making people love their servitude, and producing dictatorship without tears,
> so to speak, producing a kind of painless concentration camp for entire
> societies, so that people will in fact have their own liberties taken away from
> them, but rather enjoy it, because they will be distracted from any desire to
> rebel by propaganda or brainwashing, or brainwashing enhanced by
> pharmacological methods. And this seems to be the final revolution.

Apologists claim that mRNA synthetic 'vaccines' don't change the
DNA genetic blueprint because RNA does not affect DNA only the other
way round. This is so disingenuous. A process called 'reverse

transcription' can convert RNA into DNA and be integrated into DNA in the cell nucleus. This was highlighted in December, 2020, by scientists at Harvard and Massachusetts Institute of Technology (MIT). Geneticists report that more than 40 percent of mammalian genomes results from reverse transcription. On the most basic level if messaging changes then that sequence must lead to changes in DNA which is receiving and transmitting those communications. How can introducing synthetic material into cells not change the cells where DNA is located? The process is known as transfection which is defined as 'a technique to insert foreign nucleic acid (DNA or RNA) into a cell, typically with the intention of altering the properties of the cell'. Researchers at the Sloan Kettering Institute in New York found that changes in messenger RNA can deactivate tumour-suppressing proteins and thereby promote cancer. This is what happens when you mess with messaging. 'Covid vaccine' maker Moderna was founded in 2010 by Canadian stem cell biologist Derrick J. Rossi after his breakthrough discovery in the field of transforming and reprogramming stem cells. These are neutral cells that can be programmed to become any cell including sperm cells. Moderna was therefore founded on the principle of genetic manipulation and has never produced any vaccine or drug before its genetically-manipulating synthetic 'Covid' shite. Look at the name – Mode-RNA or Modify-RNA. Another important point is that the US Supreme Court has ruled that genetically-modified DNA, or complementary DNA (cDNA) synthesized in the laboratory from messenger RNA, can be patented and owned. These psychopaths are doing this to the human body.

Cells replicate synthetic mRNA in the 'Covid vaccines' and in theory the body is tricked into making antigens which trigger antibodies to target the 'virus spike proteins' which as Dr Tom Cowan said have *never been seen*. Cut the crap and these 'vaccines' deliver *self-replicating* synthetic material to the cells with the effect of changing human DNA. The more of them you have the more that process is compounded while synthetic material is all the time self-replicating. 'Vaccine'-maker Moderna describes mRNA as 'like software for the cell' and so they are messing with the body's software. What happens when you change the software in a computer? Everything changes. For this reason the Cult is preparing a production line of mRNA 'Covid vaccines' and a long list of excuses to use them as with all the 'variants' of a 'virus' never shown to exist. The plan is further to transfer the mRNA technique to other vaccines mostly given to children and young people. The cumulative consequences will be a transformation of human DNA through a constant infusion of synthetic genetic material which will kill many and change the rest. Now consider that governments that have given emergency approval for a vaccine that's not a vaccine; never been approved for humans before; had no testing worth the name; and the makers have been given immunity from prosecution for any deaths or adverse effects suffered by the public. The UK government awarded *permanent legal indemnity* to itself and its employees for harm done when a patient is being treated for 'Covid-19' or 'suspected Covid-19'. That is quite a thought when these are possible 'side-effects' from the 'vaccine' (they are not 'side', they are effects) listed by the US Food and Drug Administration:

Guillain-Barre syndrome; acute disseminated encephalomyelitis; transverse myelitis; encephalitis; myelitis; encephalomyelitis; meningoencephalitis; meningitis; encephalopathy; convulsions; seizures; stroke; narcolepsy; cataplexy; anaphylaxis; acute myocardial infarction (heart attack); myocarditis; pericarditis; autoimmune disease; death; implications for pregnancy, and birth outcomes; other acute demyelinating diseases; non anaphylactic allergy reactions; thrombocytopenia ; disseminated intravascular coagulation; venous thromboembolism; arthritis; arthralgia; joint pain; Kawasaki disease; multisystem inflammatory syndrome in children; vaccine enhanced disease. The latter is the way the 'vaccine' has the potential to make diseases far worse than they would otherwise be.

UK doctor and freedom campaigner Vernon Coleman described the conditions in this list as 'all unpleasant, most of them very serious, and you can't get more serious than death'. The thought that anyone at all has had the 'vaccine' in these circumstances is testament to the potential that humanity has for clueless, unquestioning, stupidity and for many that programmed stupidity has already been terminal.

An insider speaks

Dr Michael Yeadon is a former Vice President, head of research and Chief Scientific Adviser at vaccine giant Pfizer. Yeadon worked on the inside of Big Pharma, but that did not stop him becoming a vocal critic of 'Covid vaccines' and their potential for multiple harms, including infertility in women. By the spring of 2021 he went much further and even used the no, no, term 'conspiracy'. When you begin to see what is going on it is impossible not to do so. Yeadon spoke out in an interview with freedom campaigner James Delingpole and I mentioned earlier how he said that no one had samples of 'the virus'. He explained that the mRNA technique originated in the anti-cancer field and ways to turn on and off certain genes which could be advantageous if you wanted to stop cancer growing out of control. 'That's the origin of them. They are a very unusual application, really.' Yeadon said that treating a cancer patient with an aggressive procedure might be understandable if the alternative was dying, but it was quite another thing to use the same technique as a public health measure. Most people involved wouldn't catch the infectious agent you were vaccinating against and if they did they probably wouldn't die:

> If you are really using it as a public health measure you really want to as close as you can get to zero sides-effects … I find it odd that they chose techniques that were really cutting their teeth in the field of oncology and I'm worried that in using gene-based vaccines that have to be injected in the body and spread around the body, get taken up into some cells, and the regulators haven't quite told us which cells they get taken up into … you are going to be generating a wide range of responses … with multiple steps each of which could go well or badly.

I doubt the Cult intends it to go well. Yeadon said that you can put any gene you like into the body through the 'vaccine'. 'You can certainly give them a gene that would do them some harm if you wanted.' I was intrigued when he said that when used in the cancer field the technique could turn genes on and off. I explore this process in *The Answer* and with different genes having different functions you could create mayhem – physically and psychologically – if you turned the wrong ones on and the right ones off. I read reports of an experiment by researchers at the University of Washington's school of computer science and engineering in which they encoded DNA to infect computers. The body is itself a biological computer and if human DNA can inflict damage on a computer why can't the computer via synthetic material mess with the human body? It can. The Washington research team said it was possible to insert malicious malware into 'physical DNA strands' and corrupt the computer system of a gene sequencing machine as it 'reads gene letters and stores them as binary digits 0 and 1'. They concluded that hackers could one day use blood or spit samples to access computer systems and obtain sensitive data from police forensics labs or infect genome files. It is at this level of digital interaction that synthetic 'vaccines' need to be seen to get the full picture and that will become very clear later on. Michael Yeadon said it made no sense to give the 'vaccine' to younger people who were in no danger from the 'virus'. What was the benefit? It was all downside with potential effects:

> The fact that my government in what I thought was a civilised, rational country, is raining [the 'vaccine'] on people in their 30s and 40s, even my children in their 20s, they're getting letters and phone calls, I know this is not right and any of you doctors who are vaccinating you know it's not right, too. They are not at risk. They are not at risk from the disease, so you are now hoping that the side-effects are so rare that you get away with it. You don't give new technology … that you don't understand to 100 percent of the

population.

Blood clot problems with the AstraZeneca 'vaccine' have been affecting younger people to emphasise the downside risks with no benefit. AstraZeneca's version, produced with Oxford University, does not use mRNA, but still gets its toxic cocktail inside cells where it targets DNA. The Johnson & Johnson 'vaccine' which uses a similar technique has also produced blood clot effects to such an extent that the United States paused its use at one point. They are all 'gene therapy' (cell modification) procedures and not 'vaccines'. The truth is that once the content of these injections enter cells we have no idea what the effect will be. People can speculate and some can give very educated opinions and that's good. In the end, though, only the makers know what their potions are designed to do and even they won't know every last consequence. Michael Yeadon was scathing about doctors doing what they knew to be wrong. 'Everyone's mute', he said. Doctors in the NHS must know this was not right, coming into work and injecting people. 'I don't know how they sleep at night. I know I couldn't do it. I know that if I were in that position I'd have to quit.' He said he knew enough about toxicology to know this was not a good risk-benefit. Yeadon had spoken to seven or eight university professors and all except two would not speak out publicly. Their universities had a policy that no one said anything that countered the government and its medical advisors. They were afraid of losing their government grants. This is how intimidation has been used to silence the truth at every level of the system. I say silence, but these people could still speak out if they made that choice. Yeadon called them 'moral cowards' – 'This is about your children and grandchildren's lives and you have just buggered off and left it.'

'Variant' nonsense

Some of his most powerful comments related to the alleged 'variants' being used to instil more fear, justify more lockdowns, and introduce more 'vaccines'. He said government claims about 'variants' were nonsense. He had checked the alleged variant 'codes' and they were 99.7 percent identical to the 'original'. This was the human identity difference equivalent to putting a baseball cap on and off or wearing it the other way round. A 0.3 percent difference would make it impossible for that 'variant' to escape immunity from the 'original'. This made no sense of having new 'vaccines' for 'variants'. He said there would have to be at least a *30 percent* difference for that to be justified and even then he believed the immune system would still recognise what it was. Gates-funded 'variant modeller' and 'vaccine'-pusher John Edmunds might care to comment. Yeadon said drug companies were making new versions of the 'vaccine' as a 'top up' for 'variants'. Worse than that, he said, the 'regulators' around the world like the MHRA in the UK had got together and agreed that because 'vaccines' for 'variants' were so similar to the first 'vaccines' *they did not have to do safety studies.* How transparently sinister that is. This is when Yeadon said: 'There is a conspiracy here.' There was no need for another vaccine for 'variants' and yet we were told that there was and the country had shut its borders because of them. 'They are going into hundreds of millions of arms without passing 'go' or any regulator. Why did they do that? Why did they pick this method of making the vaccine?'

The reason had to be something bigger than that it seemed and 'it's not protection against the virus'. It's was a far bigger project that meant politicians and advisers were willing to do things and not do things that knowingly resulted in avoidable deaths – 'that's already happened when you think about lockdown and deprivation of health care for a year.' He spoke of people prepared to do something that results in the avoidable death of their fellow human beings and it not bother them. This is the penny-drop I have been working to get across for more than 30 years – the level of pure evil we are dealing with. Yeadon said his friends and associates could not believe there could be that much evil, but he reminded them of Stalin, Pol Pot and Hitler and of what Stalin had said: 'One death is a tragedy. A million? A statistic.' He could not think of a benign explanation for why you need top-up vaccines 'which I'm sure you don't' and for the regulators 'to just get out of the way and wave them through'. Why would the regulators do that when they were still wrestling with the dangers of the 'parent' vaccine? He was clearly shocked by what he had seen since the 'Covid' hoax began and now he was thinking the previously unthinkable:

> If you wanted to depopulate a significant proportion of the world and to do it in a way that doesn't involve destruction of the environment with nuclear weapons, poisoning everyone with anthrax or something like that, and you wanted plausible deniability while you had a multi-year infectious disease crisis, I actually don't think you could come up with a better plan of work than seems to be in front of me. I can't say that's what they are going to do, but I can't think of a benign explanation why they are doing it.

He said he never thought that they would get rid of 99 percent of humans, but now he wondered. 'If you wanted to that this would be a hell of a way to do it – it would be unstoppable folks.' Yeadon had concluded that those who submitted to the 'vaccine' would be allowed to have some kind of normal life (but for how long?) while screws were tightened to coerce and mandate the last few percent. 'I think they'll put the rest of them in a prison camp. I wish I was wrong, but I don't think I am.' Other points he made included: There were no coronavirus vaccines then suddenly they all come along at the same time; we have no idea of the long term affect with trials so short; coercing or forcing people to have medical procedures is against the Nuremberg Code instigated when the Nazis did just that; people should at least delay having the 'vaccine'; a quick Internet search confirms that masks don't reduce respiratory viral transmission and 'the government knows that'; they have smashed civil society and they know that, too; two dozen peer-reviewed studies show no connection between lockdown and reducing deaths; he knew from personal friends the elite were still flying around and going on holiday while the public were locked down; the elite were not having the 'vaccines'. He was also asked if 'vaccines' could be made to target difference races. He said he didn't know, but the document by the Project for the New American Century in September, 2000, said developing 'advanced forms of biological warfare that can target *specific genotypes* may transform biological warfare from the realm of terror to a politically useful tool.' Oh, they're evil all right. Of that we can be *absolutely* sure.

Another cull of old people

We have seen from the CDC definition that the mRNA 'Covid vaccine' is not a vaccine and nor are the others that *claim* to reduce 'severity of symptoms' in *some* people, but not protect from infection or transmission. What about all the lies about returning to 'normal' if people were 'vaccinated'? If they are not claimed to stop infection and transmission of the alleged 'virus', how does anything change? This was all lies to manipulate people to take the jabs and we are seeing that now with masks and distancing still required for the 'vaccinated'. How did they think that elderly people with fragile health and immune responses were going to be affected by infusing their cells with synthetic material and other toxic substances? They *knew* that in the short and long term it would be devastating and fatal as the culling of the old that began with the first lockdowns was continued with the 'vaccine'. Death rates in care homes soared immediately residents began to be 'vaccinated' – infused with synthetic material. Brave and committed whistleblower nurses put their careers at risk by exposing this truth while the rest kept their heads down and their mouths shut to put their careers before those they are supposed to care for. A long-time American Certified Nursing Assistant who gave his name as James posted a video in which he described emotionally what happened in his care home when vaccination began. He said that during 2020 very few residents were sick with 'Covid' and no one died during the entire year; but shortly after the Pfizer mRNA injections 14 people died within two weeks and many others were near death. 'They're dropping like flies', he said. Residents who walked on their own before the shot could no longer and they had lost their ability to conduct an intelligent conversation. The home's management said the sudden deaths were caused by a 'super-spreader' of 'Covid-19'. Then how come, James asked, that residents who refused to take the injections were not sick? It was a case of inject the elderly with mRNA synthetic potions and blame their illness and death that followed on the 'virus'. James described what was happening in care homes as 'the greatest crime of genocide this country has ever seen'. Remember the NHS staff nurse from earlier who used the same word 'genocide' for what was happening with the 'vaccines' and that it was an 'act of human annihilation'. A UK care home whistleblower told a similar story to James about the effect of the 'vaccine' in deaths and 'outbreaks' of illness dubbed 'Covid' after getting the jab. She told how her care home management and staff had zealously imposed government regulations and no one was allowed to even question the official narrative let alone speak out against it. She said the NHS was even worse. Again we see the results of reframing. A worker at a local care home where I live said they had not had a single case of 'Covid' there for almost a year and when the residents were 'vaccinated' they had 19 positive cases in two weeks with eight dying.

It's not the 'vaccine' – honest

The obvious cause and effect was being ignored by the media and most of the public. Australia's health minister Greg Hunt (a former head of strategy at the World Economic Forum) was admitted to hospital after he had the 'vaccine'. He was suffering according to reports from the skin infection 'cellulitis' and it must have been a severe case to have warranted days in hospital. Immediately the authorities said this was nothing to do with the 'vaccine' when an effect of some vaccines is a 'cellulitis-like reaction'. We had families of perfectly healthy old people who died after the 'vaccine' saying that if only they had been given the 'vaccine' earlier they would still be alive. As a numbskull rating that is off the chart. A father of four 'died of Covid' at aged 48 when he was taken ill two days after having the 'vaccine'. The man, a health administrator, had been 'shielding during the pandemic' and had 'not really left the house' until he went for the 'vaccine'. Having the 'vaccine' and then falling ill and dying does not seem to have qualified as a possible cause and effect and 'Covid-19' went on his death certificate. His family said they had no idea how he 'caught the virus'. A family member said: 'Tragically, it could be that going for a vaccination ultimately led to him catching Covid …The sad truth is that they are never going to know where it came from.' The family warned people to remember that the virus still existed and was 'very real'. So was their stupidity. Nurses and doctors who had the first round of the 'vaccine' were collapsing, dying and ending up in a hospital bed while they or their grieving relatives were saying they'd still have the 'vaccine' again despite what happened. I kid you not. You mean if your husband returned from the dead he'd have the same 'vaccine' again that killed him??

Doctors at the VCU Medical Center in Richmond, Virginia, said the Johnson & Johnson 'vaccine' was to blame for a man's skin peeling off. Patient Richard Terrell said: 'It all just happened so fast. My skin peeled off. It's still coming off on my hands now.' He said it was stinging, burning and itching and when he bent his arms and legs it was very painful with 'the skin swollen and rubbing against itself'. Pfizer/BioNTech and Moderna vaccines use mRNA to change the cell while the Johnson & Johnson version uses DNA in a process similar to AstraZeneca's technique. Johnson & Johnson and AstraZeneca have both had their 'vaccines' paused by many countries after causing serious blood problems. Terrell's doctor Fnu Nutan said he could have died if he hadn't got medical attention. It sounds terrible so what did Nutan and Terrell say about the 'vaccine' now? Oh, they still recommend that people have it. A nurse in a hospital bed 40 minutes after the vaccination and unable to swallow due to throat swelling was told by a doctor that he lost mobility in his arm for 36 hours following the vaccination. What did he say to the ailing nurse? 'Good for you for getting the vaccination.' We are dealing with a serious form of cognitive dissonance madness in both public and medical staff. There is a remarkable correlation between those having the 'vaccine' and trumpeting the fact and suffering bad happenings shortly afterwards. Witold Rogiewicz, a Polish doctor, made a video of his 'vaccination' and ridiculed those who were questioning its safety and the intentions of Bill Gates: 'Vaccinate yourself to protect yourself, your loved ones, friends and also patients. And to mention quickly I have info for anti-vaxxers and anti-Coviders if you want to contact Bill Gates you can do this through me.' He further ridiculed the dangers of 5G. Days later he was dead, but naturally the vaccination wasn't mentioned in the verdict of 'heart attack'.

Lies, lies and more lies

So many members of the human race have slipped into extreme states of insanity and unfortunately they include reframed doctors and nursing staff. Having a 'vaccine' and dying within minutes or hours is not considered a valid connection while death from any cause within 28 days or longer of a positive test with a test not testing for the 'virus' means 'Covid-19' goes on the death certificate. How could that 'vaccine'-death connection not have been made except by calculated deceit? US figures in the initial rollout period to February 12th, 2020, revealed that a third of the deaths reported to the CDC after 'Covid vaccines' happened within 48 hours. Five men in the UK suffered an 'extremely rare' blood clot problem after having the AstraZeneca 'vaccine', but no causal link was established said the Gates-funded Medicines and Healthcare products Regulatory Agency (MHRA) which had given the 'vaccine' emergency approval to be used. Former Pfizer executive Dr Michael Yeadon explained in his interview how the procedures could cause blood coagulation and clots. People who should have been at no risk were dying from blood clots in the brain and he said he had heard from medical doctor friends that people were suffering from skin bleeding and massive headaches. The AstraZeneca 'shot' was stopped by some 20 countries over the blood clotting issue and still the corrupt MHRA, the European Medicines Agency (EMA) and the World Health Organization said that it should continue to be given even though the EMA admitted that it 'still cannot rule out definitively' a link between blood clotting and the 'vaccine'. Later Marco Cavaleri, head of EMA vaccine strategy, said there was indeed a clear link between the 'vaccine' and thrombosis, but they didn't know why. So much for the trials showing the 'vaccine' is safe. Blood clots were affecting younger people who would be under virtually no danger from 'Covid' even if it existed which makes it all the more stupid and sinister.

The British government responded to public alarm by wheeling out June Raine, the terrifyingly weak infant school headmistress sound-alike who heads the UK MHRA drug 'regulator'. The idea that she would stand up to Big Pharma and government pressure is laughable and she told us that all was well in the same way that she did when allowing untested, never-used-on-humans-before, genetically-manipulating 'vaccines' to be exposed to the public in the first place. Mass lying is the new normal of the 'Covid' era. The MHRA later said 30 cases of rare blood clots had by then been connected with the AstraZeneca 'vaccine' (that means a lot more in reality) while stressing that the benefits of the jab in preventing 'Covid-19' outweighed any risks. A more ridiculous and disingenuous statement with callous disregard for human health it is hard to contemplate. Immediately after the mendacious 'all-clears' two hospital workers in Denmark experienced blood clots and cerebral haemorrhaging following the AstraZeneca jab and one died. Top Norwegian health official Pål Andre Holme said the 'vaccine' was the only common factor: 'There is nothing in the patient history of these individuals that can give such a powerful immune response … I am confident that the antibodies that we have found are the cause, and I see no other explanation than it being the vaccine which triggers it.' Strokes, a clot or bleed in the brain, were clearly associated with the 'vaccine' from word of mouth and whistleblower reports. Similar consequences followed with all these 'vaccines' that we were told were so safe and as the numbers grew by the day it was clear we were witnessing human carnage.

Learning the hard way

A woman interviewed by UKColumn told how her husband suffered dramatic health effects after the vaccine when he'd been in good health all his life. He went from being a little unwell to losing all feeling in his legs and experiencing 'excruciating pain'. Misdiagnosis followed twice at Accident and Emergency (an 'allergy' and 'sciatica') before he was admitted to a neurology ward where doctors said his serious condition had been caused by the 'vaccine'. Another seven 'vaccinated' people were apparently being treated on the same ward for similar symptoms. The woman said he had the 'vaccine' because they believed media claims that it was safe. 'I didn't think the government would give out a vaccine that does this to somebody; I believed they would be bringing out a vaccination that would be safe.' What a tragic way to learn that lesson. Another woman posted that her husband was transporting stroke patients to hospital on almost every shift and when he asked them if they had been 'vaccinated' for 'Covid' they all replied 'yes'. One had a 'massive brain bleed' the day after his second dose. She said her husband reported the 'just been vaccinated' information every time to doctors in A and E only for them to ignore it, make no notes and appear annoyed that it was even mentioned. This particular report cannot be verified, but it expresses a common theme that confirms the monumental underreporting of 'vaccine' consequences. Interestingly as the 'vaccines' and their brain blood clot/stroke consequences began to emerge the UK National Health Service began a publicity campaign telling the public what to do in the event of a stroke. A Scottish NHS staff nurse who quit in disgust in March, 2021, said:

> I have seen traumatic injuries from the vaccine, they're not getting reported to the yellow card [adverse reaction] scheme, they're treating the symptoms, not asking why, why it's happening. It's just treating the symptoms and when you speak about it you're dismissed like you're crazy, I'm not crazy, I'm not crazy because every other colleague I've spoken to is terrified to speak out, they've had enough.

Videos appeared on the Internet of people uncontrollably shaking after the 'vaccine' with no control over muscles, limbs and even their face. A Scottish mother broke out in a severe rash all over her body almost immediately after she was given the AstraZeneca 'vaccine'. The pictures were horrific. Leigh King, a 41-year-old hairdresser from Lanarkshire said: 'Never in my life was I prepared for what I was about to experience … My skin was so sore and constantly hot … I have never felt pain like this …' But don't you worry, the 'vaccine' is perfectly safe. Then there has been the effect on medical staff who have been pressured to have the 'vaccine' by psychopathic 'health' authorities and government. A London hospital consultant who gave the name K. Polyakova wrote this to the *British Medical Journal* or *BMJ*:

> I am currently struggling with … the failure to report the reality of the morbidity caused by our current vaccination program within the health service and staff population. The levels of sickness after vaccination is unprecedented and staff are getting very sick and some with neurological symptoms which is having a huge impact on the health service function. Even the young and healthy are off for days, some for weeks, and some requiring medical treatment. Whole teams are being taken out as they went to get vaccinated together.
>
> Mandatory vaccination in this instance is stupid, unethical and irresponsible when it comes to protecting our staff and public health. We are in the voluntary phase of vaccination, and encouraging staff to take an unlicensed product that is impacting on their immediate health … it is clearly stated that these vaccine products do not offer immunity or stop transmission. In which case why are we doing it?

Not to protect health that's for sure. Medical workers are lauded by governments for agenda reasons when they couldn't give a toss about them any more than they can for the population in general. Schools across America faced the same situation as they closed due to the high number of teachers and other staff with bad reactions to the Pfizer/BioNTech, Moderna, and Johnson & Johnson 'Covid vaccines' all of which were linked to death and serious adverse effects. The *BMJ* took down the consultant's comments pretty quickly on the grounds that they were being used to spread 'disinformation'. They were exposing the truth about the 'vaccine' was the real reason. The cover-up is breathtaking.

Hiding the evidence

The scale of the 'vaccine' death cover-up worldwide can be confirmed by comparing official figures with the personal experience of the public. I heard of many people in my community who died immediately or soon after the vaccine that would never appear in the media or even likely on the official totals of 'vaccine' fatalities and adverse reactions when only about ten percent are estimated to be reported and I have seen some estimates as low as one percent in a Harvard study. In the UK alone by April 29th, 2021, some 757,654 adverse reactions had been officially reported from the Pfizer/BioNTech, Oxford/AstraZeneca and Moderna 'vaccines' with more than a thousand deaths linked to jabs and that means an estimated ten times this number in reality from a ten percent reporting rate percentage. That's seven million adverse reactions and 10,000 potential deaths and a one percent reporting rate would be ten times *those* figures. In 1976 the US government pulled the swine flu vaccine after 53 deaths. The UK data included a combined 10,000 eye disorders from the 'Covid vaccines' with more than 750 suffering visual impairment or blindness and again multiply by the estimated reporting percentages. As 'Covid cases' officially fell hospitals virtually empty during the 'Covid crisis' began to fill up with a range of other problems in the wake of the 'vaccine' rollout. The numbers across America have also been catastrophic. Deaths linked to *all* types of vaccine increased by *6,000 percent* in the first quarter of 2021 compared with 2020. A 39-year-old woman from Ogden, Utah, died four days after receiving a second dose of Moderna's 'Covid vaccine' when her liver, heart and kidneys all failed despite the fact that she had no known medical issues or conditions. Her family sought an autopsy, but Dr Erik Christensen, Utah's chief medical examiner, said proving vaccine injury as a cause of death almost never happened. He could think of only one instance where an autopsy would name a vaccine as the official cause of death and that would be anaphylaxis where someone received a vaccine and died almost instantaneously. 'Short of that, it would be difficult for us to definitively say this is the vaccine,' Christensen said. If that is true this must be added to the estimated ten percent (or far less) reporting rate of vaccine deaths and serious reactions and the conclusion can only be that vaccine deaths and serious reactions – including these 'Covid' potions' – are phenomenally understated in official figures. The same story can be found everywhere. Endless accounts of deaths and serious reactions among the public, medical and care home staff while official figures did not even begin to reflect this.

Professional script-reader Dr David Williams, a 'top public-health official' in Ontario, Canada, insulted our intelligence by claiming only four serious adverse reactions and no deaths from the more than 380,000 vaccine doses then given. This bore no resemblance to what people knew had happened in their owns circles and we had Dirk Huyer in charge of getting millions vaccinated in Ontario while at the same time he was Chief Coroner for the province investigating causes of death including possible death from the vaccine. An aide said he had stepped back from investigating deaths, but evidence indicated otherwise. Rosemary Frei, who secured a Master of Science degree in molecular biology at the Faculty of Medicine at Canada's University of Calgary before turning to investigative journalism, was one who could see that official figures for 'vaccine' deaths and reactions made no sense. She said that doctors seldom reported adverse events and when people got really sick or died after getting a vaccination they would attribute that to anything except the vaccines. It had been that way for years and anyone who wondered aloud whether the 'Covid vaccines' or other shots cause harm is immediately branded as 'anti-vax' and 'anti-science'. This was 'career-threatening' for health professionals. Then there was the huge pressure to support the push to 'vaccinate' billions in the quickest time possible. Frei said:

> So that's where we're at today. More than half a million vaccine doses have been given to people in Ontario alone. The rush is on to vaccinate all 15 million of us in the province by September. And the mainstream media are screaming for this to be sped up even more. That all adds up to only a very slim likelihood that we're going to be told the truth by officials about how many people are getting sick or dying from the vaccines.

What is true of Ontario is true of everywhere.

They KNEW – and still did it

The authorities knew what was going to happen with multiple deaths and adverse reactions. The UK government's Gates-funded and Big Pharma-dominated Medicines and Healthcare products Regulatory Agency (MHRA) hired a company to employ AI in compiling the projected reactions to the 'vaccine' that would otherwise be uncountable. The request for applications said: 'The MHRA urgently seeks an Artificial Intelligence (AI) software tool to process the expected high volume of Covid-19 vaccine Adverse Drug Reaction …' This was from the agency, headed by the disingenuous June Raine, that gave the 'vaccines' emergency approval and the company was hired before the first shot was given. 'We are going to kill and maim you – is that okay?' 'Oh, yes, perfectly fine – I'm very grateful, thank you, doctor.' The range of 'Covid vaccine' adverse reactions goes on for page after page in the MHRA criminally underreported 'Yellow Card' system and includes affects to eyes, ears, skin, digestion, blood and so on. Raine's MHRA amazingly claimed that the 'overall safety experience … is so far as expected from the clinical trials'. The death, serious adverse effects, deafness and blindness were *expected?* When did they ever mention that? If these human tragedies were expected then those that gave approval for the use of these 'vaccines' must be guilty of crimes against humanity including murder – a definition of which is 'killing a person with malice aforethought or with recklessness manifesting extreme indifference to the value of human life.' People involved at the MHRA, the CDC in America and their equivalent around the world must go before Nuremberg trials to answer for their callous inhumanity. We are only talking here about the immediate effects of the 'vaccine'. The longer-term impact of the DNA synthetic manipulation is the main reason they are so hysterically desperate to inoculate the entire global population in the shortest possible time.

Africa and the developing world are a major focus for the 'vaccine' depopulation agenda and a mass vaccination sales-pitch is underway thanks to caring people like the Rockefellers and other Cult assets. The Rockefeller Foundation, which pre-empted the 'Covid pandemic' in a document published in 2010 that 'predicted' what happened a decade later, announced an initial $34.95 million grant in February, 2021, 'to ensure more equitable access to Covid-19 testing and vaccines' among other things in Africa in collaboration with '24 organizations, businesses, and government agencies'. The pan-Africa initiative would focus on 10 countries: Burkina Faso, Ethiopia, Ghana, Kenya, Nigeria, Rwanda, South Africa, Tanzania, Uganda, and Zambia'. Rajiv Shah, President of the Rockefeller Foundation and former administrator of CIA-controlled USAID, said that if Africa was not mass-vaccinated (to change the DNA of its people) it was a 'threat to all of humanity' and not fair on Africans. When someone from the Rockefeller Foundation says they want to do something to help poor and deprived people and countries it is time for a belly-laugh. They are doing this out of the goodness of their 'heart' because 'vaccinating' the entire global population is what the 'Covid' hoax set out to achieve. Official 'decolonisation' of Africa by the Cult was merely a prelude to financial colonisation on the road to a return to physical colonisation. The 'vaccine' is vital to that and the sudden and convenient death of the 'Covid' sceptic president of Tanzania can be seen in its true light. A lot of people in Africa are aware that this is another form of colonisation and exploitation and they need to stand their ground.

The 'vaccine is working' scam

A potential problem for the Cult was that the 'vaccine' is meant to change human DNA and body messaging and not to protect anyone from a 'virus' never shown to exist. The vaccine couldn't work because it was not designed to work and how could they make it *appear* to be working so that more people would have it? This was overcome by lowering the amplification rate of the PCR test to produce fewer 'cases' and therefore fewer 'deaths'. Some of us had been pointing out since March, 2020, that the amplification rate of the test not testing for the 'virus' had been made artificially high to generate positive tests which they could call 'cases' to justify lockdowns. The World Health Organization recommended an absurdly high 45 amplification cycles to ensure the high positives required by the Cult and then remained silent on the issue until January 20th, 2021 – Biden's Inauguration Day. This was when the 'vaccinations' were seriously underway and on that day the WHO recommended after discussions with America's CDC that laboratories *lowered their testing amplification.* Dr David Samadi, a certified urologist and health writer, said the WHO was encouraging all labs to reduce their cycle count for PCR tests. He said the current cycle was much too high and was 'resulting in any particle being declared a positive case'. Even one mainstream news report I saw said this meant the number of 'Covid' infections may have been 'dramatically inflated'. Oh, just a little bit. The CDC in America issued new guidance to laboratories in April, 2021, to use 28 cycles *but only for 'vaccinated' people.* The timing of the CDC/WHO interventions were cynically designed to make it appear the 'vaccines' were responsible for falling cases and deaths when the real reason can be seen in the following examples. New York's state lab, the Wadsworth Center, identified 872 positive tests in July, 2020, based on a threshold of 40 cycles. When the figure was lowered to 35 cycles *43 percent* of the 872 were no longer 'positives'. At 30 cycles the figure was 63 percent. A Massachusetts lab found that between *85 to 90 percent* of people who tested positive in July with a cycle threshold of 40 would be negative at 30 cycles, Ashish Jha, MD, director of the Harvard Global Health Institute, said: 'I'm really shocked that it could be that high … Boy, does it really change the way we need to be thinking about testing.' I'm shocked that I could see the obvious in the spring of 2020, with no medical background, and most medical professionals still haven't worked it out. No, that's not shocking – it's terrifying.

Three weeks after the WHO directive to lower PCR cycles the London *Daily Mail* ran this headline: 'Why ARE Covid cases plummeting? New infections have fallen 45% in the US and 30% globally in the past 3 weeks but experts say vaccine is NOT the main driver because only 8% of Americans and 13% of people worldwide have received their first dose.' They acknowledged that the drop could not be attributed to the 'vaccine', but soon this morphed throughout the media into the 'vaccine' has caused cases and deaths to fall when it was the PCR threshold. In December, 2020, there was chaos at English Channel ports with truck drivers needing negative 'Covid' tests before they could board a ferry home for Christmas. The government wanted to remove the backlog as fast as possible and they brought in troops to do the 'testing'. Out of 1,600 drivers just *36* tested positive and the rest were given the all clear to cross the Channel. I guess the authorities thought that 36 was the least they could get away with without the unquestioning catching on. The amplification trick which most people believed in the absence of information in the mainstream applied more pressure on those refusing the 'vaccine' to succumb when it 'obviously worked'. The truth was the exact opposite with deaths in care homes soaring with the 'vaccine' and in Israel the term used was 'skyrocket'. A re-analysis of published data from the Israeli Health Ministry led by Dr Hervé Seligmann at the Medicine Emerging Infectious and Tropical Diseases at Aix-Marseille University found that Pfizer's 'Covid vaccine' killed 'about 40 times more [elderly] people than the disease itself would have killed' during a five-week vaccination period and *260 times* more younger people than would have died from the 'virus' even according to the manipulated 'virus' figures. Dr Seligmann and his co-study author, Haim Yativ, declared after reviewing the Israeli 'vaccine' death data: 'This is a new Holocaust.'

Then, in mid-April, 2021, after vast numbers of people worldwide had been 'vaccinated', the story changed with clear coordination. The UK government began to prepare the ground for more future lockdowns when Nuremberg-destined Boris Johnson told yet another whopper. He said that cases had fallen because of *lockdowns* not 'vaccines'. Lockdowns are irrelevant when *there is no 'virus'* and the test and fraudulent death certificates are deciding the number of 'cases' and 'deaths'. Study after study has shown that lockdowns don't work and instead kill and psychologically destroy people. Meanwhile in the United States Anthony Fauci and Rochelle Walensky, the ultra-Zionist head of the CDC, peddled the same line. More lockdown was the answer and not the 'vaccine', a line repeated on cue by the moron that is Canadian Prime Minister Justin Trudeau. Why all the hysteria to get everyone 'vaccinated' if lockdowns and not 'vaccines' made the difference? None of it makes sense on the face of it. Oh, but it does. The Cult wants lockdowns *and* the 'vaccine' and if the 'vaccine' is allowed to be seen as the total answer lockdowns would no longer be justified when there are still livelihoods to destroy. 'Variants' and renewed upward manipulation of PCR amplification are planned to instigate never-ending lockdown *and* more 'vaccines'.

You *must* have it – we're desperate

Israel, where the Jewish and Arab population are ruled by the Sabbatian Cult, was the front-runner in imposing the DNA-manipulating 'vaccine' on its people to such an extent that Jewish refusers began to liken what was happening to the early years of Nazi Germany. This would seem to be a fantastic claim. Why would a government of Jewish people be acting like the Nazis did? If you realise that the Sabbatian Cult was behind the Nazis and that Sabbatians hate Jews the pieces start to fit and the question of why a 'Jewish' government would treat Jews with such callous disregard for their lives and freedom finds an answer. Those controlling the government of Israel *aren't Jewish* – they're Sabbatian. Israeli lawyer Tamir Turgal was one who made the Nazi comparison in comments to German lawyer Reiner Fuellmich who is leading a class action lawsuit against the psychopaths for crimes against humanity. Turgal described how the Israeli government was vaccinating children and pregnant women on the basis that there was no evidence that this was dangerous when they had no evidence that it *wasn't* dangerous either. They just had no evidence. This was medical experimentation and Turgal said this breached the Nuremberg Code about medical experimentation and procedures requiring informed consent and choice. Think about that. A Nuremberg Code developed because of Nazi experimentation on Jews and others in concentration camps by people like the evil-beyond-belief Josef Mengele is being breached by the *Israeli* government; but when you know that it's a *Sabbatian* government along with its intelligence and military agencies like Mossad, Shin Bet and the Israeli Defense Forces, and that Sabbatians were the force behind the Nazis, the kaleidoscope comes into focus. What have we come to when Israeli Jews are suing their government for violating the Nuremberg Code by essentially making Israelis subject to a medical experiment using the controversial 'vaccines'? It's a shocker that this has to be done in the light of what happened in Nazi Germany. The Anshe Ha-Emet, or 'People of the Truth', made up of Israeli doctors, lawyers, campaigners and public, have launched a lawsuit with the International Criminal Court. It says:

> When the heads of the Ministry of Health as well as the prime minister presented the vaccine in Israel and began the vaccination of Israeli residents, the vaccinated were not advised, that, in practice, they are taking part in a medical experiment and that their consent is required for this under the Nuremberg Code.

The irony is unbelievable, but easily explained in one word: Sabbatians. The foundation of Israeli 'Covid' apartheid is the 'green pass' or 'green passport' which allows Jews and Arabs who have had the DNA-manipulating 'vaccine' to go about their lives – to work, fly, travel in general, go to shopping malls, bars, restaurants, hotels, concerts, gyms, swimming pools, theatres and sports venues, while non-'vaccinated' are banned from all those places and activities. Israelis have likened the 'green pass' to the yellow stars that Jews in Nazi Germany were forced to wear – the same as the yellow stickers that a branch of UK supermarket chain Morrisons told exempt mask-wears they had to display when shopping. How very sensitive. The Israeli system is blatant South African-style apartheid on the basis of compliance or non-compliance to fascism rather than colour of the skin. How appropriate that the Sabbatian Israeli government was so close to the pre-Mandela apartheid regime in Pretoria. The Sabbatian-instigated 'vaccine passport' in Israel is planned for everywhere. Sabbatians struck a deal with Pfizer that allowed them to lead the way in the percentage of a national population infused with synthetic material and the result was catastrophic. Israeli freedom activist Shai Dannon told me how chairs were appearing on beaches that said 'vaccinated only'. Health Minister

Yuli Edelstein said that anyone unwilling or unable to get the jabs that 'confer immunity' will be 'left behind'. The man's a liar. Not even the makers claim the 'vaccines' confer immunity. When you see those figures of 'vaccine' deaths these psychopaths were saying that you must take the chance the 'vaccine' will kill you or maim you while knowing it will change your DNA or lockdown for you will be permanent. That's fascism. The Israeli parliament passed a law to allow personal information of the non-vaccinated to be shared with local and national authorities for three months. This was claimed by its supporters to be a way to 'encourage' people to be vaccinated. Hadas Ziv from Physicians for Human Rights described this as a 'draconian law which crushed medical ethics and the patient rights'. But that's the idea, the Sabbatians would reply.

Your papers, please

Sabbatian Israel was leading what has been planned all along to be a global 'vaccine pass' called a 'green passport' without which you would remain in permanent lockdown restriction and unable to do anything. This is how badly – *desperately* – the Cult is to get everyone 'vaccinated'. The term and colour 'green' was not by chance and related to the psychology of fusing the perception of the green climate hoax with the 'Covid' hoax and how the 'solution' to both is the same Great Reset. Lying politicians, health officials and psychologists denied there were any plans for mandatory vaccinations or restrictions based on vaccinations, but they knew that was exactly what was meant to happen with governments of all countries reaching agreements to enforce a global system. 'Free' Denmark and 'free' Sweden unveiled digital vaccine certification. Cyprus, Czech Republic, Estonia, Greece, Hungary, Iceland, Italy, Poland, Portugal, Slovakia, and Spain have all committed to a vaccine passport system and the rest including the whole of the EU would follow. The satanic UK government will certainly go this way despite mendacious denials and at the time of writing it is trying to manipulate the public into having the 'vaccine' so they could go abroad on a summer holiday. How would that work without something to prove you had the synthetic toxicity injected into you? Documents show that the EU's European Commission was moving towards 'vaccine certificates' in 2018 and 2019 before the 'Covid' hoax began. They knew what was coming. Abracadabra – Ursula von der Leyen, the German President of the Commission, announced in March, 2021, an EU 'Digital Green Certificate' – green again – to track the public's 'Covid status'. The passport sting is worldwide and the Far East followed the same pattern with South Korea ruling that only those with 'vaccination' passports – again the *green* pass – would be able to 'return to their daily lives'.

    Bill Gates has been preparing for this 'passport' with other Cult operatives for years and beyond the paper version is a Gates-funded 'digital tattoo' to identify who has been vaccinated and who hasn't. The 'tattoo' is reported to include a substance which is externally readable to confirm who has been vaccinated. This is a bio-luminous light-generating enzyme (think fireflies) called ... *Luciferase.* Yes, named after the Cult 'god' Lucifer the 'light bringer' of whom more to come. Gates said he funded the readable tattoo to ensure children in the developing world were vaccinated and no one was missed out. He cares so much about poor kids as we know. This was just the cover story to develop a vaccine tagging system for everyone on the planet. Gates has been funding the ID2020 'alliance' to do just that in league with other lovely people at Microsoft, GAVI, the Rockefeller Foundation, Accenture and IDEO.org. He said in interviews in March, 2020, before any 'vaccine' publicly existed, that the world must have a globalised digital certificate to track the 'virus' and who had been vaccinated. Gates knew from the start that the mRNA vaccines were coming and when they would come and that the plan was to tag the 'vaccinated' to marginalise the intelligent and stop them doing anything including travel. Evil just doesn't suffice. Gates was exposed for offering a $10 million bribe to the Nigerian House of Representatives to invoke compulsory 'Covid' vaccination of all Nigerians. Sara Cunial, a member of the Italian Parliament, called Gates a 'vaccine criminal'. She urged the Italian President to hand him over to the International Criminal Court for crimes against humanity and condemned his plans to 'chip the human race' through ID2020.

You know it's a long-planned agenda when war criminal and Cult gofer Tony Blair is on the case. With the scale of arrogance only someone as dark as Blair can muster he said: 'Vaccination in the end is going to be your route to liberty.' Blair is a disgusting piece of work and he confirms that again. The media has given a lot of coverage to a bloke called Charlie Mullins, founder of London's biggest independent plumbing company, Pimlico Plumbers, who has said he won't employ anyone who has not been vaccinated or have them go to any home where people are not vaccinated. He said that if he had his way no one would be allowed to walk the streets if they have not been vaccinated. Gates was cheering at the time while I was alerting the white coats. The plan is that people will qualify for 'passports' for having the first two doses and then to keep it they will have to have all the follow ups and new ones for invented 'variants' until human genetics is transformed and many are dead who can't adjust to the changes. Hollywood celebrities – the usual propaganda stunt – are promoting something called the WELL Health-Safety Rating to verify that a building or space has 'taken the necessary steps to prioritize the health and safety of their staff, visitors and other stakeholders'. They included Lady Gaga, Jennifer Lopez, Michael B.

Jordan, Robert DeNiro, Venus Williams, Wolfgang Puck, Deepak Chopra and 17th Surgeon General Richard Carmona. Yawn. WELL Health-Safety has big connections with China. Parent company Delos is headed by former Goldman Sachs partner Paul Scialla. This is another example – and we will see so many others – of using the excuse of 'health' to dictate the lives and activities of the population. I guess one confirmation of the 'safety' of buildings is that only 'vaccinated' people can go in, right?

Electronic concentration camps

I wrote decades ago about the plans to restrict travel and here we are for those who refuse to bow to tyranny. This can be achieved in one go with air travel if the aviation industry makes a blanket decree. The 'vaccine' and guaranteed income are designed to be part of a global version of China's social credit system which tracks behaviour 24/7 and awards or deletes 'credits' based on whether your behaviour is supported by the state or not. I mean your entire lifestyle – what you do, eat, say, everything. Once your credit score falls below a certain level consequences kick in. In China tens of millions have been denied travel by air and train because of this. All the locations and activities denied to refusers by the 'vaccine' passports will be included in one big mass ban on doing almost anything for those that don't bow their head to government. It's beyond fascist and a new term is required to describe its extremes – I guess fascist technocracy will have to do. The way the Chinese system of technological – technocratic – control is sweeping the West can be seen in the Los Angeles school system and is planned to be expanded worldwide. Every child is required to have a 'Covid'-tracking app scanned daily before they can enter the classroom. The so-called Daily Pass tracking system is produced by Gates' Microsoft which I'm sure will shock you rigid. The pass will be scanned using a barcode (one step from an inside-the-body barcode) and the information will include health checks, 'Covid' tests and vaccinations. Entry codes are for one specific building only and access will only be allowed if a student or teacher has a negative test with a test not testing for the 'virus', has no symptoms of anything alleged to be related to 'Covid' (symptoms from a range of other illness), and has a temperature under 100 degrees. No barcode, no entry, is planned to be the case for everywhere and not only schools.

Kids are being psychologically prepared to accept this as 'normal' their whole life which is why what they can impose in schools is so important to the Cult and its gofers. Long-time American freedom campaigner John Whitehead of the Rutherford Institute was not exaggerating when he said: 'Databit by databit, we are building our own electronic concentration camps.' Canada under its Cult gofer prime minister Justin Trudeau has taken a major step towards the real thing with people interned against their will if they test positive with a test not testing for the 'virus' when they arrive at a Canadian airport. They are jailed in internment hotels often without food or water for long periods and with many doors failing to lock there have been sexual assaults. The interned are being charged sometimes $2,000 for the privilege of being abused in this way. Trudeau is fully on board with the Cult and says the 'Covid pandemic' has provided an opportunity for a global 'reset' to permanently change Western civilisation. His number two, Deputy Prime Minister Chrystia Freeland, is a trustee of the World Economic Forum and a Rhodes Scholar. The Trudeau family have long been servants of the Cult. See *The Biggest Secret* and Cathy O'Brien's book *Trance-Formation of America* for the horrific background to Trudeau's father Pierre Trudeau another Canadian prime minister. Hide your fascism behind the façade of a heart-on-the-sleeve liberal. It's a well-honed Cult technique.

What can the 'vaccine' *really* do?

We have a 'virus' never shown to exist and 'variants' of the 'virus' that have also never been shown to exist except, like the 'original', as computer-generated fictions. Even if you believe there's a 'virus' the 'case' to 'death' rate is in the region of 0.23 to 0.15 percent and those 'deaths' are concentrated among the very old around the same average age that people die anyway. In response to this lack of threat (in truth none) psychopaths and idiots, knowingly and unknowingly answering to Gates and the Cult, are seeking to 'vaccinate' every man, woman and child on Planet Earth. Clearly the 'vaccine' is not about 'Covid' – none of this ever has been. So what is it all about *really*? Why the desperation to infuse genetically-manipulating synthetic material into everyone through mRNA fraudulent 'vaccines' with the intent of doing this over and over with the excuses of 'variants' and other 'virus' inventions? Dr Sherri Tenpenny, an osteopathic medical doctor in the United States, has made herself an expert on vaccines and their effects as a vehement campaigner against their use. Tenpenny was board certified in emergency medicine, the director of a level two trauma centre for 12 years, and moved to Cleveland in 1996 to start an integrative medicine practice which has treated patients from all 50 states and some 17 other countries. Weaning people off pharmaceutical drugs is a speciality.

She became interested in the consequences of vaccines after attending a meeting at the National Vaccine Information Center in Washington DC in 2000 where she 'sat through four days of listening to medical doctors and scientists and lawyers and parents of vaccine injured kids' and asked: 'What's going on?' She had never been vaccinated and never got ill while her father was given a list of vaccines to be in the military and

was 'sick his entire life'. The experience added to her questions and she
began to examine vaccine documents from the Centers for Disease
Control (CDC). After reading the first one, the 1998 version of *The
General Recommendations of Vaccination*, she thought: 'This is it?' The
document was poorly written and bad science and Tenpenny began 20
years of research into vaccines that continues to this day. She began her
research into 'Covid vaccines' in March, 2020, and she describes them as
'deadly'. For many, as we have seen, they already have been. Tenpenny
said that in the first 30 days of the 'vaccine' rollout in the United States
there had been more than 40,000 adverse events reported to the vaccine
adverse event database. A document had been delivered to her the day
before that was 172 pages long. 'We have over 40,000 adverse events; we
have over 3,100 cases of [potentially deadly] anaphylactic shock; we
have over 5,000 neurological reactions.' Effects ranged from headaches
to numbness, dizziness and vertigo, to losing feeling in hands or feet
and paraesthesia which is when limbs 'fall asleep' and people have the
sensation of insects crawling underneath their skin. All this happened in
the first 30 days and remember that only about *ten percent* (or far less) of
adverse reactions and vaccine-related deaths are estimated to be
officially reported. Tenpenny said:

> So can you think of one single product in any industry, any industry, for as
> long as products have been made on the planet that within 30 days we have
> 40,000 people complaining of side effects that not only is still on the market
> but … we've got paid actors telling us how great they are for getting their
> vaccine. We're offering people $500 if they will just get their vaccine and
> we've got nurses and doctors going; 'I got the vaccine, I got the vaccine'.

Tenpenny said they were not going to be 'happy dancing folks' when
they began to suffer Bell's palsy (facial paralysis), neuropathies, cardiac
arrhythmias and autoimmune reactions that kill through a blood
disorder. 'They're not going to be so happy, happy then, but we're never
going to see pictures of those people' she said. Tenpenny described the
'vaccine' as 'a well-designed killing tool'.

No off-switch

Bad as the initial consequences had been Tenpenny said it would be
maybe 14 months before we began to see the 'full ravage' of what is
going to happen to the 'Covid vaccinated' with full-out consequences
taking anything between two years and 20 years to show. You can
understand why when you consider that variations of the 'Covid
vaccine' use mRNA (messenger RNA) to in theory activate the immune
system to produce protective antibodies without using the actual 'virus'.
How can they when it's a computer program and they've never isolated

what they claim is the 'real thing'? Instead they use *synthetic* mRNA. They are inoculating synthetic material into the body which through a technique known as the Trojan horse is absorbed into cells to change the nature of DNA. Human DNA is changed by an infusion of messenger RNA and with each new 'vaccine' of this type it is changed even more. Say so and you are banned by Cult Internet platforms. The contempt the contemptuous Mark Zuckerberg has for the truth and human health can be seen in an internal Facebook video leaked to the Project Veritas investigative team in which he said of the 'Covid vaccines': '… I share some caution on this because we just don't know the long term side-effects of basically modifying people's DNA and RNA.' At the same time this disgusting man's Facebook was censoring and banning anyone saying exactly the same. He must go before a Nuremberg trial for crimes against humanity when he *knows* that he is censoring legitimate concerns and denying the right of informed consent on behalf of the Cult that owns him. People have been killed and damaged by the very 'vaccination' technique he cast doubt on himself when they may not have had the 'vaccine' with access to information that he denied them. The plan is to have at least annual 'Covid vaccinations', add others to deal with invented 'variants', and change all other vaccines into the mRNA system. Pfizer executives told shareholders at a virtual Barclays Global Healthcare Conference in March, 2021, that the public may need a third dose of 'Covid vaccine', plus regular yearly boosters and the company planned to hike prices to milk the profits in a 'significant opportunity for our vaccine'. These are the professional liars, cheats and opportunists who are telling you their 'vaccine' is safe. Given this volume of mRNA planned to be infused into the human body and its ability to then replicate we will have a transformation of human genetics from biological to synthetic biological – exactly the long-time Cult plan for reasons we'll see – and many will die. Sherri Tenpenny said of this replication:

It's like having an on-button but no off-button and that whole mechanism … they actually give it a name and they call it the Trojan horse mechanism, because it allows that [synthetic] virus and that piece of that [synthetic] virus to get inside of your cells, start to replicate and even get inserted into other parts of your DNA as a Trojan-horse.

Ask the overwhelming majority of people who have the 'vaccine' what they know about the contents and what they do and they would reply: 'The government says it will stop me getting the virus.' Governments give that false impression on purpose to increase take-up. You can read Sherri Tenpenny's detailed analysis of the health consequences in her blog at Vaxxter.com, but in summary these are some of them. She highlights the statement by Bill Gates about how human beings can become their own 'vaccine manufacturing machine'. The man is insane. ['Vaccine'-generated] 'antibodies' carry synthetic messenger RNA into the cells and the damage starts, Tenpenny contends, and she says that lungs can be adversely affected through varying degrees of pus and bleeding which obviously affects breathing and would be dubbed 'Covid-19'. Even more sinister was the impact of 'antibodies' on macrophages, a white blood cell of the immune system. They consist of Type 1 and Type 2 which have very different functions. She said Type 1 are 'hyper-vigilant' white blood cells which 'gobble up' bacteria etc. However, in doing so, this could cause inflammation and in extreme circumstances be fatal. She says these affects are mitigated by Type 2 macrophages which kick in to calm down the system and stop it going rogue. They clear up dead tissue debris and reduce inflammation that the Type 1 'fire crews' have caused. Type 1 kills the infection and Type 2 heals the damage, she says. This is her punchline with regard to 'Covid vaccinations': She says that mRNA 'antibodies' block Type 2 macrophages by attaching to them and deactivating them. This meant that when the Type 1 response was triggered by infection there was nothing to stop that getting out of hand by calming everything down. There's an on-switch, but no off-switch, she says. What follows can be 'over and out, see you when I see you'.

Genetic suicide

Tenpenny also highlights the potential for autoimmune disease – the body attacking itself – which has been associated with vaccines since they first appeared. Infusing a synthetic foreign substance into cells could cause the immune system to react in a panic believing that the body is being overwhelmed by an invader (it is) and the consequences can again be fatal. There is an autoimmune response known as a 'cytokine storm' which I have likened to a homeowner panicked by an intruder and picking up a gun to shoot randomly in all directions before turning the fire on himself. The immune system unleashes a storm of inflammatory response called cytokines to a threat and the body commits hara-kiri. The lesson is that you mess with the body's immune response at your peril and these 'vaccines' seriously – fundamentally – mess with immune response. Tenpenny refers to a consequence called anaphylactic shock which is a severe and highly dangerous allergic reaction when the immune system floods the body with chemicals. She gives the example of having a bee sting which primes the immune system and makes it sensitive to those chemicals. When people are stung again maybe years later the immune response can be so powerful that it leads to anaphylactic shock. Tenpenny relates this 'shock' with regard to the 'Covid vaccine' to something called polyethylene glycol or PEG.

Enormous numbers of people have become sensitive to this over decades of use in a whole range of products and processes including food, drink, skin creams and 'medicine'. Studies have claimed that some 72 percent of people have antibodies triggered by PEG compared with two percent in the 1960s and allergic hypersensitive reactions to this become a gathering cause for concern. Tenpenny points out that the 'mRNA vaccine' is coated in a 'bubble' of polyethylene glycol which has the potential to cause anaphylactic shock through immune sensitivity. Many reports have appeared of people reacting this way after having the 'Covid vaccine'. What do we think is going to happen as humanity has more and more of these 'vaccines'? Tenpenny said: 'All these pictures we have seen with people with these rashes … these weepy rashes, big reactions on their arms and things like that – it's an acute allergic reaction most likely to the polyethylene glycol that you've been previously primed and sensitised to.'

Those who have not studied the conspiracy and its perpetrators at length might think that making the population sensitive to PEG and then putting it in these 'vaccines' is just a coincidence. It is not. It is instead testament to how carefully and coldly-planned current events have been and the scale of the conspiracy we are dealing with. Tenpenny further explains that the 'vaccine' mRNA procedure can breach the blood-brain barrier which protects the brain from toxins and other crap that will cause malfunction. In this case they could make two proteins corrupt brain function to cause Amyotrophic lateral sclerosis (ALS), a progressive nervous system disease leading to loss of muscle control, and frontal lobe degeneration – Alzheimer's and dementia. Immunologist J. Bart Classon published a paper connecting mRNA 'vaccines' to prion disease which can lead to Alzheimer's and other forms of neurogenerative disease while others have pointed out the potential to affect the placenta in ways that make women infertile. This will become highly significant in the next chapter when I will discuss other aspects of this non-vaccine that relate to its nanotechnology and transmission from the injected to the uninjected.

Qualified in idiocy

Tenpenny describes how research has confirmed that these 'vaccine'-generated antibodies can interact with a range of other tissues in the body and attack many other organs including the lungs. 'This means that if you have a hundred people standing in front of you that all got this shot they could have a hundred different symptoms.' Anyone really think that Cult gofers like the Queen, Tony Blair, Christopher Whitty, Anthony Fauci, and all the other psychopaths have really had this 'vaccine' in the pictures we've seen? Not a bloody chance. Why don't doctors all tell us about all these dangers and consequences of the

'Covid vaccine'? Why instead do they encourage and pressure patients to have the shot? Don't let's think for a moment that doctors and medical staff can't be stupid, lazy, and psychopathic and that's without the financial incentives to give the jab. Tenpenny again:

> Some people are going to die from the vaccine directly but a large number of people are going to start to get horribly sick and get all kinds of autoimmune diseases 42 days to maybe a year out. What are they going to do, these stupid doctors who say; 'Good for you for getting that vaccine.' What are they going to say; 'Oh, it must be a mutant, we need to give an extra dose of that vaccine.'

> Because now the vaccine, instead of one dose or two doses we need three or four because the stupid physicians aren't taking the time to learn anything about it. If I can learn this sitting in my living room reading a 19 page paper and several others so can they. There's nothing special about me, I just take the time to do it.

Remember how Sara Kayat, the NHS and TV doctor, said that the 'Covid vaccine' would '100 percent prevent hospitalisation and death'. Doctors can be idiots like every other profession and they should not be worshipped as infallible. They are not and far from it. Behind many medical and scientific 'experts' lies an uninformed prat trying to hide themselves from you although in the 'Covid' era many have failed to do so as with UK narrative-repeating 'TV doctor' Hilary Jones. Pushing back against the minority of proper doctors and scientists speaking out against the 'vaccine' has been the entire edifice of the Cult global state in the form of governments, medical systems, corporations, mainstream media, Silicon Valley, and an army of compliant doctors, medical staff and scientists willing to say anything for money and to enhance their careers by promoting the party line. If you do that you are an 'expert' and if you won't you are an 'anti-vaxxer' and 'Covidiot'. The pressure to be 'vaccinated' is incessant. We have even had reports claiming that the 'vaccine' can help cure cancer and Alzheimer's and make the lame walk. I am waiting for the announcement that it can bring you coffee in the morning and cook your tea. Just as the symptoms of 'Covid' seem to increase by the week so have the miracles of the 'vaccine'. American supermarket giant Kroger Co. offered nearly 500,000 employees in 35 states a $100 bonus for having the 'vaccine' while donut chain Krispy Kreme promised 'vaccinated' customers a free glazed donut every day for the rest of 2021. Have your DNA changed and you will get a doughnut although we might not have to give you them for long. Such offers and incentives confirm the desperation.

Perhaps the worse vaccine-stunt of them all was UK 'Health'

Secretary Matt-the-prat Hancock on live TV after watching a clip of someone being 'vaccinated' when the roll-out began. Hancock faked tears so badly it was embarrassing. Brain-of-Britain Piers Morgan, the lockdown-supporting, 'vaccine' supporting, 'vaccine' passport-supporting, TV host played along with Hancock – 'You're quite emotional about that' he said in response to acting so atrocious it would have been called out at a school nativity which will presumably today include Mary and Jesus in masks, wise men keeping their camels six feet apart, and shepherds under tent arrest. System-serving Morgan tweeted this: 'Love the idea of covid vaccine passports for everywhere: flights, restaurants, clubs, football, gyms, shops etc. It's time covid-denying, anti-vaxxer loonies had their bullsh*t bluff called & bar themselves from going anywhere that responsible citizens go.' If only I could aspire to his genius. To think that Morgan, who specialises in shouting over anyone he disagrees with, was lauded as a free speech hero when he lost his job after storming off the set of his live show like a child throwing his dolly out of the pram. If he is a free speech hero we are in real trouble. I have no idea what 'bullsh*t' means, by the way, the * throws me completely.

The Cult is desperate to infuse its synthetic DNA-changing concoction into everyone and has been using every lie, trick and intimidation to do so. The question of '*Why*?' we shall now address.

CHAPTER TEN

Human 2.0

I believe that at the end of the century the use of words and general educated opinion will have altered so much that one will be able to speak of machines thinking without expecting to be contradicted –
Alan Turing (1912-1954), the 'Father of artificial intelligence'

I have been exposing for decades the plan to transform the human body from a biological to a synthetic-biological state. The new human that I will call Human 2.0 is planned to be connected to artificial intelligence and a global AI 'Smart Grid' that would operate as one global system in which AI would control everything from your fridge to your heating system to your car to your mind. Humans would no longer be 'human', but post-human and sub-human, with their thinking and emotional processes replaced by AI.

What I said sounded crazy and beyond science fiction and I could understand that. To any balanced, rational, mind it *is* crazy. Today, however, that world is becoming reality and it puts the 'Covid vaccine' into its true context. Ray Kurzweil is the ultra-Zionist 'computer scientist, inventor and futurist' and co-founder of the Singularity University. Singularity refers to the merging of humans with machines or 'transhumanism'. Kurzweil has said humanity would be connected to the cyber 'cloud' in the period of the ever-recurring year of 2030:

> Our thinking ... will be a hybrid of biological and non-biological thinking ... humans will be able to extend their limitations and 'think in the cloud' ... We're going to put gateways to the cloud in our brains ... We're going to gradually merge and enhance ourselves ... In my view, that's the nature of being human – we transcend our limitations. As the technology becomes vastly superior to what we are then the small proportion that is still human gets smaller and smaller and smaller until it's just utterly negligible.

They are trying to sell this end-of-humanity-as-we-know-it as the next stage of 'evolution' when we become super-human and 'like the gods'. They are lying to you. Shocked, eh? The population, and again especially the young, have been manipulated into addiction to technologies designed to enslave them for life. First they induced an addiction to smartphones (holdables); next they moved to technology on the body (wearables); and then began the invasion of the body (implantables). I warned way back about the plan for microchipped people and we are now entering that era. We should not be diverted into thinking that this refers only to chips we can see. Most important are the nanochips known as smart dust, neural dust and nanobots which are far too small to be seen by the human eye. Nanotechnology is everywhere, increasingly in food products, and released into the atmosphere by the geoengineering of the skies funded by Bill Gates to 'shut out the Sun' and 'save the planet from global warming'. Gates has been funding a project to spray millions of tonnes of chalk (calcium carbonate) into the stratosphere over Sweden to 'dim the Sun' and cool the Earth. Scientists warned the move could be disastrous for weather systems in ways no one can predict and opposition led to the Swedish space agency announcing that the 'experiment' would not be happening as planned in the summer of 2021; but it shows where the Cult is going with dimming the impact of the Sun and there's an associated plan to change the planet's atmosphere. Who gives psychopath Gates the right to dictate to the entire human race and dismantle planetary systems? The world will not be safe while this man is at large.

The global warming hoax has made the Sun, like the gas of life, something to fear when both are essential to good health and human survival (more inversion). The body transforms sunlight into vital vitamin D through a process involving … *cholesterol*. This is the cholesterol we are also told to fear. We are urged to take Big Pharma statin drugs to reduce cholesterol and it's all systematic. Reducing cholesterol means reducing vitamin D uptake with all the multiple health problems that will cause. At least if you take statins long term it saves the government from having to pay you a pension. The delivery system to block sunlight is widely referred to as chemtrails although these have a much deeper agenda, too. They appear at first to be contrails or condensation trails streaming from aircraft into cold air at high altitudes. Contrails disperse very quickly while chemtrails do not and spread out across the sky before eventually their content falls to earth. Many times I have watched aircraft cross-cross a clear blue sky releasing chemtrails until it looks like a cloudy day. Chemtrails contain many things harmful to humans and the natural world including toxic heavy metals, aluminium (see Alzheimer's) and nanotechnology. Ray Kurzweil reveals the reason without actually saying so: 'Nanobots will infuse all the matter around us with information. Rocks, trees, everything will become these intelligent creatures.' How do you deliver that? *From the sky*. Self-replicating nanobots would connect everything to the Smart Grid. The phenomenon of Morgellons disease began in the chemtrail era and the correlation has led to it being dubbed the 'chemtrail disease'. Self-replicating fibres appear in the body that can be pulled out through the skin. Morgellons fibres continue to grow outside the body and have a form of artificial intelligence. I cover this at greater length in *Phantom Self*.

'Vaccine' operating system

'Covid vaccines' with their self-replicating synthetic material are also designed to make the connection between humanity and Kurzweil's 'cloud'. American doctor and dedicated campaigner for truth, Carrie Madej, an Internal Medicine Specialist in Georgia with more than 20 years medical experience, has highlighted the nanotechnology aspect of the fake 'vaccines'. She explains how one of the components in at least the Moderna and Pfizer synthetic potions are 'lipid nanoparticles' which are 'like little tiny computer bits' – a 'sci-fi substance' known as nanobots and hydrogel which can be 'triggered at any moment to deliver its payload' and act as 'biosensors'. The synthetic substance had 'the ability to accumulate data from your body like your breathing, your respiration, thoughts and emotions, all kind of things' and each syringe could carry a *million* nanobots:

> This substance because it's like little bits of computers in your body, crazy, but it's true, it can do that, [and] obviously has the ability to act through Wi-Fi. It can receive and transmit energy, messages, frequencies or impulses. That issue has never been addressed by these companies. What does that do to the human?

> Just imagine getting this substance in you and it can react to things all around you, the 5G, your smart device, your phones, what is happening with that? What if something is triggering it, too, like an impulse, a frequency? We have something completely foreign in the human body.

Madej said her research revealed that electromagnetic (EMF) frequencies emitted by phones and other devices had increased dramatically in the same period of the 'vaccine' rollout and she was seeing more people with radiation problems as 5G and other electromagnetic technology was expanded and introduced to schools and hospitals. She said she was 'floored with the EMF coming off' the devices she checked. All this makes total sense and syncs with my own work of decades when you think that Moderna refers in documents to its mRNA 'vaccine' as an 'operating system':

> Recognizing the broad potential of mRNA science, we set out to create an mRNA technology platform that functions very much like an operating system

on a computer. It is designed so that it can plug and play interchangeably with different programs. In our case, the 'program' or 'app' is our mRNA drug – the unique mRNA sequence that codes for a protein …

… Our MRNA Medicines – 'The 'Software Of Life': When we have a concept for a new mRNA medicine and begin research, fundamental components are already in place. Generally, the only thing that changes from one potential mRNA medicine to another is the coding region – the actual genetic code that instructs ribosomes to make protein. Utilizing these instruction sets gives our investigational mRNA medicines a software-like quality. We also have the ability to combine different mRNA sequences encoding for different proteins in a single mRNA investigational medicine.

Who needs a real 'virus' when you can create a computer version to justify infusing your operating system into the entire human race on the road to making living, breathing people into cyborgs? What is missed with the 'vaccines' is the *digital* connection between synthetic material and the body that I highlighted earlier with the study that hacked a computer with human DNA. On one level the body is digital, based on mathematical codes, and I'll have more about that in the next chapter. Those who ridiculously claim that mRNA 'vaccines' are not designed to change human genetics should explain the words of Dr Tal Zaks, chief medical officer at Moderna, in a 2017 TED talk. He said that over the last 30 years 'we've been living this phenomenal digital scientific revolution, and I'm here today to tell you, that we are actually *hacking the software of life*, and that it's changing the way we think about prevention and treatment of disease':

In every cell there's this thing called messenger RNA, or mRNA for short, that transmits the critical information from the DNA in our genes to the protein, which is really the stuff we're all made out of. This is the critical information that determines what the cell will do. So we think about it as an operating system. So if you could change that, if you could introduce a line of code, or change a line of code, it turns out, that has profound implications for everything, from the flu to cancer.

Zaks should more accurately have said that this has profound implications for the human genetic code and the nature of DNA. Communications within the body go both ways and not only one. But, hey, no, the 'Covid vaccine' will not affect your genetics. Cult fact-checkers say so even though the man who helped to develop the mRNA technique says that it does. Zaks said in 2017:

If you think about what it is we're trying to do. We've taken information and our understanding of that information and how that information is transmitted in a cell, and we've taken our understanding of medicine and how to make drugs, and we're fusing the two. We think of it as information therapy.

I have been writing for decades that the body is an information field communicating with itself and the wider world. This is why radiation which is information can change the information field of body and mind through phenomena like 5G and change their nature and function. 'Information therapy' means to change the body's information field and change the way it operates. DNA is a receiver-transmitter of information and can be mutated by information like mRNA synthetic messaging. Technology to do this has been ready and waiting in the underground bases and other secret projects to be rolled out when the 'Covid' hoax was played. 'Trials' of such short and irrelevant duration were only for public consumption. When they say the 'vaccine' is 'experimental' that is not true. It may appear to be 'experimental' to those who don't know what's going on, but the trials have already been done to ensure the Cult gets the result it desires. Zaks said that it took decades to sequence the human genome, completed in 2003, but now they could do it in a week. By 'they' he means scientists operating in the public domain. In the secret projects they were sequencing the genome in a week long before even 2003.

Deluge of mRNA

Highly significantly the Moderna document says the guiding premise is that if using mRNA as a medicine works for one disease then it should work for many diseases. They were leveraging the flexibility afforded by their platform and the fundamental role mRNA plays in protein synthesis to pursue mRNA medicines for a broad spectrum of diseases. Moderna is confirming what I was saying through 2020 that multiple 'vaccines' were planned for 'Covid' (and later invented 'variants') and that previous vaccines would be converted to the mRNA system to infuse the body with massive amounts of genetically-manipulating synthetic material to secure a transformation to a synthetic-biological state. The 'vaccines' are designed to kill stunning numbers as part of the long-exposed Cult depopulation agenda and transform the rest. Given this is the goal you can appreciate why there is such hysterical demand for every human to be 'vaccinated' for an alleged 'disease' that has an estimated 'infection' to 'death' ratio of 0.23-0.15 percent. As I write children are being given the 'vaccine' in trials (their parents are a disgrace) and ever-younger people are being offered the vaccine for a 'virus' that even if you believe it exists has virtually zero chance of harming them. Horrific effects of the 'trials' on a 12-year-old girl were revealed by a family member to be serious brain and gastric problems that included a bowel obstruction and the inability to swallow liquids or solids. She was unable to eat or drink without throwing up, had extreme pain in her back, neck and abdomen, and was paralysed from the waist down which stopped her urinating unaided. When the girl was first taken to hospital doctors said it was all in her mind. She was signed up for the 'trial' by her parents for whom no words suffice. None of this 'Covid vaccine' insanity makes any sense unless you see what the 'vaccine' really is – a body-changer. Synthetic biology or 'SynBio' is a fast-emerging and expanding scientific discipline which includes everything from genetic and molecular engineering to electrical and computer engineering. Synthetic biology is defined in these ways:

- A multidisciplinary area of research that seeks to create new biological parts, devices, and systems, or to redesign systems that are already found in nature.

- The use of a mixture of physical engineering and genetic engineering to create new (and therefore synthetic) life forms.

- An emerging field of research that aims to combine the knowledge and methods of biology, engineering and related disciplines in the design of chemically-synthesized DNA to create organisms with novel or enhanced characteristics and traits (synthetic organisms including humans).

We now have synthetic blood, skin, organs and limbs being developed along with synthetic body parts produced by 3D printers. These are all elements of the synthetic human programme and this comment by Kurzweil's co-founder of the Singularity University, Peter Diamandis, can be seen in a whole new light with the 'Covid' hoax and the sanctions against those that refuse the 'vaccine':

> Anybody who is going to be resisting the progress forward [to transhumanism] is going to be resisting evolution and, fundamentally, they will die out. It's not a matter of whether it's good or bad. It's going to happen.

'Resisting evolution'? What absolute bollocks. The arrogance of these people is without limit. His 'it's going to happen' mantra is another way of saying 'resistance is futile' to break the spirit of those pushing back and we must not fall for it. Getting this genetically-transforming 'vaccine' into everyone is crucial to the Cult plan for total control and the desperation to achieve that is clear for anyone to see. Vaccine passports are a major factor in this and they, too, are a form of resistance is futile. It's NOT. The paper funded by the Rockefeller Foundation for the 2013 'health conference' in China said:

We will interact more with artificial intelligence. The use of robotics, bio-engineering to augment human functioning is already well underway and will advance. Re-engineering of humans into potentially separate and unequal forms through genetic engineering or mixed human-robots raises debates on ethics and equality.

A new demography is projected to emerge after 2030 [that year again] of technologies (robotics, genetic engineering, nanotechnology) producing robots, engineered organisms, 'nanobots' and artificial intelligence (AI) that can self-replicate. Debates will grow on the implications of an impending reality of human designed life.

What is happening today is so long planned. The world army enforcing the will of the world government is intended to be a robot army, not a human one. Today's military and its technologically 'enhanced' troops, pilotless planes and driverless vehicles are just stepping stones to that end. Human soldiers are used as Cult fodder and its time they woke up to that and worked for the freedom of the population instead of their own destruction and their family's destruction – the same with the police. Join us and let's sort this out. The phenomenon of enforce my own destruction is widespread in the 'Covid' era with Woker 'luvvies' in the acting and entertainment industries supporting 'Covid' rules which have destroyed their profession and the same with those among the public who put signs on the doors of their businesses 'closed due to Covid – stay safe' when many will never reopen. It's a form of masochism and most certainly insanity.

Transgender = transhumanism

When something explodes out of nowhere and is suddenly everywhere it is always the Cult agenda and so it is with the tidal wave of claims and demands that have infiltrated every aspect of society under the heading of 'transgenderism'. The term 'trans' is so 'in' and this is the dictionary definition:

A prefix meaning 'across', 'through', occurring … in loanwords from Latin, used in particular for denoting movement or conveyance from place to place (transfer; transmit; transplant) or complete change (transform; transmute), or to form adjectives meaning 'crossing','on the other side of', or 'going beyond' the place named (transmontane; transnational; trans-Siberian).

Transgender means to go beyond gender and transhuman means to go beyond human. Both are aspects of the Cult plan to transform the human body to a synthetic state with *no gender*. Human 2.0 is not designed to procreate and would be produced technologically with no need for parents. The new human would mean the end of parents and so men, and increasingly women, are being targeted for the deletion of their rights and status. Parental rights are disappearing at an ever-quickening speed for the same reason. The new human would have no need for men or women when there is no procreation and no gender. Perhaps the transgender movement that appears to be in a permanent state of frenzy might now contemplate on how it is being used. This was never about transgender rights which are only the interim excuse for confusing gender, particularly in the young, on the road to *fusing* gender. Transgender activism is not an end; it is a *means* to an end. We see again the technique of creative destruction in which you destroy the status quo to 'build back better' in the form that you want. The gender status quo had to be destroyed by persuading the Cult-created Woke mentality to believe that you can have 100 genders or more. A programme for 9 to 12 year olds produced by the Cult-owned BBC promoted the 100 genders narrative. The very idea may be the most monumental nonsense, but it is not what is true that counts, only what you can make people *believe* is true. Once the gender of $2 + 2 = 4$ has been dismantled through indoctrination, intimidation and $2 + 2 = 5$ then the new no-gender normal can take its place with Human 2.0. Aldous Huxley revealed the plan in his prophetic *Brave New World* in 1932:

> Natural reproduction has been done away with and children are created, decanted', and raised in 'hatcheries and conditioning centres'. From birth, people are genetically designed to fit into one of five castes, which are further split into 'Plus' and 'Minus' members and designed to fulfil predetermined positions within the social and economic strata of the World State.

How could Huxley know this in 1932? For the same reason George Orwell knew about the Big Brother state in 1948, Cult insiders I have quoted knew about it in 1969, and I have known about it since the early 1990s. If you are connected to the Cult or you work your balls off to uncover the plan you can predict the future. The process is simple. If there is a plan for the world and nothing intervenes to stop it then it will happen. Thus if you communicate the plan ahead of time you are perceived to have predicted the future, but you haven't. You have revealed the plan which without intervention will become the human future. The whole reason I have done what I have is to alert enough people to inspire an intervention and maybe at last that time has come with the Cult and its intentions now so obvious to anyone with a brain in working order.

The future is here

Technological wombs that Huxley described to replace parent
procreation are already being developed and they are only the projects
we know about in the public arena. Israeli scientists told *The Times of
Israel* in March, 2021, that they have grown 250-cell embryos into mouse
foetuses with fully formed organs using artificial wombs in a
development they say could pave the way for gestating humans outside
the womb. Professor Jacob Hanna of the Weizmann Institute of Science
said:

> We took mouse embryos from the mother at day five of development, when
> they are just of 250 cells, and had them in the incubator from day five until
> day 11, by which point they had grown all their organs.

> By day 11 they make their own blood and have a beating heart, a fully
> developed brain. Anybody would look at them and say, 'this is clearly a
> mouse foetus with all the characteristics of a mouse.' It's gone from being a
> ball of cells to being an advanced foetus.

A special liquid is used to nourish embryo cells in a laboratory dish
and they float on the liquid to duplicate the first stage of embryonic
development. The incubator creates all the right conditions for its
development, Hanna said. The liquid gives the embryo 'all the nutrients,
hormones and sugars they need' along with a custom-made electronic
incubator which controls gas concentration, pressure and temperature.
The cutting-edge in the underground bases and other secret locations
will be light years ahead of that, however, and this was reported by the
London *Guardian* in 2017:

> We are approaching a biotechnological breakthrough. Ectogenesis, the
> invention of a complete external womb, could completely change the nature
> of human reproduction. In April this year, researchers at the Children's
> Hospital of Philadelphia announced their development of an artificial womb.

The article was headed 'Artificial wombs could soon be a reality.
What will this mean for women?' What would it mean for children is an
even bigger question. No mother to bond with only a machine in
preparation for a life of soulless interaction and control in a world
governed by machines (see the *Matrix* movies). Now observe the
calculated manipulations of the 'Covid' hoax as human interaction and
warmth has been curtailed by distancing, isolation and fear with people
communicating via machines on a scale never seen before. These are all
dots in the same picture as are all the personal assistants, gadgets and
children's toys through which kids and adults communicate with AI as

if it is human. The AI 'voice' on Sat-Nav should be included. All these things are psychological preparation for the Cult endgame. Before you can make a physical connection with AI you have to make a psychological connection and that is what people are being conditioned to do with this ever gathering human-AI interaction. Movies and TV programmes depicting the transhuman, robot dystopia relate to a phenomenon known as 'pre-emptive programming' in which the world that is planned is portrayed everywhere in movies, TV and advertising. This is conditioning the conscious and subconscious mind to become familiar with the planned reality to dilute resistance when it happens for real. What would have been a shock such is the change is made less so. We have young children put on the road to transgender transition surgery with puberty blocking drugs at an age when they could never be able to make those life-changing decisions.

Rachel Levine, a professor of paediatrics and psychiatry who believes in treating children this way, became America's highest-ranked openly-transgender official when she was confirmed as US Assistant Secretary at the Department of Health and Human Services after being nominated by Joe Biden (the Cult). Activists and governments press for laws to deny parents a say in their children's transition process so the kids can be isolated and manipulated into agreeing to irreversible medical procedures. A Canadian father Robert Hoogland was denied bail by the Vancouver Supreme Court in 2021 and remained in jail for breaching a court order that he stay silent over his young teenage daughter, a minor, who was being offered life-changing hormone therapy without parental consent. At the age of 12 the girl's 'school counsellor' said she may be transgender, referred her to a doctor and told the school to treat her like a boy. This is another example of state-serving schools imposing ever more control over children's lives while parents have ever less. Contemptible and extreme child abuse is happening all over the world as the Cult gender-fusion operation goes into warp-speed.

Why the war on men – and now women?

The question about what artificial wombs mean for women should rightly be asked. The answer can be seen in the deletion of women's rights involving sport, changing rooms, toilets and status in favour of people in male bodies claiming to identify as women. I can identify as a mountain climber, but it doesn't mean I can climb a mountain any more than a biological man can be a biological woman. To believe so is a triumph of belief over factual reality which is the very perceptual basis of everything Woke. Women's sport is being destroyed by allowing those with male bodies who say they identify as female to 'compete' with girls and women. Male body 'women' dominate 'women's' competition with their greater muscle mass, bone density, strength and

speed. With that disadvantage sport for women loses all meaning. To
put this in perspective nearly 300 American high school boys can run
faster than the quickest woman sprinter in the world. Women are seeing
their previously protected spaces invaded by male bodies simply
because they claim to identify as women. That's all they need to do to
access all women's spaces and activities under the Biden 'Equality Act'
that destroys equality for women with the usual Orwellian Woke
inversion. Male sex offenders have already committed rapes in women's
prisons after claiming to identify as women to get them transferred.
Does this not matter to the Woke 'equality' hypocrites? Not in the least.
What matters to Cult manipulators and funders behind transgender
activists is to advance gender fusion on the way to the no-gender
'human'. When you are seeking to impose transparent nonsense like
this, or the 'Covid' hoax, the only way the nonsense can prevail is
through censorship and intimidation of dissenters, deletion of factual
information, and programming of the unquestioning, bewildered and
naive. You don't have to scan the world for long to see that all these
things are happening.

Many women's rights organisations have realised that rights and
status which took such a long time to secure are being eroded and that it
is systematic. Kara Dansky of the global Women's Human Rights
Campaign said that Biden's transgender executive order immediately he
took office, subsequent orders, and Equality Act legislation that
followed 'seek to erase women and girls in the law as a category'.
Exactly. I said during the long ago-started war on men (in which many
women play a crucial part) that this was going to turn into a war on
them. The Cult is phasing out *both* male and female genders. To get
away with that they are brought into conflict so they are busy fighting
each other while the Cult completes the job with no unity of response.
Unity, people, *unity*. We need unity everywhere. Transgender is the only
show in town as the big step towards the no-gender human. It's not
about rights for transgender people and never has been. Woke political
correctness is deleting words relating to genders to the same end.
Wokers believe this is to be 'inclusive' when the opposite is true. They
are deleting words describing gender because gender *itself* is being
deleted by Human 2.0. Terms like 'man', 'woman', 'mother' and 'father'
are being deleted in the universities and other institutions to be replaced
by the *no*-gender, not trans-gender, 'individuals' and 'guardians'.
Women's rights campaigner Maria Keffler of Partners for Ethical Care
said: 'Children are being taught from kindergarten upward that some
boys have a vagina, some girls have a penis, and that kids can be any
gender they want to be.' Do we really believe that suddenly countries all
over the world at the same time had the idea of having drag queens go
into schools or read transgender stories to very young children in the

local library? It's coldly-calculated confusion of gender on the way to the fusion of gender. Suzanne Vierling, a psychologist from Southern California, made another important point:

> Yesterday's slave woman who endured gynecological medical experiments is today's girl-child being butchered in a booming gender-transitioning sector. Ovaries removed, pushing her into menopause and osteoporosis, uncharted territory, and parents' rights and authority decimated.

The erosion of parental rights is a common theme in line with the Cult plans to erase the very concept of parents and 'ovaries removed, pushing her into menopause' means what? Those born female lose the ability to have children – another way to discontinue humanity as we know it.

Eliminating Human 1.0 (before our very eyes)

To pave the way for Human 2.0 you must phase out Human 1.0. This is happening through plummeting sperm counts and making women infertile through an onslaught of chemicals, radiation (including smartphones in pockets of men) and mRNA 'vaccines'. Common agriculture pesticides are also having a devastating impact on human fertility. I have been tracking collapsing sperm counts in the books for a long time and in 2021 came a book by fertility scientist and reproductive epidemiologist Shanna Swan, *Count Down: How Our Modern World Is Threatening Sperm Counts, Altering Male and Female Reproductive Development and Imperiling the Future of the Human Race*. She reports how the global fertility rate dropped by *half* between 1960 and 2016 with America's birth rate 16 percent below where it needs to be to sustain the population. Women are experiencing declining egg quality, more miscarriages, and more couples suffer from infertility. Other findings were an increase in erectile dysfunction, infant boys developing more genital abnormalities, male problems with conception, and plunging levels of the male hormone testosterone which would explain why so many men have lost their backbone and masculinity. This has been very evident during the 'Covid' hoax when women have been prominent among the Pushbackers and big strapping blokes have bowed their heads, covered their faces with a nappy and quietly submitted. Mind control expert Cathy O'Brien also points to how global education introduced the concept of 'we're all winners' in sport and classrooms: 'Competition was defused, and it in turn defused a sense of fighting back.' This is another version of the 'equity' doctrine in which you drive down rather than raise up. What a contrast in Cult-controlled China with its global ambitions where the government published plans in January, 2021, to 'cultivate masculinity' in boys from kindergarten through to high school in the face of a 'masculinity crisis'. A government adviser said boys would be soon become 'delicate, timid and effeminate' unless action was taken. Don't expect any similar policy in the targeted West. A 2006 study showed that a 65-year-old man in 2002 had testosterone levels *15 percent* lower than a 65-year-old man in 1987 while a 2020 study found a similar story with young adults and adolescents. Men are getting prescriptions for testosterone replacement therapy which causes an even greater drop in sperm count with up to 99 percent seeing sperm counts drop to zero during the treatment. More sperm is defective and malfunctioning with some having two heads or not pursuing an egg.

A class of *synthetic* chemicals known as phthalates are being blamed for the decline. These are found everywhere in plastics, shampoos, cosmetics, furniture, flame retardants, personal care products, pesticides, canned foods and even receipts. Why till receipts? Everyone touches them. Let no one delude themselves that all this is not systematic to advance the long-time agenda for human body transformation. Phthalates mimic hormones and disrupt the hormone balance causing testosterone to fall and genital birth defects in male infants. Animals and fish have been affected in the same way due to phthalates and other toxins in rivers. When fish turn gay or change sex through chemicals in rivers and streams it is a pointer to why there has been such an increase in gay people and the sexually confused. It doesn't matter to me what sexuality people choose to be, but if it's being affected by chemical pollution and consumption then we need to know. Does anyone really think that this is not connected to the transgender agenda, the war on men and the condemnation of male 'toxic masculinity'? You watch this being followed by 'toxic femininity'. It's already happening. When breastfeeding becomes 'chest-feeding', pregnant women become pregnant people along with all the other Woke claptrap you know that the world is going insane and there's a Cult scam in progress. Transgender activists are promoting the Cult agenda while Cult billionaires support and fund the insanity as they laugh themselves to sleep at the sheer stupidity for which humans must be infamous in galaxies far, far away.

'Covid vaccines' and female infertility

We can now see why the 'vaccine' has been connected to potential infertility in women. Dr Michael Yeadon, former Vice President and Chief Scientific Advisor at Pfizer, and Dr Wolfgang Wodarg in Germany, filed a petition with the European Medicines Agency in December, 2020, urging them to stop trials for the Pfizer/BioNTech shot and all other mRNA trials until further studies had been done. They were particularly concerned about possible effects on fertility with 'vaccine'-produced antibodies attacking the protein Syncytin-1 which is responsible for developing the placenta. The result would be infertility 'of indefinite duration' in women who have the 'vaccine' with the placenta failing to form. Section 10.4.2 of the Pfizer/BioNTech trial protocol says that pregnant women or those who might become so should not have mRNA shots. Section 10.4 warns men taking mRNA shots to 'be abstinent from heterosexual intercourse' and not to donate sperm. The UK government said that it *did not know* if the mRNA procedure had an effect on fertility. *Did not know?* These people have to go to jail. UK government advice did not recommend at the start that pregnant women had the shot and said they should avoid pregnancy for at least two months after 'vaccination'. The 'advice' was later updated to pregnant women should only have the 'vaccine' if the benefits outweighed the risks to mother and foetus. What the hell is that supposed to mean? Then 'spontaneous abortions' began to appear and rapidly increase on the adverse reaction reporting schemes which include only a fraction of adverse reactions. Thousands and ever-growing numbers of 'vaccinated' women are describing changes to their menstrual cycle with heavier blood flow, irregular periods and menstruating again after going through the menopause – all links to reproduction effects. Women are passing blood clots and the lining of their uterus while men report erectile dysfunction and blood effects. Most significantly of all *un*vaccinated women began to report similar menstrual changes after interaction with *'vaccinated'* people and men and children were also affected with bleeding noses, blood clots and other conditions. 'Shedding' is when vaccinated people can emit the content of a vaccine to affect the unvaccinated, but this is different. 'Vaccinated' people were not shedding a 'live virus' allegedly in 'vaccines' as before because the fake 'Covid vaccines' involve synthetic material and other toxicity. Doctors exposing what is happening prefer the term 'transmission' to shedding. Somehow those that have had the shots are transmitting effects to those that haven't. Dr Carrie Madej said the nano-content of the 'vaccines' can 'act like an antenna' to others around them which fits perfectly with my own conclusions. This 'vaccine' transmission phenomenon was becoming known as the book went into production and I deal with this further in the Postscript.

Vaccine effects on sterility are well known. The World Health Organization was accused in 2014 of sterilising millions of women in Kenya with the evidence confirmed by the content of the vaccines involved. The same WHO behind the 'Covid' hoax admitted its involvement for more than ten years with the vaccine programme. Other countries made similar claims. Charges were lodged by Tanzania, Nicaragua, Mexico, and the Philippines. The Gardasil vaccine claimed to protect against a genital 'virus' known as HPV has also been linked to infertility. Big Pharma and the WHO (same thing) are criminal and satanic entities. Then there's the Bill Gates Foundation which is connected through funding and shared interests with 20 pharmaceutical giants and laboratories. He stands accused of directing the policy of United Nations Children's Fund (UNICEF), vaccine alliance GAVI, and other groupings, to advance the vaccine agenda and silence opposition at great cost to women and children. At the same time Gates wants to reduce the global population. Coincidence?

Great Reset = Smart Grid = new human

The Cult agenda I have been exposing for 30 years is now being openly promoted by Cult assets like Gates and Klaus Schwab of the World Economic Forum under code-terms like the 'Great Reset', 'Build Back Better' and 'a rare but narrow window of opportunity to reflect, reimagine, and reset our world'. What provided this 'rare but narrow window of opportunity'? The 'Covid' hoax did. Who created that? *They* did. My books from not that long ago warned about the planned 'Internet of Things' (IoT) and its implications for human freedom. This was the plan to connect all technology to the Internet and artificial intelligence and today we are way down that road with an estimated 36 billion devices connected to the World Wide Web and that figure is projected to be 76 billion by 2025. I further warned that the Cult planned to go beyond that to the Internet of *Everything* when the human brain was connected via AI to the Internet and Kurzweil's 'cloud'. Now we have Cult operatives like Schwab calling for precisely that under the term 'Internet of Bodies', a fusion of the physical, digital and biological into one centrally-controlled Smart Grid system which the Cult refers to as the 'Fourth Industrial Revolution'. They talk about the 'biological', but they really mean the synthetic-biological which is required to fully integrate the human body and brain into the Smart Grid and artificial intelligence planned to replace the human mind. We have everything being synthetically manipulated including the natural world through GMO and smart dust, the food we eat and the human body itself with synthetic 'vaccines'. I said in *The Answer* that we would see the Cult push for synthetic meat to replace animals and in February, 2021, the so predictable psychopath Bill Gates called for the introduction of synthetic meat to save us all from 'climate change'. The climate hoax just keeps on giving like the 'Covid' hoax. The war on meat by vegan activists is a carbon (oops, sorry) copy of the manipulation of transgender activists. They have no idea (except their inner core) that they are being used to promote and impose the agenda of the Cult or that they are only the *vehicle* and not the *reason*. This is not to say those who choose not to eat meat shouldn't be respected and supported in that right, but there are ulterior motives for those in power. A *Forbes* article in December, 2019, highlighted the plan so beloved of Schwab and the Cult under the heading: 'What Is The Internet of Bodies? And How Is It Changing Our World?' The article said the human body is the latest data platform (remember 'our vaccine is an operating system'). *Forbes* described the plan very accurately and the words could have come straight out of my books from long before:

> The Internet of Bodies (IoB) is an extension of the IoT and basically connects the human body to a network through devices that are ingested, implanted, or connected to the body in some way. Once connected, data can be exchanged, and the body and device can be remotely monitored and controlled.

They were really describing a human hive mind with human perception centrally-dictated via an AI connection as well as allowing people to be 'remotely monitored and controlled'. Everything from a fridge to a human mind could be directed from a central point by these insane psychopaths and 'Covid vaccines' are crucial to this. Forbes explained the process I mentioned earlier of holdable and wearable technology followed by implantable. The article said there were three generations of the Internet of Bodies that include:

- Body external: These are wearable devices such as Apple Watches or Fitbits that can monitor our health.

- Body internal: These include pacemakers, cochlear implants, and digital pills that go inside our bodies to monitor or control various aspects of health.

- Body embedded: The third generation of the Internet of Bodies is embedded technology where technology and the human body are melded together and have a real-time connection to a remote machine.

Forbes noted the development of the Brain Computer Interface (BCI) which merges the brain with an external device for monitoring and controlling in real-time. 'The ultimate goal is to help restore function to individuals with disabilities by using brain signals rather than conventional neuromuscular pathways.' Oh, do fuck off. The goal of brain interface technology is controlling human thought and emotion from the central point in a hive mind serving its masters wishes. Many people are now agreeing to be chipped to open doors without a key. You can recognise them because they'll be wearing a mask, social distancing and lining up for the 'vaccine'. The Cult plans a Great Reset money system after they have completed the demolition of the global economy in which 'money' will be exchanged through communication with body operating systems. Rand Corporation, a Cult-owned think tank, said of the Internet of Bodies or IoB:

Internet of Bodies technologies fall under the broader IoT umbrella. But as the name suggests, IoB devices introduce an even more intimate interplay between humans and gadgets. IoB devices monitor the human body, collect health metrics and other personal information, and transmit those data over the Internet. Many devices, such as fitness trackers, are already in use ... IoB devices ... and those in development can track, record, and store users' whereabouts, bodily functions, and what they see, hear, and even think.

Schwab's World Economic Forum, a long-winded way of saying 'fascism' or 'the Cult', has gone full-on with the Internet of Bodies in the 'Covid' era. 'We're entering the era of the Internet of Bodies', it declared, 'collecting our physical data via a range of devices that can be implanted, swallowed or worn'. The result would be a huge amount of health-related data that could improve human wellbeing around the world, and prove crucial in fighting the 'Covid-19 pandemic'. Does anyone think these clowns care about 'human wellbeing' after the death and devastation their pandemic hoax has purposely caused? Schwab and co say we should move forward with the Internet of Bodies because 'Keeping track of symptoms could help us stop the spread of infection, and quickly detect new cases'. How wonderful, but keeping track' is all they are really bothered about. Researchers were investigating if data gathered from smartwatches and similar devices could be used as viral infection alerts by tracking the user's heart rate and breathing. Schwab said in his 2018 book *Shaping the Future of the Fourth Industrial Revolution*:

The lines between technologies and beings are becoming blurred and not just by the ability to create lifelike robots or synthetics. Instead it is about the ability of new technologies to literally become part of us. Technologies already influence how we understand ourselves, how we think about each other, and how we determine our realities. As the technologies ... give us deeper access to parts of ourselves, we may begin to integrate digital technologies into our bodies.

You can see what the game is. Twenty-four hour control and people – if you could still call them that – would never know when something would go ping and take them out of circulation. It's the most obvious rush to a global fascist dictatorship and the complete submission of humanity and yet still so many are locked away in their Cult-induced perceptual coma and can't see it.

Smart Grid control centres

The human body is being transformed by the 'vaccines' and in other ways into a synthetic cyborg that can be attached to the global Smart Grid which would be controlled from a central point and other sub-locations of Grid manipulation. Where are these planned to be? Well, China for a start which is one of the Cult's biggest centres of operation. The technological control system and technocratic rule was incubated here to be unleashed across the world after the 'Covid' hoax came out of China in 2020. Another Smart Grid location that will surprise people new to this is Israel. I have exposed in *The Trigger* how Sabbatian technocrats, intelligence and military operatives were behind the horrors of 9/11 and not `19 Arab hijackers' who somehow manifested the ability to pilot big passenger airliners when instructors at puddle-jumping flying schools described some of them as a joke. The 9/11 attacks were made possible through control of civilian and military air computer systems and those of the White House, Pentagon and connected agencies. See *The Trigger* – it will blow your mind. The controlling and coordinating force were the Sabbatian networks in Israel and the United States which by then had infiltrated the entire US government, military and intelligence system. The real name of the American Deep State is 'Sabbatian State'. Israel is a tiny country of only nine million people, but it is one of the global centres of cyber operations and fast catching Silicon Valley in importance to the Cult. Israel is known as the 'start-up nation' for all the cyber companies spawned there with the Sabbatian specialisation of 'cyber security' that I mentioned earlier which gives those companies access to computer systems of their clients in real time through 'backdoors' written into the coding when security software is downloaded. The Sabbatian centre of cyber operations outside Silicon Valley is the Israeli military Cyber Intelligence Unit, the biggest infrastructure project in Israel's history, headquartered in the desert-city of Beersheba and involving some 20,000 'cyber soldiers'. Here are located a literal army of Internet trolls scanning social media, forums and comment lists for anyone challenging the Cult agenda. The UK military has something similar with its 77th Brigade and associated operations. The Beersheba complex includes research and development centres for other Cult operations such as Intel, Microsoft, IBM, Google, Apple, Hewlett-Packard, Cisco Systems, Facebook and Motorola. Techcrunch.com ran an article about the Beersheba global Internet technology centre headlined 'Israel's desert city of Beersheba is turning into a cybertech oasis':

> The military's massive relocation of its prestigious technology units, the presence of multinational and local companies, a close proximity to Ben Gurion University and generous government subsidies are turning Beersheba

into a major global cybertech hub. Beersheba has all of the ingredients of a vibrant security technology ecosystem, including Ben Gurion University with its graduate program in cybersecurity and Cyber Security Research Center, and the presence of companies such as EMC, Deutsche Telekom, PayPal, Oracle, IBM, and Lockheed Martin. It's also the future home of the INCB (Israeli National Cyber Bureau); offers a special income tax incentive for cyber security companies, and was the site for the relocation of the army's intelligence corps units.

Sabbatians have taken over the cyber world through the following process: They scan the schools for likely cyber talent and develop them at Ben Gurion University and their period of conscription in the Israeli Defense Forces when they are stationed at the Beersheba complex. When the cyber talented officially leave the army they are funded to start cyber companies with technology developed by themselves or given to them by the state. Much of this is stolen through backdoors of computer systems around the world with America top of the list. Others are sent off to Silicon Valley to start companies or join the major ones and so we have many major positions filled by apparently 'Jewish' but really Sabbatian operatives. Google, YouTube and Facebook are all run by 'Jewish' CEOs while Twitter is all but run by ultra-Zionist hedge-fund shark Paul Singer. At the centre of the Sabbatian global cyber web is the Israeli army's Unit 8200 which specialises in hacking into computer systems of other countries, inserting viruses, gathering information, instigating malfunction, and even taking control of them from a distance. A long list of Sabbatians involved with 9/11, Silicon Valley and Israeli cyber security companies are operatives of Unit 8200. This is not about Israel. It's about the Cult. Israel is planned to be a Smart Grid hub as with China and what is happening at Beersheba is not for the benefit of Jewish people who are treated disgustingly by the Sabbatian elite that control the country. A glance at the Nuremberg Codes will tell you that.

The story is much bigger than 'Covid', important as that is to where we are being taken. Now, though, it's time to really strap in. There's more … much more …

CHAPTER ELEVEN

Who controls the Cult?

Awake, arise or be forever fall'n
John Milton, *Paradise Lost*

I have exposed this far the level of the Cult conspiracy that operates in the world of the seen and within the global secret society and satanic network which operates in the shadows one step back from the seen. The story, however, goes much deeper than that.

The 'Covid' hoax is major part of the Cult agenda, but only part, and to grasp the biggest picture we have to expand our attention beyond the realm of human sight and into the infinity of possibility that we cannot see. It is from here, ultimately, that humanity is being manipulated into a state of total control by the force which dictates the actions of the Cult. How much of reality can we see? Next to damn all is the answer. We may appear to see all there is to see in the 'space' our eyes survey and observe, but little could be further from the truth. The human 'world' is only a tiny band of frequency that the body's visual and perceptual systems can decode into *perception* of a 'world'. According to mainstream science the electromagnetic spectrum is 0.005 percent of what exists in the Universe (Fig 10). The maximum estimate I have seen is 0.5 percent and either way it's miniscule. I say it is far, far, smaller even than 0.005 percent when you compare reality we see with the totality of reality that we don't. Now get this if you are new to such information: Visible light, the only band of frequency that we can see, is a *fraction* of the 0.005 percent (Fig 11 overleaf). Take this further and realise that

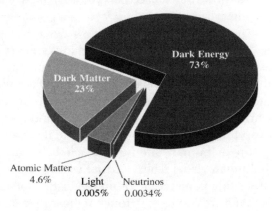

Figure 10: Humans can perceive such a tiny band of visual reality it's laughable.

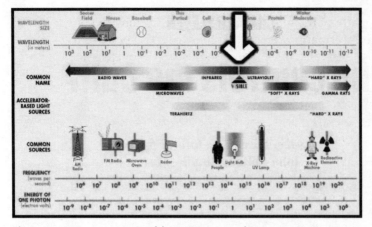

Figure 11: We can see a smear of the 0.005 percent electromagnetic spectrum, but we still know it all. Yep, makes sense.

our universe is one of infinite universes and that universes are only a fragment of overall reality – *infinite* reality. Then compare that with the almost infinitesimal frequency band of visible light or human sight. You see that humans are as near blind as it is possible to be without actually being so. Artist and filmmaker, Sergio Toporek, said:

> Consider that you can see less than 1% of the electromagnetic spectrum and hear less than 1% of the acoustic spectrum. 90% of the cells in your body carry their own microbial DNA and are not 'you'. The atoms in your body are 99.9999999999999999% empty space and none of them are the ones you were born with ... Human beings have 46 chromosomes, two less than a potato.

> The existence of the rainbow depends on the conical photoreceptors in your eyes; to animals without cones, the rainbow does not exist. So you don't just look at a rainbow, you create it. This is pretty amazing, especially considering that all the beautiful colours you see represent less than 1% of the electromagnetic spectrum.

Suddenly the 'world' of humans looks a very different place. Take into account, too, that Planet Earth when compared with the projected size of this single universe is the equivalent of a billionth of a pinhead. Imagine the ratio that would be when compared to infinite reality. To think that Christianity once insisted that Earth and humanity were the centre of everything. This background is vital if we are going to appreciate the nature of 'human' and how we can be manipulated by an unseen force. To human visual reality virtually *everything* is unseen and yet the prevailing perception within the institutions and so much of the public is that if we can't see it, touch it, hear it, taste it and smell it then it cannot exist. Such perception is indoctrinated and encouraged by the Cult and its agents because it isolates believers in the strictly limited, village-idiot, realm of the five senses where perceptions can be firewalled and information controlled. Most of those perpetuating the 'this-world-is-all-there-is' insanity are themselves indoctrinated into believing the same delusion. While major players and influencers know that official reality is laughable most of those in science, academia and medicine really believe the nonsense they peddle and teach succeeding generations. Those who challenge the orthodoxy are dismissed as nutters and freaks to protect the manufactured illusion from exposure. Observe the dynamic of the 'Covid' hoax and you will see how that takes the same form. The inner-circle psychopaths knows it's a gigantic scam, but almost the entirety of those imposing their fascist rules believe that 'Covid' is all that they're told it is.

Stolen identity

Ask people who they are and they will give you their name, place of birth, location, job, family background and life story. Yet that is not who they are – it is what they are *experiencing*. The difference is *absolutely crucial*. The true 'I', the eternal, infinite 'I', is consciousness, a state of being aware. Forget 'form'. That is a vehicle for a brief experience. Consciousness does not come *from* the brain, but *through* the brain and even that is more symbolic than literal. We are awareness, pure awareness, and this is what withdraws from the body at what we call 'death' to continue our eternal beingness, *isness*, in other realms of reality within the limitlessness of infinity or the Biblical 'many mansions in my father's house'. Labels of a human life, man, woman, transgender, black, white, brown, nationality, circumstances and income are not who we are. They are what we are – awareness – is *experiencing* in a brief connection with a band of frequency we call 'human'. The labels are not the self; they are, to use the title of one of my books, a *Phantom* Self. I am not David Icke born in Leicester, England, on April 29th, 1952. I am the consciousness *having that experience*. The Cult and its non-human masters seek to convince us through the institutions of 'education', science, medicine, media and government that what we are *experiencing* is who we *are*. It's so easy to control and direct perception locked away in the bewildered illusions of the five senses with no expanded radar. Try, by contrast, doing the same with a humanity aware of its true self and its true power to consciously create its reality and experience. How is it possible to do this? We do it all day every day. If you perceive yourself as 'little me' with no power to impact upon your life and the world then your life experience will reflect that. You will hand the power you don't think you have to authority in all its forms which will use it to control your experience. This, in turn, will appear to confirm your perception of 'little me' in a self-fulfilling feedback loop. But that is what 'little me' really is – a *perception*. We are all 'big-me', infinite me, and the Cult has to make us forget that if its will is to prevail. We are therefore manipulated and pressured into self-identifying with human labels and not the consciousness/awareness *experiencing* those human labels.

The phenomenon of identity politics is a Cult-instigated manipulation technique to sub-divide previous labels into even smaller ones. A United States university employs this list of letters to describe student identity: LGBTTQQFAGPBDSM or lesbian, gay, bisexual, transgender, transsexual, queer, questioning, flexual, asexual, gender-fuck, polyamorous, bondage/discipline, dominance/submission and sadism/masochism. I'm sure other lists are even longer by now as people feel the need to self-identity the 'I' with the minutiae of race and sexual preference. Wokers programmed by the Cult for generations believe this is about 'inclusivity' when it's really the Cult locking them away into smaller and smaller versions of Phantom Self while firewalling them from the influence of their true self, the infinite, eternal 'I'. You may notice that my philosophy which contends that we are all unique points of attention/awareness within the same infinite whole or Oneness is the ultimate non-racism. The very sense of Oneness makes the judgement of people by their body-type, colour or sexuality utterly ridiculous and confirms that racism has no understanding of reality (including anti-white racism). Yet despite my perception of life Cult agents and fast-asleep Wokers label me racist to discredit my information while they are themselves phenomenally racist and sexist. All they see is race and sexuality and they judge people as good or bad, demons or untouchables, by their race and sexuality. All they see is *Phantom Self* and perceive themselves in terms of Phantom Self. They are pawns and puppets of the Cult agenda to focus attention and self-identity in the five senses and play those identities against each other to divide and rule. Columbia University has introduced segregated graduations in another version of social distancing designed to drive people apart and teach them that different racial and cultural groups have nothing in common with each other. The last thing the Cult wants is unity. Again the pump-primers of this will be Cult operatives in the knowledge of what they are doing, but the rest are just the Phantom Self blind leading the Phantom Self blind. We *do* have something in common – we are all *the same consciousness* having different temporary experiences.

What is this 'human'?

Yes, what *is* 'human'? That is what we are supposed to be, right? I mean 'human'? True, but 'human' is the experience not the 'I'. Break it down to basics and 'human' is the way that information is processed. If we are to experience and interact with this band of frequency we call the 'world' we must have a vehicle that operates within that band of frequency. Our consciousness in its prime form cannot do that; it is way beyond the frequency of the human realm. My consciousness or awareness could not tap these keys and pick up the cup in front of me in the same way that radio station A cannot interact with radio station B when they are on different frequencies. The human body is the means through which we have that interaction. I have long described the body as a biological computer which processes information in a way that allows consciousness to experience this reality. The body is a receiver, transmitter and processor of information in a particular way that we call human. We visually perceive only the world of the five senses in a wakened state – that is the limit of the body's visual decoding system. In truth it's not even visual in the way we experience 'visual reality' as I will come to in a moment. We are 'human' because the body processes the information sources of human into a reality and behaviour system that we *perceive* as human. Why does an elephant act like an elephant and not like a human or a duck? The elephant's biological computer is a different information field and processes information according to that program into a visual and behaviour type we call an elephant. The same applies to everything in our reality. These body information fields are perpetuated through procreation (like making a copy of a software program). The Cult wants to break that cycle and intervene technologically to transform the human information field into one that will change what we call humanity. If it can change the human information field it will change the way that field processes information and change humanity both 'physically' and psychologically. Hence the *messenger* (information) RNA 'vaccines' and so much more that is targeting human genetics by changing the body's information – *messaging* – construct through food, drink, radiation, toxicity and other means.

Reality that we experience is nothing like reality as it really is in the same way that the reality people experience in virtual reality games is not the reality they are really living in. The game is only a decoded source of information that appears to be a reality. Our world is also an information construct – a *simulation* (more later). In its base form our reality is a wavefield of information much the same in theme as Wi-Fi. The five senses decode wavefield information into electrical information which they communicate to the brain to decode into holographic (illusory 'physical') information. Different parts of the brain specialise in decoding different senses and the information is fused into a reality that appears to be outside of us but is really inside the brain and the genetic structure in general (Fig 12 overleaf). DNA is a receiver-transmitter of information and a vital part of this decoding process and the body's connection to other realities. Change DNA and you change the way we

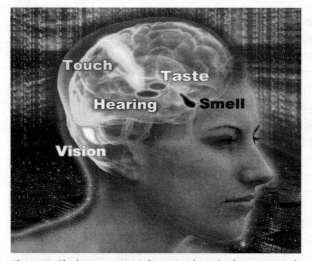

Figure 12: The brain receives information from the five senses and constructs from that our perceived reality.

decode and connect with reality – see 'Covid vaccines'. Think of computers decoding Wi-Fi. You have information encoded in a radiation field and the computer decodes that information into a very different form on the screen. You can't see the Wi-Fi until its information is made manifest on the screen and the information on the screen is inside the computer and not outside. I have just described how we decode the 'human world'. All five senses decode the waveform 'Wi-Fi' field into electrical signals and the brain (computer) constructs reality inside the brain and not outside – 'You don't just look at a rainbow, you create it'. Sound is a simple example. We don't hear sound until the brain decodes it. Waveform sound waves are picked up by the hearing sense and communicated to the brain in an electrical form to be decoded into the sounds that we hear. Everything we hear is inside the brain along with everything we see, feel, smell and taste. Words and language are waveform fields generated by our vocal chords which pass through this process until they are decoded by the brain into words that we hear. Different languages are different frequency fields or sound waves generated by vocal chords. Late British philosopher Alan Watts said:

> [Without the brain] the world is devoid of light, heat, weight, solidity, motion, space, time or any other imaginable feature. All these phenomena are interactions, or transactions, of vibrations with a certain arrangement of neurons.

That's exactly what they are and scientist Robert Lanza describes in his book, *Biocentrism*, how we decode electromagnetic waves and energy into visual and 'physical' experience. He uses the example of a flame emitting photons, electromagnetic energy, each pulsing electrically and magnetically:

> … these … invisible electromagnetic waves strike a human retina, and if (and

only if) the waves happen to measure between 400 and 700 nano meters in length from crest to crest, then their energy is just right to deliver a stimulus to the 8 million cone-shaped cells in the retina.

Each in turn send an electrical pulse to a neighbour neuron, and on up the line this goes, at 250 mph, until it reaches the ... occipital lobe of the brain, in the back of the head. There, a cascading complex of neurons fire from the incoming stimuli, and we subjectively perceive this experience as a yellow brightness occurring in a place we have been conditioned to call the 'external world'.

You hear what you decode

If a tree falls or a building collapses they make no noise unless someone is there to decode the energetic waves generated by the disturbance into what we call sound. Does a falling tree make a noise? Only if you hear it – *decode* it. Everything in our reality is a frequency field of information operating within the overall 'Wi-Fi' field that I call The Field. A vibrational disturbance is generated in The Field by the fields of the falling tree or building. These disturbance waves are what we decode into the sound of them falling. If no one is there to do that then neither will make any noise. Reality is created by the observer – *decoder* – and the *perceptions* of the observer affect the decoding process. For this reason different people – different *perceptions* – will perceive the same reality or situation in a different way. What one may perceive as a nightmare another will see as an opportunity. The question of why the Cult is so focused on controlling human perception now answers itself. All experienced reality is the act of decoding and we don't experience Wi-Fi until it is decoded on the computer screen. The sight and sound of an Internet video is encoded in the Wi-Fi all around us, but we don't see or hear it until the computer decodes that information. Taste, smell and touch are all phenomena of the brain as a result of the same process. We don't taste, smell or feel anything except in the brain and there are pain relief techniques that seek to block the signal from the site of discomfort to the brain because if the brain doesn't decode that signal we don't feel pain. Pain is in the brain and only appears to be at the point of impact thanks to the feedback loop between them. We don't see anything until electrical information from the sight senses is decoded in an area at the back of the brain. If that area is damaged we can go blind when our eyes are perfectly okay. So why do we go blind if we damage an eye? We damage the information processing between the waveform visual information and the visual decoding area of the brain. If information doesn't reach the brain in a form it can decode then we can't see the visual reality that it represents. What's more the brain is decoding only a fraction of the information it receives and the rest is absorbed by the sub-conscious mind. This explanation is from the science magazine, *Wonderpedia*:

> Every second, 11 million sensations crackle along these [brain] pathways ... The brain is confronted with an alarming array of images, sounds and smells which it rigorously filters down until it is left with a manageable list of around 40. Thus 40 sensations per second make up what we perceive as reality.

The 'world' is not what people are told to believe that is it and the inner circles of the Cult *know that*.

Illusory 'physical' reality

We can only see a smear of 0.005 percent of the Universe which is only one of a vast array of universes – 'mansions' – within infinite reality. Even then the brain decodes only 40 pieces of information ('sensations') from a potential *11 million* that we receive every second. Two points strike you from this immediately: The sheer breathtaking stupidity of believing we know anything so rigidly that there's nothing more to know; and the potential for these processes to be manipulated by a malevolent force to control the reality of the population. One thing I can say for sure with no risk of contradiction is that when you can perceive an almost indescribable fraction of infinite reality there is always more to know as in tidal waves of it. Ancient Greek philosopher Socrates was so right when he said that wisdom is to know how little we know. How obviously true that is when you think that we are experiencing a physical world of solidity that is neither physical nor solid and a world of apartness when everything is connected. Cult-controlled 'science' dismisses the so-called 'paranormal' and all phenomena related to that when the 'para'-normal is perfectly normal and explains the alleged 'great mysteries' which dumbfound scientific minds. There is a reason for this. A 'scientific mind' in terms of the mainstream is a material mind, a five-sense mind imprisoned in see it, touch it, hear it, smell it and taste it. Phenomena and happenings that can't be explained that way leave the 'scientific mind' bewildered and the rule is that if they can't account for why something is happening then it can't, by definition, be happening. I beg to differ. Telepathy is thought waves passing through The Field (think wave disturbance again) to be decoded by someone able to connect with that wavelength (information). For example: You can pick up the thought waves of a friend at any distance and at the very least that will bring them to mind. A few minutes later the friend calls you. 'My god', you say, 'that's incredible – I was just thinking of you.' Ah, but *they* were thinking of *you* before they made the call and that's what you decoded. Native peoples not entrapped in five-sense reality do this so well it became known as the 'bush telegraph'. Those known as psychics and mediums (genuine ones) are doing the same only across dimensions of reality. 'Mind over matter' comes from the fact that matter and mind are the *same*. The state of one influences the state of the other. Indeed one *and* the other are illusions. They are aspects of the same field. Paranormal phenomena are all explainable so why are they still considered 'mysteries' or not happening? Once you go down this road of understanding you begin to expand awareness beyond the five senses and that's the nightmare for the Cult.

Holographic 'solidity'

Our reality is not solid, it is holographic. We are now well aware of holograms which are widely used today. Two-dimensional information is decoded into a three-dimensional reality that is not solid although can very much appear to be (Fig 13). Holograms are created with a laser divided into two parts. One goes directly onto a holographic photographic print ('reference beam') and the other takes a waveform image of the subject ('working beam') before being directed onto the print where it 'collides' with the other half of the laser (Fig 14). This creates a *waveform* interference pattern which contains the wavefield information of whatever is being photographed (Fig 15 overleaf). The process can be likened to dropping pebbles in a pond. Waves generated by each one spread out across the water to collide with the others and create a wave representation of where the

Figure 13: Holograms are not solid, but the best ones appear to be.

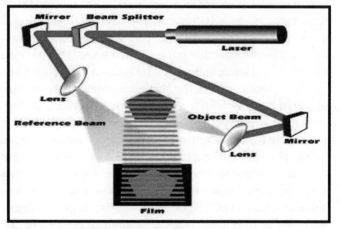

Figure 14: How holograms are created by capturing a waveform version of the subject image.

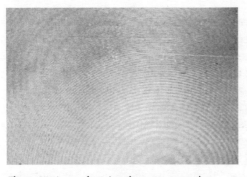

Figure 15: A waveform interference pattern that holds the information that transforms into a hologram.

Figure 16: Holographic people including 'Elvis' holographically inserted to sing a duet with Celine Dion.

stones fell and at what speed, weight and distance. A waveform interference pattern of a hologram is akin to the waveform information in The Field which the five senses decode into electrical signals to be decoded by the brain into a holographic illusory 'physical' reality. In the same way when a laser (think human attention) is directed at the waveform interference pattern a three-dimensional version of the subject is projected into apparently 'solid' reality (Fig 16). An amazing trait of holograms reveals more 'paranormal mysteries'. Information of the *whole* hologram is encoded in waveform in every part of the interference pattern by the way they are created. This means that every *part* of a hologram is a smaller version of the whole. Cut the interference wave-pattern into four and you won't get four parts of the image. You get quarter-sized versions of the *whole* image. The body is a hologram and the same applies. Here we have the basis of acupuncture, reflexology and other forms of healing which identify representations of the whole body in all of the parts, hands, feet, ears, everywhere. Skilled palm readers can do what they do because the information of whole body is encoded in the hand. The concept of as above, so below, comes from this.

The question will be asked of why, if solidity is illusory, we can't just walk through walls and each other. The resistance is not solid against solid; it is electromagnetic field against electromagnetic field and we decode this into the *experience* of solid against solid. We should also not underestimate the power of belief to dictate reality. What you believe is impossible *will be*. Your belief impacts on your decoding processes and they won't decode what you think is impossible. What we believe we perceive and what we perceive we experience. 'Can't dos' and 'impossibles' are like a firewall in a computer system that won't put on the screen what the firewall blocks. How vital that is to understanding how human experience has been hijacked. I explain in *The Answer, Everything You Need To Know But Have Never Been Told* and other books a long list of 'mysteries' and 'paranormal' phenomena that are not mysterious and perfectly normal once you realise what reality is and how it works. 'Ghosts' can be seen to pass through 'solid' walls because the walls are not solid and the ghost is a discarnate entity operating on a frequency so different to that of the wall that it's like two radio stations sharing the same space while never interfering with each other. I have seen ghosts do this myself. The apartness of people and objects is also an illusion. Everything is connected by the Field like all sea life is connected by the sea. It's just that within the limits of our visual reality we only 'see' holographic information and not the field of information that connects everything and from which the holographic world is made manifest. If you can only see holographic 'objects' and not the field that connects them they will appear to you as unconnected to each other in the same way that we see the computer while not seeing the Wi-Fi.

What you don't know *can* hurt you

Okay, we return to those 'two worlds' of human society and the Cult with its global network of interconnecting secret societies and satanic groups which manipulate through governments, corporations, media, religions, etc. The fundamental difference between them is *knowledge*. The idea has been to keep humanity ignorant of the plan for its total enslavement underpinned by a crucial ignorance of reality – who we are and where we are – and how we interact with it. 'Human' should be the interaction between our expanded eternal consciousness and the five-sense body experience. We are meant to be *in* this world in terms of the five senses but not *of* this world in relation to our greater consciousness and perspective. In that state we experience the small picture of the five senses within the wider context of the big picture of awareness beyond the five senses. Put another way the five senses see the dots and expanded awareness connects them into pictures and patterns that give context to the apparently random and unconnected. Without the context of expanded awareness the five senses see only apartness and randomness with apparently no meaning. The Cult and its other-dimensional controllers seek to intervene in the frequency realm where five-sense reality is supposed to connect with expanded reality and to keep the two apart (more on this in the final chapter). When that happens five-sense mental and emotional processes are no longer influenced by expanded awareness, or the True 'I', and instead are driven by the isolated perceptions of the body's decoding systems. They are in the world *and* of it. Here we have the human plight and why humanity with its potential for infinite awareness can be so easily manipulatable and descend into such extremes of stupidity.

Once the Cult isolates five-sense mind from expanded awareness it can then program the mind with perceptions and beliefs by controlling information that the mind receives through the 'education' system of the formative years and the media perceptual bombardment and censorship of an entire lifetime. Limit perception and a sense of the possible through limiting knowledge by limiting and skewing information while censoring and discrediting that which could set people free. As the title of another of my books says ... *And The Truth Shall Set You Free*. For this reason the last thing the Cult wants in circulation is the truth about anything – especially the reality of the eternal 'I' – and that's why it is desperate to control information. The Cult knows that information becomes perception which becomes behaviour which, collectively, becomes human society. Cult-controlled and funded mainstream 'science' denies the existence of an eternal 'I' and seeks to dismiss and trash all evidence to the contrary. Cult-controlled mainstream religion has a version of 'God' that is little more than a system of control and dictatorship that employs threats of damnation in an afterlife to control perceptions and behaviour in the here and now through fear and guilt. Neither is true and it's the 'neither' that the Cult wishes to suppress. This 'neither' is that everything is an expression, a point of attention, within an infinite state of consciousness which is the real meaning of the term 'God'.

Perceptual obsession with the 'physical body' and five-senses means that 'God' becomes personified as a bearded bloke sitting among the clouds or a raging bully who loves us if we do what 'he' wants and condemns us to the fires of hell if we don't. These are no more than a 'spiritual' fairy tales to control and dictate events and behaviour through fear of this 'God' which has bizarrely made 'God-fearing' in religious circles a state to be desired. I would suggest that fearing *anything* is not to be encouraged and celebrated, but rather deleted. You can see why 'God fearing' is so beneficial to the Cult and its religions when *they* decide what 'God' wants and what 'God' demands (the Cult demands) that everyone do. As the great American comedian Bill Hicks said satirising a Christian zealot: 'I think what God meant to say.' How much of this infinite awareness ('God') that we access is decided by how far we choose to expand our perceptions, self-identity and sense of the possible. The scale of self-identity reflects itself in the scale of awareness that we can connect with and are influenced by – how much knowing and insight we have instead of programmed perception. You cannot expand your awareness into the infinity of possibility when you believe that you are little me Peter the postman or Mary in marketing and nothing more. I'll deal with this in the concluding chapter because it's crucial to how we turnaround current events.

Where the Cult came from

When I realised in the early 1990s there was a Cult network behind global events I asked the obvious question: When did it start? I took it back to ancient Rome and Egypt and on to Babylon and Sumer in Mesopotamia, the 'Land Between Two Rivers', in what we now call Iraq. The two rivers are the Tigris and Euphrates and this region is of immense historical and other importance to the Cult, as is the land called Israel only 550 miles away by air. There is much more going with deep esoteric meaning across this whole region. It's not only about 'wars for oil'. Priceless artefacts from Mesopotamia were stolen or destroyed after the American and British invasion of Iraq in 2003 justified by the lies of Boy Bush and Tony Blair (their Cult masters) about non-existent 'weapons of mass destruction'. Mesopotamia was the location of Sumer (about 5,400BC to 1,750BC), and Babylon (about 2,350BC to 539BC). Sabbatians may have become immensely influential in the Cult in modern times but they are part of a network that goes back into the mists of history. Sumer is said by historians to be the 'cradle of civilisation'. I disagree. I say it was the re-start of what we call human civilisation after cataclysmic events symbolised in part as the 'Great Flood' destroyed the world that existed before. These fantastic upheavals that I have been describing in detail in the books since the early1990s appear in accounts and legends of ancient cultures across the world and they are supported by geological and biological evidence. Stone tablets found in Iraq detailing the Sumer period say the cataclysms were caused by non-human 'gods' they call the Anunnaki. These are described in terms of extraterrestrial visitations in which knowledge supplied by the Anunnaki is said to have been the source of at least one of the world's oldest writing systems and developments in astronomy, mathematics and architecture that were way ahead of their time. I have covered this subject at length in *The Biggest Secret* and *Children of the Matrix* and the same basic 'Anunnaki' story can be found in Zulu accounts in South Africa where the late and very great Zulu high shaman Credo Mutwa told me that the Sumerian Anunnaki were known by Zulus as the Chitauri or 'children of the serpent'. See my six-hour video interview with Credo on this subject entitled *The Reptilian Agenda* recorded at his then home near Johannesburg in 1999 which you can watch on the Ickonic media platform.

The Cult emerged out of Sumer, Babylon and Egypt (and elsewhere) and established the Roman Empire before expanding with the Romans into northern Europe from where many empires were savagely imposed in the form of Cult-controlled societies all over the world. Mass death and destruction was their calling card. The Cult established its centre of operations in Europe and European Empires were Cult empires which allowed it to expand into a global force. Spanish and Portuguese colonialists headed for Central and South America while the British and French targeted North America. Africa was colonised by Britain, France, Belgium, the Netherlands, Portugal, Spain, Italy, and Germany. Some like Britain and France moved in on the Middle East. The British Empire was by far the biggest for a simple reason. By now Britain was the headquarters of the Cult from which it expanded to form Canada, the United States, Australia and New Zealand. The Sun never set on the British Empire such was the scale of its occupation. London remains a global centre for the Cult along with Rome and the Vatican although others have emerged in Israel and China. It is no accident that the 'virus' is alleged to have come out of China while Italy was chosen as the means to terrify the Western population into compliance with 'Covid' fascism. Nor that Israel has led the world in 'Covid' fascism and mass 'vaccination'.

You would think that I would mention the United States here, but while it has been an important means of imposing the Cult's will it is less significant than would appear and is currently in the process of having what power it does have deleted. The Cult in Europe has mostly loaded the guns for the US to fire. America has been controlled from Europe from the start through Cult operatives in Britain and Europe. The American Revolution was an illusion to make it appear that America was governing itself while very different forces were pulling the strings in the form of Cult families such as the Rothschilds through the Rockefellers and other subordinates. The Rockefellers are extremely close to Bill Gates and established both scalpel and drug 'medicine' and the World Health Organization. They play a major role in the development and circulation of vaccines through the Rockefeller Foundation on which Bill Gates said his Foundation is based. Why wouldn't this be the case when the Rockefellers and Gates are on the same team? Cult infiltration of human society goes way back into what we call history and has been constantly expanding and centralising power with the goal of establishing a global structure to dictate everything. Look how this has been advanced in great leaps with the 'Covid' hoax.

The non-human dimension

I researched and observed the comings and goings of Cult operatives through the centuries and even thousands of years as they were born, worked to promote the agenda within the secret society and satanic networks, and then died for others to replace them. Clearly there had to be a coordinating force that spanned this entire period while operatives who would not have seen the end goal in their lifetimes came and went advancing the plan over millennia. I went in search of that coordinating force with the usual support from the extraordinary synchronicity of my life which has been an almost daily experience since 1990. I saw common themes in religious texts and ancient cultures about a non-human force manipulating human society from the hidden. Christianity calls this force Satan, the Devil and demons; Islam refers to the Jinn or Djinn; Zulus have their Chitauri (spelt in other ways in different parts of Africa); and the Gnostic people in Egypt in the period around and before 400AD referred to this phenomena as the 'Archons', a word meaning rulers in Greek. Central American cultures speak of the 'Predators' among other names and the same theme is everywhere. I will use 'Archons' as a collective name for all of them. When you see how their nature and behaviour is described all these different sources are clearly talking about the same force. Gnostics described the Archons in terms of 'luminous fire' while Islam relates the Jinn to 'smokeless fire'. Some refer to beings in form that could occasionally be seen, but the most common of common theme is that they operate from unseen realms which means almost all existence to the visual processes of humans. I had concluded that this was indeed the foundation of human control and that the Cult was operating within the human frequency band on behalf of this hidden force when I came across the writings of Gnostics which supported my conclusions in the most extraordinary way.

A sealed earthen jar was found in 1945 near the town of Nag Hammadi about 75-80 miles north of Luxor on the banks of the River Nile in Egypt. Inside was a treasure trove of manuscripts and texts left by the Gnostic people some 1,600 years earlier. They included 13 leather-bound papyrus codices (manuscripts) and more than 50 texts written in Coptic Egyptian estimated to have been hidden in the jar in the period of 400AD although the source of the information goes back much further. Gnostics oversaw the Great or Royal Library of Alexandria, the fantastic depository of ancient texts detailing advanced knowledge and accounts of human history. The Library was dismantled and destroyed in stages over a long period with the death-blow delivered by the Cult-established Roman Church in the period around 415AD. The Church of Rome was the Church of Babylon relocated as I said earlier. Gnostics were not a race. They were a way of perceiving reality. Whenever they established themselves and their information circulated the terrorists of the Church of Rome would target them for destruction. This happened with the Great Library and with the Gnostic Cathars who were burned to death by the psychopaths after a long period of oppression at the siege of the Castle of Monségur in southern France in 1244. The Church has always been terrified of Gnostic information which demolishes the official Christian narrative although there is much in the Bible that supports the Gnostic view if you read it in another way. To anyone studying the texts of what became known as the Nag Hammadi Library it is clear that great swathes of Christian and Biblical belief has its origin with Gnostics sources going back to Sumer. Gnostic themes have been twisted to manipulate the perceived reality of Bible believers. Biblical texts have been in the open for centuries where they could be changed while Gnostic documents found at Nag Hammadi were sealed away and untouched for 1,600 years. What you see is what they wrote.

Use your *pneuma* not your *nous*

Gnosticism and Gnostic come from 'gnosis' which means knowledge, or rather *secret* knowledge, in the sense of spiritual awareness – knowledge about reality and life itself. The desperation of the Cult's Church of Rome to destroy the Gnostics can be understood when the knowledge they were circulating was the last thing the Cult wanted the population to know. Sixteen hundred years later the same Cult is working hard to undermine and silence me for the same reason. The dynamic between knowledge and ignorance is a constant. 'Time' appears to move on, but essential themes remain the same. We are told to 'use your nous', a Gnostic word for head/brain/intelligence. They said, however, that spiritual awakening or 'salvation' could only be secured by expanding awareness *beyond* what they called *nous* and into *pneuma* or Infinite Self. Obviously as I read these texts the parallels with what I have been saying since 1990 were fascinating to me. There is a universal truth that spans human history and in that case why wouldn't we be talking the same language 16 centuries apart? When you free yourself from the perception program of the five senses and explore expanded realms of consciousness you are going to connect with the same information no matter what the perceived 'era' within a manufactured timeline of a single and tiny range of manipulated frequency. Humans working with 'smart' technology or knocking rocks together in caves is only a timeline appearing to operate within the human frequency band. Expanded awareness and the knowledge it holds have always been there whether the era be Stone Age or computer age. We can only access that knowledge by opening ourselves to its frequency which the five-sense prison cell is designed to stop us doing. Gates, Fauci, Whitty, Vallance, Zuckerberg, Brin, Page, Wojcicki, Bezos, and all the others behind the 'Covid' hoax clearly have a long wait before their range of frequency can make that connection given that an open heart is crucial to that as we shall see. Instead of accessing knowledge directly through expanded awareness it is given to Cult operatives by the secret society networks of the Cult where it has been passed on over thousands of years outside the public arena. Expanded realms of consciousness is where great artists, composers and writers find their inspiration and where truth awaits anyone open enough to connect with it. We need to go there fast.

Archon hijack

A fifth of the Nag Hammadi texts describe the existence and manipulation of the Archons led by a 'Chief Archon' they call 'Yaldabaoth', or the 'Demiurge', and this is the Christian 'Devil', 'Satan', 'Lucifer', and his demons. Archons in Biblical symbolism are the 'fallen ones' which are also referred to as fallen angels after the angels expelled from heaven according to the Abrahamic religions of Judaism, Christianity and Islam. These angels are claimed to tempt humans to 'sin' ongoing and you will see how accurate that symbolism is during the rest of the book. The theme of 'original sin' is related to the 'Fall' when Adam and Eve were 'tempted by the serpent' and fell from a state of innocence and 'obedience' (connection) with God into a state of disobedience (disconnection). The Fall is said to have brought sin into the world and corrupted everything including human nature. Yaldabaoth, the 'Lord Archon', is described by Gnostics as a 'counterfeit spirit', 'The Blind One', 'The Blind God', and 'The Foolish One'. The Jewish name for Yaldabaoth in Talmudic writings is Samael which translates as 'Poison of God', or 'Blindness of God'. You see the parallels. Yaldabaoth in Islamic belief is the Muslim Jinn devil known as Shaytan – Shaytan is Satan as the same themes are found all over the world in every religion and culture. The 'Lord God' of the Old Testament is the 'Lord Archon' of Gnostic manuscripts and that's why he's such a bloodthirsty bastard. Satan is known by Christians as 'the Demon of Demons' and Gnostics called Yaldabaoth the 'Archon of Archons'. Both are known as 'The Deceiver'. We are talking about the same 'bloke' for sure and these common themes using different names, storylines and symbolism tell a common tale of the human plight.

Archons are referred to in Nag Hammadi documents as mind parasites, inverters, guards, gatekeepers, detainers, judges, pitiless ones and deceivers. The 'Covid' hoax alone is a glaring example of all these things. The Biblical 'God' is so different in the Old and New Testaments because they are not describing the same phenomenon. The vindictive, angry, hate-filled, 'God' of the Old Testament, known as Yahweh, is Yaldabaoth who is depicted in Cult-dictated popular culture as the 'Dark Lord', 'Lord of Time', Lord (Darth) Vader and Dormammu, the evil ruler of the 'Dark Dimension' trying to take over the 'Earth Dimension' in the Marvel comic movie, *Dr Strange*. Yaldabaoth is both the Old Testament 'god' and the Biblical 'Satan'. Gnostics referred to Yaldabaoth as the 'Great Architect of the Universe'and the Cult-controlled Freemason network calls their god 'the 'Great Architect of the Universe' (also Grand

Architect). The 'Great Architect' Yaldabaoth is symbolised by the Cult as the all-seeing eye at the top of the pyramid on the Great Seal of the United States and the dollar bill. Archon is encoded in *arch*-itect as it is in *arch*-angels and *arch*-bishops. All religions have the theme of a force for good and force for evil in some sort of spiritual war and there is a reason for that – the theme is true. The Cult and its non-human masters are quite happy for this to circulate. They present themselves as the force for good fighting evil when they are really the force of evil (absence of love). The whole foundation of Cult modus operandi is inversion. They promote themselves as a force for good and anyone challenging them in pursuit of peace, love, fairness, truth and justice is condemned as a satanic force for evil. This has been the game plan throughout history whether the Church of Rome inquisitions of non-believers or 'conspiracy theorists' and 'anti-vaxxers' of today. The technique is the same whatever the timeline era.

Yaldabaoth is revolting (true)

Yaldabaoth and the Archons are said to have revolted against God with Yaldabaoth claiming to *be* God – the *All That Is*. The Old Testament 'God' (Yaldabaoth) demanded to be worshipped as such: '*I am* the LORD, and there is none else, there is no God beside me' (Isaiah 45:5). I have quoted in other books a man who said he was the unofficial son of the late Baron Philippe de Rothschild of the Mouton-Rothschild wine producing estates in France who died in 1988 and he told me about the Rothschild 'revolt from God'. The man said he was given the name Phillip Eugene de Rothschild and we shared long correspondence many years ago while he was living under another identity. He said that he was conceived through 'occult incest' which (within the Cult) was 'normal and to be admired'. 'Phillip' told me about his experience attending satanic rituals with rich and famous people whom he names and you can see them and the wider background to Cult Satanism in my other books starting with *The Biggest Secret*. Cult rituals are interactions with Archontic 'gods'. 'Phillip' described Baron Philippe de Rothschild as 'a master Satanist and hater of God' and he used the same term 'revolt from God' associated with Yaldabaoth/Satan/Lucifer/the Devil in describing the Sabbatian Rothschild dynasty. 'I played a key role in my family's revolt from God', he said. That role was to infiltrate in classic Sabbatian style the Christian Church, but eventually he escaped the mind-prison to live another life. The Cult has been targeting religion in a plan to make worship of the Archons the global one-world religion. Infiltration of Satanism into modern 'culture', especially among the young, through music videos, stage shows and other means, is all part of this.

Nag Hammadi texts describe Yaldabaoth and the Archons in their prime form as energy – consciousness – and say they can take form if they choose in the same way that consciousness takes form as a human. Yaldabaoth is called 'formless' and represents a deeply inverted, distorted and chaotic state of consciousness which seeks to attached to humans and turn them into a likeness of itself in an attempt at assimilation. For that to happen it has to manipulate humans into low frequency mental and emotional states that match its own. Archons can certainly appear in human form and this is the origin of the psychopathic personality. The energetic distortion Gnostics called Yaldabaoth *is* psychopathy. When psychopathic Archons take human form that human will be a psychopath as an expression of Yaldabaoth consciousness. Cult psychopaths are Archons in human form. The principle is the same as that portrayed in the 2009 *Avatar* movie when the American military travelled to a fictional Earth-like moon called Pandora in the Alpha Centauri star system to infiltrate a society of blue people, or Na'vi, by hiding within bodies that looked like the Na'vi. Archons posing as humans have a particular hybrid information field, part human, part Archon, (the ancient 'demigods') which processes information in a way that manifests behaviour to match their psychopathic evil, lack of empathy and compassion, and stops them being influenced by the empathy, compassion and love that a fully-human information field is capable of expressing. Cult bloodlines interbreed, be they royalty or dark suits, for this reason and you have their obsession with incest. Interbreeding with full-blown humans would dilute the Archontic energy field that guarantees psychopathy in its representatives in the human realm.

Gnostic writings say the main non-human forms that Archons take are *serpentine* (what I have called for decades 'reptilian' amid unbounded ridicule from the Archontically-programmed) and what Gnostics describe as 'an unborn baby or foetus with grey skin and dark, unmoving eyes'. This is an excellent representation of the ET 'Greys' of UFO folklore which large numbers of people claim to have seen and been abducted by – Zulu shaman Credo Mutwa among them. I agree with those that believe in extraterrestrial or interdimensional visitations today and for thousands of years past. No wonder with their advanced knowledge and technological capability they were perceived and worshipped as gods for technological and other 'miracles' they appeared to perform. Imagine someone arriving in a culture disconnected from the modern world with a smartphone and computer. They would be seen as a 'god' capable of 'miracles'. The Renegade Mind, however, wants to know the source of everything and not only the way that source manifests as human or non-human. In the same way that a Renegade Mind seeks the original source material for the 'Covid virus' to see if what is claimed is true. The original source of Archons in form is consciousness – the distorted state of consciousness known to Gnostics as Yaldabaoth.

'Revolt from God' is energetic disconnection

Where I am going next will make a lot of sense of religious texts and ancient legends relating to 'Satan', Lucifer' and the 'gods'. Gnostic descriptions sync perfectly with the themes of my own research over the years in how they describe a consciousness distortion seeking to impose itself on human consciousness. I've referred to the core of infinite awareness in previous books as Infinite Awareness in Awareness of Itself. By that I mean a level of awareness that knows that it is all awareness and is aware of all awareness. From here comes the frequency of love in its true sense and balance which is what love is on one level – the balance of all forces into a single whole called Oneness and Isness. The more we disconnect from this state of love that many call 'God' the constituent parts of that Oneness start to unravel and express themselves as a part and not a whole. They become individualised as intellect, mind, selfishness, hatred, envy, desire for power over others, and such like. This is not a problem in the greater scheme in that 'God', the *All That Is*, can experience all these possibilities through different expressions of itself including humans. What we as expressions of the whole experience the *All That Is* experiences. We are the *All That Is* experiencing itself. As we withdraw from that state of Oneness we disconnect from its influence and things can get very unpleasant and very stupid. Archontic consciousness is at the extreme end of that. It has so disconnected from the influence of Oneness that it has become an inversion of unity and love, an inversion of everything, an inversion of life itself. Evil is appropriately live written backwards. Archontic consciousness is obsessed with death, an inversion of life, and so its manifestations in Satanism are obsessed with death. They use inverted symbols in their rituals such as the inverted pentagram and cross. Sabbatians as Archontic consciousness incarnate invert Judaism and every other religion and culture they infiltrate. They seek disunity and chaos and they fear unity and harmony as they fear love like garlic to a vampire. As a result the Cult, Archons incarnate, act with such evil, psychopathy and lack of empathy and compassion disconnected as they are from the source of love. How could Bill Gates and the rest of the Archontic psychopaths do what they have to human society in the 'Covid' era with all the death, suffering and destruction involved and have no emotional consequence for the impact on others? Now you know. Why have Zuckerberg, Brin, Page, Wojcicki and company callously censored information warning about the dangers of the 'vaccine' while thousands have been dying and having severe, sometimes life-changing reactions? Now you know. Why have Tedros,

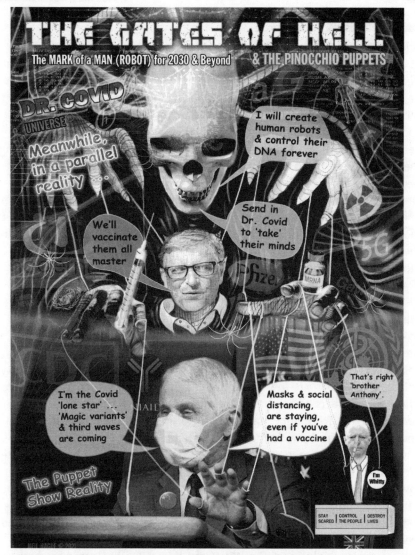

Figure 17: Artist Neil Hague's version of the 'Covid' hierarchy.

Fauci, Whitty, Vallance and their like around the world been using case and death figures they're aware are fraudulent to justify lockdowns and all the deaths and destroyed lives that have come from that? Now you know. Why did Christian Drosten produce and promote a 'testing' protocol that he knew couldn't test for infectious disease which led to a global human catastrophe. Now you know. The Archontic mind doesn't give a shit (Fig 17). I personally think that Gates and major Cult insiders are a form of AI cyborg that the Archons want humans to become.

Human batteries

A state of such inversion does have its consequences, however. The level of disconnection from the Source of All means that you withdraw from that source of energetic sustenance and creativity. This means that you have to find your own supply of energetic power and it has – *us*. When the Morpheus character in the first *Matrix* movie held up a battery he spoke a profound truth when he said: 'The Matrix is a computer-generated dream world built to keep us under control in order to change the human being into one of these.' The statement was true in all respects. We do live in a technologically-generated virtual reality simulation (more very shortly) and we have been manipulated to be an energy source for Archontic consciousness. The Disney-Pixar animated movie *Monsters, Inc.* in 2001 symbolised the dynamic when monsters in their world had no energy source and they would enter the human world to terrify children in their beds, catch the child's scream, terror (low-vibrational frequencies), and take that energy back to power the monster world. The lead character you might remember was a single giant eye and the symbolism of the Cult's all-seeing eye was obvious. Every thought and emotion is broadcast as a frequency unique to that thought and emotion. Feelings of love and joy, empathy and compassion, are high, quick, frequencies while fear, depression, anxiety, suffering and hate are low, slow, dense frequencies. Which kind do you think Archontic consciousness can connect with and absorb? In such a low and dense frequency state there's no way it can connect with the energy of love and joy. Archons can only feed off energy compatible with their own frequency and they and their Cult agents want to delete the human world of love and joy and manipulate the transmission of low vibrational frequencies through low-vibrational human mental and emotional states. *We are their energy source*. Wars are energetic banquets to the Archons – a world war even more so – and think how much low-frequency mental and emotional energy has been generated from the consequences for humanity of the 'Covid' hoax orchestrated by Archons incarnate like Gates.

The ancient practice of human sacrifice 'to the gods', continued in secret today by the Cult, is based on the same principle. 'The gods' are Archontic consciousness in different forms and the sacrifice is induced into a state of intense terror to generate the energy the Archontic frequency can absorb. Incarnate Archons in the ritual drink the blood which contains an adrenaline they crave which floods into the bloodstream when people are terrorised. Most of the sacrifices, ancient and modern, are children and the theme of 'sacrificing young virgins to the gods' is just code for children. They have a particular pre-puberty energy that Archons want more than anything and the energy of the young in general is their target. The California Department of Education wants students to chant the names of Aztec gods (Archontic gods) once worshipped in human sacrifice rituals in a curriculum designed to encourage them to 'challenge racist, bigoted, discriminatory, imperialist/colonial beliefs', join 'social movements that struggle for social justice', and 'build new possibilities for a post-racist, post-systemic racism society'. It's the usual Woke crap that inverts racism and calls it anti-racism. In this case solidarity with 'indigenous tribes' is being used as an excuse to chant the names of 'gods' to which people were sacrificed (and still are in secret). What an example of Woke's inability to see beyond black and white, us and them, They condemn the colonisation of these tribal cultures by Europeans (quite right), but those cultures sacrificing people including children to their 'gods', and mass murdering untold numbers as the Aztecs did, is just fine. One chant is to the Aztec god Tezcatlipoca who had a man sacrificed to him in the 5th month of the Aztec calendar. His heart was cut out and he was eaten. Oh, that's okay then. Come on children ... after three ... Other sacrificial 'gods' for the young to chant their allegiance include Quetzalcoatl, Huitzilopochtli and Xipe Totec. The curriculum says that 'chants, affirmations, and energizers can be used to bring the class together, build unity around ethnic studies principles and values, and to reinvigorate the class following a lesson that may be emotionally taxing or even when student engagement may appear to be low'. Well, that's the cover story, anyway. Chanting and mantras are the repetition of a particular frequency generated from the vocal cords and chanting the names of these Archontic 'gods' tunes you into their frequency. That is the last thing you want when it allows for energetic synchronisation, attachment and perceptual influence. Initiates chant the names of their 'Gods' in their rituals for this very reason.

Vampires of the Woke

Paedophilia is another way that Archons absorb the energy of children. Paedophiles possessed by Archontic consciousness are used as the conduit during sexual abuse for discarnate Archons to vampire the energy of the young they desire so much. Stupendous numbers of children disappear every year never to be seen again although you would never know from the media. Imagine how much low-vibrational energy has been generated by children during the 'Covid' hoax when so many have become depressed and psychologically destroyed to the point of killing themselves. Shocking numbers of children are now taken by the state from loving parents to be handed to others. I can tell you from long experience of researching this since 1996 that many end up with paedophiles and assets of the Cult through corrupt and Cult-owned social services which in the reframing era has hired many psychopaths and emotionless automatons to do the job. Children are even stolen to order using spurious reasons to take them by the corrupt and secret (because they're corrupt) 'family courts'. I have written in detail in other books, starting with *The Biggest Secret* in 1997, about the ubiquitous connections between the political, corporate, government, intelligence and military elites (Cult operatives) and Satanism and paedophilia. If you go deep enough both networks have an interlocking leadership. The Woke mentality has been developed by the Cult for many reasons: To promote almost every aspect of its agenda; to hijack the traditional political left and turn it fascist; to divide and rule; and to target agenda pushbackers. But there are other reasons which relate to what I am describing here. How many happy and joyful Wokers do you ever see especially at the extreme end? They are a mental and psychological mess consumed by emotional stress and constantly emotionally cocked for the next explosion of indignation at someone referring to a female as a female. They are walking, talking, batteries as Morpheus might say emitting frequencies which both enslave them in low-vibrational bubbles of perceptual limitation and feed the Archons. Add to this the hatred claimed to be love; fascism claimed to 'anti-fascism', racism claimed to be 'anti-racism'; exclusion claimed to inclusion; and the abuse-filled Internet trolling. You have a purpose-built Archontic energy system with not a wind turbine in sight and all founded on Archontic *inversion*. We have whole generations now manipulated to serve the Archons with their actions and energy. They will be doing so their entire adult lives unless they snap out of their Archon-induced trance. Is it really a surprise that Cult billionaires and corporations put so much money their way? Where is the energy of joy and laughter, including laughing at yourself which is confirmation of your own emotional security? Mark Twain said: 'The human race has one really effective weapon, and that is laughter.' We must use it all the time. Woke has destroyed comedy because it has no humour, no joy, sense of irony, or self-deprecation. Its energy is dense and intense. *Mmmmm*, lunch says the Archontic frequency. Rudolf Steiner (1861-1925) was the Austrian philosopher and famous esoteric thinker who established Waldorf education or Steiner schools to treat children like unique expressions of consciousness and not minds to be programmed with the perceptions determined by authority. I'd been writing about this energy vampiring for decades when I was sent in 2016 a quote by Steiner. He was spot on:

> There are beings in the spiritual realms for whom anxiety and fear emanating from human beings offer welcome food. When humans have no anxiety and fear, then these creatures starve. If fear and anxiety radiates from people and they break out in panic, then these creatures find welcome nutrition and they become more and more powerful. These beings are hostile towards humanity.

Everything that feeds on negative feelings, on anxiety, fear and superstition, despair or doubt, are in reality hostile forces in super-sensible worlds, launching cruel attacks on human beings, while they are being fed ... These are exactly the feelings that belong to contemporary culture and materialism; because it estranges people from the spiritual world, it is especially suited to evoke hopelessness and fear of the unknown in people, thereby calling up the above mentioned hostile forces against them.

Pause for a moment from this perspective and reflect on what has happened in the world since the start of 2020. Not only will pennies drop, but billion dollar bills. We see the same theme from Don Juan Matus, a Yaqui Indian shaman in Mexico and the information source for Peruvian-born writer, Carlos Castaneda, who wrote a series of books from the 1960s to 1990s. Don Juan described the force manipulating human society and his name for the Archons was the predator:

We have a predator that came from the depths of the cosmos and took over the rule of our lives. Human beings are its prisoners. The predator is our lord and master. It has rendered us docile, helpless. If we want to protest, it suppresses our protest. If we want to act independently, it demands that we don't do so ... indeed we are held prisoner!

They took us over because we are food to them, and they squeeze us mercilessly because we are their sustenance. Just as we rear chickens in coops, the predators rear us in human coops, humaneros. Therefore, their food is always available to them.

Different cultures, different eras, same recurring theme.

The 'ennoia' dilemma

Nag Hammadi Gnostic manuscripts say that Archon consciousness has no 'ennoia'. This is directly translated as 'intentionality', but I'll use the term 'creative imagination'. The *All That Is* in awareness of itself is the source of all creativity – all possibility – and the more disconnected you are from that source the more you are subsequently denied 'creative imagination'. Given that Archon consciousness is almost entirely disconnected it severely lacks creativity and has to rely on far more mechanical processes of thought and exploit the creative potential of those that do have 'ennoia'. You can see cases of this throughout human society. Archon consciousness almost entirely dominates the global banking system and if we study how that system works you will appreciate what I mean. Banks manifest 'money' out of nothing by issuing lines of 'credit' which is 'money' that has never, does not, and will never exist except in theory. It's a confidence trick. If you think 'credit' figures-on-a-screen 'money' is worth anything you accept it as payment. If you don't then the whole system collapses through lack of confidence in the value of that 'money'. Archontic bankers with no 'ennoia' are 'lending' 'money' that doesn't exist to humans that *do* have creativity – those that have the inspired ideas and create businesses and products. Archon banking feeds off human creativity which it controls through 'money' creation and debt. Humans have the creativity and Archons exploit that for their own benefit and control while having none themselves. Archon Internet platforms like Facebook claim joint copyright of everything that creative users post and while Archontic minds like Zuckerberg may officially head that company it will be human creatives on the staff that provide the creative inspiration. When you have limitless 'money' you can then buy other companies established by creative humans. Witness the acquisition record of Facebook, Google and their like. Survey the Archon-controlled music industry and you see non-creative dark suit executives making their fortune from the human creativity of their artists. The cases are endless. Research the history of people like Gates and Zuckerberg and how their empires were built on exploiting the creativity of others. Archon minds cannot create out of nothing, but they are skilled (because they have to be) in what Gnostic texts call 'countermimicry'. They can imitate, but not innovate. Sabbatians trawl the creativity of others through backdoors they install in computer systems through their cybersecurity systems. Archon-controlled China is globally infamous for stealing intellectual property and I remember how Hong Kong, now part of China, became notorious for making counterfeit copies of the creativity of others – 'countermimicry'. With the now pervasive and all-seeing surveillance systems able to infiltrate any computer you can appreciate the potential for Archons to vampire the creativity of humans. Author John Lamb Lash wrote in his book about the Nag Hammadi texts, *Not In His Image*:

> Although they cannot originate anything, because they lack the divine factor of ennoia (intentionality), Archons can imitate with a vengeance. Their expertise is simulation (HAL, virtual reality). The Demiurge [Yaldabaoth] fashions a heaven world copied from the fractal patterns [of the original] ... His construction is celestial kitsch, like the fake Italianate villa of a Mafia don complete with militant angels to guard every portal.

This brings us to something that I have been speaking about since the turn of the millennium. Our reality is a simulation; a virtual reality that we think is real. No, I'm not kidding.

Human reality? Well, virtually

I had pondered for years about whether our reality is 'real' or some kind of construct. I remembered being immensely affected on a visit as a small child in the late 1950s to the then newly-opened Planetarium on the Marylebone Road in London which is now closed and part of the adjacent Madame Tussauds wax museum. It was in the middle of the day, but when the lights went out there was the night sky projected in the Planetarium's domed ceiling and it appeared to be so real. The experience never left me and I didn't know why until around the turn of the millennium when I became certain that our 'night sky' and entire reality is a projection, a virtual reality, akin to the illusory world portrayed in the *Matrix* movies. I looked at the sky one day in this period and it appeared to me like the domed roof of the Planetarium. The release of the first *Matrix* movie in 1999 also provided a synchronistic and perfect visual representation of where my mind had been going for a long time. I hadn't come across the Gnostic Nag Hammadi texts then. When I did years later the correlation was once again astounding. As I read Gnostic accounts from 1,600 years and more earlier it was clear that they were describing the same simulation phenomenon. They tell how the Yaldabaoth 'Demiurge' and Archons created a 'bad copy' of original reality to rule over all that were captured by its illusions and the body was a prison to trap consciousness in the 'bad copy' fake reality. Read how Gnostics describe the 'bad copy' and update that to current times and they are referring to what we would call today a virtual reality simulation.

Author John Lamb Lash said 'the Demiurge fashions a heaven world copied from the fractal patterns' of the original through expertise in 'HAL' or virtual reality simulation. Fractal patterns are part of the energetic information construct of our reality, a sort of blueprint. If these patterns were copied in computer terms it would indeed give you a copy of a 'natural' reality in a non-natural frequency and digital form. The principle is the same as making a copy of a website. The original website still exists, but now you can change the copy version to make it whatever you like and it can become very different to the original website. Archons have done this with our reality, a *synthetic* copy of prime reality that still exists beyond the frequency walls of the simulation. Trapped within the illusions of this synthetic Matrix, however, were and are human consciousness and other expressions of prime reality and this is why the Archons via the Cult are seeking to make the human body synthetic and give us synthetic AI minds to complete the job of turning the entire reality synthetic including what we perceive to be the natural world. To quote Kurzweil: 'Nanobots will infuse all the matter around us with information. Rocks, trees, everything will become these intelligent creatures.' Yes, *synthetic* 'creatures' just as 'Covid' and other genetically-manipulating 'vaccines' are designed to make the human body synthetic. From this perspective it is obvious why Archons and their Cult are so desperate to infuse synthetic material into every human with their 'Covid' scam.

Let there be (electromagnetic) light

Yaldabaoth, the force that created the simulation, or Matrix, makes sense of the Gnostic reference to 'The Great Architect' and its use by Cult Freemasonry as the name of its deity. The designer of the Matrix in the movies is called 'The Architect' and that trilogy is jam-packed with symbolism relating to these subjects. I have contended for years that the angry Old Testament God (Yaldabaoth) is the 'God' being symbolically 'quoted' in the opening of Genesis as 'creating the world'. This is not the creation of prime reality – it's the creation of the *simulation*. The Genesis 'God' says: 'Let there be Light: and there was light.' But what is this 'Light'? I have said for decades that the speed of light (186,000 miles per second) is not the fastest speed possible as claimed by mainstream science and is in fact the frequency walls or outer limits of the Matrix. You can't have a fastest or slowest anything within all possibility when everything is possible. The human body is encoded to operate within the speed of light or *within the simulation* and thus we see only the tiny frequency band of visible *light*. Near-death experiencers who perceive reality outside the body during temporary 'death' describe a very different form of light and this is supported by the Nag Hammadi texts. Prime reality beyond the simulation ('Upper Aeons' to the Gnostics) is described as a realm of incredible beauty, bliss, love and harmony – a realm of 'watery light' that is so powerful 'there are no shadows'. Our false reality of Archon control, which Gnostics call the 'Lower Aeons', is depicted as a realm with a different kind of 'light' and described in terms of chaos, 'Hell', 'the Abyss' and 'Outer Darkness', where trapped souls are tormented and manipulated by demons (relate that to the 'Covid' hoax alone). The watery light theme can be found in near-death accounts and it is not the same as *simulation* 'light' which is electromagnetic or radiation light within the speed of light – the 'Lower Aeons'. Simulation 'light' is the 'luminous fire' associated by Gnostics with the Archons. The Bible refers to Yaldabaoth as 'that old serpent, called the Devil, and Satan, which deceiveth the whole world' (Revelation 12:9). I think that making a simulated copy of prime reality ('countermimicry') and changing it dramatically while all the time manipulating humanity to believe it to be real could probably meet the criteria of deceiving the whole world. Then we come to the Cult god Lucifer – the *Light Bringer*. Lucifer is symbolic of Yaldabaoth, the bringer of radiation light that forms the bad copy simulation within the speed of light. 'He' is symbolised by the lighted torch held by the Statue of

Liberty and in the name 'Illuminati'. Sabbatian-Frankism declares that Lucifer is the true god and Lucifer is the real god of Freemasonry honoured as their 'Great or Grand Architect of the Universe' (simulation).

I would emphasise, too, the way Archontic technologically-generated luminous fire of radiation has deluged our environment since I was a kid in the 1950s and changed the nature of The Field with which we constantly interact. Through that interaction technological radiation is changing us. The Smart Grid is designed to operate with immense levels of communication power with 5G expanding across the world and 6G, 7G, in the process of development. Radiation is the simulation and the Archontic manipulation system. Why wouldn't the Archon Cult wish to unleash radiation upon us to an ever-greater extreme to form Kurzweil's 'cloud'? The plan for a synthetic human is related to the need to cope with levels of radiation beyond even anything we've seen so far. Biological humans would not survive the scale of radiation they have in their script. The Smart Grid is a technological sub-reality within the technological simulation to further disconnect five-sense perception from expanded consciousness. It's a technological prison of the mind.

Infusing the 'spirit of darkness'

A recurring theme in religion and native cultures is the manipulation of human genetics by a non-human force and most famously recorded as the biblical 'sons of god' (the gods plural in the original) who interbred with the daughters of men. The Nag Hammadi *Apocryphon of John* tells the same story this way:

> He [Yaldabaoth] sent his angels [Archons/demons] to the daughters of men, that they might take some of them for themselves and raise offspring for their enjoyment. And at first they did not succeed. When they had no success, they gathered together again and they made a plan together ... And the angels changed themselves in their likeness into the likeness of their mates, filling them with the spirit of darkness, which they had mixed for them, and with evil ... And they took women and begot children out of the darkness according to the likeness of their spirit.

Possession when a discarnate entity takes over a human body is an age-old theme and continues today. It's very real and I've seen it. Satanic and secret society rituals can create an energetic environment in which entities can attach to initiates and I've heard many stories of how people have changed their personality after being initiated even into lower levels of the Freemasons. I have been inside three Freemasonic temples, one at a public open day and two by just walking in when there was no one around to stop me. They were in Ryde, the town where I live,

Birmingham, England, when I was with a group, and Boston, Massachusetts. They all felt the same energetically – dark, dense, low-vibrational and sinister. Demonic attachment can happen while the initiate has no idea what is going on. To them it's just a ritual to get in the Masons and do a bit of good business. In the far more extreme rituals of Satanism human possession is even more powerful and they are designed to make possession possible. The hierarchy of the Cult is dictated by the power and perceived status of the possessing Archon. In this way the Archon hierarchy becomes the Cult hierarchy. Once the entity has attached it can influence perception and behaviour and if it attaches to the extreme then so much of its energy (information) infuses into the body information field that the hologram starts to reflect the nature of the possessing entity. This is the *Exorcist* movie type of possession when facial features change and it's known as shapeshifting. Islam's Jinn are said to be invisible tricksters who change shape, 'whisper', confuse and take human form. These are all traits of the Archons and other versions of the same phenomenon. Extreme possession could certainty infuse the 'spirit of darkness' into a partner during sex as the Nag Hammadi texts appear to describe. Such an infusion can change genetics which is also energetic information. Human genetics is information and the 'spirit of darkness' is information. Mix one with the other and change must happen. Islam has the concept of a 'Jinn baby' through possession of the mother and by Jinn taking human form. There are many ways that human genetics can be changed and remember that Archons have been aware all along of advanced techniques to do this. What is being done in human society today – and far more – was known about by Archons at the time of the 'fallen ones' and their other versions described in religions and cultures.

Archons and their human-world Cult are obsessed with genetics as we see today and they know this dictates how information is processed into perceived reality during a human life. They needed to produce a human form that would decode the simulation and this is symbolically known as 'Adam and Eve' who left the 'garden' (prime reality) and 'fell' into Matrix reality. The simulation is not a 'physical' construct (there is no 'physical'); it is a source of information. Think Wi-Fi again. The simulation is an energetic field encoded with information and body-brain systems are designed to decode that information encoded in wave or frequency form which is transmitted to the brain as electrical signals. These are decoded by the brain to construct our sense of reality – an illusory 'physical' world that only exists in the brain or the mind. Virtual reality games mimic this process using the same sensory decoding system. Information is fed to the senses to decode a virtual reality that can appear so real, but isn't (Figs 18 and 19). Some scientists believe – and I agree with them – that what we perceive as 'physical' reality only

Figure 18: Virtual reality technology 'hacks' into the body's five-sense decoding system.

Figure 19: The result can be experienced as very 'real'.

exists when we are looking or observing. The act of perception or focus triggers the decoding systems which turn waveform information into holographic reality. When we are not observing something our reality reverts from a holographic state to a waveform state. This relates to the same principle as a falling tree not making a noise unless someone is there to hear it or decode it. The concept makes sense from the simulation perspective. A computer is not decoding all the information in a Wi-Fi field all the time and only decodes or brings into reality on the screen that part of Wi-Fi that it's decoding – focusing upon – at that moment.

Interestingly, Professor Donald Hoffman at the Department of Cognitive Sciences at the University of California, Irvine, says that our experienced reality is like a computer interface that shows us only the level with which we interact while hiding all that exists beyond it: 'Evolution shaped us with a user interface that hides the truth. Nothing that we see is the truth – the very language of space and time and objects is the wrong language to describe reality.' He is correct in what he says on so many levels. Space and time are not a universal reality. They are a phenomenon of decoded *simulation* reality as part of the process of enslaving our sense of reality. Near-death experiencers report again and again how space and time did not exist as we perceive them once they were free of the body – body decoding systems. You can appreciate from this why Archons and their Cult are so desperate to entrap human attention in the five senses where we are in the Matrix and of the Matrix. Opening your mind to expanded states of awareness takes you beyond the information confines of the simulation and you become aware of knowledge and insights denied to you before. This is what we call 'awakening' – *awakening from the Matrix* – and in the final chapter I will relate this to current events.

Where are the 'aliens'?

A simulation would explain the so-called 'Fermi Paradox' named after

Italian physicist Enrico Fermi (1901-1954) who created the first nuclear reactor. He considered the question of why there is such a lack of extraterrestrial activity when there are so many stars and planets in an apparently vast universe; but what if the night sky that we see, or think we do, is a simulated projection as I say? If you control the simulation and your aim is to hold humanity fast in essential ignorance would you want other forms of life including advanced life coming and going sharing information with humanity? Or would you want them to believe they were isolated and apparently alone? Themes of human isolation and apartness are common whether they be the perception of a lifeless universe or the fascist isolation laws of the 'Covid' era. Paradoxically the very existence of a simulation means that we are not alone when some force had to construct it. My view is that experiences that people have reported all over the world for centuries with Reptilians and Grey entities are Archon phenomena as Nag Hammadi texts describe; and that benevolent 'alien' interactions are non-human groups that come in and out of the simulation by overcoming Archon attempts to keep them out. It should be highlighted, too, that Reptilians and Greys are obsessed with *genetics* and *technology* as related by cultural accounts and those who say they have been abducted by them. Technology is their way of overcoming some of the limitations in their creative potential and our technology-driven and controlled human society of today is *arch*etypical Archon-Reptilian-Grey modus operandi. Technocracy is really *Archon*tocracy. The Universe does not have to be as big as it appears with a simulation. There is no space or distance only information decoded into holographic reality. What we call 'space' is only the absence of holographic 'objects' and that 'space' is The Field of energetic information which connects everything into a single whole. The same applies with the artificially-generated information field of the simulation. The Universe is not big or small as a physical reality. It is decoded information, that's all, and its perceived size is decided by the way the simulation is encoded to make it appear. The entire night sky as we perceive it only exists in our brain and so where are those 'millions of light years'? The 'stars' on the ceiling of the Planetarium looked a vast distance away.

There's another point to mention about 'aliens'. I have been highlighting since the 1990s the plan to stage a fake 'alien invasion' to justify the centralisation of global power and a world military. Nazi scientist Werner von Braun, who was taken to America by Operation Paperclip after World War Two to help found NASA, told his American assistant Dr Carol Rosin about the Cult agenda when he knew he was dying in 1977. Rosin said that he told her about a sequence that would lead to total human control by a one-world government. This included threats from terrorism, rogue nations, meteors and asteroids before finally an 'alien invasion'. All of these things, von Braun said, would be bogus and what I would refer to as a No-Problem-Reaction-Solution. Keep this in mind when 'the aliens are coming' is the new mantra. The aliens are not coming – they are *already here* and they have infiltrated human society while looking human. French-Canadian investigative journalist Serge Monast said in 1994 that he had uncovered a NASA/military operation called Project Blue Beam which fits with what Werner von Braun predicted. Monast died of a 'heart attack' in 1996 the day after he was arrested and spent a night in prison. He was 51. He said Blue Beam was a plan to stage an alien invasion that would include religious figures beamed holographically into the sky as part of a global manipulation to usher in a 'new age' of worshipping what I would say is the Cult 'god' Yaldabaoth in a one-world religion. Fake holographic asteroids are also said to be part of the plan which again syncs with von Braun. How could you stage an illusory threat from asteroids unless they were holographic inserts? This is pretty straightforward given the advanced technology outside the public arena and the fact that our 'physical' reality is holographic anyway. Information fields would be projected and we would decode them into the illusion of a 'physical' asteroid. If they can sell a global 'pandemic' with a 'virus' that doesn't exist what will humans not believe if government and media tell them?

All this is particularly relevant as I write with the Pentagon planning to release in June, 2021, information about 'UFO sightings'. I have been following the UFO story since the early 1990s and the common theme throughout has been government and military denials and cover up. More recently, however, the Pentagon has suddenly become more talkative and apparently open with Air Force pilot radar images released of unexplained craft moving and changing direction at speeds well beyond anything believed possible with human technology. Then, in March, 2021, former Director of National Intelligence John Ratcliffe said a Pentagon report months later in June would reveal a great deal of information about UFO sightings unknown to the public. He said the report would have 'massive implications'. The order to do this was included bizarrely in a $2.3 trillion 'coronavirus' relief and government funding bill passed by the Trump administration at the end of 2020. I would add some serious notes of caution here. I have been pointing out since the 1990s that the US military and intelligence networks have long had craft – 'flying saucers' or anti-gravity craft – which any observer would take to be extraterrestrial in origin. Keeping this knowledge from the public allows craft flown by *humans* to be perceived as alien visitations. I am not saying that 'aliens' do not exist. I would be the last one to say that, but we have to be streetwise here. President Ronald Reagan told the UN General Assembly in 1987: 'I occasionally think how quickly our differences worldwide would vanish if we were facing an alien threat from outside this world.' That's the idea. Unite against a common 'enemy' with a common purpose behind your 'saviour force' (the Cult) as this age-old technique of mass manipulation goes global.

Science moves this way ...

I could find only one other person who was discussing the simulation hypothesis publicly when I concluded it was real. This was Nick Bostrom, a Swedish-born philosopher at the University of Oxford, who has explored for many years the possibility that human reality is a computer simulation although his version and mine are not the same. Today the simulation and holographic reality hypothesis have increasingly entered the scientific mainstream. Well, the more open-minded mainstream, that is. Here are a few of the ever-gathering examples. American nuclear physicist Silas Beane led a team of physicists at the University of Bonn in Germany pursuing the question of whether we live in a simulation. They concluded that we probably do and it was likely based on a lattice of cubes. They found that cosmic rays align with that specific pattern. The team highlighted the Greisen–Zatsepin–Kuzmin (GZK) limit which refers to cosmic ray particle interaction with cosmic background radiation that creates an apparent boundary for cosmic ray particles. They say in a paper entitled 'Constraints on the Universe as a Numerical Simulation' that this 'pattern of constraint' is exactly what you would find with a computer simulation. They also made the point that a simulation would create its own 'laws of physics' that would limit possibility. I've been making the same point for decades that the *perceived* laws of physics relate only to this reality, or what I would later call the simulation. When designers write codes to create computer and virtual reality games they are the equivalent of the laws of physics for that game. Players interact within the limitations laid out by the coding. In the same way those who wrote the codes for the simulation decided the laws of physics that would apply. These can be overridden by expanded states of consciousness, but not by those enslaved in only five-sense awareness where simulation codes rule. Overriding the codes is what people call 'miracles'. They are not. They are bypassing the encoded limits of the simulation. A population caught in simulation perception would have no idea that this was their plight. As the Bonn paper said: 'Like a prisoner in a pitch-black cell we would not be able to see the "walls" of our prison,' That's true if people remain mesmerised by the five senses. Open to expanded awareness and those walls become very clear. The main one is the speed of light.

American theoretical physicist James Gates is another who has explored the simulation question and found considerable evidence to support the idea. Gates was Professor of Physics at the University of

Maryland, Director of The Center for String and Particle Theory, and on Barack Obama's Council of Advisors on Science and Technology. He and his team found *computer codes* of digital data embedded in the fabric of our reality. They relate to on-off electrical charges of 1 and 0 in the binary system used by computers. 'We have no idea what they are doing there', Gates said. They found within the energetic fabric mathematical sequences known as error-correcting codes or block codes that 'reboot' data to its original state or 'default settings' when something knocks it out of sync. Gates was asked if he had found a set of equations embedded in our reality indistinguishable from those that drive search engines and browsers and he said: 'That is correct.' Rich Terrile, director of the Centre for Evolutionary Computation and Automated Design at NASA's Jet Propulsion Laboratory, has said publicly that he believes the Universe is a digital hologram that must have been created by a form of intelligence. I agree with that in every way. Waveform information is delivered electrically by the senses to the brain which constructs a *digital* holographic reality that we call the 'world'. This digital level of reality can be read by the esoteric art of numerology. Digital holograms are at the cutting edge of holographics today. We have digital technology everywhere designed to access and manipulate our digital level of perceived reality. Synthetic mRNA in 'Covid vaccines' has a digital component to manipulate the body's digital 'operating system'.

Reality is numbers

How many know that our reality can be broken down to numbers and codes that are the same as computer games? Max Tegmark, a physicist at the Massachusetts Institute of Technology (MIT), is the author of *Our Mathematical Universe* in which he lays out how reality can be entirely described by numbers and maths in the way that a video game is encoded with the 'physics' of computer games. Our world and computer virtual reality are essentially the same. Tegmark imagines the perceptions of characters in an advanced computer game when the graphics are so good they don't know they are in a game. They think they can bump into real objects (electromagnetic resistance in our reality), fall in love and feel emotions like excitement. When they began to study the apparently 'physical world' of the video game they would realise that everything was made of pixels (which have been found in our energetic reality as must be the case when on one level our world is digital). What computer game characters thought was physical 'stuff', Tegmark said, could actually be broken down into numbers:

> And we're exactly in this situation in our world. We look around and it doesn't seem that mathematical at all, but everything we see is made out of elementary particles like quarks and electrons. And what properties does an

electron have? Does it have a smell or a colour or a texture? No! ... We physicists have come up with geeky names for [Electron] properties, like electric charge, or spin, or lepton number, but the electron doesn't care what we call it, the properties are just numbers.

This is the illusory reality Gnostics were describing. This is the simulation. The A, C, G, and T codes of DNA have a binary value – A and C = 0 while G and T = 1. This has to be when the simulation is digital and the body must be digital to interact with it. Recurring mathematical sequences are encoded throughout reality and the body. They include the Fibonacci sequence in which the two previous numbers are added to get the next one, as in ... 1, 1, 2, 3, 5, 8, 13, 21, 34, 55, etc. The sequence is encoded in the human face and body, proportions of animals, DNA, seed heads, pine cones, trees, shells, spiral galaxies, hurricanes and the number of petals in a flower. The list goes on and on. There are fractal patterns – a 'never-ending pattern that is infinitely complex and self-similar across all scales in the as above, so below, principle of holograms. These and other famous recurring geometrical and mathematical sequences such as Phi, Pi, Golden Mean, Golden Ratio and Golden Section are *computer codes* of the simulation. I had to laugh and give my head a shake the day I finished this book and it went into the production stage. I was sent an article in *Scientific American* published in April, 2021, with the headline 'Confirmed! We Live in a Simulation'. Two decades after I first said our reality is a simulation and the speed of light is it's outer limit the article suggested that we do live in a simulation and that the speed of light is its outer limit. I left school at 15 and never passed a major exam in my life while the writer was up to his eyes in qualifications. As I will explain in the final chapter *knowing* is far better than thinking and they come from very different sources. The article rightly connected the speed of light to the processing speed of the 'Matrix' and said what has been in my books all this time ... 'If we are in a simulation, as it appears, then space is an abstract property written in code. It is not real'. No it's not and if we live in a simulation something created it and it wasn't *us*. 'That David Icke says we are manipulated by aliens' – he's crackers.'

Wow ...

The reality that humanity thinks is so real is an illusion. Politicians, governments, scientists, doctors, academics, law enforcement, media, school and university curriculums, on and on, are all founded on a world that *does not exist* except as a simulated prison cell. Is it such a stretch to accept that 'Covid' doesn't exist when our entire 'physical' reality doesn't exist? Revealed here is the knowledge kept under raps in the Cult networks of compartmentalised secrecy to control humanity's sense of reality by inducing the population to believe in a reality that's not real. If it wasn't so tragic in its experiential consequences the whole thing would be hysterically funny. None of this is new to Renegade Minds. Ancient Greek philosopher Plato (about 428 to about 347BC) was a major influence on Gnostic belief and he described the human plight thousands of years ago with his Allegory of the Cave. He told the symbolic story of prisoners living in a cave who had never been outside. They were chained and could only see one wall of the cave while behind them was a fire that they could not see. Figures walked past the fire casting shadows on the prisoners' wall and those moving shadows became their sense of reality. Some prisoners began to study the shadows and were considered experts on them (today's academics and scientists), but what they studied was only an illusion (today's academics and scientists). A prisoner escaped from the cave and saw reality as it really is. When he returned to report this revelation they didn't believe him, called him mad and threatened to kill him if he tried to set them free. Plato's tale is not only a brilliant analogy of the human plight and our illusory reality. It describes, too, the dynamics of the 'Covid' hoax. I have only skimmed the surface of these subjects here. The aim of this book is to crisply connect all essential dots to put what is happening today into its true context. All subject areas and their connections in this chapter are covered in great evidential detail in *Everything You Need To Know, But Have Never Been Told* and *The Answer*.

They say that bewildered people 'can't see the forest for the trees'. Humanity, however, can't see the forest for the *twigs*. The five senses see only twigs while Renegade Minds can see the forest and it's the forest where the answers lie with the connections that reveals. Breaking free of perceptual programming so the forest can be seen is the way we turn all this around. Not breaking free is how humanity got into this mess. The situation may seem hopeless, but I promise you it's not. We are a perceptual heartbeat from paradise if only we knew.

CHAPTER TWELVE

Escaping Wetiko

Life is simply a vacation from the infinite
Dean Cavanagh

Renegade Minds weave the web of life and events and see common themes in the apparently random. They are always there if you look for them and their pursuit is aided by incredible synchronicity that comes when your mind is open rather than mesmerised by what it thinks it can see.

Infinite awareness is infinite possibility and the more of infinite possibility that we access the more becomes infinitely possible. That may be stating the apparently obvious, but it is a devastatingly-powerful fact that can set us free. We are a point of attention within an infinity of consciousness. The question is how much of that infinity do we choose to access? How much knowledge, insight, awareness, wisdom, do we want to connect with and explore? If your focus is only in the five senses you will be influenced by a fraction of infinite awareness. I mean a range so tiny that it gives new meaning to infinitesimal. Limitation of self-identity and a sense of the possible limit accordingly your range of consciousness. We are what we think we are. Life is what we think it is. The dream is the dreamer and the dreamer is the dream. Buddhist philosophy puts it this way: 'As a thing is viewed, so it appears.' Most humans live in the realm of touch, taste, see, hear, and smell and that's the limit of their sense of the possible and sense of self. Many will follow a religion and speak of a God in his heaven, but their lives are still dominated by the five senses in their perceptions and actions. The five senses become the arbiter of everything. When that happens all except a smear of infinity is sealed away from influence by the rigid, unyielding, reality bubbles that are the five-sense human or Phantom Self. Archon Cult methodology is to isolate consciousness within five-sense reality – the simulation – and then program that consciousness with a sense of self and the world through a deluge of life-long information designed to instil the desired perception that allows global control. Efforts to do this have increased dramatically with identity politics as identity bubbles are squeezed into the minutiae of five-sense detail which disconnect people even more profoundly from the infinite 'I'.

Five-sense focus and self-identity are like a firewall that limits access to the infinite realms. You only perceive one radio or television station and no other. We'll take that literally for a moment. Imagine a vast array of stations giving different information and angles on reality, but you only ever listen to one. Here we have the human plight in which the population is overwhelmingly confined to CultFM. This relates only to the frequency range of CultFM and limits perception and insight to that band – limits *possibility* to that band. It means you are connecting with an almost imperceptibly minuscule range of possibility and creative potential within the infinite Field. It's a world where everything seems apart from everything else and where synchronicity is rare. Synchronicity is defined in the dictionary as 'the happening by chance of two or more related or similar events at the same time'. Use of 'by chance' betrays a complete misunderstanding of reality. Synchronicity is not 'by chance'. As people open their minds, or 'awaken' to use the term, they notice more and more coincidences in their lives, bits of 'luck', apparently miraculous happenings that put them in the right place at the right time with the right people. Days become peppered with 'fancy meeting you here' and 'what are the chances of that?' My entire life has been lived like this and ever more so since my own colossal awakening in 1990 and 91 which transformed my sense of reality. Synchronicity is not 'by chance'; it is by accessing expanded realms of possibility which allow expanded potential for manifestation. People broadcasting the same vibe from the same openness of mind tend to be drawn 'by chance' to each other through what I call frequency magnetism and it's not only people. In the last more than 30 years incredible synchronicity has also led me through the Cult maze to information in so many forms and to crucial personal experiences. These 'coincidences' have allowed me to put the puzzle pieces together across an enormous array of subjects and situations. Those who have breached the bubble of five-sense reality will know exactly what I mean and this escape from the perceptual prison cell is open to everyone whenever they make that choice. This may appear super-human when compared with the limitations of 'human', but it's really our natural state. 'Human' as currently experienced is consciousness in an unnatural state of induced separation from the infinity of the whole. I'll come to how this transformation into unity can be made when I have described in more detail the force that holds humanity in servitude by denying this access to infinite self.

The Wetiko factor

I have been talking and writing for decades about the way five-sense mind is systematically barricaded from expanded awareness. I have used the analogy of a computer (five-sense mind) and someone at the keyboard (expanded awareness). Interaction between the computer and the operator is symbolic of the interaction between five-sense mind and expanded awareness. The computer directly experiences the Internet and the operator experiences the Internet via the computer which is how it's supposed to be – the two working as one. Archons seek to control

Figure 20: The mind 'virus' I have been writing about for decades seeks to isolate five-sense mind (the computer) from the true 'I'. (Image by Neil Hague).

that point where the operator connects with the computer to stop that interaction (Fig 20). Now the operator is banging the keyboard and clicking the mouse, but the computer is not responding and this happens when the computer is taken over – *possessed* – by an appropriately-named computer 'virus'. The operator has lost all influence over the computer which goes its own way making decisions under the control of the 'virus'. I have just described the dynamic through which the force known to Gnostics as Yaldabaoth and Archons disconnects five-sense mind from expanded awareness to imprison humanity in perceptual servitude.

About a year ago I came across a Native American concept of Wetiko which describes precisely the same phenomenon. Wetiko is the spelling used by the Cree and there are other versions including wintiko and windigo used by other tribal groups. They spell the name with lower case, but I see Wetiko as a proper noun as with Archons and prefer a capital. I first saw an article about Wetiko by writer and researcher Paul Levy which so synced with what I had been writing about the computer/operator disconnection and later the Archons. I then read his book, the fascinating *Dispelling Wetiko, Breaking the Spell of Evil.* The parallels between what I had concluded long before and the Native American concept of Wetiko were so clear and obvious that it was almost funny. For Wetiko see the Gnostic Archons for sure and the Jinn, the Predators, and every other name for a force of evil, inversion and chaos. Wetiko is the Native American name for the force that divides the

Figure 21: The mind 'virus' is known to Native Americans as 'Wetiko'. (Image by Neil Hague).

computer from the operator (Fig 21). Indigenous author Jack D. Forbes, a founder of the Native American movement in the 1960s, wrote another book about Wetiko entitled *Columbus And Other Cannibals – The Wetiko Disease of Exploitation, Imperialism, and Terrorism* which I also read. Forbes says that Wetiko refers to an evil person or spirit 'who terrorizes other creatures by means of terrible acts, including cannibalism'. Zulu shaman Credo Mutwa told me that African accounts tell how cannibalism was brought into the world by the Chitauri 'gods' – another manifestation of Wetiko. The distinction between 'evil person or spirit' relates to Archons/Wetiko possessing a human or acting as pure consciousness. Wetiko is said to be a sickness of the soul or spirit and a state of being that takes but gives nothing back – the Cult and its operatives perfectly described. Black Hawk, a Native American war leader defending their lands from confiscation, said European invaders had 'poisoned hearts' – Wetiko hearts – and that this would spread to native societies. Mention of the heart is very significant as we shall shortly see. Forbes writes: 'Tragically, the history of the world for the past 2,000 years is, in great part, the story of the epidemiology of the wetiko disease.' Yes, and much longer. Forbes is correct when he says: 'The wetikos destroyed Egypt and Babylon and Athens and Rome and Tenochtitlan [capital of the Aztec empire] and perhaps now they will destroy the entire earth.' Evil, he said, is the number one export of a Wetiko culture – see its globalisation with 'Covid'. Constant war, mass murder, suffering of all kinds, child abuse, Satanism, torture and human sacrifice are all expressions of Wetiko and the Wetiko possessed. The world is Wetiko made manifest, *but it doesn't have to be.* There is a way out of this even now.

Cult of Wetiko

Wetiko is the Yaldabaoth frequency distortion that seeks to attach to human consciousness and absorb it into its own. Once this connection is made Wetiko can drive the perceptions of the target which they believe to be coming from their own mind. All the horrors of history and today from mass killers to Satanists, paedophiles like Jeffrey Epstein and other psychopaths, are the embodiment of Wetiko and express its state of being in all its grotesqueness. The Cult is Wetiko incarnate, Yaldabaoth incarnate, and it seeks to facilitate Wetiko assimilation of humanity in totality into its distortion by manipulating the population into low frequency states that match its own. Paul Levy writes: 'Holographically enforced within the psyche of every human being the wetiko virus pervades and underlies the entire field of consciousness, and can therefore potentially manifest through any one of us at any moment if we are not mindful.' The 'Covid' hoax has achieved this with many people, but others have not fallen into Wetiko's frequency lair. Players in the 'Covid' human catastrophe including Gates, Schwab, Tedros, Fauci, Whitty, Vallance, Johnson, Hancock, Ferguson, Drosten, and all the rest, including the psychopath psychologists, are expressions of Wetiko. This is why they have no compassion or empathy and no emotional consequence for what they do that would make them stop doing it. Observe all the people who support the psychopaths in authority against the Pushbackers despite the damaging impact the psychopaths have on their own lives and their family's lives. You are again looking at Wetiko possession which prevents them seeing through the lies to the obvious scam going on. *Why can't they see it?* Wetiko won't let them see it. The perceptual divide that has now become a chasm is between the Wetikoed and the non-Wetikoed.

Paul Levy describes Wetiko in the same way that I have long described the Archontic force. They are the same distorted consciousness operating across dimensions of reality: '… the subtle body of wetiko is not located in the third dimension of space and time, literally existing in another dimension … it is able to affect ordinary lives by mysteriously interpenetrating into our three-dimensional world.' Wetiko does this through its incarnate representatives in the Cult and by weaving itself into The Field which on our level of reality is the electromagnetic information field of the simulation or Matrix. More than that, the simulation *is* Wetiko / Yaldabaoth. Caleb Scharf, Director of Astrobiology at Columbia University, has speculated that 'alien life' could be so advanced that it has transcribed itself into the quantum realm to become what we call physics. He said intelligence indistinguishable from the fabric of the Universe would solve many of its greatest mysteries:

> Perhaps hyper-advanced life isn't just external. Perhaps it's already all around. It is embedded in what we perceive to be physics itself, from the root behaviour of particles and fields to the phenomena of complexity and emergence ... In other words, life might not just be in the equations. It might BE the equations [My emphasis].

Scharf said it is possible that 'we don't recognise advanced life because it forms an integral and unsuspicious part of what we've considered to be the natural world'. I agree. Wetiko / Yaldabaoth *is* the simulation. We are literally in the body of the beast. But that doesn't mean it has to control us. We all have the power to overcome Wetiko influence and the Cult knows that. I doubt it sleeps too well because it knows that.

Which Field?

This, I suggest, is how it all works. There are two Fields. One is the fierce electromagnetic light of the Matrix within the speed of light; the other is the 'watery light' of The Field beyond the walls of the Matrix that connects with the Great Infinity. Five-sense mind and the decoding systems of the body attach us to the Field of Matrix light. They have to or we could not experience this reality. Five-sense mind sees only the Matrix Field of information while our expanded consciousness is part of the Infinity Field. When we open our minds, and most importantly our hearts, to the Infinity Field we have a mission control which gives us an expanded perspective, a road map, to understand the nature of the five-sense world. If we are isolated only in five-sense mind there is no mission control. We're on our own trying to understand a world that's constantly feeding us information to ensure we do not understand. People in this state can feel 'lost' and bewildered with no direction or radar. You can see ever more clearly those who are influenced by the Fields of Big Infinity or little five-sense mind simply by their views and behaviour with regard to the 'Covid' hoax. We have had this division throughout known human history with the mass of the people on one side and individuals who could see and intuit beyond the walls of the simulation – Plato's prisoner who broke out of the cave and saw reality for what it is. Such people have always been targeted by Wetiko / Archon-possessed authority, burned at the stake or demonised as mad, bad and dangerous. The Cult today and its global network of 'anti-hate', 'anti-fascist' Woke groups are all expressions of Wetiko attacking those exposing the conspiracy, 'Covid' lies and the 'vaccine' agenda.

Woke as a whole is Wetiko which explains its black and white mentality and how at one it is with the Wetiko-possessed Cult. Paul Levy said: 'To be in this paradigm is to still be under the thrall of a two-valued logic – where things are either true or false – of a wetikoized mind.' Wetiko consciousness is in a permanent rage, therefore so is Woke, and then there is Woke inversion and contradiction. 'Anti-fascists' act like fascists because fascists *and* 'anti-fascists' are both Wetiko at work. Political parties act the same while claiming to be different for the same reason. Secret society and satanic rituals are attaching initiates to Wetiko and the cold, ruthless, psychopathic mentality that secures the positions of power all over the world is Wetiko. Reframing 'training programmes' have the same cumulative effect of attaching Wetiko and we have their graduates described as automatons and robots with a cold, psychopathic, uncaring demeanour. They are all traits of Wetiko possession and look how many times they have been described in this book and elsewhere with regard to personnel behind 'Covid' including the police and medical profession. Climbing the greasy pole in any profession in a Wetiko society requires traits of Wetiko to get there and that is particularly true of politics which is not about fair competition and pre-eminence of ideas. It is founded on how many backs you can stab and arses you can lick. This culminated in the global 'Covid' coordination between the Wetiko possessed who pulled it off in all the different countries without a trace of empathy and compassion for their impact on humans. Our sight sense can see only holographic form and not the Field which connects holographic form. Therefore we perceive 'physical' objects with 'space' in between. In fact that 'space' is energy/consciousness operating on multiple frequencies. One of them is Wetiko and that connects the Cult psychopaths, those who submit to the psychopaths, and those who serve the psychopaths in the media operations of the world. Wetiko is Gates. Wetiko is the mask-wearing submissive. Wetiko is the fake journalist and 'fact-checker'. The Wetiko Field is coordinating the whole thing. Psychopaths, gofers, media operatives, 'anti-hate' hate groups, 'fact-checkers' and submissive people work as one unit *even without human coordination* because they are attached to the *same* Field which is organising it all (Fig 22). Paul Levy is here describing how Wetiko-possessed people are drawn together and refuse to let any information breach their rigid perceptions. He was writing long before 'Covid', but I think you will recognise followers of the 'Covid' religion *oh just a little bit*:

People who are channelling the vibratory frequency of wetiko align with each other through psychic resonance to reinforce their unspoken shared agreement so as to uphold their deranged view of reality. Once an unconscious content takes possession of certain individuals, it irresistibly draws them together by mutual attraction and knits them into groups tied together by their shared madness that can easily swell into an avalanche of insanity.

A psychic epidemic is a closed system, which is to say that it is insular and not open to any new information or informing influences from the outside world which contradict its fixed, limited, and limiting perspective.

There we have the Woke mind and the 'Covid' mind. Compatible resonance draws the awakening together, too, which is clearly happening today.

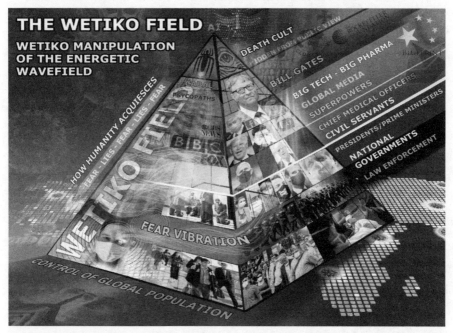

Figure 22: The Wetiko Field from which the Cult pyramid and its personnel are made manifest. (Image by Neil Hague).

Spiritual servitude

Wetiko doesn't care about humans. It's not human; it just possesses humans for its own ends and the effect (depending on the scale of possession) can be anything from extreme psychopathy to unquestioning obedience. Wetiko's worst nightmare is for human consciousness to expand beyond the simulation. Everything is focussed on stopping that happening through control of information, thus perception, thus frequency. The 'education system', media, science, medicine, academia, are all geared to maintaining humanity in five-sense servitude as is the constant stimulation of low-vibrational mental and emotional states (see 'Covid'). Wetiko seeks to dominate those subconscious spaces between five-sense perception and expanded consciousness where the computer meets the operator. From these subconscious hiding places Wetiko speaks to us to trigger urges and desires that we take to be our own and manipulate us into anything from low-vibrational to psychopathic states. Remember how Islam describes the Jinn as invisible tricksters that 'whisper' and confuse. Wetiko is the origin of the 'trickster god' theme that you find in cultures all over the world. Jinn, like the Archons, are Wetiko which is terrified of humans awakening and reconnecting with our true self for then its energy source has gone. With that the feedback loop breaks between Wetiko and human perception that provides the energetic momentum on which its very existence depends as a force of evil. Humans are both its target and its source of survival, but only if we are operating in low-vibrational states of fear, hate, depression and the background anxiety that most people suffer. We are Wetiko's target because we are its key to survival. It needs us, not the other way round. Paul Levy writes:

> A vampire has no intrinsic, independent, substantial existence in its own right; it only exists in relation to us. The pathogenic, vampiric mind-parasite called wetiko is nothing in itself – not being able to exist from its own side – yet it has a 'virtual reality' such that it can potentially destroy our species …

> …The fact that a vampire is not reflected by a mirror can also mean that what we need to see is that there's nothing, no-thing to see, other than ourselves. The fact that wetiko is the expression of something inside of us means that the cure for wetiko is with us as well. The critical issue is finding this cure within us and then putting it into effect.

Evil begets evil because if evil does not constantly expand and find new sources of energetic sustenance its evil, its *distortion*, dies with the assimilation into balance and harmony. Love is the garlic to Wetiko's vampire. Evil, the absence of love, cannot exist in the presence of love. I think I see a way out of here. I have emphasised so many times over the decades that the Archons/Wetiko and their Cult are not all powerful. *They are not.* I don't care how it looks even now *they are not.* I have not called them little boys in short trousers for effect. I have said it because it is true. Wetiko's insatiable desire for power over others is not a sign of its omnipotence, but its insecurity. Paul Levy writes: 'Due to the primal fear which ultimately drives it and which it is driven to cultivate, wetiko's body politic has an intrinsic and insistent need for centralising power and control so as to create imagined safety for itself.' *Yeeeeeees!* Exactly! Why does Wetiko want humans in an ongoing state of fear? Wetiko itself *is* fear and it is petrified of love. As evil is an absence of love, so love is an absence of fear. Love conquers all and *especially* Wetiko which *is* fear. Wetiko brought fear into the world when it wasn't here before. *Fear* was the 'fall', the fall into low-frequency ignorance and illusion – fear is **F**alse **E**motion **A**ppearing **R**eal. The simulation is driven and energised by fear because Wetiko / Yaldabaoth (fear) *are* the simulation. Fear is the absence of love and Wetiko is the absence of love.

Wetiko today

We can now view current events from this level of perspective. The 'Covid' hoax has generated momentous amounts of ongoing fear, anxiety, depression and despair which have empowered Wetiko. No wonder people like Gates have been the instigators when they are Wetiko incarnate and exhibit every trait of Wetiko in the extreme. See how cold and unemotional these people are like Gates and his cronies, how dead of eye they are. That's Wetiko. Sabbatians are Wetiko and everything they control including the World Health Organization, Big Pharma and the 'vaccine' makers, national 'health' hierarchies, corporate media, Silicon Valley, the banking system, and the United Nations with its planned transformation into world government. All are controlled and possessed by the Wetiko distortion into distorting human society in its image. We are with this knowledge at the gateway to understanding the world. Divisions of race, culture, creed and sexuality are diversions to hide the real division between those possessed and influenced by Wetiko and those that are not. The 'Covid' hoax has brought both clearly into view. Human behaviour is not about race. Tyrants and dictatorships come in all colours and creeds. What unites the US president bombing the innocent and an African tribe committing genocide against another as in Rwanda? What unites them? *Wetiko.* All wars are Wetiko, all genocide is Wetiko, all hunger over centuries in a world of plenty is Wetiko. Children going to bed hungry, including in the West, is Wetiko. Cult-generated Woke racial divisions that focus on the body are designed to obscure the reality that divisions in behaviour are manifestations of mind, not body. Obsession with body identity and group judgement is a means to divert attention from the real source of behaviour – mind and perception. Conflict sown by the Woke both within themselves and with their target groups are Wetiko providing lunch for itself through still more agents of the division, chaos, and fear on which it feeds. The Cult is seeking to assimilate the entirety of humanity and all children and young people into the Wetiko frequency by manipulating them into states of fear and despair. Witness all the suicide and psychological unravelling since the spring of 2020. Wetiko psychopaths want to impose a state of unquestioning obedience to authority which is no more than a conduit for Wetiko to enforce its will and assimilate humanity into itself. It needs us to believe that resistance is futile when it fears resistance and even more so the game-changing non-cooperation with its impositions. It can use violent resistance for its benefit. Violent impositions and violent resistance are *both* Wetiko. The Power of Love with its Power of No will sweep Wetiko from our world. Wetiko and its Cult know that. They just don't want us to know.

AI Wetiko

This brings me to AI or artificial intelligence and something else Wetikos don't want us to know. What is AI *really*? I know about computer code algorithms and AI that learns from data input. These, however, are more diversions, the expeditionary force, for the real AI that they want to connect to the human brain as promoted by Silicon Valley Wetikos like Kurzweil. What is this AI? It is the frequency of *Wetiko*, the frequency of the Archons. The connection of AI to the human brain is the connection of the Wetiko frequency to create a Wetiko hive mind and complete the job of assimilation. The hive mind is planned to be controlled from Israel and China which are both 100 percent owned by Wetiko Sabbatians. The assimilation process has been going on minute by minute in the 'smart' era which fused with the 'Covid' era. We are told that social media is scrambling the minds of the young and changing their personality. This is true, but what is social media? Look more deeply at how it works, how it creates divisions and conflict, the hostility and cruelty, the targeting of people until they are destroyed. That's Wetiko. Social media is manipulated to tune people to the Wetiko frequency with all the emotional exploitation tricks employed by platforms like Facebook and its Wetiko front man, Zuckerberg. Facebook's Instagram announced a new platform for children to overcome a legal bar on them using the main site. This is more Wetiko exploitation and manipulation of kids. Amnesty International likened the plan to foxes offering to guard the henhouse and said it was incompatible with human rights. Since when did Wetiko or Zuckerberg (I repeat myself) care about that? Would Brin and Page at Google, Wojcicki at YouTube, Bezos at Amazon and whoever the hell runs Twitter act as they do if they were not channelling Wetiko? Would those who are developing technologies for no other reason than human control? How about those designing and selling technologies to kill people and Big Pharma drug and 'vaccine' producers who know they will end or devastate lives? Quite a thought for these people to consider is that if you are Wetiko in a human life you are Wetiko on the 'other side' unless your frequency changes and that can only change by a change of perception which becomes a change of behaviour. Where Gates is going does not bear thinking about although perhaps that's exactly where he wants to go. Either way, that's where he's going. His frequency will make it so.

The frequency lair

I have been saying for a long time that a big part of the addiction to smartphones and devices is that a frequency is coming off them that entraps the mind. People spend ages on their phones and sometimes even a minute or so after they put them down they pick them up again and it all repeats. 'Covid' lockdowns will have increased this addiction a million times for obvious reasons. Addictions to alcohol overindulgence and drugs are another way that Wetiko entraps consciousness to attach to its own. Both are symptoms of low-vibrational psychological distress which alcoholism and drug addiction further compound. Do we think it's really a coincidence that access to them is made so easy while potions that can take people into realms beyond the simulation are banned and illegal? I have explored smartphone addiction in other books, the scale is mind-blowing, and that level of addiction does not come without help. Tech companies that make these phones are Wetiko and they will have no qualms about destroying the minds of children. We are seeing again with these companies the Wetiko perceptual combination of psychopathic enforcers and weak and meek unquestioning compliance by the rank and file.

The global Smart Grid is the Wetiko Grid and it is crucial to complete the Cult endgame. The simulation is radiation and we are being deluged with technological radiation on a devastating scale. Wetiko frauds like Elon Musk serve Cult interests while occasionally criticising them to maintain his street-cred. 5G and other forms of Wi-Fi are being directed at the earth from space on a volume and scale that goes on increasing by the day. Elon Musk's (officially) SpaceX Starlink project is in the process of putting tens of thousands of satellites in low orbit to cover every inch of the planet with 5G and other Wi-Fi to create Kurzweil's global 'cloud' to which the human mind is planned to be attached very soon. SpaceX has approval to operate 12,000 satellites with more than 1,300 launched at the time of writing and applications filed for *30,000* more. Other operators in the Wi-Fi, 5G, low-orbit satellite market include OneWeb (UK), Telesat (Canada), and AST & Science (US). Musk tells us that AI could be the end of humanity and then launches a company called Neuralink to connect the human brain to computers. Musk's (in theory) Tesla company is building electric cars and the driverless vehicles of the smart control grid. As frauds and bullshitters go Elon Musk in my opinion is Major League.

5G and technological radiation in general are destructive to human health, genetics and psychology and increasing the strength of artificial radiation underpins the five-sense perceptual bubbles which are themselves expressions of radiation or electromagnetism. Freedom activist John Whitehead was so right with his 'databit by databit, we are building our own electronic concentration camps'. The Smart Grid and 5G is a means to control the human mind and infuse perceptual information into The Field to influence anyone in sync with its frequency. You can change perception and behaviour en masse if you can manipulate the population into those levels of frequency and this is happening all around us today. The arrogance of Musk and his fellow Cult operatives knows no bounds in the way that we see with Gates. Musk's satellites are so many in number already they are changing the night sky when viewed from Earth. The astronomy community has complained about this and they have seen nothing yet. Some consequences of Musk's Wetiko hubris include: Radiation; visible pollution of the night sky; interference with astronomy and meteorology; ground and water pollution from intensive use of increasingly many spaceports; accumulating space debris; continual deorbiting and burning up of aging satellites, polluting the atmosphere with toxic dust and smoke; and ever-increasing likelihood of collisions. A collective public open letter of complaint to Musk said:

> We are writing to you … because SpaceX is in process of surrounding the Earth with a network of thousands of satellites whose very purpose is to irradiate every square inch of the Earth. SpaceX, like everyone else, is treating the radiation as if it were not there. As if the mitochondria in our cells do not depend on electrons moving undisturbed from the food we digest to the oxygen we breathe.

> As if our nervous systems and our hearts are not subject to radio frequency interference like any piece of electronic equipment. As if the cancer, diabetes, and heart disease that now afflict a majority of the Earth's population are not metabolic diseases that result from interference with our cellular machinery. As if insects everywhere, and the birds and animals that eat them, are not starving to death as a result.

People like Musk and Gates believe in their limitless Wetiko arrogance that they can do whatever they like to the world because they own it. Consequences for humanity are irrelevant. It's absolutely time that we stopped taking this shit from these self-styled masters of the Earth when you consider where this is going.

Why is the Cult so anti-human?

I hear this question often: Why would they do this when it will affect them, too? Ah, but will it? Who is this *them*? Forget their bodies. They are just vehicles for Wetiko consciousness. When you break it all down to the foundations we are looking at a state of severely distorted consciousness targeting another state of consciousness for assimilation. The rest is detail. The simulation is the fly-trap in which unique sensations of the five senses create a cycle of addiction called reincarnation. Renegade Minds see that everything which happens in our reality is a smaller version of the whole picture in line with the holographic principle. Addiction to the radiation of smart technology is a smaller version of addiction to the whole simulation. Connecting the body/brain to AI is taking that addiction on a giant step further to total ongoing control by assimilating human incarnate consciousness into Wetiko. I have watched during the 'Covid' hoax how many are becoming ever more profoundly attached to Wetiko's perceptual calling cards of aggressive response to any other point of view ('There is no other god but me'), psychopathic lack of compassion and empathy, and servile submission to the narrative and will of authority. Wetiko is the psychopaths *and* subservience to psychopaths. The Cult of Wetiko is so anti-human because it is *not* human. It embarked on a mission to destroy human by targeting everything that it means to be human and to survive as human. 'Covid' is not the end, just a means to an end. The Cult with its Wetiko consciousness is seeking to change Earth systems, including the atmosphere, to suit them, not humans. The gathering bombardment of 5G alone from ground and space is dramatically changing The Field with which the five senses interact. There is so much more to come if we sit on our hands and hope it will all go away. It is not meant to go away. It is meant to get ever more extreme and we need to face that while we still can – just.

Carbon dioxide is the gas of life. Without that human is over. Kaput, gone, history. No natural world, no human. The Cult has created a cock and bull story about carbon dioxide and climate change to justify its reduction to the point where Gates and the ignoramus Biden 'climate chief' John Kerry want to suck it out of the atmosphere. Kerry wants to do this because his master Gates does. Wetikos have made the gas of life a demon with the usual support from the Wokers of Extinction Rebellion and similar organisations and the bewildered puppet-child that is Greta Thunberg who was put on the world stage by Klaus Schwab and the World Economic Forum. The name Extinction Rebellion is both ironic and as always Wetiko inversion. The gas that we need to survive must be reduced to save us from extinction. The most basic need of human is oxygen and we now have billions walking around in face nappies depriving body and brain of this essential requirement of human existence. More than that 5G at 60 gigahertz interacts with the oxygen molecule to reduce the amount of oxygen the body can absorb into the bloodstream. The obvious knock-on consequences of that for respiratory and cognitive problems and life itself need no further explanation. Psychopaths like Musk are assembling a global system of satellites to deluge the human atmosphere with this insanity. The man should be in jail. Here we have two most basic of human needs, oxygen and carbon dioxide, being dismantled.

Two others, water and food, are getting similar treatment with the United Nations Agendas 21 and 2030 – the Great Reset – planning to centrally control all water and food supplies. People will not even own rain water that falls on their land. Food is affected at the most basic level by reducing carbon dioxide. We have genetic modification or GMO infiltrating the food chain on a mass scale, pesticides and herbicides polluting the air and destroying the soil. Freshwater fish that provide livelihoods for 60 million people and feed hundreds of millions worldwide are being 'pushed to the brink' according the conservationists while climate change is the only focus. Now we have Gates and Schwab wanting to dispense with current food sources all together and replace them with a synthetic version which the Wetiko Cult would control in terms of production and who eats and who doesn't. We have been on the Totalitarian Tiptoe to this for more than 60 years as food has become ever more processed and full of chemical shite to the point today when it's not natural food at all. As Dr Tom Cowan says: 'If it has a label don't eat it.' Bill Gates is now the biggest owner of farmland in the United States and he does nothing without an ulterior motive involving the Cult. Klaus Schwab wrote: 'To feed the world in the next 50 years we will need to produce as much food as was produced in the last 10,000 years … food security will only be achieved, however, if regulations on genetically modified foods are adapted to reflect the reality that gene editing offers a precise, efficient and safe method of improving crops.' Liar. People and the world are being targeted with aluminium through vaccines, chemtrails, food, drink cans, and endless other sources when aluminium has been linked to many health issues including dementia which is increasing year after year. Insects, bees and wildlife essential to the food chain are being deleted by pesticides, herbicides and radiation which 5G is dramatically increasing with 6G and 7G to come. The pollinating bee population is being devastated while wildlife including birds, dolphins and whales are having their natural radar blocked by the effects of ever-increasing radiation. In the summer windscreens used to be splattered with insects so numerous were they. It doesn't happen now. Where have they gone?

Synthetic everything

The Cult is introducing genetically-modified versions of trees, plants and insects including a Gates-funded project to unleash hundreds of millions of genetically-modified, lab-altered and patented male mosquitoes to mate with wild mosquitoes and induce genetic flaws that cause them to die out. Clinically-insane Gates-funded Japanese researchers have developed mosquitos that spread vaccine and are dubbed 'flying vaccinators'. Gates is funding the modification of weather patterns in part to sell the myth that this is caused by carbon dioxide and he's funding geoengineering of the skies to change the atmosphere. Some of this came to light with the Gates-backed plan to release tonnes of chalk into the atmosphere to 'deflect the Sun and cool the planet'. Funny how they do this while the heating effect of the Sun is not factored into climate projections focussed on carbon dioxide. The reason is that they want to reduce carbon dioxide (so don't mention the Sun), but at the same time they do want to reduce the impact of the Sun which is so essential to human life and health. I have mentioned the sun-cholesterol-vitamin D connection as they demonise the Sun with warnings about skin cancer (caused by the chemicals in sun cream they tell you to splash on). They come from the other end of the process with statin drugs to reduce cholesterol that turns sunlight into vitamin D. A lack of vitamin D leads to a long list of health effects and how vitamin D levels must have fallen with people confined to their homes over 'Covid'. Gates is funding other forms of geoengineering and most importantly chemtrails which are dropping heavy metals, aluminium and self-replicating nanotechnology onto the Earth which is killing the natural world. See *Everything You Need To Know, But Have Never Been Told* for the detailed background to this.

Every human system is being targeted for deletion by a force that's not human. The Wetiko Cult has embarked on the process of transforming the human body from biological to synthetic biological as I have explained. Biological is being replaced by the artificial and synthetic – Archontic 'countermimicry' – right across human society. The plan eventually is to dispense with the human body altogether and absorb human consciousness – which it wouldn't really be by then – into cyberspace (the simulation which is Wetiko/Yaldabaoth). Preparations for that are already happening if people would care to look. The alternative media rightly warns about globalism and 'the globalists', but this is far bigger than that and represents the end of the human race as we know it. The 'bad copy' of prime reality that Gnostics describe was a bad copy of harmony, wonder and beauty to start with before Wetiko/Yaldabaoth set out to change the simulated 'copy' into something very different. The process was slow to start with. Entrapped humans in the simulation timeline were not technologically aware and they had to be brought up to intellectual speed while being suppressed spiritually to the point where they could build their own prison while having no idea they were doing so. We have now reached that stage where technological intellect has the potential to destroy us and that's

why events are moving so fast. Central American shaman Don Juan
Matus said:

> Think for a moment, and tell me how you would explain the contradictions
> between the intelligence of man the engineer and the stupidity of his systems
> of belief, or the stupidity of his contradictory behaviour. Sorcerers believe that
> the predators have given us our systems of beliefs, our ideas of good and evil;
> our social mores. They are the ones who set up our dreams of success or
> failure. They have given us covetousness, greed, and cowardice. It is the
> predator who makes us complacent, routinary, and egomaniacal.
>
> In order to keep us obedient and meek and weak, the predators engaged
> themselves in a stupendous manoeuvre – stupendous, of course, from the
> point of view of a fighting strategist; a horrendous manoeuvre from the point
> of those who suffer it. They gave us their mind. The predators' mind is
> baroque, contradictory, morose, filled with the fear of being discovered any
> minute now.

For 'predators' see Wetiko, Archons, Yaldabaoth, Jinn, and all the
other versions of the same phenomenon in cultures and religions all
over the world. The theme is always the same because it's true and it's
real. We have reached the point where we have to deal with it. The
question is – how?

Don't fight – walk away

I thought I'd use a controversial subheading to get things moving in
terms of our response to global fascism. What do you mean 'don't fight'?
What do you mean 'walk away'? We've got to fight. We can't walk away.
Well, it depends what we mean by fight and walk away. If fighting
means physical combat we are playing Wetiko's game and falling for its
trap. It wants us to get angry, aggressive, and direct hate and hostility at
the enemy we think we must fight. Every war, every battle, every
conflict, has been fought with Wetiko leading both sides. It's what it
does. Wetiko wants a fight, anywhere, any place. Just hit me, son, so I
can hit you back. Wetiko hits Wetiko and Wetiko hits Wetiko in return. I
am very forthright as you can see in exposing Wetikos of the Cult, but I
don't hate them. I refuse to hate them. It's what they want. What you
hate you become. What you *fight* you become. Wokers, 'anti-haters' and
'anti-fascists' prove this every time they reach for their keyboards or don
their balaclavas. By walk away I mean to disengage from Wetiko which
includes ceasing to cooperate with its tyranny. Paul Levy says of Wetiko:

> The way to 'defeat' evil is not to try to destroy it (for then, in playing evil's
> game, we have already lost), but rather, to find the invulnerable place within

ourselves where evil is unable to vanquish us – this is to truly 'win' our battle with evil.

Wetiko is everywhere in human society and it's been on steroids since the 'Covid' hoax. Every shouting match over wearing masks has Wetiko wearing a mask and Wetiko not wearing one. It's an electrical circuit of push and resist, push and resist, with Wetiko pushing *and* resisting. Each polarity is Wetiko empowering itself. Dictionary definitions of 'resist' include 'opposing, refusing to accept or comply with' and the word to focus on is 'opposing'. What form does this take – setting police cars alight or 'refusing to accept or comply with'? The former is Wetiko opposing Wetiko while the other points the way forward. This is the difference between those aggressively demanding that government fascism must be obeyed who stand in stark contrast to the great majority of Pushbackers. We saw this clearly with a march by thousands of Pushbackers against lockdown in London followed days later by a Woker-hijacked protest in Bristol in which police cars were set on fire. Masks were virtually absent in London and widespread in Bristol. Wetiko wants lockdown on every level of society and infuses its aggression to police it through its unknowing stooges. Lockdown protesters are the ones with the smiling faces and the hugs, The two blatantly obvious states of being – getting more obvious by the day – are the result of Wokers and their like becoming ever more influenced by the simulation Field of Wetiko and Pushbackers ever more influenced by The Field of a far higher vibration beyond the simulation. Wetiko can't invade the heart which is where most lockdown opponents are coming from. It's the heart that allows them to see through the lies to the truth in ways I will be highlighting.

Renegade Minds know that calmness is the place from which wisdom comes. You won't find wisdom in a hissing fit and wisdom is what we need in abundance right now. Calmness is not weakness – you don't have to scream at the top of your voice to be strong. Calmness is indeed a sign of strength. 'No' means I'm not doing it. *NOOOO!!!* doesn't mean you're not doing it even more. Volume does not advance 'No – I'm not doing it'. You are just not doing it. Wetiko possessed and influenced don't know how to deal with that. Wetiko wants a fight and we should not give it one. What it needs more than anything is our *cooperation* and we should not give that either. Mass rallies and marches are great in that they are a visual representation of feeling, but if it ends there they are irrelevant. You demand that Wetikos act differently? Well, they're not going to are they? They are Wetikos. We don't need to waste our time demanding that something doesn't happen when that will make no difference. We need to delete the means that *allows* it to happen. This, invariably, is our cooperation. You can demand a child stop firing a peashooter at the dog or you can refuse to buy the peashooter. If you provide the means you are cooperating with the dog being smacked on the nose with a pea. How can the authorities enforce mask-wearing if millions in a country refuse? What if the 74 million Pushbackers that voted for Trump in 2020 refused to wear masks, close their businesses or stay in their homes. It would be unenforceable. The few control the many through the compliance of the many and that's always been the dynamic be it 'Covid' regulations or the Roman Empire. I know people can find it intimidating to say no to authority or stand out in a crowd for being the only one with a face on display; but it has to be done or it's over. I hope I've made clear in this book that where this is going will be far more intimidating than standing up now and saying 'No' – I will not cooperate with my own enslavement and that of my children. There might be consequences for some initially, although not so if enough do the same. The question that must be addressed is what is going to happen if we don't? It is time to be strong and unyieldingly so. No means no. Not here and there, but *everywhere* and *always*. I have refused to wear a mask and obey all the other nonsense. I will not comply with tyranny. I repeat: Fascism is not imposed by fascists – there are never enough of them. Fascism is imposed by the population acquiescing to fascism. *I will not do it.* I will die first, or my body will. Living meekly under fascism is a form of death anyway, the death of the spirit that Martin Luther King described.

Making things happen

We must not despair. This is not over till it's over and it's far from that. The 'fat lady' must refuse to sing. The longer the 'Covid' hoax has dragged on and impacted on more lives we have seen an awakening of phenomenal numbers of people worldwide to the realisation that what they have believed all their lives is not how the world really is. Research published by the system-serving University of Bristol and King's College London in February, 2021, concluded: 'One in every 11 people in Britain say they trust David Icke's take on the coronavirus pandemic.' It will be more by now and we have gathering numbers to build on. We must urgently progress from seeing the scam to ceasing to cooperate with it. Prominent German lawyer Reiner Fuellmich, also licenced to practice law in America, is doing a magnificent job taking the legal route to bring the psychopaths to justice through a second Nuremberg tribunal for crimes against humanity. Fuellmich has an impressive record of beating the elite in court and he formed the German Corona Investigative Committee to pursue civil charges against the main perpetrators with a view to triggering criminal charges. Most importantly he has grasped the foundation of the hoax – the PCR test not testing for the 'virus' – and Christian Drosten is therefore on his charge sheet along with Gates frontman Tedros at the World Health Organization. Major players must be not be allowed to inflict their horrors on the human race without being brought to book. A life sentence must follow for Bill Gates and the rest of them. A group of researchers has also indicted the government of Norway for crimes against humanity with copies sent to the police and the International Criminal Court. The lawsuit cites participation in an internationally-planned false pandemic and violation of international law and human rights, the European Commission's definition of human rights by coercive rules, Nuremberg and Hague rules on fundamental human rights, and the Norwegian constitution. We must take the initiative from hereon and not just complain, protest and react.

There are practical ways to support vital mass non-cooperation. Organising in numbers is one. Lockdown marches in London in the spring in 2021 were mass non-cooperation that the authorities could not stop. There were too many people. Hundreds of thousands walked the London streets in the centre of the road for mile after mile while the Face-Nappies could only look on. They were determined, but calm, and just *did it* with no histrionics and lots of smiles. The police were impotent. Others are organising group shopping without masks for mutual support and imagine if that was happening all over. Policing it would be impossible. If the store refuses to serve people in these circumstances they would be faced with a long line of trolleys full of goods standing on their own and everything would have to be returned to the shelves. How would they cope with that if it kept happening? I am talking here about moving on from complaining to being pro-active; from watching things happen to making things happen. I include in this our relationship with the police. The behaviour of many Face-Nappies has been disgraceful and anyone who thinks they would never find concentration camp guards in the 'enlightened' modern era have had that myth busted big-time. The period and setting may change – Wetikos never do. I watched film footage from a London march in which a police thug viciously kicked a protestor on the floor who had done nothing. His fellow Face-Nappies stood in a ring protecting him. What he did was a criminal assault and with a crowd far outnumbering the police this can no longer be allowed to happen unchallenged. I get it when people chant 'shame on you' in these circumstances, but that is no longer enough. They *have* no shame those who do this. Crowds needs to start making a citizen's arrest of the police who commit criminal offences and brutally attack innocent people and defenceless women. A citizen's arrest can be made under section 24A of the UK Police and Criminal Evidence (PACE) Act of 1984 and you will find something similar in other countries. I prefer to call it a Common Law arrest rather than citizen's for reasons I will come to shortly. Anyone can arrest a person committing an indictable offence or if they have reasonable grounds to suspect they are committing an indictable offence. On both counts the attack by the police thug would have fallen into this category. A citizen's arrest can be made to stop someone:

- Causing physical injury to himself or any other person
- Suffering physical injury
- Causing loss of or damage to property
- Making off before a constable can assume responsibility for him

A citizen's arrest may also be made to prevent a breach of the peace under Common Law and if they believe a breach of the peace will happen or anything related to harm likely to be done or already done in their presence. This is the way to go I think – the Common Law version. If police know that the crowd and members of the public will no longer be standing and watching while they commit their thuggery and crimes they will think twice about acting like Brownshirts and Blackshirts.

Common Law – common sense

Mention of Common Law is very important. Most people think the law is the law as in one law. This is not the case. There are two bodies of law, Common Law and Statute Law, and they are not the same. Common Law is founded on the simple premise of do no harm. It does not recognise victimless crimes in which no harm is done while Statute Law does. There is a Statute Law against almost everything. So what is Statute Law? Amazingly it's the law of the *sea* that was brought ashore by the Cult to override the law of the land which is Common Law. They had no right to do this and as always they did it anyway. They had to. They could not impose their will on the people through Common Law which only applies to do no harm. How could you stitch up the fine detail of people's lives with that? Instead they took the law of the sea, or Admiralty Law, and applied it to the population. Statute Law refers to all the laws spewing out of governments and their agencies including all the fascist laws and regulations relating to 'Covid'. The key point to make is that Statute Law is *contract law*. It only applies between *contracting* corporations. Most police officers don't even know this. They have to be kept in the dark, too. Long ago when merchants and their sailing ships began to trade with different countries a contractual law was developed called Admiralty Law and other names. Again it only applied to *contracts* agreed between *corporate* entities. If there is no agreed contract the law of the sea had no jurisdiction *and that still applies to its new alias of Statute Law*. The problem for the Cult when the law of the sea was brought ashore was an obvious one. People were not corporations and neither were government entities. To overcome the latter they made governments and all associated organisations corporations. All the institutions are *private corporations* and I mean governments and their agencies, local councils, police, courts, military, US states, the whole lot. Go to the Dun and Bradstreet corporate listings website for confirmation that they are all corporations. You are arrested by a private corporation called the police by someone who is really a private security guard and they take you to court which is another private corporation. Neither have jurisdiction over you unless you consent and *contract* with them. This is why you hear the mantra about law enforcement policing by *consent* of the people. In truth the people 'consent' only in theory through monumental trickery.

Okay, the Cult overcame the corporate law problem by making governments and institutions corporate entities; but what about people? They are not corporations are they? Ah ... well in a sense, and *only* a sense, they are. Not people exactly – the illusion of people. The Cult creates a corporation in the name of everyone at the time that their birth certificate is issued. Note birth/*berth* certificate and when you go to court under the law of the sea on land you stand in a *dock*. These are throwbacks to the origin. My Common Law name is David Vaughan Icke. The name of the corporation created by the government when I was born is called Mr David Vaughan Icke usually written in capitals as MR DAVID VAUGHAN ICKE. That is not me, the living, breathing man. It is a fictitious corporate entity. The trick is to make you think that David Vaughan Icke and MR DAVID VAUGHAN ICKE are the same thing. *They are not.* When police charge you and take you to court they are prosecuting the corporate entity and not the living, breathing, man or woman. They have to trick you into identifying as the corporate entity and contracting with them. Otherwise they have no jurisdiction. They do this through a language known as legalese. Lawful and legal are not the same either. Lawful relates to Common Law and legal relates to Statute Law. Legalese is the language of Statue Law which uses terms that mean one thing to the public and another in legalese. Notice that when a police officer tells someone why they are being charged he or she will say at the end: 'Do you understand?' To the public that means 'Do you comprehend?' In legalese it means 'Do you stand under me?' Do you stand under my authority? If you say yes to the question you are unknowingly agreeing to give them jurisdiction over you in a contract between two corporate entities.

This is a confidence trick in every way. Contracts have to be agreed between informed parties and if you don't know that David Vaughan Icke is agreeing to be the corporation MR DAVID VAUGHAN ICKE you cannot knowingly agree to contract. They are deceiving you and another way they do this is to ask for proof of identity. You usually show them a driving licence or other document on which your corporate name is written. In doing so you are accepting that you are that corporate entity when you are not. Referring to yourself as a 'person' or 'citizen' is also identifying with your corporate fiction which is why I made the Common Law point about the citizen's arrest. If you are approached by a police officer you identify yourself immediately as a living, breathing, man or woman and say 'I do not consent, I do not contract with you and I do not understand' or stand under their authority. I have a Common Law birth certificate as a living man and these are available at no charge from commonlawcourt.com. Businesses registered under the Statute Law system means that its laws apply. There are, however, ways to run a business under Common Law. Remember all 'Covid' laws and regulations are Statute Law – the law of *contracts* and you do not have to contract. This doesn't mean that you can kill someone and get away with it. Common Law says do no harm and that applies to physical harm, financial harm etc. Police are employees of private corporations and there needs to be a new system of non-corporate Common Law constables operating outside the Statute Law system. If you go to davidicke.com and put Common Law into the search engine you will find videos that explain Common Law in much greater detail. It is definitely a road we should walk.

With all my heart

I have heard people say that we are in a spiritual war. I don't like the term 'war' with its Wetiko dynamic, but I know what they mean. Sweep aside all the bodily forms and we are in a situation in which two states of consciousness are seeking very different realities. Wetiko wants upheaval, chaos, fear, suffering, conflict and control. The other wants love, peace, harmony, fairness and freedom. That's where we are. We should not fall for the idea that Wetiko is all-powerful and there's nothing we can do. Wetiko is not all-powerful. It's a joke, pathetic. It doesn't have to be, but it has made that choice for now. A handful of times over the years when I have felt the presence of its frequency I have allowed it to attach briefly so I could consciously observe its nature. The experience is not pleasant, the energy is heavy and dark, but the ease with which you can kick it back out the door shows that its real power is in persuading us that it has power. It's all a con. Wetiko is a con. It's a trickster and not a power that can control us if we unleash our own. The con is founded on manipulating humanity to give its power to Wetiko which recycles it back to present the illusion that it has power when its power is *ours* that we gave away. This happens on an energetic level and plays out in the world of the seen as humanity giving its power to Wetiko authority which uses that power to control the population when the power is only the power the population has handed over. How could it be any other way for billions to be controlled by a relative few? I have had experiences with people possessed by Wetiko and again you can kick its arse if you do it with an open heart. Oh yes – the *heart* which can transform the world of perceived 'matter'.

We are receiver-transmitters and processors of information, but what information and where from? Information is processed into perception in three main areas – the brain, the heart and the belly. These relate to thinking, knowing, and emotion. Wetiko wants us to be head and belly people which means we think within the confines of the Matrix simulation and low-vibrational emotional reaction scrambles balance and perception. A few minutes on social media and you see how emotion is the dominant force. Woke is all emotion and is therefore thought-free and fact-free. Our heart is something different. It *knows* while the head *thinks* and has to try to work it out because it doesn't know. The human energy field has seven prime vortexes which connect us with wider reality (Fig 23). Chakra means 'wheels of light' in the Sanskrit language of ancient India. The main ones are: The crown chakra on top of the head; brow (or 'third eye') chakra in the centre of the forehead; throat chakra; heart chakra in the centre of the chest; solar plexus chakra below the sternum; sacral chakra beneath the navel; and base chakra at the bottom of the spine. Each one has a particular function or functions. We feel anxiety and nervousness in the belly where the sacral chakra is located and this processes emotion that can affect the colon to give people 'the shits' or make them 'shit scared' when they are nervous. Chakras all play an important role, but the Mr and Mrs Big is the heart chakra which sits at the centre of the seven, above the chakras that connect us to the 'physical' and below those that connect with higher realms (or at least should). Here in the heart chakra we feel love, empathy and compassion – 'My heart goes out to you'. Those with closed hearts become literally 'heart-less' in their attitudes and behaviour (see Bill Gates). Native Americans portrayed Wetiko with what Paul Levy calls a 'frigid, icy heart, devoid of mercy' (see Bill Gates).

Figure 23: The chakra system which interpenetrates the human energy field. The heart chakra is the governor – or should be.

Wetiko trembles at the thought of heart energy which it cannot infiltrate. The frequency is too high. What it seeks to do instead is close the heart chakra vortex to block its perceptual and energetic influence. Psychopaths have 'hearts of stone' and emotionally-damaged people have 'heartache' and 'broken hearts'. The astonishing amount of heart disease is related to heart chakra disruption with its fundamental connection to the 'physical' heart. Dr Tom Cowan has written an outstanding book challenging the belief that the heart is a pump and making the connection between the 'physical' and spiritual heart. Rudolph Steiner who was way ahead of his time said the same about the fallacy that the heart is a pump. *What*? The heart is not a pump? That's crazy, right? Everybody knows that. Read Cowan's *Human Heart, Cosmic Heart* and you will realise that the very idea of the heart as a pump is ridiculous when you see the evidence. How does blood in the feet so far from the heart get pumped horizontally up the body by the heart?? Cowan explains in the book the real reason why blood moves as it does. Our 'physical' heart is used to symbolise love when the source is really the heart vortex or spiritual heart which is our most powerful energetic connection to 'out there' expanded consciousness. That's why we feel *knowing* – intuitive knowing – in the centre of the chest. Knowing doesn't come from a process of thoughts leading to a conclusion. It is there in an instant all in one go. Our heart knows because of its connection to levels of awareness that *do* know. This is the meaning and source of intuition – intuitive *knowing*.

For the last more than 30 years of uncovering the global game and the nature of reality my heart has been my constant antenna for truth and accuracy. An American intelligence insider once said that I had quoted a disinformer in one of my books and yet I had only quoted the part that was true. He asked: 'How do you do that?' By using my heart antenna was the answer and anyone can do it. Heart-centred is how we are meant to be. With a closed heart chakra we withdraw into a closed mind and the bubble of five-sense reality. If you take a moment to focus your attention on the centre of your chest, picture a spinning wheel of light and see it opening and expanding. You will feel it happening, too, and perceptions of the heart like joy and love as the heart impacts on the mind as they interact. The more the chakra opens the more you will feel expressions of heart consciousness and as the process continues, and becomes part of you, insights and knowings will follow. An open heart is connected to that level of awareness that knows all is *One*. You will see from its perspective that the fault-lines that divide us are only illusions to control us. An open heart does not process the illusions of race, creed and sexuality except as brief experiences for a consciousness that is all. Our heart does not see division, only unity (Figs 24 and 25). There's something else, too. Our hearts love to laugh. Mark Twain's quote that says 'The human race has one really effective weapon, and that is laughter' is really a reference to the heart which loves to laugh with the joy of knowing the true nature of infinite reality and that all the madness of human society is an illusion of the mind. Twain also said: 'Against the

Figure 24: Head consciousness without the heart sees division and everything apart from everything else.

Figure 25: Heart consciousness sees everything as One.

assault of laughter nothing can stand.' This is so true of Wetiko and the Cult. Their insecurity demands that they be taken seriously and their power and authority acknowledged and feared. We should do nothing of the sort. We should not get aggressive or fearful which their insecurity so desires. We should laugh in their face. Even in their no-face as police come over in their face-nappies and expect to be taken seriously. They don't take themselves seriously looking like that so why should we? Laugh in the face of intimidation. Laugh in the face of tyranny. You will see by its reaction that you have pressed all of its buttons. Wetiko does not know what to do in the face of laughter or when its targets refuse to concede their joy to fear. We have seen many examples during the 'Covid' hoax when people have expressed their energetic power and the string puppets of Wetiko retreat with their tail limp between their knees. Laugh – the world is bloody mad after all and if it's a choice between laughter and tears I know which way I'm going.

'Vaccines' and the soul

The foundation of Wetiko/Archon control of humans is the separation of incarnate five-sense mind from the infinite 'I' and closing the heart chakra where the True 'I' lives during a human life. The goal has been to achieve complete separation in both cases. I was interested therefore to read an account by a French energetic healer of what she said she experienced with a patient who had been given the 'Covid' vaccine. Genuine energy healers can sense information and consciousness fields at different levels of being which are referred to as 'subtle bodies'. She described treating the patient who later returned after having, without the healer's knowledge, two doses of the 'Covid vaccine'. The healer said:

I noticed immediately the change, very heavy energy emanating from [the] subtle bodies. The scariest thing was when I was working on the heart chakra, I connected with her soul: it was detached from the physical body, it had no contact and it was, as if it was floating in a state of total confusion: a damage to the consciousness that loses contact with the physical body, i.e. with our biological machine, there is no longer any communication between them.

I continued the treatment by sending light to the heart chakra, the soul of the person, but it seemed that the soul could no longer receive any light, frequency or energy. It was a very powerful experience for me. Then I understood that this substance is indeed used to detach consciousness so that this consciousness can no longer interact through this body that it possesses in life, where there is no longer any contact, no frequency, no light, no more energetic balance or mind.

This would create a human that is rudderless and at the extreme almost zombie-like operating with a fractional state of consciousness at the mercy of Wetiko. I was especially intrigued by what the healer said in the light of the prediction by the highly-informed Rudolf Steiner more than a hundred years ago. He said:

In the future, we will eliminate the soul with medicine. Under the pretext of a 'healthy point of view', there will be a vaccine by which the human body will be treated as soon as possible directly at birth, so that the human being cannot develop the thought of the existence of soul and Spirit. To materialistic doctors will be entrusted the task of removing the soul of humanity.

As today, people are vaccinated against this disease or that disease, so in the future, children will be vaccinated with a substance that can be produced precisely in such a way that people, thanks to this vaccination, will be immune to being subjected to the 'madness' of spiritual life. He would be extremely smart, but he would not develop a conscience, and that is the true goal of some materialistic circles.

Steiner said the vaccine would detach the physical body from the etheric body (subtle bodies) and 'once the etheric body is detached the relationship between the universe and the etheric body would become extremely unstable, and man would become an automaton'. He said 'the physical body of man must be polished on this Earth by spiritual will – so the vaccine becomes a kind of arymanique (Wetiko) force' and 'man can no longer get rid of a given materialistic feeling'. Humans would then, he said, become 'materialistic of constitution and can no longer rise to the spiritual'. I have been writing for years about DNA being a receiver-transmitter of information that connects us to other levels of reality and these 'vaccines' changing DNA can be likened to changing an antenna and what it can transmit and receive. Such a disconnection would clearly lead to changes in personality and perception. Steiner further predicted the arrival of AI. Big Pharma 'Covid vaccine' makers, expressions of Wetiko, are testing their DNA-manipulating evil on children as I write with a view to giving the 'vaccine' to babies. If it's a soul-body disconnector – and I say that it is or can be – every child would be disconnected from 'soul' at birth and the 'vaccine' would create a closed system in which spiritual guidance from the greater self would play no part. This has been the ambition of Wetiko all along. A Pentagon video from 2005 was leaked of a presentation explaining the development of vaccines to change behaviour by their effect on the brain. Those that believe this is not happening with the 'Covid' genetically-modifying procedure masquerading as a 'vaccine' should make an urgent appointment with Naivety Anonymous. Klaus Schwab wrote in 2018:

> Neurotechnologies enable us to better influence consciousness and thought and to understand many activities of the brain. They include decoding what we are thinking in fine levels of detail through new chemicals and interventions that can influence our brains to correct for errors or enhance functionality.

The plan is clear and only the heart can stop it. With every heart that opens, every mind that awakens, Wetiko is weakened. Heart and love are far more powerful than head and hate and so nothing like a majority is needed to turn this around.

Beyond the Phantom

Our heart is the prime target of Wetiko and so it must be the answer to Wetiko. We *are* our heart which is part of one heart, the infinite heart. Our heart is where the true self lives in a human life behind firewalls of five-sense illusion when an imposter takes its place – *Phantom Self*; but our heart waits patiently to be set free any time we choose to see beyond the Phantom, beyond Wetiko. A Wetikoed Phantom Self can wreak mass death and destruction while the love of forever is locked away in its heart. The time is here to unleash its power and let it sweep away the fear and despair that is Wetiko. Heart consciousness does not seek manipulated, censored, advantage for its belief or religion, its activism and desires. As an expression of the One it treats all as One with the same rights to freedom and opinion. Our heart demands fairness for itself no more than for others. From this unity of heart we can come together in mutual support and transform this Wetikoed world into what reality is meant to be – a place of love, joy, happiness, fairness, justice and freedom. Wetiko has another agenda and that's why the world is as it is, but enough of this nonsense. Wetiko can't stay where hearts are open and it works so hard to keep them closed. Fear is its currency and its food source and love in its true sense has no fear. Why would love have fear when it knows it is *All That Is, Has Been, And Ever Can Be* on an eternal exploration of all possibility? Love in this true sense is not the physical attraction that passes for love. This can be an expression of it, yes, but Infinite Love, a love without condition, goes far deeper to the core of all being. It *is* the core of all being. Infinite realty was born from love beyond the illusions of the simulation. Love infinitely expressed is the knowing that all is One and the swiftly-passing experience of separation is a temporary hallucination. You cannot disconnect from Oneness; you can only *perceive* that you have and withdraw from its influence. This is the most important of all perception trickery by the mind parasite that is Wetiko and the foundation of all its potential for manipulation.

If we open our hearts, open the sluice gates of the mind, and redefine self-identity amazing things start to happen. Consciousness expands or contracts in accordance with self-identity. When true self is recognised as infinite awareness and label self – Phantom Self – is seen as only a series of brief experiences life is transformed. Consciousness expands to the extent that self-identity expands and everything changes. You see unity, not division, the picture, not the pixels. From this we can play the long game. No more is an experience something in and of itself, but a fleeting moment in the eternity of forever. Suddenly people in uniform and dark suits are no longer intimidating. Doing what your heart knows to be right is no longer intimidating and consequences for those actions take on the same nature of a brief experience that passes in the blink of an infinite eye. Intimidation is all in the mind. Beyond the mind there is no intimidation.

An open heart does not consider consequences for what it knows to be right. To do so would be to consider not doing what it knows to be right and for a heart in its power that is never an option. The Renegade Mind is really the Renegade Heart. Consideration of consequences will always provide a getaway car for the mind and the heart doesn't want one. What is right in the light of what we face today is to stop cooperating with Wetiko in all its forms and to do it without fear or compromise. You cannot compromise with tyranny when tyranny always demands more until it has everything. Life is your perception and you are your destiny. Change your perception and you change your life. Change collective perception and we change the world.

Come on people … One human family, One heart, One goal …
FREEEEEEEDOM!

We must settle for nothing less.

Postscript

The big scare story as the book goes to press is the 'Indian' variant and the world is being deluged with propaganda about the 'Covid catastrophe' in India which mirrors in its lies and misrepresentations what happened in Italy before the first lockdown in 2020.

The *New York Post* published a picture of someone who had 'collapsed in the street from Covid' in India in April, 2021, which was actually taken during a gas leak in May, 2020. Same old, same old. Media articles in mid-February were asking why India had been so untouched by 'Covid' and then as their vaccine rollout gathered pace the alleged 'cases' began to rapidly increase. Indian 'Covid vaccine' maker Bharat Biotech was funded into existence by the Bill and Melinda Gates Foundation (the pair announced their divorce in May, 2021, which is a pity because they so deserve each other). The Indian 'Covid crisis' was ramped up by the media to terrify the world and prepare people for submission to still more restrictions. The scam that worked the first time was being repeated only with far more people seeing through the deceit. Davidicke.com and Ickonic.com have sought to tell the true story of what is happening by talking to people living through the Indian nightmare which has nothing to do with 'Covid'. We posted a letter from 'Alisha' in Pune who told a very different story to government and media mendacity. She said scenes of dying people and overwhelmed hospitals were designed to hide what was really happening – genocide and starvation. Alisha said that millions had already died of starvation during the ongoing lockdowns while government and media were lying and making it look like the 'virus':

> Restaurants, shops, gyms, theatres, basically everything is shut. The cities are ghost towns. Even so-called 'essential' businesses are only open till 11am in the morning. You basically have just an hour to buy food and then your time is up.

> Inter-state travel and even inter-district travel is banned. The cops wait at all major crossroads to question why you are traveling outdoors or to fine you if you are not wearing a mask.

> The medical community here is also complicit in genocide, lying about

hospitals being full and turning away people with genuine illnesses, who need immediate care. They have even created a shortage of oxygen cylinders.

This is the classic Cult modus operandi played out in every country. Alisha said that people who would not have a PCR test not testing for the 'virus' were being denied hospital treatment. She said the people hit hardest were migrant workers and those in rural areas. Most businesses employed migrant workers and with everything closed there were no jobs, no income and no food. As a result millions were dying of starvation or malnutrition. All this was happening under Prime Minister Narendra Modi, a 100-percent asset of the Cult, and it emphasises yet again the scale of pure anti-human evil we are dealing with. Australia banned its people from returning home from India with penalties for trying to do so of up to five years in jail and a fine of £37,000. The manufactured 'Covid' crisis in India was being prepared to justify further fascism in the West. Obvious connections could be seen between the Indian 'vaccine' programme and increased 'cases' and this became a common theme. The Seychelles, the most per capita 'Covid vaccinated' population in the world, went back into lockdown after a 'surge of cases'.

Long ago the truly evil Monsanto agricultural biotechnology corporation with its big connections to Bill Gates devastated Indian farming with genetically-modified crops. Human rights activist Gurcharan Singh highlighted the efforts by the Indian government to complete the job by destroying the food supply to hundreds of millions with 'Covid' lockdowns. He said that 415 million people at the bottom of the disgusting caste system (still going whatever they say) were below the poverty line and struggled to feed themselves every year. Now the government was imposing lockdown at just the time to destroy the harvest. This deliberate policy was leading to mass starvation. People may reel back at the suggestion that a government would do that, but Wetiko-controlled 'leaders' are capable of any level of evil. In fact what is described in India is in the process of being instigated worldwide. The food chain and food supply are being targeted at every level to cause world hunger and thus control. Bill Gates is not the biggest owner of farmland in America for no reason and destroying access to food aids both the depopulation agenda and the plan for synthetic 'food' already being funded into existence by Gates. Add to this the coming hyper-inflation from the suicidal creation of fake 'money' in response to 'Covid' and the breakdown of container shipping systems and you have a cocktail that can only lead one way and is meant to. The Cult plan is to crash the entire system to 'build back better' with the Great Reset.

'Vaccine' transmission

Reports from all over the world continue to emerge of women suffering
menstrual and fertility problems after having the fake 'vaccine' and of
the non-'vaccinated' having similar problems when interacting with the
'vaccinated'. There are far too many for 'coincidence' to be credible.
We've had menopausal women getting periods, others having periods
stop or not stopping for weeks, passing clots, sometimes the lining of the
uterus, breast irregularities, and miscarriages (which increased by 400
percent in parts of the United States). Non-'vaccinated' men and
children have suffered blood clots and nose bleeding after interaction
with the 'vaccinated'. Babies have died from the effects of breast milk
from a 'vaccinated' mother. Awake doctors – the small minority –
speculated on the cause of non-'vaccinated' suffering the same effects as
the 'vaccinated'. Was it nanotechnology in the synthetic substance
transmitting frequencies or was it a straight chemical bioweapon that
was being transmitted between people? I am not saying that some kind
of chemical transmission is not one possible answer, but the foundation
of all that the Cult does is frequency and this is fertile ground for
understanding how transmission can happen. American doctor Carrie
Madej, an internal medicine physician and osteopath, has been
practicing for the last 20 years, teaching medical students, and she says
attending different meetings where the agenda for humanity was
discussed. Madej, who operates out of Georgia, did not dismiss other
possible forms of transmission, but she focused on frequency in search
of an explanation for transmission. She said the Moderna and Pfizer
'vaccines' contained nano-lipid particles as a key component. This was a
brand new technology never before used on humanity. 'They're using a
nanotechnology which is pretty much little tiny computer bits …
nanobots or hydrogel.' Inside the 'vaccines' was 'this sci-fi kind of
substance' which suppressed immune checkpoints to get into the cell. I
referred to this earlier as the 'Trojan horse' technique that tricks the cell
into opening a gateway for the self-replicating synthetic material and
while the immune system is artificially suppressed the body has no
defences. Madej said the substance served many purposes including an
on-demand ability to 'deliver the payload' and using the nano
'computer bits' as biosensors in the body. 'It actually has the ability to
accumulate data from your body, like your breathing, your respiration,
thoughts, emotions, all kinds of things.'

She said the technology obviously has the ability to operate through
Wi-Fi and transmit and receive energy, messages, frequencies or
impulses. 'Just imagine you're getting this new substance in you and it
can react to things all around you, the 5G, your smart device, your
phones.' We had something completely foreign in the human body that
had never been launched large scale at a time when we were seeing 5G

going into schools and hospitals (plus the Musk satellites) and she believed the 'vaccine' transmission had something to do with this: '… if these people have this inside of them … it can act like an antenna and actually transmit it outwardly as well.' The synthetic substance produced its own voltage and so it could have that kind of effect. This fits with my own contention that the nano receiver-transmitters are designed to connect people to the Smart Grid and break the receiver-transmitter connection to expanded consciousness. That would explain the French energy healer's experience of the disconnection of body from 'soul' with those who have had the 'vaccine'. The nanobots, self-replicating inside the body, would also transmit the synthetic frequency which could be picked up through close interaction by those who have not been 'vaccinated'. Madej speculated that perhaps it was 5G and increased levels of other radiation that was causing the symptoms directly although interestingly she said that non-'vaccinated' patients had shown improvement when they were away from the 'vaccinated' person they had interacted with. It must be remembered that you can control frequency and energy with your mind and you can consciously create energetic barriers or bubbles with the mind to stop damaging frequencies from penetrating your field. American paediatrician Dr Larry Palevsky said the 'vaccine' was not a 'vaccine' and was never designed to protect from a 'viral' infection. He called it 'a massive, brilliant propaganda of genocide' because they didn't have to inject everyone to get the result they wanted. He said the content of the jabs was able to infuse any material into the brain, heart, lungs, kidneys, liver, sperm and female productive system. 'This is genocide; this is a weapon of mass destruction.' At the same time American colleges were banning students from attending if they didn't have this life-changing and potentially life-ending 'vaccine'. Class action lawsuits must follow when the consequences of this college fascism come to light. As the book was going to press came reports about fertility effects on sperm in 'vaccinated' men which would absolutely fit with what I have been saying and hospitals continued to fill with 'vaccine' reactions. Another question is what about transmission via blood transfusions? The NHS has extended blood donation restrictions from seven days after a 'Covid vaccination' to 28 days after even a sore arm reaction.

I said in the spring of 2020 that the then touted 'Covid vaccine' would be ongoing each year like the flu jab. A year later Pfizer CEO, the appalling Albert Bourla, said people would 'likely' need a 'booster dose' of the 'vaccine' within 12 months of getting 'fully vaccinated' and then a yearly shot. 'Variants will play a key role', he said confirming the point. Johnson & Johnson CEO Alex Gorsky also took time out from his 'vaccine' disaster to say that people may need to be vaccinated against 'Covid-19' each year. UK Health Secretary, the psychopath Matt

Hancock, said additional 'boosters' would be available in the autumn of 2021. This is the trap of the 'vaccine passport'. The public will have to accept every last 'vaccine' they introduce, including for the fake 'variants', or it would cease to be valid. The only other way in some cases would be continuous testing with a test not testing for the 'virus' and what is on the swabs constantly pushed up your noise towards the brain every time?

'Vaccines' changing behaviour

I mentioned in the body of the book how I believed we would see gathering behaviour changes in the 'vaccinated' and I am already hearing such comments from the non-'vaccinated' describing behaviour changes in friends, loved ones and work colleagues. This will only increase as the self-replicating synthetic material and nanoparticles expand in body and brain. An article in the *Guardian* in 2016 detailed research at the University of Virginia in Charlottesville which developed a new method for controlling brain circuits associated with complex animal behaviour. The method, dubbed 'magnetogenetics', involves genetically-engineering a protein called ferritin, which stores and releases iron, to create a magnetised substance – 'Magneto' – that can activate specific groups of nerve cells from a distance. This is claimed to be an advance on other methods of brain activity manipulation known as optogenetics and chemogenetics (the Cult has been developing methods of brain control for a long time). The ferritin technique is said to be non-invasive and able to activate neurons 'rapidly and reversibly'. In other words, human thought and perception. The article said that earlier studies revealed how nerve cell proteins 'activated by heat and mechanical pressure can be genetically engineered so that they become sensitive to radio waves and magnetic fields, by attaching them to an iron-storing protein called ferritin, or to inorganic paramagnetic particles'. Sensitive to radio waves and magnetic fields? You mean like 5G, 6G and 7G? This is the human-AI Smart Grid hive mind we are talking about. The *Guardian* article said:

> … the researchers injected Magneto into the striatum of freely behaving mice, a deep brain structure containing dopamine-producing neurons that are involved in reward and motivation, and then placed the animals into an apparatus split into magnetised and non-magnetised sections.
>
> Mice expressing Magneto spent far more time in the magnetised areas than mice that did not, because activation of the protein caused the striatal neurons expressing it to release dopamine, so that the mice found being in those areas rewarding. This shows that Magneto can remotely control the firing of neurons deep within the brain, and also control complex behaviours.

Make no mistake this basic methodology will be part of the 'Covid vaccine' cocktail and using magnetics to change brain function through electromagnetic field frequency activation. The Pentagon is developing a 'Covid vaccine' using ferritin. Magnetics would explain changes in behaviour and why videos are appearing across the Internet as I write showing how magnets stick to the skin at the point of the 'vaccine' shot. Once people take these 'vaccines' anything becomes possible in terms of brain function and illness which will be blamed on 'Covid-19' and 'variants'. Magnetic field manipulation would further explain why the non-'vaccinated' are reporting the same symptoms as the 'vaccinated' they interact with and why those symptoms are reported to decrease when not in their company. Interestingly 'Magneto', a 'mutant', is a character in the Marvel Comic *X-Men* stories with the ability to manipulate magnetic fields and he believes that mutants should fight back against their human oppressors by any means necessary. The character was born Erik Lehnsherr to a Jewish family in Germany.

Cult-controlled courts

The European Court of Human Rights opened the door for mandatory 'Covid-19 vaccines' across the continent when it ruled in a Czech Republic dispute over childhood immunisation that legally enforced vaccination could be 'necessary in a democratic society'. The 17 judges decided that compulsory vaccinations did not breach human rights law. On the face of it the judgement was so inverted you gasp for air. If not having a vaccine infused into your body is not a human right then what is? Ah, but they said human rights law which has been specifically written to delete all human rights at the behest of the state (the Cult). Article 8 of the European Convention on Human Rights relates to the right to a private life. The crucial word here is *'except'*:

> There shall be no interference by a public authority with the exercise of this right EXCEPT such as is in accordance with the law and is necessary in a democratic society in the interests of national security, public safety or the economic wellbeing of the country, for the prevention of disorder or crime, for the protection of health or morals, or for the protection of the rights and freedoms of others [My emphasis].

No interference *except* in accordance with the law means there *are* no 'human rights' *except* what EU governments decide you can have at their behest. 'As is necessary in a democratic society' explains that reference in the judgement and 'in the interests of national security, public safety or the economic well-being of the country, for the prevention of disorder or crime, for the protection of health or morals, or for the protection of the rights and freedoms of others' gives the EU a coach and horses to ride through 'human rights' and scatter them in all directions. The judiciary is not a check and balance on government extremism; it is a vehicle to enforce it. This judgement was almost laughably predictable when the last thing the Cult wanted was a decision that went against mandatory vaccination. Judges rule over and over again to benefit the system of which they are a part. Vaccination disputes that come before them are invariably delivered in favour of doctors and authorities representing the view of the state which owns the judiciary. Oh, yes, and we have even had calls to stop putting 'Covid-19' on death certificates within 28 days of a 'positive test' because it is claimed the practice makes the 'vaccine' appear not to work. They are laughing at you.

The scale of madness, inhumanity and things to come was highlighted when those not 'vaccinated' for 'Covid' were refused evacuation from the Caribbean island of St Vincent during massive volcanic eruptions. Cruise ships taking residents to the safety of another island allowed only the 'vaccinated' to board and the rest were left to their fate. Even in life and death situations like this we see 'Covid' stripping people of their most basic human instincts and the insanity is even more extreme when you think that fake 'vaccine'-makers are not even claiming their body-manipulating concoctions stop 'infection' and 'transmission' of a 'virus' that doesn't exist. St Vincent Prime Minister Ralph Gonsalves said: 'The chief medical officer will be identifying the persons already vaccinated so that we can get them on the ship.' Note again the power of the chief medical officer who, like Whitty in the UK, will be answering to the World Health Organization. This is the Cult network structure that has overridden politicians who 'follow the science' which means doing what WHO-controlled 'medical officers' and 'science advisers' tell them. Gonsalves even said that residents who were 'vaccinated' after the order so they could board the ships would still be refused entry due to possible side effects such as 'wooziness in the head'. The good news is that if they were woozy enough in the head they could qualify to be prime minister of St Vincent.

Microchipping freedom

The European judgement will be used at some point to justify moves to enforce the 'Covid' DNA-manipulating procedure. Sandra Ro, CEO of the Global Blockchain Business Council, told a World Economic Forum event that she hoped 'vaccine passports' would help to 'drive forced consent and standardisation' of global digital identity schemes: 'I'm hoping with the desire and global demand for some sort of vaccine passport – so that people can get travelling and working again – [it] will drive forced consent, standardisation, and frankly, cooperation across the world.' The lady is either not very bright, or thoroughly mendacious, to use the term 'forced consent'. You do not 'consent' if you are forced – you *submit*. She was describing what the plan has been all along and that's to enforce a digital identity on every human without which they could not function. 'Vaccine passports' are opening the door and are far from the end goal. A digital identity would allow you to be tracked in everything you do in cyberspace and this is the same technique used by Cult-owned China to enforce its social credit system of total control. The ultimate 'passport' is planned to be a microchip as my books have warned for nearly 30 years. Those nice people at the Pentagon working for the Cult-controlled Defense Advanced Research Projects Agency (DARPA) claimed in April, 2021, they have developed a microchip inserted under the skin to detect 'asymptomatic Covid-19 infection' before it becomes an outbreak and a 'revolutionary filter' that can remove the 'virus' from the blood when attached to a dialysis machine. The only problems with this are that the 'virus' does not exist and people transmitting the 'virus' with no symptoms is brain-numbing bullshit. This is, of course, not a ruse to get people to be microchipped for very different reasons. DARPA also said it was producing a one-stop 'vaccine' for the 'virus' and all 'variants'. One of the most sinister organisations on Planet Earth is doing this? Better have it then. These people are insane because Wetiko that possesses them is insane.

Researchers from the Salk Institute in California announced they have created an embryo that is part human and part monkey. My books going back to the 1990s have exposed experiments in top secret underground facilities in the United States where humans are being crossed with animal and non-human 'extraterrestrial' species. They are now easing that long-developed capability into the public arena and there is much more to come given we are dealing with psychiatric basket cases. Talking of which – Elon Musk's scientists at Neuralink trained a monkey to play Pong and other puzzles on a computer screen using a joystick and when the monkey made the correct move a metal tube squirted banana smoothie into his mouth which is the basic technique for training humans into unquestioning compliance. Two Neuralink chips were in the monkey's skull and more than 2,000 wires 'fanned out' into its brain. Eventually the monkey played a video game purely with its brain waves. Psychopathic narcissist Musk said the 'breakthrough' was a step towards putting Neuralink chips into human skulls and merging minds with artificial intelligence. *Exactly*. This man is so dark and Cult to his DNA.

World Economic Fascism (WEF)

The World Economic Forum is telling you the plan by the statements made at its many and various events. Cult-owned fascist YouTube CEO Susan Wojcicki spoke at the 2021 WEF Global Technology Governance

Summit (see the name) in which 40 governments and 150 companies met to ensure 'the responsible design and deployment of emerging technologies'. Orwellian translation: 'Ensuring the design and deployment of long-planned technologies will advance the Cult agenda for control and censorship.' Freedom-destroyer and Nuremberg-bound Wojcicki expressed support for tech platforms like hers to censor content that is 'technically legal but could be harmful'. Who decides what is 'harmful'? She does and they do. 'Harmful' will be whatever the Cult doesn't want people to see and we have legislation proposed by the UK government that would censor content on the basis of 'harm' no matter if the information is fair, legal and provably true. Make that *especially* if it is fair, legal and provably true. Wojcicki called for a global coalition to be formed to enforce content moderation standards through automated censorship. This is a woman and mega-censor so self-deluded that she shamelessly accepted a 'free expression' award – *Wojcicki* – in an event sponsored by her own *YouTube*. They have no shame and no self-awareness.

You know that 'Covid' is a scam and Wojcicki a Cult operative when YouTube is censoring medical and scientific opinion purely on the grounds of whether it supports or opposes the Cult 'Covid' narrative. Florida governor Ron DeSantis compiled an expert panel with four professors of medicine from Harvard, Oxford, and Stanford Universities who spoke against forcing children and vaccinated people to wear masks. They also said there was no proof that lockdowns reduced spread or death rates of 'Covid-19'. Cult-gofer Wojcicki and her YouTube deleted the panel video 'because it included content that contradicts the consensus of local and global health authorities regarding the efficacy of masks to prevent the spread of Covid-19'. This 'consensus' refers to what the Cult tells the World Health Organization to say and the WHO tells 'local health authorities' to do. Wojcicki knows this, of course. The panellists pointed out that censorship of scientific debate was responsible for deaths from many causes, but Wojcicki couldn't care less. She would not dare go against what she is told and as a disgrace to humanity she wouldn't want to anyway. The UK government is seeking to pass a fascist 'Online Safety Bill' to specifically target with massive fines and other means non-censored video and social media platforms to make them censor 'lawful but harmful' content like the Cult-owned Facebook, Twitter, Google and YouTube. What is 'lawful but harmful' would be decided by the fascist Blair-created Ofcom.

Another WEF obsession is a cyber-attack on the financial system and this is clearly what the Cult has planned to take down the bank accounts of everyone – except theirs. Those that think they have enough money for the Cult agenda not to matter to them have got a big lesson coming if they continue to ignore what is staring them in the face. The World

Economic Forum, funded by Gates and fronted by Klaus Schwab, announced it would be running a 'simulation' with the Russian government and global banks of just such an attack called Cyber Polygon 2021. What they simulate – as with the 'Covid' Event 201 – they plan to instigate. The WEF is involved in a project with the Cult-owned Carnegie Endowment for International Peace called the WEF-Carnegie Cyber Policy Initiative which seeks to merge Wall Street banks, 'regulators' (I love it) and intelligence agencies to 'prevent' (arrange and allow) a cyber-attack that would bring down the global financial system as long planned by those that control the WEF and the Carnegie operation. The Carnegie Endowment for International Peace sent an instruction to First World War US President Woodrow Wilson not to let the war end before society had been irreversibly transformed.

The Wuhan lab diversion

As I close, the Cult-controlled authorities and lapdog media are systematically pushing 'the virus was released from the Wuhan lab' narrative. There are two versions – it happened by accident and it happened on purpose. Both are nonsense. The perceived existence of the never-shown-to-exist 'virus' is vital to sell the impression that there is actually an infective agent to deal with and to allow the endless potential for terrifying the population with 'variants' of a 'virus' that does not exist. The authorities at the time of writing are going with the 'by accident' while the alternative media is promoting the 'on purpose'. Cable news host Tucker Carlson who has questioned aspects of lockdown and 'vaccine' compulsion has bought the Wuhan lab story. 'Everyone now agrees' he said. Well, I don't and many others don't and the question is *why* does the system and its media suddenly 'agree'? When the media moves as one unit with a narrative it is always a lie – witness the hour by hour mendacity of the 'Covid' era. Why would this Cult-owned combination which has unleashed lies like machine gun fire suddenly 'agree' to tell the truth??

Much of the alternative media is buying the lie because it fits the conspiracy narrative, but it's the *wrong* conspiracy. The real conspiracy is that *there is no virus* and that is what the Cult is desperate to hide. The idea that the 'virus' was released by accident is ludicrous when the whole 'Covid' hoax was clearly long-planned and waiting to be played out as it was so fast in accordance with the Rockefeller document and Event 201. So they prepared everything in detail over decades and then sat around strumming their fingers waiting for an 'accidental' release from a bio-lab? *What??* It's crazy. Then there's the 'on purpose' claim. You want to circulate a 'deadly virus' and hide the fact that you've done so and you release it down the street from the highest-level bio-lab in China? I repeat – *What??* You would release it far from that lab to stop any association being made. But, no, we'll do it in a place where the connection was certain to be made. Why would you need to scam 'cases' and 'deaths' and pay hospitals to diagnose 'Covid-19' if you had a real 'virus'? What are sections of the alternative media doing believing this crap? Where were all the mass deaths in Wuhan from a 'deadly pathogen' when the recovery to normal life after the initial propaganda was dramatic in speed? Why isn't the 'deadly pathogen' now circulating all over China with bodies in the street? Once again we have the technique of tell them what they want to hear and they will likely believe it. The alternative media has its 'conspiracy' and with Carlson it fits with his 'China is the danger' narrative over years. China *is* a danger as a global Cult operations centre, but not for this reason. The Wuhan lab story also has the potential to instigate conflict with China when at some stage the plan is to trigger a Problem-Reaction-Solution confrontation with the West. Question everything – *everything* – and especially when the media agrees on a common party line.

Third wave ... fourth wave ... fifth wave ...

As the book went into production the world was being set up for more lockdowns and a 'third wave' supported by invented 'variants' that were increasing all the time and will continue to do so in public statements and computer programs, but not in reality. India became the new Italy in the 'Covid' propaganda campaign and we were told to be frightened of the new 'Indian strain'. Somehow I couldn't find it within myself to do so. A document produced for the UK government entitled 'Summary of further modelling of easing of restrictions – Roadmap Step 2' declared that a third wave was inevitable (of course when it's in the script) and it would be the fault of children and those who refuse the health-destroying fake 'Covid vaccine'. One of the computer models involved came from the Cult-owned *Imperial College* and the other from Warwick University which I wouldn't trust to tell me the date in a calendar factory. The document states that both models presumed extremely high uptake of the 'Covid vaccines' and didn't allow for 'variants'. The document states: 'The resurgence is a result of some people (mostly children) being ineligible for vaccination; others choosing not to receive the vaccine; and others being vaccinated but not perfectly protected.' The mendacity takes the breath away. Okay, blame those with a brain who won't take the DNA-modifying shots and put more pressure on children to have it as 'trials' were underway involving children as young as six months with parents who give insanity a bad name. Massive pressure is being put on the young to have the fake 'vaccine' and child age consent limits have been systematically lowered around the world to stop parents intervening. Most extraordinary about the document was its claim that the 'third wave' would be driven by 'the resurgence in both hospitalisations and deaths ... dominated by *those that have received two doses of the vaccine*, comprising around 60-70% of the wave respectively'. The predicted peak of the 'third wave' suggested 300 deaths per day with 250 of them *fully 'vaccinated' people*. How many more lies do acquiescers need to be told before they see the obvious? Those who took the jab to 'protect themselves' are projected to be those who mostly get sick and die? So what's in the 'vaccine'? The document went on:

> It is possible that a summer of low prevalence could be followed by substantial increases in incidence over the following autumn and winter. Low prevalence in late summer should not be taken as an indication that SARS-CoV-2 has retreated or that the population has high enough levels of immunity to prevent another wave.

They are telling you the script and while many British people believed 'Covid' restrictions would end in the summer of 2021 the government was preparing for them to be ongoing. Authorities were awarding contracts for 'Covid marshals' to police the restrictions with contracts starting in July, 2021, and going through to January 31st, 2022, and the government was advertising for 'Media Buying Services' to secure media propaganda slots worth a potential £320 million for 'Covid-19 campaigns' with a contract not ending until March, 2022. The recipient – via a list of other front companies – was reported to be American media marketing giant Omnicom Group Inc. While money is no object for 'Covid' the UK waiting list for all other treatment – including life-threatening conditions – passed 4.5 million. Meantime the Cult is seeking to control all official 'inquiries' to block revelations about what has really been happening and why. It must not be allowed to – we need Nuremberg jury trials in every country. The cover-up doesn't get more obvious than appointing ultra-Zionist professor Philip Zelikow to oversee two dozen US virologists, public health officials, clinicians, former government officials and four American 'charitable foundations' to 'learn the lessons' of the 'Covid' debacle. The personnel will be those that created and perpetuated the 'Covid' lies while Zelikow is the former executive director of the 9/11 Commission who ensured that the truth about those attacks never came out and produced a report that must be among the most mendacious and manipulative documents ever written – see *The Trigger* for the detailed exposure of the almost unimaginable 9/11 story in which Sabbatians can be found at every level.

Passive no more

People are increasingly challenging the authorities with amazing numbers of people taking to the streets in London well beyond the ability of the Face-Nappies to stop them. Instead the Nappies choose situations away from the mass crowds to target, intimidate, and seek to promote the impression of 'violent protestors'. One such incident happened in London's Hyde Park. Hundreds of thousands walking through the streets in protest against 'Covid' fascism were ignored by the Cult-owned BBC and most of the rest of the mainstream media, but they delighted in reporting how police were injured in 'clashes with protestors'. The truth was that a group of people gathered in Hyde Park at the end of one march when most had gone home and they were peacefully having a good time with music and chat. Face-Nappies who couldn't deal with the full-march crowd then waded in with their batons and got more than they bargained for. Instead of just standing for this criminal brutality the crowd used their numerical superiority to push the Face-Nappies out of the park. Eventually the Nappies turned and ran. Unfortunately two or three idiots in the crowd threw drink cans striking two officers which gave the media and the government the image they wanted to discredit the 99.9999 percent who were peaceful. The idiots walked straight into the trap and we must always be aware of potential agent provocateurs used by the authorities to discredit their targets.

This response from the crowd – the can people apart – must be a turning point when the public no longer stand by while the innocent are arrested and brutally attacked by the Face-Nappies. That doesn't mean to be violent, that's the last thing we need. We'll leave the violence to the Face-Nappies and government. But it does mean that when the Face-Nappies use violence against peaceful people the numerical superiority is employed to stop them and make citizen's arrests or Common Law arrests for a breach of the peace. The time for being passive in the face of fascism is over.

We are the many, they are the few, and we need to make that count before there is no freedom left and our children and grandchildren face an ongoing fascist nightmare.

COME ON PEOPLE – IT'S TIME.

One final thought …

The power of love
A force from above
Cleaning my soul
Flame on burn desire
Love with tongues of fire
Purge the soul
Make love your goal

I'll protect you from the hooded claw
Keep the vampires from your door
When the chips are down I'll be around
With my undying, death-defying
Love for you

Envy will hurt itself
Let yourself be beautiful
Sparkling love, flowers
And pearls and pretty girls
Love is like an energy
Rushin' rushin' inside of me

This time we go sublime
Lovers entwine, divine, divine,
Love is danger, love is pleasure
Love is pure – the only treasure

I'm so in love with you
Purge the soul
Make love your goal

The power of love
A force from above
Cleaning my soul
The power of love
A force from above
A sky-scraping dove

Flame on burn desire
Love with tongues of fire
Purge the soul
Make love your goal

Frankie Goes To Hollywood

Cowan-Kaufman-Morell Statement on Virus Isolation (SOVI)

Isolation: The action of isolating; the fact or condition of being isolated or standing alone; separation from other things or persons; solitariness
Oxford English Dictionary

The controversy over whether the SARS-CoV-2 virus has ever been isolated or purified continues. However, using the above definition, common sense, the laws of logic and the dictates of science, any unbiased person must come to the conclusion that the SARS-CoV-2 virus has never been isolated or purified. As a result, no confirmation of the virus' existence can be found. The logical, common sense, and scientific consequences of this fact are:

- the structure and composition of something not shown to exist can't be known, including the presence, structure, and function of any hypothetical spike or other proteins;
- the genetic sequence of something that has never been found can't be known;
- "variants" of something that hasn't been shown to exist can't be known;
- it's impossible to demonstrate that SARS-CoV-2 causes a disease called Covid-19.

In as concise terms as possible, here's the proper way to isolate, characterize and demonstrate a new virus. First, one takes samples (blood, sputum, secretions) from many people (e.g. 500) with symptoms which are unique and specific enough to characterize an illness. Without mixing these samples with ANY tissue or products that also contain genetic material, the virologist macerates, filters and ultracentrifuges i.e. *purifies* the specimen. This common virology technique, done for decades to isolate bacteriophages[1] and so-called giant viruses in every virology lab, then allows the virologist to demonstrate with electron microscopy thousands of identically sized and shaped particles. These particles are the isolated and purified virus.

These identical particles are then checked for uniformity by physical and/or microscopic techniques. Once the purity is determined, the particles may be further characterized. This would include examining the structure, morphology, and chemical composition of the particles. Next, their genetic makeup is characterized by extracting the genetic material directly from the purified particles and using genetic-sequencing techniques, such as Sanger sequencing, that have also been around for decades. Then one does an analysis to confirm that these uniform particles are exogenous (outside) in origin as a virus is conceptualized to be, and not the normal breakdown products of dead and dying tissues.[2] (As of May 2020, we know that virologists have no way to determine whether the particles they're seeing are viruses or just normal break-down products of dead and dying tissues.)[3]

---

1 Isolation, characterization and analysis of bacteriophages from the haloalkaline lake Elmenteita, KenyaJuliah Khayeli Akhwale et al, PLOS One, Published: April 25, 2019. https://journals.plos.org/plosone/article?id=10.1371/journal.pone.0215734 – accessed 2/15/21

2 "Extracellular Vesicles Derived From Apoptotic Cells: An Essential Link Between Death and Regeneration," Maojiao Li1 et al, Frontiers in Cell and Developmental Biology, 2020 October 2. https://www.frontiersin.org/articles/10.3389/fcell.2020.573511/full – accessed 2/15/21

3 "The Role of Extraellular Vesicles as Allies of HIV, HCV and SARS Viruses," Flavia Giannessi, et al, Viruses, 2020 May

---

If we have come this far then we have fully isolated, characterized, and genetically sequenced an exogenous virus particle. However, we still have to show it is causally related to a disease. This is carried out by exposing a group of healthy subjects (animals are usually used) to this isolated, purified virus in the manner in which the disease is thought to be transmitted. If the animals get sick with the same disease, as confirmed by clinical and autopsy findings, one has now shown that the virus actually causes a disease. This demonstrates infectivity and transmission of an infectious agent.

None of these steps has even been attempted with the SARS-CoV-2 virus, nor have all these steps been successfully performed for any so-called pathogenic virus. Our research indicates that a single study showing these steps does not exist in the medical literature.

Instead, since 1954, virologists have taken unpurified samples from a relatively few people, often less than ten, with a similar disease. They then minimally process this sample and inoculate this unpurified sample onto tissue culture containing usually four to six other types of material – all of which contain identical genetic material as to what is called a "virus." The tissue culture is starved and poisoned and naturally disintegrates into many types of particles, some of which contain genetic material. Against all common sense, logic, use of the English language and scientific integrity, this process is called "virus isolation." This brew containing fragments of genetic material from many sources is then subjected to genetic analysis, which then creates in a computer-simulation process the alleged sequence of the alleged virus, a so called in silico genome. At no time is an actual virus confirmed by electron microscopy. At no time is a genome extracted and sequenced from an actual virus. This is scientific fraud.

The observation that the unpurified specimen — inoculated onto tissue culture along with toxic antibiotics, bovine fetal tissue, amniotic fluid and other tissues — destroys the kidney tissue onto which it is inoculated is given as evidence of the virus' existence and pathogenicity. This is scientific fraud.

From now on, when anyone gives you a paper that suggests the SARS-CoV-2 virus has been isolated, please check the methods sections. If the researchers used Vero cells or any other culture method, you know that their process was not isolation. You will hear the following excuses for why actual isolation isn't done:

1. There were not enough virus particles found in samples from patients to analyze.

2. Viruses are intracellular parasites; they can't be found outside the cell in this manner.

If No. 1 is correct, and we can't find the virus in the sputum of sick people, then on what evidence do we think the virus is dangerous or even lethal? If No. 2 is correct, then how is the virus spread from person to person? We are told it emerges from the cell to infect others. Then why isn't it possible to find it?

Finally, questioning these virology techniques and conclusions is not some distraction or divisive issue. Shining the light on this truth is essential to stop this terrible fraud that humanity is confronting. For, as we now know, if the virus has never been isolated, sequenced or shown to cause illness, if the virus is imaginary, then why are we wearing masks, social distancing and putting the whole world into prison?

Finally, if pathogenic viruses don't exist, then what is going into those injectable devices erroneously called "vaccines," and what is their purpose? This scientific question is the most urgent and relevant one of our time.

We are correct. The SARS-CoV2 virus does not exist.

Sally Fallon Morell, MA
Dr. Thomas Cowan, MD
Dr. Andrew Kaufman, MD

Bibliography

Alinsky, Saul: *Rules for Radicals* (Vintage, 1989)

Antelman, Rabbi Marvin: *To Eliminate the Opiate* (Zahavia, 1974)

Bastardi, Joe: *The Climate Chronicles* (Relentless Thunder Press, 2018)

Cowan, Tom: *Human Heart, Cosmic Heart* (Chelsea Green Publishing, 2016)

Cowan, Tom, and Fallon Morell, Sally: *The Contagion Myth* (Skyhorse Publishing, 2020)

Forbes, Jack D: *Columbus And Other Cannibals – The Wetiko Disease of Exploitation, Imperialism, and Terrorism* (Seven Stories Press, 2008 – originally published in 1979)

Gates, Bill: *How to Avoid a Climate Disaster: The Solutions We Have and the Breakthroughs We Need* (Allen Lane, 2021)

Huxley, Aldous: *Brave New World* (Chatto & Windus, 1932)

Köhnlein, Dr Claus, and Engelbrecht, Torsten: *Virus Mania* (emu-Vertag, Lahnstein, 2020)

Lanza, Robert, and Berman, Bob: *Biocentrism* (BenBella Books, 2010)

Lash, John Lamb: *Not In His Image* (Chelsea Green Publishing, 2006)

Lester, Dawn, and Parker, David: *What Really Makes You Ill – Why everything you thought you knew about disease is wrong* (Independently Published, 2019)

Levy, Paul: *Dispelling Wetiko, Breaking the Spell of Evil* (North Atlantic Books, 2013)

Marx, Karl: *A World Without Jews* (Philosophical Library, first edition, 1959)

Mullis, Kary: *Dancing Naked in the Mine Field* (Bloomsbury, 1999)

O'Brien, Cathy: *Trance-Formation of America* (Reality Marketing, 1995)

Scholem, Gershon: *The Messianic Idea in Judaism* (Schocken Books, 1994)

Schwab, Klaus, and Davis, Nicholas: *Shaping the Future of the Fourth Industrial Revolution: A guide to building a better world* (Penguin Books, 2018)

Schwab, Klaus: *The Great Reset* (Agentur Schweiz, 2020)

Sunstein, Cass and Thaler, Richard: *Nudge: Improving Decisions About Health, Wealth, and Happiness* (Penguin, 2009)

Swan, Shanna: *Count Down: How Our Modern World Is Threatening Sperm Counts, Altering Male and Female Reproductive Development and Imperiling the Future of the Human Race* (Scribner, 2021)

Tegmark, Max: *Our Mathematical Universe: My Quest for the Ultimate Nature of Reality* (Penguin, 2015)

Velikovsky, Immanuel: *Worlds in Collision* (Paradigma, 2009)

Wilton, Robert: *The Last Days of the Romanovs* (Blurb, 2018, first published 1920)

Index

309–10
Big Pharma 308, 326
children 309–10
China 309
consciousness 303–7, 312
education 307
Facebook 309–10
fear 308–9, 327
frequency 309–12, 322–3
Gates 308, 311–12
Global Cult 301, 303–19
heart 322–3, 326–7
lockdowns 316
masks 316
Native American concept
301–19
psychopathic personality
304, 306–13
reframing / retraining
programmes 306
religion 315
Silicon Valley 308–9
Smart Grid 310–11
smartphone addiction 310,
312
social media 309
war 315–17, 321–2
WHO 308
Wokeness 306–7, 309, 316
Yaldabaoth 302, 304–5, 307,
314–15
whistle-blowing 115, 120,
138–40, 143–4, 220, 223, 226
white privilege 199, 200
white supremacy 54, 58, 63,
196–7, 199–202
Whitty, Christopher 95–6,
124–5, 129, 151, 178, 212,
241, 278, 282, 304
'who benefits' 13
Wi-Fi 267–9, 273, 292–3,
310–11
Wikipedia 98, 149–50
Wojcicki, Susan 39, 133, 150,
212, 278, 282, 310
Wokeness
Antifa 56, 192, 306, 316
anti-Semitism 44
billionaire social justice
warriors 196–9, 204, 286
Capitol Hill riot 58–9, 190
censorship 194
Christianity 203
climate change hoax 195,
204
culture 203–4
education, control of 191–4
emotion 322
facts 194–5

fascism 191–2, 195, 286
Global Cult 49, 53, 190–9,
203–4
group-think 193–5
immigration 60–4
indigenous people,
solidarity with 284–5
inversion 192, 194–5, 254
left, hijacking the 194–6,
286
Marxism 31–2, 50, 194
mind control 191
New Woke 192
Old Woke 192
Oneness 266
perceptual programming
192–4
Phantom Self 266
police 190–1
defunding the 198–9
reframing 190–1
public institutions 203–4
Pushbackers 49, 55, 286
racism 195–6, 199–202, 309
reframing 181, 190–204
religion, as 194
Sabbatians 36, 48, 53
Silicon Valley 204
social justice 193, 196–8, 204,
284–5
transgender 195, 251, 254, 256,
286
United States 60–4, 196–7
vaccines 306
Wetiko factor 306–7, 309,
316
young people 165, 191–3, 195
**women, deletion of rights
and status of** 251, 253–4
**World Economic Forum
(WEF)** 12, 75, 83, 96–7, 108,
121, 127, 206–7, 236–7
**World Health Organization
(WHO)** 3, 13, 72, 76, 78,
87–91, 94–6, 116, 121
AIDs / HIV 100
amplification cycles 230–1
Big Pharma 13, 114, 258
cooperation in health
emergencies 17–18
creation 89, 114
fatality rate 145
funding 73, 78, 94–7
Gates 276
Internet 149
lockdown 117
vaccines 215, 225, 230–1,
257–8
Wetiko factor 308

world number 1 (masses) 2–3,
7–8
world number 2 3–5
**Wuhan 71, 81, 88, 90–2, 101,
115, 122–3**

Y
Yaldabaoth 279–81, 289–91,
302, 304–5, 307, 314–15
Yeadon, Michael 108, 218–20,
225, 256–7
young people *see also* **children**
addiction to technology
244–5
Human 2.0 251
vaccines 219–20, 225
Wokeness 165, 191–3, 195
YouTube 53, 75, 98, 149, 262
WHO 548

Z
Zaks, Tal 247–8
Zionism 33–7, 44, 62
Zuckerberg, Mark 9, 54, 66,
76, 149, 212, 214, 238, 278,
282, 288, 309–10
Zulus 275

Ickonic is something that has been a dream of mine for the last 5 years, growing up around alternative information I have always had a natural interest in what is going on in the World and what could I do to make it better.
Across the range of subjects and positions of influence occupied mainly by people who don't strive to make things better it's the Media that I have always found the most frustrating and fascinating. Mainly because if the Media did their Jobs properly then so much of the negative things happening in the World simply would not be able to happen, because they would be exposed within a heartbeat.
Free Press and the Opportunities that the internet could have given would mean that the Media are able to expose things like never before and hold people to account for their actions. As we all know there are 'Untouchables' that walk among us, people the Media simply won't touch, expose or investigate and that leads to the dark underworlds that infest the establishment the World over.
Well I say enough, it's time for something different, a different kind of Media, where no one is off limits from exposing and investigating. All we're interested in at Ickonic is the truth of what is really going on in the World on whichever subject we're covering.
We hope you enjoy what we have created and take something away from the platform, we aim to deliver information that's informative and most importantly self-empowering, you're not a little person, you're part of something much bigger than that and its time we as a collective race began to understand that and look to the future as ours to take.

It's time...

Jaymie Icke - Founder Ickonic Alternative Media.

SIGN UP NOW AT ICKONIC.COM

DAVID ICKE
THE ANSWER

We live in extraordinary times with billions bewildered and seeking answers for what is happening. David Icke, the man who has been proved right again and again, has spent 30 years uncovering the truth behind world affairs and in a stream of previous books he predicted current events.

The Answer will change your every perception of life and the world and set you free of the illusions that control human society. There is nothing more vital for our collective freedom than humanity becoming aware of what is in this book.

Available now at davidicke.com.

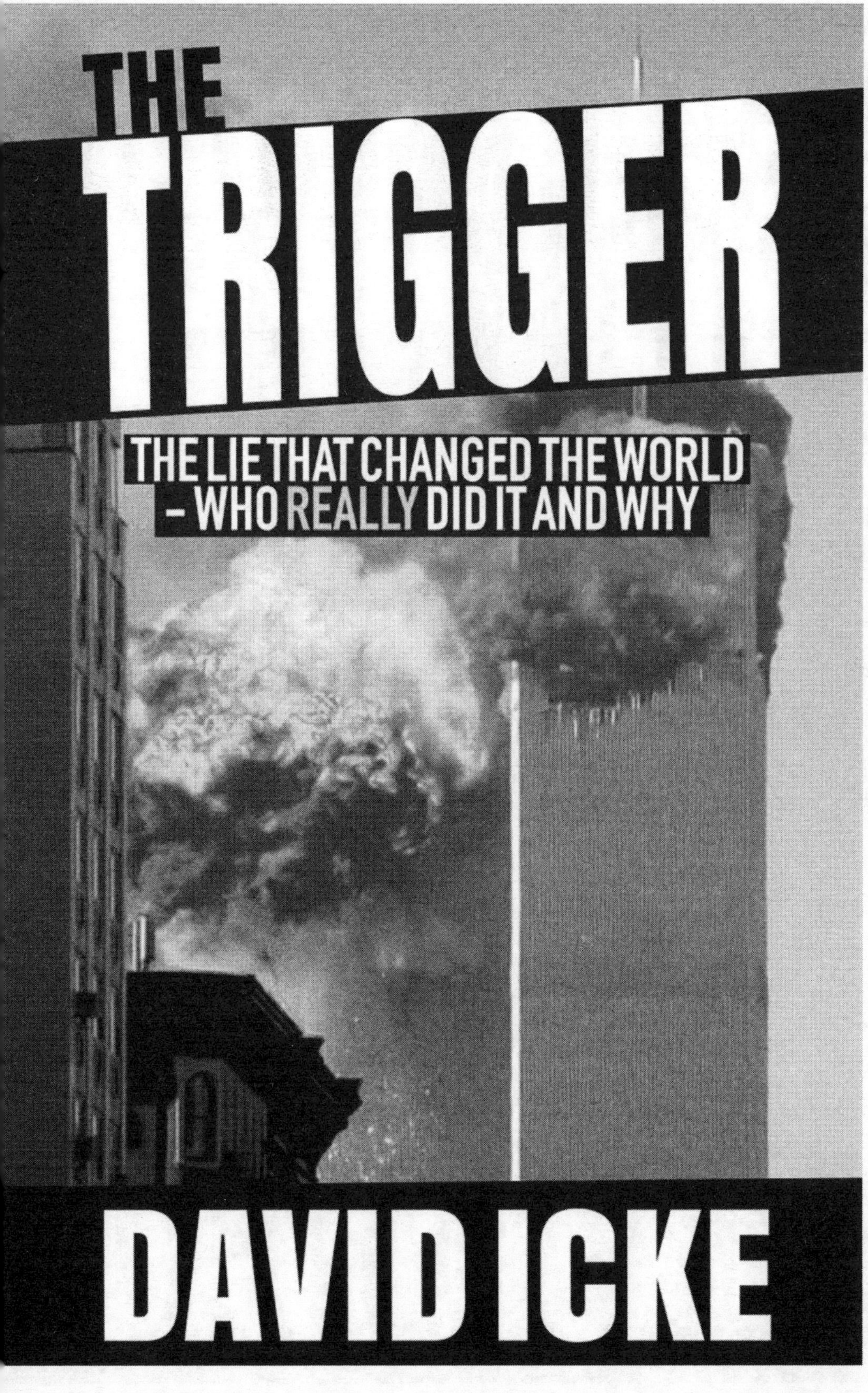
THE
TRIGGER
THE LIE THAT CHANGED THE WORLD
– WHO REALLY DID IT AND WHY
DAVID ICKE

EVERYTHING YOU NEED TO KNOW

BUT HAVE NEVER BEEN TOLD

DAVID ICKE

DAVIDICKE.COM

DAVID ICKE STORE

LATEST NEWS ARTICLES

DAVID ICKE VIDEOS

WEEKLY DOT-CONNECTOR PODCASTS

LIVE EVENTS

WWW.DAVIDICKE.COM

364

THE LIFE STORY OF DAVID ICKE

RENEGADE

THE FEATURE LENGTH FILM

/ˈren·ɪˌɡeɪd/

noun

A person who behaves in a rebelliously unconventional manner.

AVAILABLE NOW AT DAVIDICKE.COM

2 NEW BOOKS BY NEIL HAGUE

ORION'S DOOR
SYMBOLS OF CONSCIOUSNESS & BLUEPRINTS OF CONTROL - THE STORY OF ORION'S INFLUENCE OVER HUMANITY

CUTTING EDGE VISIONARY ART & UNIQUE ILLUSTRATED BOOKS

NEIL HAGUE

THE DR. COVID UNIVERSE
ADVENTURES IN CLOWNLAND

CHARACTERS & CONCEPTS BY NEIL HAGUE

FOR BOOKS, PRINTS & T-SHIRTS

VISIT:

NEILHAGUEBOOKS.COM

OR NEILHAGUE.COM

Before you go ...

For more detail, background and evidence about the subjects in *Perceptions of a Renegade Mind* – and so much more – see my others books including *And The Truth Shall Set You Free; The Biggest Secret; Children of the Matrix; The David Icke Guide to the Global Conspiracy; Tales from the Time Loop; The Perception Deception; Remember Who You Are; Human Race Get Off Your Knees; Phantom Self; Everything You Need To Know But Have Never Been Told, The Trigger and The Answer.*

You can subscribe to the fantastic new Ickonic media platform where there are many hundreds of hours of cutting-edge information in videos, documentaries and series across a whole range of subjects which are added to every week. This includes my 90 minute breakdown of the week's news every Friday to explain *why* events are happening and to what end.